The Bureaucratic Labor Market

The Case of the Federal Civil Service

PLENUM STUDIES IN WORK AND INDUSTRY

Series Editors:
Ivar Berg, *University of Pennsylvania, Philadelphia, Pennsylvania*
and Arne L. Kalleberg, *University of North Carolina, Chapel Hill, North Carolina*

WORK AND INDUSTRY
Structures, Markets, and Processes
Arne L. Kalleberg and Ivar Berg

THE BUREAUCRATIC LABOR MARKET
The Case of the Federal Civil Service
Thomas A. DiPrete

ENSURING MINORITY SUCCESS IN CORPORATE MANAGEMENT
Edited by Donna E. Thompson and Nancy DiTomaso

INDUSTRIES, FIRMS, AND JOBS
Sociological and Economic Approaches
Edited by George Farkas and Paula England

MATERNAL EMPLOYMENT AND CHILDREN'S DEVELOPMENT
Longitudinal Research
Edited by Adele Eskeles Gottfried and Allan W. Gottfried

THE STATE AND THE LABOR MARKET
Edited by Samuel Rosenberg

WORKERS, MANAGERS, AND TECHNOLOGICAL CHANGE
Emerging Patterns of Labor Relations
Edited by Daniel B. Cornfield

A Continuation Order Plan is available for this series. A continuation order will bring delivery of each
new volume immediately upon publication. Volumes are billed only upon actual shipment. For further
information please contact the publisher.

The Bureaucratic Labor Market

The Case of the Federal Civil Service

Thomas A. DiPrete

Duke University
Durham, North Carolina

With a Foreword by
Arthur L. Stinchcombe

Plenum Press • New York and London

Library of Congress Cataloging in Publication Data

DiPrete, Thomas Albert, 1950–
   The bureaucratic labor market: the case of the federal civil service / Thomas A.
DiPrete.
     p.   cm.—(Plenum studies in work and industry)
     Bibliography: p.
     Includes index.
     ISBN 0-306-43184-X
     1. United States—Officials and employees—Promotions. 2. Civil service positions—
United States—Classification. 3. Occupational mobility—United States. I. Title. II.
Series.
JK768.D56   1989   89-35450
353.001′03—dc20   CIP

© 1989 Plenum Press, New York
A Division of Plenum Publishing Corporation
233 Spring Street, New York, N.Y. 10013

Printed in the United States of America

Foreword

A description of the jobs in a labor force, an "occupational" description of it, is an abstraction for describing the flow of concrete work that goes through one or more employing organizations; the flow of work probably changes at a higher speed than the system for abstracting a description of its occupations and jobs. A career system is an abstraction for describing the flow of workers through a system of occupations or jobs, and thus is doubly removed from the flow of work. The federal civil service, however, ties many of the incentives and much of the authority to the flow of work through the abstractions of its career system, and still more of them through its system of job descriptions. The same dependence of the connection between reward and performance on abstractions about jobs and careers characterizes most white-collar work in large organizations.

The system of abstractions from the flow of work of the federal civil service, described here by Thomas A. DiPrete, is an institution, a set of valued social practices created in a long and complex historical process. The system is widely imitated, especially in American state and local governments, but also in the white-collar parts of many large private corporations and nonprofit organizations and to some degree by governments abroad. DiPrete has done us a great service in studying the historical origins of this system of abstractions, especially of the career abstractions. He then studies the relation of the career abstractions built into the institution to the actual demography of movements of employees into, through, and out of that system.

It is important to keep in mind the relation between the labor market that is studied here and the total labor market for governmental work. In 1985 civilian governmental employees made up about 14.5 percent of the civilian labor force; adding in the military brings government employment to about 16 percent of the total labor force. (All fig-

ures in this paragraph are from the *Statistical Abstract of the United States,*
1987.) Total federal employees constitute about 27 percent of total governmental employees, with the other three-quarters being state and local employees. Federal civilian employees are about three-fifths of total
federal employment—the other two-fifths being in the military—so
federal civilian employees account for about 16 percent of total government employees.* To get some idea of what this 16 percent figure
means, there were about 15 percent more teachers employed by local
governments than federal civil servants in 1985. In total the federal civil
service labor market studied here made up about 2.5 percent of the labor
force in 1985.

   While such figures help remind us that an understanding of internal
labor markets in American government entails studies of schools, arm-
ies, and police forces, as well of the federal civil service, it undersells the
importance of DiPrete's monograph. The system for analysis of individual productivity in the federal civil service, and its use in the distribution of wages and other incentives, have been the result of specific
study, legislation, and regulation development and implementation
over the last two centuries. The sequence of institutional development
for the civil service is better recorded than that for any other such system, so the kinds of influences that shape the system of analysis of
productivity of labor can be much better identified. That explicitness and
the fullness of records themselves partly explain why the system has
been so widely imitated by state and local governments, and why parts
of it have been widely adopted by private organizations.

   Furthermore, the federal civil service system generates some of the
best data we have on the demography of movements through it, so the
relation between the conception and the reality, between the institutionalized abstraction and the labor market experience, can be better
studied here than almost anywhere else.

   Of course the system of activities analyzed in terms of this system
can itself often change very rapidly. For example, from 1941 to 1945 the
percentage of the civilian labor force who were civil employees of the
federal government about tripled, then from 1945 to 1950 it about halved
again. Clearly this was because many activities were being carried out in
1945 that were not carried out in 1941 nor in 1950. While there were
substantial changes in the system of abstractions for describing what

---

*A little less than 2 percent of civilian employees of the federal government are employed
  in the legislative and judicial branches, and so are not under the civil service. Legislators
  and judges were probably a larger proportion of federal employment in the early days of
  DiPrete's story.

jobs and careers people had during the war, and changes (partly changes back) again immediately afterward, the changes in the institutions did not keep up with the radical fluctuations in activities. But to explore these deeper relations between the system of abstractions by which we agree to describe federal jobs and careers and the evolution of activities of the government as an organization, we need for a solid basis the description of the institution, and of the flow of people through it that DiPrete has given us.

I believe this book makes the federal civil service the best studied labor market in the world

Arthur L. Stinchcombe
Department of Sociology
Northwestern University
Evanston, Illinois

Preface

In John Dunlop's seminal paper, "The Task of Contemporary Wage Theory," he argued that job clusters ("a stable group of job classifications or work assignments within a firm") were a major determinant of the wage structure of a society. Doeringer and Piore later built on this concept in their study of internal labor markets when they introduced the notion of a "mobility cluster," by which they meant the groupings of jobs within which an employee is customarily upgraded, downgraded, transferred, and laid off. Both formulations assert that the formal linkages of jobs in position classification systems will affect job mobility, and that these linkages are maintained through customary as well as technical considerations. Because both technology and custom are flexible, these clusters can change over time, though in the short run they are stable. Sociologists later picked up on these ideas and began using internal labor markets as a major explanatory variable in their studies of social mobility.

The formulation of the internal labor market was sufficiently vague, however, to raise the question of how strong an impact job ladders—the formal (as opposed to the empirical) manifestation of mobility clusters—actually had on job mobility. It raised the possibility that mobility clusters might vary in the extent to which their formal structure controlled job mobility. If so, then this variation would itself be explainable. The obvious place to look for an explanation was in the factors that created mobility clusters in the first place, namely technology and custom. One of the insights found throughout the sociological literature is that "custom" shapes the way that actors formulate and weigh alternatives when making decisions, including technological decisions. But, whereas cross-sectional comparisons can do a reasonable job of measuring certain technological differences, the shaping forces of custom are more difficult to measure. However, it made sense to suppose that this shaping process would reveal itself in the history of these job ladders. In other words, an explanation of the links between job ladders and job mobility, and particularly of variation in the nature of these links, might be found in the processes that gave rise to these formal structures.

This chain of reasoning formed the basis for the research program that led to the present volume. The focus on the white-collar job ladders of the federal government was dictated partly by my interest in white-collar jobs and partly by the availability of data, both statistical and historical. Although a case study, even one involving a set of agencies that today employ about 3 million workers, is by definition restricted in scope, the similarities in the organization of white-collar work in bureaucratized organizations throughout the country made it likely that insights developed in this study could be generalized beyond the case on which they were based.

Like most studies, this one has origins that precede the specific intellectual question around which it is organized. Donald J. Treiman sparked my initial interest in the study of social mobility while I was a graduate student at Columbia. Burton Singer later introduced me to the subject of internal labor markets. Although my dissertation research under Singer was primarily of a methodological nature, our many substantive discussions on the impact of internal labor markets on social mobility ultimately led to the present volume.

My major recently acquired debt is to Whitman T. Soule. Aside from coauthoring the paper on which Chapter 10 is based, he coauthored an earlier paper in which some of the ideas developed here first found expression. In numerous conversations on personal policies and their impact on the lives of working men and women, he provided insights as useful as anything I have read on the subject. I would also like to thank Patrick Kit-Ling Cheung for early research assistance, which was particularly useful in the preparation of Chapter 8.

Financial support for this research was provided first by a small grant from the Spencer Foundation and then by National Science Foundation grant SES-8308896. The Center for Advanced Study in the Behavioral Sciences provided me with a congenial environment for doing the historical research contained in this book. While at the Center, I made use of materials from the Johnson Library of Government Documents and the Hoover Library, both at Stanford University. I did additional research at the Joseph Regenstein Library at the University of Chicago and the Library of the Office of Personnel Management in Washington, D.C. Bruce Harley, one of the librarians at the Behavioral Sciences Center, was particularly helpful. I was afraid he would rebel at my incessant requests for more material, but he was always understanding. Several civil servants in the U.S. Office of Personnel Management provided answers to specific questions that arose in the course of my work.

I also received helpful suggestions or comments from a number of other persons during the course of this research, including Jim Baron, Paul DiMaggio, Sally Ewing, Burke Grandjean, David Halle, Terry Halliday, Dennis Hogan, David Hollinger, Morris Janowitz, Arne Kalleberg, Edward Laumann, Gardner Lindzey, Ralph Nenni, Barbara Reskin, Mary Ryan, Gerald Salancik, Richard Simpson, Aage Sorensen, Arthur Stinchcombe, and Dennis Thompson. A special word of thanks to Allan Silver. While I was a graduate student at Columbia, he and I had many conversations about civil service systems as a topic in the study of political sociology. Though I did not anticipate it at the time, these exchanges nicely complemented my quantitative inclinations to provide a foundation for the writing of this book. I am also grateful to Burke Grandjean and Patricia Taylor for providing me with access to their extract from the Federal Personnel Statistics File and the Central Personnel Data File. Last but not least, I would like to thank my wife Katherine Ewing and my daughter Julia for putting up with me during the writing of this book. It goes without saying that I take ultimate responsibility for the opinions, conclusions, and recommendations expressed in its pages.

Thomas A. DiPrete
Durham, North Carolina

Contents

PART III. JOB LADDERS AND CAREER OUTCOMES

Chapter 10
**Conclusion: Structures and Outcomes in Bureaucratic Labor
Markets** **259**

Appendix
**The Occupational Content of Clerical and Administrative Work:
1920 to the Present** **277**

1

Structural Explanations for Inequality and Mobility in Bureaucratized Organizations

INTRODUCTION

Sociology has traditionally analyzed the problem of social inequality through the framework of class structure or through the study of mechanisms that produce status inheritance in modern as well as traditional societies. But in recent years, a new approach to the classic problem has emerged from studies of the life chances of working men and women. It is now recognized that the structure of labor markets plays a principal role in the generation and maintenance of social inequality.

The new focus on labor market structures contrasts with earlier approaches to the study of inequality, particularly those within quantitative sociology. Early quantitative research in social mobility (Glass 1954; Carlsson 1958; Svalastoga 1959; Lipset and Bendix 1959) attempted to measure the extent of association between the status of parents and their children but did not seriously investigate the structures that produced this association. The status attainment school of stratification, in contrast, began the systematic examination of these mediating institutional structures. However, its attention centered largely on the educational system and the process by which family resources and background affected academic success.

Even the early status attainment models took account of the significant social mobility during the course of an individual's years in the labor force (Blau and Duncan 1967; Sewell and Hauser 1975). Status attainment researchers showed that educational attainment affected one's first job and that educational attainment and first job both had influence on a worker's later occupational status. But this work also showed that minority status harmed one's chances for success, even when education and first job were controlled (Blau and Duncan 1967). Scholars later showed that women were disadvantaged as well (Wolf and Fligstein 1979; Rosenfeld 1980; Marini 1980; Sewell, Hauser, and Wolf 1980). Why did this pattern exist?

Sociologists have traditionally been skeptical of the view that social inequality was simply a by-product of an efficient market economy. By the later 1970s, many sociologists became convinced that inequality could not be adequately explained through the study of family background and educational attainment either. The rediscovery of 1940s and 1950s institutional economics and the emergence of poverty as a social policy in the 1960s and 1970s caused sociologists to expand their research to include the systematic study of labor markets. Most sociologists and institutional economists now attribute a substantial portion of the continued levels of race and gender inequality to these structures.

The first and best known paradigm for the structuralist revival is known as dual labor market theory and its close cousin, dual economy theory. These early models of segmentation are now viewed as too simplistic and limited to be adequate.[1] Their failings, however, should not obscure the now-established consensus in sociology that markets are segmented and that this segmentation has implications for social inequality.

In any general treatment of market segmentation, internal labor markets (ILMs) must receive a central focus. These structures are not markets in the classical sense but rather "administrative units . . . within which the pricing and allocation of labor is governed." Ideal-typical conceptions of internal labor markets conceptualize ILMs as consisting of job ladders "with entry only at the bottom" and "movement up the ladder" (Althauser and Kalleberg 1981: 130). The dualism literature stressed the advantages that workers had in these protected arenas—which together comprise the so-called primary labor market—compared with those who had unstable, low-paying jobs in the so-called secondary labor market. But these advantages, however real, should not over-

---

[1]Scholars have criticized the dual approach for its descriptive character, its vague theoretical formulations, its inconsistent operationalizations, and the porous character of its boundaries to labor mobility (Cain 1976; Zucker and Rosenstein 1981; Rumberger and Carnoy 1980; D'Amico and Brown 1982; Hodson and Kaufman 1982; Rosenfeld 1983).

shadow the substantial inequality that exists within the primary labor market as well.

That the jobs on a job ladder are unequal is hardly a revelation. But what is less obvious is the implication of any given system of job ladders for social mobility. One of the principal functions of job ladders is to facilitate advancement from entry level to more rewarding positions in the organization. But the number of good jobs in any organization is limited. Of necessity, the job ladders of internal labor markets block mobility for some as they encourage it for others. In particular, the tendency for white-collar job ladders to be organized into tiers (Piore 1975) might play a major role in the shaping of career mobility. The job ladders of clerical, subprofessional or sales work start near the bottom of the organization and have low ceilings. To reach the upper levels of an organization, an employee must secure a position on a professional or administrative job ladder. The criteria for recruitment to entry positions, the length of job ladders, and opportunity for moving from one ladder to another all play a role in shaping career outcomes. These issues are particularly salient to the study of gender and racial inequality because women and minorities are disproportionately located on the job ladders of the lower tier.

To understand the precise role of internal labor markets in shaping social inequality, we need to know the answers to several questions, some rather technical, and others more interpretive. Technical questions concern the relationship between the structure of job ladders and job mobility. How accessible are the entry ports of the upper tier to lower-tier workers? How often do employees cross the boundaries between one job ladder and another? Is the upper tier closed to those who did not complete college? Does permeability differ by type of job? Is the boundary sharp, or is there a transition zone separating the upper from the lower tier? Lying behind technical questions such as these is the broader question of why the system of job ladders has taken the form it now holds. This broader question is complementary to the more technical ones just raised because the forces that shape the internal labor markets of bureaucratized organizations are integral parts of any comprehensive explanation of the effects of job ladders on individual-level outcomes, and ultimately on social inequality. Although no one research effort can definitively address all these questions, this book attempts to provide answers for one important setting, that is, the agencies and departments of the U.S. federal government. As this book will argue, developments in the federal civil service both affected and reflected developments in the American labor market as a whole.

INSTITUTIONAL VERSUS TECHNICAL THEORIES OF ORGANIZATIONAL LABOR MARKETS

In their 1971 book, *Internal Labor Markets and Manpower Analysis*, Doeringer and Piore attributed the structure of internal labor markets to three principal causes: (1) skill specificity, (2) on-the-job training, and (3) customary law.[2] They argued at the time that these three concerns were "not envisioned in conventional economic theory" (Doeringer and Piore 1971: 13). Economic models have grown more sophisticated since then and incorporated not only skill specificity and on-the-job training but other technical factors as well. But the third of Doeringer and Piore's determinants, the role of "custom" and other noneconomic factors, is largely the province of sociological research.

Neoclassical economists have viewed the development of internal labor markets as economically rational responses to market contingencies. Firms come into existence because of the advantages of team production over individual production. But team production makes it difficult for management to pay workers a wage equal to their marginal products because the marginal product of individual team members is too difficult to measure (Alchian and Demsetz 1972). Economists classify ILMs as incentive systems based on the tournament rather than the piece-rate model (Williamson 1975, 1985; Lazear and Rosen 1981; Rosen 1985; see also Rosenbaum 1979) that solve the problems created by team production. Firms reward productive workers with promotions and the chance to play in new tournaments for still higher stakes. Competitors for promotions are thus motivated to improve their productivity and are deterred from opportunistic behavior. Furthermore, economists have argued that tournament models provide justification for the sharply higher rewards at the top of the hierarchy (Lazear and Rosen 1981; Rosen 1985). In some versions, these models justify the creation of boundaries to restrict competition for vacancies to homogeneous groups of workers (Rosen 1985; see also Turner 1960). Finally, hierarchies provide a system for training workers efficiently while reducing turnover and thereby keeping the necessity of retraining at a minimum (Ross 1958; Doeringer and Piore 1971).

Sociological explanations for the origin and development of ILMs do not ignore the importance of technical considerations but have looked beyond them to the role of institutional and political factors as

---

[2]Strictly speaking, their work applies only to blue-collar internal labor markets. However, later research on white-collar internal labor markets has focused on similar issues (e.g., Osterman 1984).

well (see Althauser 1987 for a useful survey).[3] Industrial conflict theories differ from technical, market-based theories in hypothesizing that ILMs grew out of the industrial conflict, and potential conflict, of management and workers (Edwards 1979; Jacoby 1983). Political theories see outcomes as a consequence of legislation or administrative actions by the state. Institutional theories attribute the development of ILMs to the development of the personnel department and of personnel specialists.

The very existence of a short list of alternative theories is proof of scholarly progress in this area. However, it is unlikely that definitive answers will be obtained by a further paring of this list in search of a universal origins theory, be it economic, political, or institutional in character. First, it is unlikely that the same theory will provide a viable explanation for ILMs in all the different segments that make up an economy. But, more importantly, the factors on Althauser's short list of competing origin theories contain not only alternative environmental forces shaping organizational responses but also alternative mechanisms by which organizations could respond to environmental pressure. In particular, the role of the personnel office in shaping outcomes must be interpreted both as a response to certain environmental forces and as the way an organization would respond to environmental contingencies in general. In other words, it both mediates other forces and plays an independent role in shaping outcomes.

The mediating role of the personnel department is easy to see. The state, the market, and the presence of unions place environmental constraints on organizations seeking to attain objectives, whether the objective is profitability or some more substantive goal. From the rational decision perspective, the personnel department would respond to the employment aspects of these constraints in a way that is consistent with the organization's goals; that is, would play the role of the rational actor for the organization. But personnel departments are not purely rational actors. Institutionalization theory hypothesizes that the establishment and operation of the personnel office constitutes a distinct force shaping employment relations, one not reducible to market forces, industrial relations, or state action.

Institutionalization theory argues that organizational practices develop in response to an organization's need to maintain social legitimacy. To quote Tolbert and Zucker (1983: 25), "institutionalization re-

---

[3]Althauser summarized the principal origins theories of ILMs as (1) a consequence of core–periphery organization, (2) an outcome of struggles between workers and management, (3) the development of personnel departments, formalized rule structures, and the rise of bureaucratic control, (4) firm-specific skills, (5) on-the-job training, and (6) employer needs for renewable supplies of otherwise scarce, highly skilled workers.

fers to the process through which components of formal structure become widely accepted as both appropriate and necessary, and serve to legitimate organizations." Origin theories involving the personnel department naturally would stress institutional over technical considerations, especially given their connection with the more general phenomena of bureaucratization and professionalization (see, for example, Meyer and Rowan 1977; DiMaggio and Powell 1983; Baron et al. 1986).

Institutionalization theory relies heavily on the proposition that the institutionalized "solution," and the efficient solution to an organizational problem are generally quite different. Pfeffer and Cohen (1984: 555), for instance, wrote that

> Once a practice becomes institutionalized . . . , prediction of adoption versus nonadoption depends much less on efficiency criteria than on the unit's position in the interorganizational information network, its need for legitimacy, and the normative sanctions it would confront if it failed to conform to generalized expectations. Institutionalization may lead to the adoption of practices that are, therefore, quite uncorrelated with efficiency.

The claim that structural development is only weakly connected to efficiency considerations is the clearest difference between institutionalization theory and theories that link organizational development to technical or market forces.

Meyer and Rowan (1977) argued that institutionalized solutions would generally be incapable of addressing technical problems efficiently, for three reasons. First, they asserted, institutionalized rules are primarily oriented toward ritual significance, not toward operational effectiveness. Second, institutionalized rules are "couched at high levels of generalization, . . . whereas technical activities vary with specific, unstandardized, and possibly unique conditions" (p. 355). Third, the institutionalized elements themselves might be inconsistent. This view that institutionalization is in conflict with technical rationality led them to view organizations as lying on a continuum, with institutionalized organizations at one end and organizations "under strong output controls" at the other (Meyer and Rowan 1977: 354).

The tension between the legitimate and the efficient, Meyer and Rowan further argued, creates problems for operating officials, problems that they described as "structural inconsistency" in institutionalized organizations. Structural inconsistency results from the organization's inconsistent needs for technical efficiency and for social legitimacy. The hypothesis of structural inconsistency leads to predictions about the form that day-to-day organizational activity will take. First, organizations resist external monitoring, which might uncover the extent of inefficiency involved in ceremonial adherence to legitimate standards for organizing particular activities. Instead, the organization encourages both internal participants and external observers to maintain both "confidence and good faith" regarding the organization's performance. Second, to the extent necessary, organizational members decouple actual activities from the activities one might expect if the organization maintained "rigid conformity to institutionalized prescriptions" (p. 356). This allows the activities of the organization to "vary in response to practical considerations" (p. 357), whereas this variation is hidden from outsiders, who might view it as undermining the organization's legitimacy.

In discussions such as Meyer and Rowan's, the assumption persists that adherence to institutional prescriptions will often be inefficient. But although institutional and technical constraints no doubt are often mutually inconsistent, one risks undercutting the utility of the institutionalization approach by stressing the conflict too much. Instead, it is arguable that the supposed conflict arises from a theoretical misunderstanding about how technical constraints operate. This misunderstanding concerns the problem of how organizational actors interpret their environment. It assumes that in highly competitive environments, rational actors can accurately diagnose and solve technical problems, whereas in institutionalized environments, the need to maintain legitimacy precludes organizations from effectively solving technical problems. But if the search process for solutions is inherently interpretive and if the forces of institutionalization are at work in formulating operating strategies in even the most competitive environments, then the relationship between the institutional and the technical is not simply one of opposition. Instead, it is arguable that the process of search and implementation, even in environments where technical considerations are important, inherently involves institutionalization as a force that shapes the processes of search and organizational decision making.

Even scholars who have underplayed the role of institutionalization in organizational development have argued that organizational problem solving is never optimal in any objective sense. Herbert Simon (1945–1957) reasoned that because organizations do not have the processing capacity to find optimal solutions, they must content themselves with solutions that are merely satisfactory; that is, they must satisfice. In Simon's formulation, of course, satisficing is a form of rational decision making that takes information costs into account along with other considerations. As such, it does not apparently resemble the picture of ritual conformity to an established cultural model, which is suggested by institutionalization theory. But if institutionalization theory is broadened to recognize that plastic and dynamic cultural models can shape decision making without eliminating the possibility of choice, then the complementarities between institutional and more technical theories of organizational development become more visible. The independent contribution of institutionalization theory then becomes the specification of what might be termed the *option space* from which choice and implementation is made.

One predisposed to technical theories of development might question the assumption that the framework within which search and implementation occurs has much bearing on the final form of organizational structures. In the spirit of DiMaggio and Powell's (1983) competitive isomorphism model, one might predict that the configuration of costs and benefits for alternative solutions would lead different decision makers to arrive at the same answer. This is often an implicit assumption in economic models for the development of ILMs; by showing the market rationality of ILMs, they implicitly or explicitly claim to have explained their origins. This approach to the origins problem would be fine if the search for solutions to problems is unproblematic, if options for choice are given, and if the rational decision maker makes his or her choice in a way consistent with his or her goal of maximizing profitability. But if different solutions produce roughly comparable results and if decision makers satisfice instead of maximize, then these assumptions are unrealistic. If competitive pressures are weaker than market-based models assume, then the range of possible solutions grows even further. As the range of possible variation grows, so too does interest in the process that gave rise to any particular solution. It is here that sociological approaches can play an important role.

Indirect evidence for how institutional forces can partly explain the structure of employment relationships comes from available studies of how these relationships are organized cross-nationally. Consider, for example, the issue of how organizational rank is defined. In France (Maurice, Sellier, and Silvestre 1986), the United States (Suskin 1977; Henderson 1979), and the private sector in Britain (Dore 1973; Lupton and Bowey 1974), position is determined by attributes of the job. In Japan (Dore 1973), Germany (Maurice *et al.* 1982), and the public sector in Britain (Gladden 1967), employees have a personal rank or status apart from the particular position they happen to be working in. The basis for this rank is not everywhere the same, however. In the British civil service, for example, one obtains membership in the elite civil service through examination. In Germany's private sector, an employee's professional credential or apprenticeship certificate determines his or her status. In Japan, employers use personal rank to reward seniority without having to give an employee more responsibility than the employee can manage (Dore 1973: 68).

There are also differences in the relationship between education and recruitment. Granick (1972), for instance, showed that the patterns of recruitment to top management positions differ greatly in France, England, and the United States. English firms recruit a large portion of their management from the ranks of high-school graduates. People entering the bottom ranks of management have had a reasonably good chance of moving to top management positions (see also Acton Society Trust 1956). But in France, top managers are almost always graduates from the *grande ecole*. Middle managers have had little chance to move into the ranks of top management. The United States falls midway between these two cases. A much larger proportion of new middle managers have college degrees than in England, but the boundary between top and middle management is not as rigid as in France. In Germany, advancement to managerial jobs has been possible for those who obtain the right professional credentials through the extensive system of adult education.[4] The stress in Germany on credentials, however, apparently restricts seniority-based promotions, in contrast to the situation in France (Maurice et al. 1986). In Japan, virtually all managers have university degrees, which they obtained before they started working.

The organization of public administration also exhibits cross-national variation. Chapman (1959) reported in the late 1950s that civil servants in Spain, Italy, and Denmark simply could not advance from middle to upper civil service class jobs. Employees in these countries also had trouble moving from the lower to the middle class because of the rigid educational requirements for higher jobs. German workers could sometimes cross tier boundaries, but Chapman reported that only Britain and France had set up formal procedures to make such promotions easier (also see Suleiman, 1971; Rose, 1984; Cassese 1984; Valenzuela 1984). American civil servants have had an easier time advancing through the ranks than their British counterparts. American scientists and engineers have advanced to top administrative jobs, also in contrast with the British case. Moreover, lateral entry is a more important route into civil service jobs in the United States than in most European countries (Van Riper 1958; Chapman 1959; Mosher 1965; Reimer 1965; Heclo 1977, 1984).

Such cross-national variation suggests that the technical character of

[4]Obtaining additional credentials at midcareer is also a mobility route in Britain (Dore 1973: 46).

work does not by itself control the personnel structures that evolved to match workers and jobs. "Generalized social values, norms, and roles," operating through the "existence of social models and premises concerning what organizations 'can and should be'" also are important (Lammers and Hickson 1979: 403). Although technical considerations constrain organizational development, these constraints are too weak to force convergence in industrial forms (Clark 1979).

A supporter of the unproblematic search model might counter that the different solutions are each maximally efficient for their own particular environments. For example, one might argue that the adult educational systems of France and Germany are so different that employers in the two countries would be foolish to structure promotion and training decisions in the same way (Maurice *et al.* 1986). For another example, American employers have an incentive to use job analysis and rank-in-the-job classification systems in order to maintain compliance with terms of the Equal Pay Act of 1963 and Title VII of the Civil Rights Act (Henderson 1979).

Such counterarguments, although reasonable to a point, do not make a compelling case against institutional explanations. The implicit claim that institutional forces shape the external environment within which companies operate, without shaping the way they go about solving environmental problems, is dubious on its face. Moreover, recent comparative studies of economic performance would question both the proposition that employment relationships are equally efficient in the capitalist countries of East Asia, North America, and Europe and the proposition that any differences could be ascribed entirely to external actors such as the state (e.g., Magaziner and Reich 1982; Thurow 1985; Piore and Sabel 1984). However, one can side with institutionalization theory in this debate without succumbing to its tendency to exaggerate the cultural at the expense of the technical (see, e.g., Perrow 1985), as if, for example, the Japanese lifetime employment system was a "purely cultural" phenomenon, with only an accidental relationship to the standard of efficient production (cf., e.g., Aoki 1984). Instead, with suitable modifications, one can combine the advantages of each school into a more satisfying explanation for the development of organizational structures such as internal labor markets. To do this, one must look beyond the superficial contradictions to the evidence that organizational development often results from an interplay between the two forces. The search for a useful synthesis can best start by examining the basis for legitimacy in institutionalized environments.

Meyer and Rowan reported in their seminal (1977) article on institutionalization that a strong ideological connection often exists between efficiency and legitimation. This connection exists because, as Ellul (1964) had argued earlier, the myths that legitimize particular ways of organizing activity often claim that the structures in question *are* efficient; in Western capitalist culture, the attainment of legitimacy often rests on this claim. But if claims regarding efficiency are necessary for a particular organizational form, policy, or procedure to achieve legitimacy, then it follows that the structure in question has claims to being a technology, which differs from physical technologies because of the difficulty of making efficiency comparisons with competing technologies.

Because institutionalized structures often have a claim to being technologies designed to efficiently solve certain problems, it is reasonably clear that no general statement can be made about the level of efficiency of any particular institutionalized solution. As Meyer, Scott, and Deal (1983) noted in their discussion of "some unresolved theoretical problems" in the study of institutionalization:

> Technologies become institutionalized in their own right. Further, rationalized institutional arrangements in society often come to spell out and enforce technologies of action (whether objectively or socially defined as efficacious) in great detail. Hence institutional environments may not always lead to a decoupling of organizational structure from technical activities . . . .
> Our theory is very ambiguous here. Will the resultant organizational activities be tightly or loosely coupled? Are the two processes really at odds much of the time in organizational life? (Meyer *et al.* 1983: 61–62)

What is the basis, then, of the idea that institutional structures can be "quite uncorrelated" with efficiently designed procedures? Meyer and Rowan in effect hypothesized that institutionalized structures had two properties that interfered with efficiency. First, institutionalized rules are stated at high levels of generality. Second, Meyer and Rowan assumed that these values would substantially limit the discretion of an official trying to conform with them. These two considerations justify their argument that the institutional and the efficient solution to a particular problem might differ. The generality of institutionalized rules clashes with the specific, unique quality of real-world situations. In addition, their confining quality precludes a flexible response by organizational members who try both to respond to practical problems and to stay within the rules. Without these two qualities—rules that are stated at a high level of generality but that are confining if adhered to—there would be no need for the decoupling response that Meyer and Rowan predicted to resolve structural inconsistency. It therefore follows that the discrepancies one would expect between the predictions of a rational search model and an institutional model depend upon the applicability of Meyer and Rowan's assumptions to actual situations.

I would argue that the applicability of these assumptions would itself vary, depending upon the situation in question. This variation can be specified in terms of three contingencies. First, recall that institutionalized rules typically contain some official justification that supports their claim to legitimacy. This justification may be seen as the formulation of an official problem to which these rules provide an official solution. Therefore, the first contingency concerns the extent to which the legitimate solution efficiently solves the official problem it is intended for. An idealized solution may or may not be the right way to solve an idealized problem. If the idealized solution is inappropriate for the idealized problem, one would not expect real-world implementations of this solution to be useful in solving the real-world problems corresponding to the textbook ideal.

The second contingency concerns the relationship between the official problem that the legitimate practice is ostensibly a solution for and the real-world problems that confront organizations that adopt this solution. Meyer and Rowan assumed high variability in real-world manifestations of idealized problems. But the extent of variability across problem areas may itself be variable. For some problems, abstract solutions may be generally inefficient, whereas for other problems, they may produce technically acceptable results.

The third contingency concerns the extent and ways in which the officially defined problem constrains organizational behavior. Institutionalization theory assumes that structure is generally confining—otherwise, there would be no need for the "decoupling" response that Meyer and Rowan saw as the way to resolve the inconsistency between the technical and the institutional. But this assumption may not hold in many situations. Ronald Dworkin's (1967) analysis of the constraints that law places on behavior provides a useful framework for understanding this issue.

Dworkin distinguished the concepts of rules, principles, and policies according to the constraint on behavior each produced. By his usage, principles are standards to be followed as a requirement of fairness, policies are standards that set out some goal to be reached, whereas rules have an all-or-nothing quality; if applicable, they are completely constraining, though they may require officials to exercise discretion in interpreting the facts before the rule is applied. Although he intended these terms to apply to constraints on decision making in the law, they apply to organizations also, by suggesting varying levels of constraint implied by different types of structures and varying levels in the quality of the fit between institutionalized structures and an organization's technical problems. For example, a loosely constraining set of institutionalized guidelines may contribute to the efficient solution of a particular type of organizational problem, even one whose specific manifestations vary. In this case, a manager would be able to retain a certain flexibility in handling a particular issue without risking organizational legitimacy. If the institutionalized structure imposed rules in Dworkin's sense, then the level of flexibility would depend upon the freedom the manager had to make factual determinations. The extent to which such constraints interfered with efficiency would depend upon whether efficiency was a function of the factual determination—in which case there would be no conflict—or whether the procedure itself was inefficient. In the latter case, a conflict between legitimacy and efficiency would exist, and decoupling or some other response might be necessary.

The purpose of this discussion has not been to suggest practical ways of evaluating and explaining the efficiency of various institutionalized structures. As I noted earlier, the efficiency properties of institutionalized technologies may be difficult to determine. It rather is to support the claim that the connection between technical forces, the process of institutionalization, and the effect of institutionalized structures on outcomes is more complex than usually realized, and to justify a particular synthesis for explaining the current structure of white-collar internal labor markets, as well as similar structures designed at least ostensibly for the solution of technical or market problems.

The assumption underlying most economic models of employment relationships is that the search process leading to development and implementation is unproblematic; hence the interesting question is to show how a particular structure is efficient. The answer to this question is implicitly taken to be the explanation for its development. The assumption often underlying the institutionalization literature is that cultural forces are so powerful and monolithic that the implementation of structure is again unproblematic, though its implementation is usually too abstract, too confining, and too unresponsive to technical needs to be instrumental in accomplishing its official purpose. In this case, the spreading implementation of the cultural model and any resulting structural inconsistencies are the focus of interest. Consider instead a situation in which institutionalized solutions are not monolithic, at least during the early development of the structures in question. Consider further the possibility that the developing institutionalized solutions are at least partially responsive to technical considerations, though not so responsive as to prevent alternative, competing solutions from coexisting in a struggle for legitimacy. If option sets rather than monolithic models dominate early development, then a different set of questions arise. These questions include (1) the origins of the emerging option set; (2) how the emerging option set constrained the early search process of organizational decision makers; (3) how the option set was shaped by (a) the early experience and interpretation of this experience by pioneering implementers and (b) by other relevant sociopolitical forces that create what in effect would be a competition among the alternatives of the option set; (4) the outcome of this competition for the mature form of the cultural model that provides guidance and legitimacy for later implementation; and (5) the relationship between structure and outcomes, which itself might generally be a consequence of the process that shaped the evolution of the option set, that is, the path as well as the destination of organizational development.

The applicability of this approach for understanding the development of ILMs depends upon the assumption that multiple, competing models existed and that each had claims to legitimacy as a technically viable strategy for organizing white-collar work. At least in the American case, this condition is probably satisfied. Three competing sources of legitimacy stand out: (1) the scientific management movement, (2) the professionalization movement, and (3) a long-standing tradition supporting the proposition that office workers at almost any level can learn their trade better on the job than in school. Although each has influenced the development of job ladders, none has so thoroughly controlled its development and implementation as to eliminate the influence of the other two.

The scientific management movement was a principal contributor to the development of personnel management in American business (Hawley 1979). The proponents of scientific management asserted that the actions of people as well as of mechanisms could be engineered to increase efficiency. This engineering, they claimed, could not only determine the best way to perform specific job tasks through time and motion studies but also the best way to bundle tasks into jobs and to select the right person to fill a given job. A principal result of the scientific management orientation to problem solving was that American personnel systems tended to emphasize position classification systems based upon rank-in-the-job, rather than European style rank-in-the-man systems (Baruch 1944; Heclo 1984). Rank-in-the-job systems naturally led to the construction of job ladders. However, it is fair to say that scientific management *per se* never produced anything approaching a detailed set of principles for the production of job ladders. Its specific principles for the organization of production were rarely implemented, even by corporations that claimed to be doing so (Edwards 1979). Eventually, with the advent of the human relations movement, it fell into disrepute, though scholars disagree about its lasting influence (see, e.g., Haber 1964; Merkle 1980).

Another major influence on the organization of white-collar work in the United States has been the rise of professionalism (Larson 1977; Kocka 1980). In the usual sociological formulation, a profession is an occupation whose performance requires scientific or technical knowledge best learned in a university education and whose incumbents have a self-awareness of the occupation as a community, with a professional association, a service orientation, and a code of ethics. However, as Johnson (1972), Larson (1977), and others (see, e.g., Haskell 1984) have emphasized, the specific way that work of a particular type is organized over time is not simply a function of its place in the technical division of labor. Sociocultural and political factors create alternative forms of organizations even when the technical constraints are roughly similar. Kocka (1980), for example, noted that the democratic tradition of the United States places a high value on specialized competence and condemns privileges, titles, and monopolies. As a consequence, he argued, white-collar workers in the United States found the professional model for shaping their self-identity more conducive than a status model based upon broad distinctions between blue collar and white collar, as in Germany.

A specialized professional model, would, if fully realized, lead to the development of occupational internal labor markets, where the occupation itself controlled entry through its control of the procedures for learning the trade. But the existence of the professional model did not guarantee its acceptance for all occupations for which claims were made. The market position of any particular occupation, the interests and resources of universities and employers, and the response of the general public and the state tempered the precise influence of the professional model on the organization of work. In some cases, for example, retail store clerks, there was too large a gap between the occupation's claim to specialized competence and the low skill requirements needed to do the job. In other cases, for example, managers, administrators, and to some extent social workers and engineers, the occupation had no effective way of wresting complete control over training and selection from the large and powerful employers for whom many incumbents worked. Professionalization, in short, has had a broad influence on the organization of work, but its influence has often fallen short of complete dominance.

A third influence on the organization of management and administration in the United States, one in tension with the forces of professionalization, is the American "antiintellectual" (Hofstadter 1964) tradition that champions the value of practical experience over the theoretical knowledge taught in universities. Even such currently well-established professions as medicine had to overcome resistance to its claims to authority from the leveling democratic culture of nineteenth-century America (Starr 1982; see also Haskell 1977). Resistance to the professionalization of management was even greater, given the general American view that success in business came from good business judgment. This talent might be discovered and nurtured through on-the-job training, but it could not be taught in college. In the words of Andrew Carnegie, "college education, as it exists, is fatal to success in that domain" (quoted in Veysey 1965:13–14). To this day, observers question the professional status of administration and management even as others assert its existence.

The existence of multiple models from which legitimacy might be drawn has important implications for the development and impact of white-collar job ladders. In a world in which technical needs were such that one solution completely dominated others and where legitimation was obtained largely through appeals to efficiency, I would expect that form to gain exclusive legitimacy and to be applied universally. A more accurate description of the process of decision making and implementation of white-collar internal labor markets, however, may be that multiple actors formulated these structures out of a set of limited options, each of which had some claim to legitimacy and each of which was favored by particular actors who had the resources to influence results. This view differs from the search model in emphasizing the limitations that legitimacy considerations place on the option set that receives serious consideration or can realistically be promoted by one or another of the interested parties. This competition for control of implementation, which was sometimes muted and other times intense, combined with practical concerns to shape further development both of the models in the option set and of the structures themselves. In other words, cultural and other factors can create variation both in the option sets struggling for legitimacy in different contexts and in the ultimate form the legitimate structures take.

The existence of multiple models for organizing work raises the question of how much variation to expect in the structure of different white-collar occupations and in the implications of internal labor market structures for actual personnel decisions about recruitment and promotion. As I pointed out earlier, various spokesmen, either for occupational groups themselves or for interested parties, have claimed relevance for the professional model for a wide range of white-collar occupations. However, as much of the literature on professions has argued, the legitimacy of this claim has not been institutionalized equally across the range of occupations for whom the claim has been made. For some occupations, laws stipulate that incumbents must have particular educational credentials. But even many commonly accepted professions do not have this level of social closure. Freidson (1986), for instance, pointed out that companies are not generally required to hire engineers, nurses, librarians, accountants, and social workers on the basis of credentials, even though these occupations are commonly thought of as professions. Employers also have discretion in the educational requirements they set for managers and administrators, whose professional status remains ambiguous, despite the increased prominence of business school and the MBA degree in the United States.[5]

Because competing models for the organization of work have shaped the institutionalization of internal labor markets, explanations for the precise form these structures would take, especially in the case of office work, are not always simple. On the one hand, the combination of scientific management and professionalism predicts the establishment of job ladders that are organized around occupations, that define ranks in terms of jobs rather than people, and that are tiered, where the tiering is justified in terms of the educational requirements of jobs. However, these institutional solutions have had to compete with other traditions that question the worth of education for office work and that value on-the-job experience instead. As a result, it is possible for different syntheses of these alternatives to emerge, creating tiers between upper-level managerial/administrative work and lower-level clerical work that are more or less porous to employee movement.

The existence of multiple options for structuring white-collar ILMs allows both technical and sociopolitical forces to influence their development. Consider, for instance, the relationship between the supply of education among young job seekers and the development of credentialism, defined to mean that employers prefer highly educated job applicants, even when their training is not specifically useful for the job in question (Berg 1970; Collins 1979). Economists arguing against the credentialism theory have hypothesized that employers use education as a

[5]When I use the word *administrative* in this book, it is meant to apply to higher-level office work, including both managerial and administrative. Technically speaking, of course, administrators are staff specialists, whereas managers design organizational policy and direct its execution. See, for example, Henderson (1979) for a good summary of the differences.

screen, that is, as a source of information about the applicant's general capabilities. If the highly educated are generally more capable, it might make sense for employers to favor them and then give them specific training on the job. An increase in the proportion of young people with college degrees might make college a more useful screen and motivate employers to require college for administrative jobs. This development might further institutionalize tier boundaries and lead to an excessive reliance on this source of manpower at the expense of the subset of existing lower-level employees who are capable of handling more responsible work. The promotion rate, in other words, might depend upon how much legitimacy this alternative option retained.

To understand the distribution of legitimacy across alternatives, one must analyze the interests and conflicts that would influence this distribution. Although the effect of union–management struggles on the structure of white-collar job ladders is more questionable than is its impact on blue-collar internal labor markets (Edwards 1979; Jacoby 1983), they still might have some importance. Discrimination, and the civil rights movement that emerged to fight it, is also a potentially important element. Institutionalization theory suggests that the legitimate option set constrains the form of these struggles but does not preclude conflict from shaping the evolving option set as well.

The existence of multiple principles of legitimacy and of competing interpretations of how these principles should be applied raises questions not only about the form of job ladders but about their impact on employee mobility, and on the proper interpretation of this impact. Institutionalization theory, in its usual form, might interpret the relationship between the structures that define internal labor markets and actual patterns of movement as a test of the extent to which decoupling has occurred, that is, as a test of the ability of these structures to fulfill the technical mission that supposedly justifies their existence. Although this description may be adequate in certain respects, it has shortcomings as well. From the institutionalization perspective, decoupling is most likely where strong pressures for conformity to a legitimate model combine with technical inadequacy of this model. But in a world that lacks a strong consensus on the "right" way to structure promotion systems, the extent to which operating officials are constrained to hire and promote only within job ladders and to prohibit movement across tiers is an open question. Going back to Dworkin's language, the rules of internal labor markets may in some cases bind behavior with rules but in others serve only as guidelines. In the latter case, ILMs might still influence organizational behavior, but their exact effects would be less predictable and subject to greater manipulation by actors with an interest in behavioral outcomes. Social legitimacy for structures that function only as guidelines may permit a certain amount of cross-organization variability in their effects as well. The precise determination of the impact of job ladder boundaries on employee movement is a question best answered through empirical analysis.

This discussion suggests an outline for describing the development of a tiered system of job ladders, which can be stated as a set of hypotheses:

1. There are many ways for organizing work. Alternative strategies may be similarly efficient. Environments are too complex and change too rapidly for any process of experimentation or comparison to reveal which alternative is optimally efficient. Instead, organizational decisions on the matter depend upon the very few models for organizing work that are culturally legitimate at the time.

2. The number of culturally available methods for organizing an activity will generally be variable. At some times and for some situations, only one legitimate solution may present itself. At other times and for other solutions, the number of possibilities may be larger. The number of such models is not random, but itself is explainable in terms of larger social forces.

3. The scientific management movement caused internal labor markets to be organized around hierarchies of jobs, rather than of people. Pay and position were job related. However, scientific management left open the question of the particular form that job ladders would take and of the extent to which they would control employee mobility.

4. The process of professionalization has affected the development of white-collar internal labor markets for nonprofessional as well as for professional work. Its effect has generally been to differentiate work in particular functional areas into upper and lower tiers, and to associate upper tier work with college or university graduation. However, the closure implied by tier boundaries may vary substantially, depending upon the strength of societal forces that constrain the way positions in any given occupation are filled.

5. The availability of multiple options for structuring work constrains the development of job ladders. The precise form these job ladders will take is an outcome of a political process, where

management, employees, professional groups, universities, and
the state may all play a role. Their form will also depend on the
results of early experimentation with job ladders.

6. Changes in the distribution of higher education probably affected the development of tier boundaries. The practice of using
   college degrees as a screen, coupled with the expansion of the
   education system, might institutionalize tier boundaries.

7. Race and gender inequality did not create the labor market tiers
   that characterize the organization of white-collar work in organizations. But they articulate well with these tiers and may have
   reinforced them. Conversely, changes in patterns of racial and
   gender segregation could affect the organization of internal labor
   markets as well.

8. The implications of job ladders for employee movement will depend upon their configuration, the constraints or influences they
   place on the behavior of managers, and the practical considerations that managers must also take into account when filling
   vacancies.

PUBLIC VERSUS PRIVATE SECTOR ORGANIZATIONS

Ideally, one would examine the validity of these hypotheses with
data from a representative sample of bureaucratized organizations. Unfortunately, the data requirements and other resources necessary for
such an analysis are prohibitive. This book instead takes a case study
approach to the problem. It examines the development of tiered job
ladders in the federal civil service of the United States. The federal
government is the nation's largest employer, and its personnel policies
are highly visible. The findings of this book are therefore likely to be
important simply because of the influence the government has had on
developments elsewhere. But because this book focuses on a single
employer, the issue of how generalizable the findings are likely to be
will also arise and should be addressed at the outset.

A useful way to approach this question is to isolate the characteristics of the federal government that are most likely to influence the
development of its personnel policies. First, it is large, and like virtually all large organizations it is bureaucratically organized (Blau and
Schoenherr 1971). Second, its activities are not structured by a profit
motive. The question arises whether federal personnel policy is similar
to that of other large organizations, or whether it is similar only to the
subset of large organizations that can be found in the public sector.

Clearly, this question cannot receive a definitive answer here because it ultimately depends upon the existence of multiple studies as comprehensive as the one attempted here. Nonetheless, we know enough about the character of public and private personnel systems to arrive at a tentative answer.

First, we know that bureaucratic personnel policies are a characteristic of large organizations, not just of large public ones. Pfeffer and Cohen (1984) found, for instance, that whereas government organizations were more likely to make use of internal labor markets than private-sector firms, this difference disappeared once the presence of a personnel department was controlled. Most workers in the United States have worked for firms with personnel departments since the 1930s (Jacoby 1983; Baron *et al.* 1986). By 1954, 85% of establishments with more than 250 employees had a centralized personnel department (National Industrial Conference Board [NICB] 1954: 119). The percentage has undoubtedly increased further since then (National Industrial Conference Board 1965: 68; National Industrial Conference Board 1966: 203).

Furthermore, it is likely that the personnel departments in the public and the private sector will organize personnel practices in roughly similar ways. Cohen and Pfeffer (1986), showed with their sample of 306 Bay Area establishments that "public trust" establishments, which included governmental organizations as well as certain other service establishments, were more likely to require college degrees for a benchmark set of occupations, were more likely to be selective in other ways, and were more likely to use tests. However, these differences disappeared when Cohen and Pfeffer included a control for the existence of a personnel department. Thus, the form of recruiting is shaped not by sector, but by level of bureaucratization as indicated by the presence of a personnel department. Authors such as Cohen and Pfeffer and Stinchcombe (1979) have used industrial typologies that combined government organizations with private sector industries such as banks and insurance companies. Their actions are recognitions that bureaucratization and the type of work performed may be as important as the "public" quality of the organization in determining personnel practices and career mobility.

These arguments notwithstanding, it must be recognized that the government's unique character will affect its labor markets. The literature on organizational development predicts that the forces of institutionalization should have had a relatively stronger influence on personnel developments in the federal civil service than in private-sector firms, and technical factors should have had relatively less importance. This difference may affect not only the rules regarding recruitment and promotion but also the extent to which managers follow these rules or decouple behavior under particular circumstances. It must be emphasized, however, that the justification for a study of personnel practices and outcomes in the federal civil service does not rest simply upon its representativeness. In an economy as diverse as the American one, there is no such thing as a single representative organization. The historical position of the federal civil service as a model for other organizations, when combined with the availability of data for studying it, provide ample justification by themselves for a study such as this. It joins other studies of employment policies and practices in individual firms (Bartholomew 1973; Kanter 1977; Stewman and Konda 1983; Rosenbaum 1984; Pfeffer and Cohen 1984; Baron *et al.* 1986) in laying the groundwork for future comparative research.

Many scholars have studied the federal civil service in the past. Some tracked the development of public personnel management as an outgrowth of the civil service reform movement (Mosher *et al.* 1950; Van Riper 1958; Rosenbloom 1971, 1977; Nigro and Nigro 1976; Shafritz *et al.* 1981). This study treats such issues only to the extent that they affected organizational stratification, whether in form or practice. Another group of studies investigated the political power of higher civil servants (Lowi 1969; Heclo 1977; Seidman 1980). In contrast, this study focuses on the organization of work, not the political power of the bureaucracy. Studies of bureaucratic power have naturally focused on the highest positions of the civil service, where power is concentrated. This study concerns the entire hierarchy, which is numerically dominated by the lower- and middle-level jobs. But it will also show that the organization of high-level jobs in an organization can affect the organization of work throughout the white-collar hierarchy.

THE CHANGING STRUCTURE OF WHITE-COLLAR WORK IN THE FEDERAL GOVERNMENT: AN OVERVIEW

Earlier in this chapter, I formulated a set of loosely stated hypotheses regarding the development of job ladders for white-collar jobs. The following chapters provide the details to substantiate them. Before proceeding, however, it is useful to more closely relate them to the specific case of the federal government by previewing the principal themes that shaped the development of a tiered system of job ladders in the federal government. This preview is the subject of the present section.

Three major changes have occurred in the organization of white-collar work in the federal government during the past century. Each change has had important implications for organizational inequality and mobility. First, the federal civil service has grown enormously in the past century, though at an uneven rate. Second, with this growth has come substantial change in both the composition of white-collar work and the shape of the government hierarchy. The upper-level professional and administrative ranks grew even more rapidly than the work force of the government as a whole. Third, the specification of the civil service hierarchy itself has changed in response to the development and application of standardized position classification systems, a development linked to the rise of scientific management in the United States.

If all federal hiring was done at the bottom grades and vacancies were generally filled by promotion, the changing shape of the grade structure would have greatly increased promotional opportunities for employees entering the system in the bottom, clerical grades. However, other forces have worked to counter this tendency. The process of professionalization resulted in the bifurcation of job ladders for both scientific and office work into an upper and a lower tier. Its effects on the organization of scientific positions and such professions as law or medicine have been greater than its effects on the administrative positions of government. Agencies limited access to professional positions to applicants with college degrees early in the present century. But the link between education and administrative careers was never formalized to the same extent, even though personnel officers in government generally placed greater weight on educational qualifications than their counterparts in the private sector did. Until the post-World-War II era, administrative positions were not clearly distinguished from clerical positions, and the structure of "services" in the civil service reflected that fact. But as a result of the professionalization of management, a distinction between clerical and administrative work was gradually institutionalized in the structure of job ladders. Management created a two-tier job ladder system for clerical and administrative work to parallel the tiered system for professional and subprofessional work.

One could reasonably argue that the separation of administrative from clerical work has a technical justification. According to this argument, the changing character of work in bureaucratized organizations such as the federal agencies created new administrative occupations. This new work was analytical in character and based on a body of formal knowledge. In this way, the argument goes, one can distinguish it from routinized, structured clerical tasks. Therefore, it properly belongs on separate job ladders.

But this argument is not by itself adequate to explain how tiers have developed. Neither clerical work nor administrative work is unitary in character. On the contrary, each exhibits substantial internal hetero-geneity. Such heterogeneity begs the question of where the boundary between the hierarchies should be drawn, or why any boundary should be drawn at all. The legitimacy of the professional model, the desire of management to enhance recruitment of college graduates, and the corre-sponding desire to introduce more controls over the promotion of lower-level employees are all part of the answer to this question.

The development of a two-tier personnel system in both the profes-sional and administrative sectors of government would obviously have important implications for the character of organizational careers. It would especially affect the lower-ranking employees, who have pre-dominantly been women and minorities in the postwar era. However, the actual impact of this development depends upon the precise char-acter of rules regarding recruitment and promotion. Personnel policies and practices could make job ladder boundaries either absolute barriers to movement or irrelevant terminology. In practice, their effect lay be-tween these extremes. Furthermore, the effects of the clerical–admin-istrative boundary and the subprofessional–professional boundary on personnel actions have not been the same. The clerical–administrative boundary has not been institutionalized to the same extent as the sub-professional–professional one. As a result, the rules regarding admin-istrative careers have been and remain more ambiguous, more conten-tious, and more open to policy initiatives than the rules regarding professional careers.

A civil service run according to merit principle is a professional civil service. The modifier "professional" emphasizes the neutral, compe-tent, career-oriented aspects of the service. The civil service is also pro-fessional in a more specific sense. It places greater weight on educational credentials than most private sector employers do (Collins 1979; Kocka 1980; Cohen and Pfeffer 1986). And, as Freidson (1986) argued, it is the requirement for college credentials that is the practical measure of whether a job can be considered to be a professional position.

But underneath this umbrella of professionalism there is still room for both a "professional" and a "nonprofessional" interpretation of the principles that should govern hiring and promotion decisions.[6] The "professional" perspective stressed the existence of qualitative dif-ferences between skill requirements for positions, the importance of

[6]These are my terms for the two perspectives; those who have supported the *nonprofessional* perspective on personnel management would naturally claim that their stance is consistent with a *professional* civil service. Such a claim is necessary to legitimize their stance, by making it symbolically compatible with the values of a merit system.

formal knowledge, and the need to recruit from universities. It also feared the harm to organizational efficiency that might come when officials promote employees past their level of competence. Supporters of the "professional" perspective assumed that this level would vary inversely with educational attainment and length of service in lower-level white-collar jobs. The "nonprofessional" perspective stressed the uniform progression in skill requirements between low- and high-level jobs, the value of practical experience, and the benefits of promotion policies to overall employee morale. Academics, particularly the Progressive era and New Deal reformers, and the emerging personnel management profession favored the "professional" perspective. Employee unions, veterans, and most recently civil rights and women's groups have favored the "nonprofessional" perspective.

The support of union officials and civil rights groups at various times in history for what I have described as the "nonprofessional" perspective does not contradict their obvious interest in high status for their constituencies. The federal civil service union in particular has actively promoted the status of the service throughout its history. However, professionalism has an exclusionary as well as a status-enhancing aspect. Those who concluded that such exclusionary policies were not in their interest have, not surprisingly, opposed them, even as they supported other policies that they perceived to be status enhancing.

Present-day personnel structures are in effect a shifting compromise between competing positions. The resulting policies combine with practical needs arising from organizational growth, its demographic structure, and the external labor market to define the implications of formal job ladders for civil service careers. The tension or conflict most salient at any given time was not always the same. In the early days of civil service reform, the key issue was the proper balance between patronage and merit principles. Supporters of patronage believed that the party structure, and hence the American democracy, depended for its viability on patronage. Civil service reformers thought that the party system as it then existed was a threat to democracy, largely because it kept government from developing greater administrative capacity to deal with modern social problems. The end of patronage politics and the installation of a merit civil service was their solution to the problem. In the middle were those who believed that the best government combined the two.

Later, other conflicts developed. One such conflict concerned the relative value of on-the-job training in lower governmental positions as opposed to college education as the best preparation for middle- and upper-level administrative positions. A second conflict concerned the proportion of lower-level employees who had the ability and temperament to do higher-level work. A third concerned the costs and benefits of providing training to civil servants at government expense, both to improve their ability to do their current job and to improve their prospects for advancement.

One's position on these issues depended in part on one's conception of what administrative work consisted of. Some argued that administrative work was largely a function of skill in dealing with people (i.e., personality) and organizational knowledge learned on the job; as such it was not highly related to education. Others argued that it was largely a function of intelligence. A third view was that administration was a secondary function of high-level technical jobs. Training for such jobs must therefore be primarily technical. A fourth view was that administrative skill came from a broad outlook on life learned through the right upbringing and through a liberal education. Technical skills were not necessarily unimportant, but they were a secondary priority. Finally, a fifth view was that administrative science was a profession of the same order as medicine and law and was properly learned through study at a university.

Debates about the nature of administration continued through much of the century, though they took a different form after World War II. In the 1930s and again in the 1950s, the question of the nature of administrative work became intertwined with competing conceptions about the nature of the state and the relationship between politics and administration. Debates about whether to set up an administrative class in the 1930s or a senior civil service in the 1950s turned on political differences as much as on disputes about the best training for administrative work. In the 1930s those who favored a strong articulation between a liberal arts college education and recruitment into administrative jobs were the same people who favored the creation of a strong state. Their vision of an administrative class was never realized. However, by the postwar period, the number of college graduates was much larger than in the 1930s. The Civil Service Commission (CSC) saw these young people as a major source of talent for filling even the more routine administrative jobs, which by then were proliferating in the federal government.

The principal controversy of the 1960s and 1970s concerned equal employment opportunity (EEO). The equal employment opportunity issue has of course affected employment relationships throughout the society. Even within the civil service, it arguably overshadowed the establishment of a Senior Executive Service in 1978. Earlier debates over the structure of job ladders concerned the relevance of educational credentials for recruitment into government jobs. In contrast, debates about EEO focused on disparities in the distribution of women, minorities, and white males in government positions. The conflict over EEO was superficially very different from earlier arguments about personnel policies during the Progressive and later the New Deal years. But a closer look shows the two to be very similar. One position, the non-professional one, argued for the opening of higher-level positions to those lower in the hierarchy, where employees capable of higher-level work could be found. It also viewed experience in these jobs as adequate preparation. Additional training, sometimes in specially designed "bridge" jobs, could fill remaining gaps in a lower-level worker's preparation. A second position, the professional one, tended to view lower-level employees as unqualified for higher-level positions. Either view could be framed to conform to merit principles. After all, both views accepted technical competence and fairness as the proper guidelines for personnel decisions. But they interpreted these terms differently. They also differed in their judgment of how much discrimination there was in the federal service.

The link between the structure of job ladders and outcomes depends not only on the rules and regulations governing recruitment and promotion decisions but also on management discretion. The amount of managerial discretion varies from one setting to another, typically being higher in private than in public bureaucracies. But even in a highly bureaucratized system of personnel management such as that found in the federal civil service, management has substantial discretion over personnel decisions. Extensive rules exist, but for the most part they provide only guidelines for the final decision. These guidelines themselves are part of the formal structure of the organization. Together with the demographic structure of the organization, the market environment, and broader cultural influences, they will affect personnel outcomes. Empirical analysis of personnel flows is necessary to pin down the link between structure and outcomes in a modern-day bureaucratic personnel system.

Chapters 2–4 are devoted to an analysis of changes in the white-collar hierarchy of the federal civil service and to the formal implications of these changes for organizational stratification and mobility. Chapter 2 focuses on organizational demography; it documents quantitatively the changing distribution of jobs by grade and by type in the federal government and shows the mathematical implications of this change for promotion rates, in the absence of shifts in recruitment policies. Chapter 3 discusses in more qualitative terms the development of the clerical–administrative boundary, whereas the Appendix analyzes position-classification standards for the years between 1920 and the present to show what the bifurcation of administrative and clerical work meant in the formal language of job analysis.

Chapters 4–6 address the question of the origins of the system of personnel rules and regulations that governed how these positions were to be filled. Chapter 4 discusses early personnel management in the federal civil service and the procedures developed by the civil service commission in the early years of the merit system for filling vacancies and for handling the subject of promotions. Chapter 5 discusses how scientific management and progressivism shaped the early development of job ladders and how the emerging question of whether administrative work was an extension of clerical work or a profession in its own right shaped proposals for structuring nonprofessional careers. Chapter 6 documents the dispute between proponents and opponents of the idea of an "administrative class" for the United States and how elements of that debate shaped the compromise that led to the implementation in the postwar period of a tiered system of job ladders for both professional and administrative jobs in the federal civil service.

The third part of this book uses quantitative analysis to determine the extent to which formal job ladders constrain employee movement, the extent to which these constraints have varied in recent years, and the implications of the structure of job ladders for the promotion of white males, women and minorities. Chapter 7 examines the link between formal job ladders and the way vacancies are filled. It looks at the question in substantial detail for a small number of bureaus and then shows that similar patterns exist in the civil service as a whole. Chapter 8 examines the impact of the equal employment opportunity movement on the job-ladder structure and on mobility from the lower to the upper tier. Chapter 9 then investigates the determinants of advancement in white-collar job ladders, the extent to which women and minorities are disadvantaged in the competition for advancement, and the ability of structural factors to account for these disadvantages. It also explores the linkages between initial assignment and advancement in a bureaucratic labor market operating under rules that are, in a formal sense, gender and race neutral.

I

THE STRUCTURE OF WHITE-COLLAR JOB LADDERS

2

The Hierarchy of White-Collar Work

CHANGES IN THE COMPOSITION OF THE LABOR FORCE

The changed composition of white-collar work in the federal government is only one manifestation of the remarkable transformation the American labor force as a whole has undergone during the present century. During this period, the American work force increased in size from 28 million to over 100 million. At the start of the century, almost half of these workers made their living by farming, but fewer than 1 in 20 are farmers today (U.S. Bureau of the Census 1975, 1980). But the most relevant change for present purposes is the rise to prominence of the white-collar worker. In 1900, only 18% of American workers were white-collar workers. By 1980, that proportion passed 50% as the American economy became a service economy (U.S. Bureau of the Census 1986).

Within the white-collar group, important compositional changes have occurred as well. Overall growth in the lower nonmanual occupations has exceeded growth in upper nonmanual occupations. In 1900, only 17% of white-collar workers could be classified as clerical and kindred workers. By 1970 that proportion had grown to nearly 38%. Most of the change occurred early in the century, but the clerical proportion of the white-collar work force continued to grow after that, albeit slowly: 37.2% of white-collar workers 14 and over in 1970 were clerical workers, as compared with 34% in 1950, 31% in 1940, or 30% in 1930 (U.S. Bureau of the Census 1975: Table D, 182–232). Since that time, the proportion of white-collar workers in clerical jobs has decreased slightly, and experts predict this decrease to continue for the rest of the century.[1] But this decrease notwithstanding, the category of clerical workers is a substantially larger proportion of the white-collar work force now than it was at the turn of the century.

The professional and administrative sectors have also grown enormously, both absolutely, and as a percentage of the labor force. In 1900, only 4.3% of the experienced civilian labor force (ECLF) 14 years of age and over were in professional, technical, or kindred occupations, with another 5.8% in the manager, officials, and proprietor occupational group. By 1950, 17% of the ECLF were in these two categories combined, whereas by 1970, 21% were so employed (U.S. Bureau of the Census 1975).[2] As a percentage of all white-collar occupations, however, the manager, official and proprietor category has slowly declined from 33% to 17%, a consequence of the diminishing importance of self-employment in the economy (Featherman and Hauser 1978), at least until the early 1970s (Blau 1987). In contrast, the percentage of white-collar employees in professional, technical, and kindred employees, after remaining roughly constant for the first half of the century, began growing steadily from 1950 on. It will probably keep growing for the foreseeable future (Kutscher 1987).

The work force of the federal government has also changed considerably during the twentieth century, though in different ways than the nation's work force as a whole. Its average growth rate actually exceeds that of the total work force, but this average hides substantial variance. In 1901, there were approximately 230,000 civil servants in the employment of the executive branch of the federal government. The number of executive branch employees nearly doubled between 1901 and 1917. It nearly doubled again in a single year during World War I, reaching 844,000 in 1918. After the war, the service shrank to 550,000 by 1921 and remained more or less at that level until the beginning of the Great Depression. During the depression years, the size of the executive

---

[1]The proportion decreased from 37.5% of the civilian labor force 16 years and older in 1970 to 36.2% in 1980. The Bureau of Labor Statistics predicts that the overall percentage of "administrative support workers, including clerical" will decline slightly from 17.7% in 1986 to 16.6% in the year 2000. When white-collar workers—technicians, salesworkers, executive, administrative, and managerial workers, professional workers, and administrative support workers, including clerical—instead of the labor force as a whole is used as the base, the percentage declines from 32.9% to 29.7% (Kutscher 1987). Other changes, such as a marked rise in the proportion of part-time workers, many of whom are clerical workers, are also important (Deutermann and Brown 1978). But these other chances are only of secondary interest here.

[2]For each calculation, the census occupation codes for the particular census year were employed.

branch grew steadily, reaching 1,000,000 in 1940. Tremendous expansion occurred during the 1940s because of World War II, and the executive civil service reached 3,786,000 in 1945. It gradually declined to 2,000,000 in 1950 but then grew again because of the Korean War to about 2.5 million. After the war it declined only gradually. Between 1955 and 1965, it grew at a slow but steady pace, nearly reaching the 2.5 million mark again. Another spurt during the Vietnam War brought the total to 3 million by the end of that decade. After a small decline at the beginning of the 1970s, the executive civil service remained roughly constant at about 2,800,000 until the present time. Because of its uneven growth, the share of American workers employed by the federal government has ranged from 1% to about 7%, with 3% being the current figure (U.S. Bureau of the Census 1975, 1986).

Within the federal government, the share of jobs held by white-collar workers has remained stable at about 80% throughout the twentieth century.[3] But the occupational composition of these white-collar jobs has not been stable. The proportion of white-collar workers classified as administrative or professional has grown, and this growth exceeds the level for the nation's total white-collar sector. As a consequence, the proportion of government workers in higher graded positions has increased enormously.

Growth in the professional and administrative sectors of the federal work force has not been synchronous. The professional work force grew quickly early in the century. Growth in administrative occupations jumped after World War II. In 1896, only 2.3% of the civilian positions in the federal civil service were in professional, scientific, or technical areas (U.S. Civil Service Commission [CSC] 1938). But by 1928, 16% of government positions were professional (U.S. Personnel Classification Board [PCB] 1931: Table 8).[4] The proportion of professionals has continued to increase. Whereas 19% of white-collar positions required professional training in 1957, the percentage of professional positions, as opposed to administrative, technical, clerical, or "other" (mostly security) workers, reached 21% by the middle 1970s and 23% by 1983.[5]

---

[3]It was 83% around 1900 (Van Riper 1959: 163) and 78% in 1983 (U.S. OPM 1983). Currently about 1,500,000 employees work in classified white-collar positions outside the postal service (U.S. Office of Personnel Management 1983).

[4]These figures exclude the postal service.

[5]Beginning in the early 1970s, the Civil Service Commission grouped white-collar jobs into one of five "PATCO" classifications, which is an acronym for the five types of work just mentioned. All percentages presented in this chapter exclude postal employees from the base. The general schedule excludes postal workers and certain other small groups of white-collar workers.

The distinction between administrative and clerical work was not well developed at the turn of the century. Consequently, no data exist to support a comparison of the relative size of these two groups from the turn of the century to the present time. But data for more recent times make clear that the proportion of office workers classified as administrative has grown rapidly during the postwar era. Census data show that 27.3% of the clerical–administrative group in the civil service were classified as managers or officials in 1970, compared with only 20.3% in 1950.[6] In contrast, the ratio of managers, officials, and proprietors to clerical workers fell during this period in the economy as a whole (U.S. Bureau of the Census 1950, 1970)[7] In recent years, the administrative segment of the federal civil service has continued to grow faster than other segments; it accounted for 28% of white-collar civil servants in 1983, compared with 25% in 1975 (U.S. Office of Personnel Management [OPM] 1983).

As the occupational composition of the civil service has changed, so has its hierarchical composition. Federal agencies have classified an ever-growing proportion of jobs to the higher ranks of the service, and an ever-shrinking proportion to the clerical ranks. Over-time comparisons can most easily be made between years after 1949, when the current system of civil service grades was introduced. In 1950, 67% of white-collar employees were in grades GS-6 or below, which is the range where clerical jobs are typically classified. But by 1983, only 38% of white-collar employees were in grades GS-6 or below (U.S. OPM 1938).[8] Clearly, the proportion of low-level workers was diminishing during these years.

[6]1950 was the first year in which the census reported separate statistics for federal workers, who previously had not been distinguished from state and local government workers.

[7]The CSC commented on this divergent trend in a 1964 publication, *Federal Workforce Outlook, Fiscal Years 1965–68*. The report noted that "federal white-collar employment . . . is growing significantly less rapidly than is total white-collar employment in the national work force as a whole . . . [but while] 'professional, technical and kindred' employment is growing at a rate equal to 14.2% over the 1964–1968 period [in the economy as a whole] . . . federal employment in such higher graded occupations is expected to grow 17.4% during the same period. . . . Current growth rates for 'clerical and kindred' employment in the national work force are equivalent to a 11.4% increase over the 1964–1968 period. In sharp contrast, Federal lower-graded growth over the same period is estimated at a scant 2.7%."

[8]A relatively small portion of this increase has been ascribed to "overgrading," by managers to obtain higher salaries for their subordinates (U.S. Comptroller General 1975b). OPM does not count members of the Senior Executive Service, which began in 1978, in its general schedule totals. The Senior Executive Service contained 6,924 workers as of 9/30/83 according to the Office of Personnel Management (personal communication).

Table 2.1
Salary/Grade Relationships for the
Subprofessional, Clerical, Administrative
and Fiscal, and Professional Service,
1923–1928[a]

$900–1260	S-1		
1140–1500	S-2	CAF-1	
1320–1680	S-3	CAF-2	
1500–1860	S-4	CAF-3	
1680–2040	S-5	CAF-4	
1860–2400	S-6	CAF-5	P-1
2100–2700	S-7	CAF-6	
2400–3000	S-8	CAF-7	P-2
2700–3300		CAF-8	
3000–3600		CAF-9	P-3
3300–3900		CAF-10	
3800–5000		CAF-11	P-4
5200–6000		CAF-12	P-5
6000–7500		CAF-13	P-6
7500		CAF-14	P-7
—		CAF-15	P-8
—		CAF-16	P-9

[a]The salary scale quoted in this table is from the
Classification Act of 1923. In 1928, the Welch Act
added grades CAF-15, CAF-16, P-8, and P-9 to the
top of the grade hierarchy.

We can get a better perspective on the transformation of the federal
service if we extend the comparison back to 1923, when Congress authorized the first systematic classification system for civil servants. It
grouped the covered work force into one of five separate "services,"
which lasted until the Classification Act of 1949.[9] Three of these services
contained white-collar workers. The act divided the professional and
scientific service into 7 grades (P-1 through P-7), the subprofessional
service into 8 (SP-1 through SP-8), and the clerical, administrative, and
fiscal service into 14 (CAF-1 through CAF-14). Grades were not in general equivalent across the services; a P-1 employee earned a much higher
salary than did an SP-1 or a CAF-1 employee. However, we can equate
grades based on their salaries, as shown in Table 2.1.

Congress has changed the 1923 grade structure twice since then.
The Welch Act of 1928 added two grades to the top of both the CAF and

[9]In addition, many workers were not covered by the act and were paid under different
authorities.

Table 2.2
Correspondence between the Grade
Systems Used before and after the
Passage of the Classification Act of 1949

S-1			GS-1
S-2	CAF-1		GS-1
S-3	CAF-2		GS-2
S-4	CAF-3		GS-3
S-5	CAF-4		GS-4
S-6	CAF-5	P-1	GS-5
S-7	CAF-6		GS-6
S-8	CAF-7	P-2	GS-7
	CAF-8		GS-8
	CAF-9	P-3	GS-9
	CAF-10		GS-10
	CAF-11	P-4	GS-11
	CAF-12	P-5	GS-12
	CAF-13	P-6	GS-13
	CAF-14	P-7	GS-14
	CAF-15	P-8	GS-15
	CAF-16	P-9	GS-16
			GS-17
			GS-18

the professional services. Then in 1949, Congress passed the Classification Act of 1949, which instituted a new system for grading white-collar jobs. This new system, which is still in place, collapsed the three separate white-collar pay systems into a single schedule. It also established a translation table for the purpose of reclassifying employees into the new set of grades. By using the translations shown in Table 2.2, it is possible to compare the grade structure of the civil service from the time of the Welch At of 1928 to the present.[10]

Figure 2.1 shows the extent to which the government's white-collar work force has shifted from one dominated by lower-graded employees to one dominated by higher-graded employees. In the contemporary service, journeymen-level professional and administrative jobs are generally located in grades GS-11 and higher. In 1928, only 9% of employees in the departmental and field service were in grades equivalent to GS-11

[10]Over-time comparisons are complicated by the change in coverage of the classification act from 1923 to 1949. Although the civil service was growing during this time, more employees were falling under the act as well. Thus, any comparisons must be viewed as approximate.

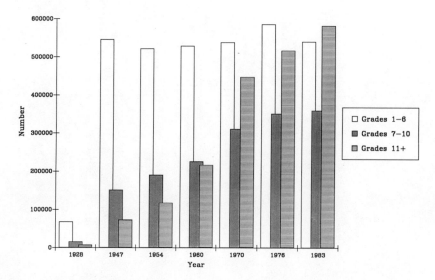

Figure 2.1. Grade distribution of federal civil service full-time white-collar workers, excluding the postal service, by year.

or higher.[11] By the middle 1970s, 31% of white-collar employees were at these grade levels, and by 1983 the proportion had grown to 42% (U.S. CSC 1976a; U.S. OPM 1983).

If we focus solely on comparisons involving nonprofessional employees, a similar story can be told: The growth of administrative employees far outstripped the growth of lower-level employees during the last 50 years. Only 4%, or 2,488 out of 63,001 employees in the Clerical, Administrative and Fiscal Service were classified at grades CAF-11 or higher in 1928 (U.S. PCB 1929: Table 1; 1931: Table 10). The proportion at this level went up only slightly, to 4.4% in 1937.[12] By 1947, the proportion of such high-ranked civil servants in the departmental service had risen to 6% (U.S. Congress, Senate 1948: 410).[13] Thus the proportion of employees at these levels increased at a gradual rate from 1923 to 1947.

[11]Grades equivalent to GS-11 include positions at grades CAF-11 and higher in the clerical, administrative, and fiscal service after 1928, the year the Welch Act was passed, and grades P-4 and higher in the old professional service. See the translations in Table 2.2.

[12]In the department service, 1,738 out of 49,158 were at CAF-11 or higher; 1,750 out of 30,982 were so classified in the field service. Note, however, that these statistics omit the emergency agencies, which had their own pay systems (President's Committee on Civil Service Improvement 1941a).

[13]These percentages are based on 115,306 departmental employees in the clerical, administrative, and fiscal service, and 551,788 in the total government service.

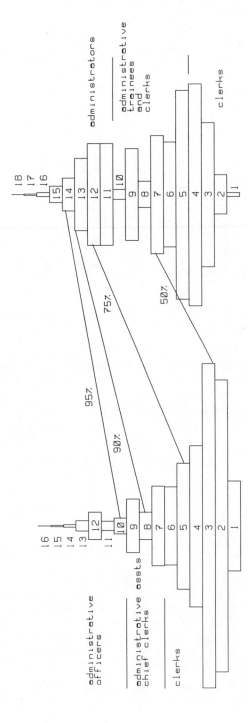

Figure 2.2 The clerical-administration grade structure, 1928 and 1976. The 1928 distribution is based on all CAF employees in the departmental and field service. The 1976 distribution is based on all employees in the general clerical and administrative, the personnel, the accounting and budget, and the business and industry occupational groups. The lines connecting the two diagrams connect the median grade, and the 75%, the 90%, and the 95% points of each distribution.

But during the next 25 years, growth in these levels far outstripped growth at the lower levels. By the middle 1970s, roughly one fourth of clerical, administrative, and fiscal employees were at grades GS-11 or higher.[14] The combination of government growth and compositional change lifted the number of administrative jobs at grades 11 and higher from about 2,500 at the end of the 1920s to roughly 250,000 by the middle 1970s.[15] In other words, in the space of 50 years, the number of administrative-level employees increased by a factor of about 100, whereas the white-collar civil service as a whole (except for the postal service) increased by only a factor of about 15.[16]

This remarkable change over about 50 years in the composition of clerical–administrative jobs is shown in more detail in Figure 2.2. The width of the bars at each grade level stands for the proportion of civil servants located at that grade. The left diagram shows the composition of the Clerical, Administrative and Fiscal Service in 1928, under the Welch system. The right diagram shows the grade composition in four major clerical/administrative occupational groups: general clerical and administrative, personnel, accounting and budget, and business and industry. The 1928 system has the form of a pyramid with a very wide base, the modal grade being CAF-2. The 1976 diagram is more similar to a diamond in shape (the modal grade being grade 4). A more eye-catching difference is the large proportion of positions above grade 9 in 1976 compare with 1928, when the higher grades were comparatively unpopulated. The long sharp spire of 1928 became a relatively squat pyramid by 1976, as administrators at these levels proliferated.

FORMAL IMPLICATIONS OF THE CHANGE FOR PROMOTIONS

The changing shape of the civil service grade hierarchy has certain formal implications for promotion rates, which can illustrate how the

---

[14]The Classification Act of 1949 merged the services, a fact that makes exact comparisons difficult. The comparisons presented here use all employees located in the general administrative, clerical and officer services, the personnel management and industrial relations, the accounting and budget, and the business and industry occupational groups in 1976. Of these employees, 25.3% were classified at grade GS-11 or higher at this time (U.S. CSC 1976a)

[15]172,000 of which are located in the occupational groups listed before namely general administrative, personnel, accounting, and business and industry.

[16]In 1928, there were 36,000 employees in the three white-collar services in Washington and 57,500 in the field, compared with about 1,400,000 total employees in the general schedule by the middle 1970s (U.S. PCB 1931: Table 8; U.S. CSC 1976a).

changing shape of government would have affected promotion rates in the absence of other factors. In a closed internal labor market, where outsiders can enter only at the bottom, the rate of upward movement would depend upon the rate of exit from higher grades (because of retirement, resignation, and so forth), the rate of growth, and the distribution of growth among the grades of the hierarchy. Stewman and Konda (1983) have shown that the probability of promotion from grade i to grade $i+1$ takes the following form:

$$p_{i,i+1} = \sum_{j=i}^{K} s_{j,i}[p_{j,0} + rm_j]$$

where $s_{j,i}$ is the ratio of the number of positions at grade j to the number of positions at grade i, K is the highest grade in the system, $p_{j,0}$ is the rate of separation from grade j, r is the overall rate of growth, and m_j is the proportion of this growth which occurred at grade j.

The extent to which one's chance for a promotion would depend upon the shape of the grade distribution can be most easily seen if we assume no growth and equal exit probabilities at all grades. Under these circumstances, the preceding formula reduces to the following:

$$p^*_{i,i+} = c \sum_{j=i}^{K} s_{j,i} = c * \text{MGR}$$

where $p^*_{i,i+1}$ is the probability under the preceding assumptions, and c is the (assumed constant) exit probability. Stewman and Konda called the sum of the grade ratios of all higher grades to the one of interest the multiple grade ratio (MGR). The promotion probability varies directly with this quantity.

A comparison of multiple grade ratios for 1928 and 1976 shows that the changing shape of the civil service hierarchy created a force for upward mobility. *Ceteris paribus,* this force would have sharply raised promotion rates at the bottom of the service, where clerical and subprofessional workers are located. The extent of change predicted under the previously mentioned assumptions is graphically demonstrated in Figure 2.3. The two diagrams in this figure show the size of the multiple grade ratios at each grade in the civil service in 1928 and 1976.[17] The

[17]They correspond to the Venturi tubes of Stewman and Konda (1983).

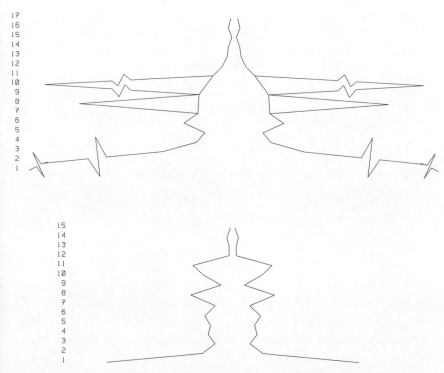

Figure 2.3. Multiple grade ratios, 1928 and 1976. The width of the figure shows the relative size of the multiple grade ratio for each grade in the CAF service in 1928 (below), and in the general clerical and administrative, personnel, accounting and budget, and business and industry occupational groups in 1976 (above). A broken line signifies a multiple grade ratio that was too large to represent in proper proportion in this figure.

greater the width, the greater would be the level of upward mobility under the all-other-things-being-equal assumptions that I discussed before.[18]

Neither diagram shows a smooth pattern, but there are some common features to the two diagrams. First, the MGR is largest at the very bottom of both hierarchies. The MGR remains reasonably large at several high grades before tapering to a point at the top of the grade struc-

---

[18]Namely, no growth, all entry limited to the bottom grade, and exit probabilities constant at higher grades. The jagged lines indicate extremely large multiple grade ratios, which were compressed in order to show the other MGRs on a reasonable scale.

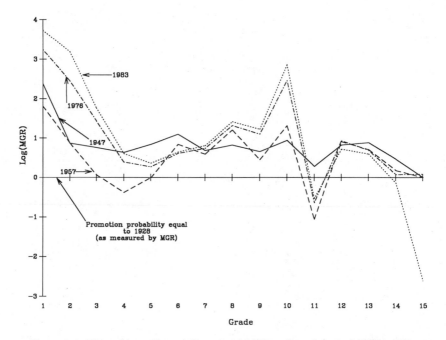

Figure 2.4. Natural logarithm of the ratio of MGR at four dates to MGR in 1928.

ture.[19] However, the two diagrams differ greatly in the level of opportunity suggested for lower-level employees. Aside from the jags at
grades CAF-8 and CAF-11, the 1928 diagram could fit inside the 1976
one. The level of opportunity for advancement as measured by the
multiple grade ratio is much higher in the more recent time period.

Figure 2.4 gives another demonstration of how the changing shape
of the white-collar hierarchy would have increased promotion rates if
compensating changes were absent. This figure shows the natural logarithm of the ratio of the MGR for selected years (specifically 1947, 1957,

---

[19]Also, both diagrams show unevenness in the middle-grade levels. The sharply jagged
character of the 1976 figure reflects the fact that administrative trainees in fact typically
enter the system at an odd-numbered grade and progress two grades at a time until they
reach grade 11. Thus, the even-numbered grades are underpopulated and have ar-
tificially high MGRs. The CSC had not formalized the two-grade interval for administrative jobs in the 1920s. However, the table of salary correspondence between professional and CAF salaries suggests that a rough correspondence between administrative
and professional grades may already have started evolving at that time.

1976, and 1983), to the MGR for 1928, by grade.[20] Figure 2.4 shows that
the changing shape of the civil service hierarchy implies increasingly
higher promotion probabilities for employees in all of the grades below
the journeymen level, and especially in the lowest civil service grades.[21]

Did opportunity for promotion out of the clerical ranks actually
increase to the extent suggested by the previously mentioned figures?
The answer is almost certainly *no*. First of all, the preceding calculations
are based on the unrealistic assumptions first that turnover is uniform at
all grades and second that no growth occurred. We have already seen
how high the growth in the federal government was during these years.
The turnover rate in government also varied during the first third of the
century.[22] These factors might significantly alter the actual level of the
promotion probability at each grade.

But a factor of possibly greater importance still was the changing
organization of job ladders during these years. The promotion probabilities computed here depend upon a critical assumption, namely that
entry into the civil service system occurred only at the bottom. But this
assumption never characterized government recruitment.[23] Instead,
federal agencies have filled vacancies at all levels both by recruitment
and by promotion. Some recruits entered the civil service soon after the
completion of school. During the first half of the century, they generally
entered the ranks either at the lowest professional grade if they were
professionals or else at a low clerical grade if they were not. They would
then advance through the system. Eventually, they would either leave
the service for better opportunities elsewhere or else would reached
their career plateau. A second type of recruit has traditionally come from
the ranks of experienced workers in the private sector. These recruits

[20]The 1947 data are most directly comparable to the 1928 data, because they include the
entire CAF work force, as did the 1928 data. The MGRs for 1956, 1976, and 1983 were
computed for employees in certain occupational groups dominated by administrative
and clerical employees, specifically the general clerical and administrative group, the
personnel and industrial relations group, the accounting and budget group, and the
business and industry occupational group (U.S. PCB 1929: Table 1; 1931, Table 10; U.S.
Congress, Senate 1948: 410; U.S. CSC 1957a, 1976a; U.S. OPM 1983).

[21]The graphed points are the log of the ratios; this was done to keep them on a reasonable
scale.

[22]Generally speaking, it was high by modern standards, though generally less than the
turnover rate in private industry, and higher in the lower grades than the upper grades.
See Brissenden (1929), Mitchell (1952), and various annual reports of the U.S. CSC for
information on federal turnover.

[23]A rule to this effect was actually incorporated in the 1882 reform bill introduced by
Senator Pendleton. But he deleted it from the final bill before it was passed.

entered the system at a level that roughly corresponded with their previous work experience outside the civil service.

But this pattern of recruitment changed after World War II. The gradual professionalization of administration created a new route into the civil service. Young college graduates entered the government at grades above the ranks of most clerical workers, grades that were entry portals into newly separated administrative job ladders. Much of the apparently increased opportunity for clerical workers that is shown in Figures 2.3 and 2.4 was, in reality, increased opportunity for young college graduates. Opportunity for a clerical worker to reach a given grade in the system probably rose from the 1920s to the 1980s but certainly not to the extent suggested by the multiple grade ratios. Whether opportunity for a subprofessional worker to reach a professional job rose or fell is not clear, but it is certainly small at present, despite the growth in the proportion of civil service positions designated as professional.

The changing recruitment picture corresponded to a changing organization of job ladders and particularly of office work job ladders. It also corresponded to a changed conception of what clerical work consisted of. As administrative jobs proliferated in the government, the traditional conception of these positions as a superior type of clerical work became outmoded. Administration came to be seen as a function distinct from clerical work. This new way of organizing work transformed the top of the clerical hierarchy. It shifted the boundary between clerical and administrative work downwards and split the hierarchy of office work into separate hierarchies of administrative and clerical work.

SUMMARY

The federal civil service has grown enormously from 1900 to the present, though at an uneven rate. Important compositional changes occurred within the federal service as well. The proportion of civil service positions defined as clerical has steadily decreased, whereas the proportion defined as administrative—which includes managerial jobs—or professional has increased. Along with this change has come a marked increase in the average grade of civil service positions. The changing grade distribution of civil service jobs has important formal implications for promotion chances. If recruitment patterns had not changed, the increased proportion of administrative and professional jobs would have increased career opportunities for employees entering the service at the bottom grades. However, the structure of job ladders, and hence the pattern of recruitment, also changed. It is likely that changes in recruitment patterns largely offset the increased promotion chances implied by the changing occupational and grade distribution.

3

The Clerical–Administrative Boundary

INTRODUCTION

Several scholars have argued that the socioeconomic ranking of occupations has been relatively stable over time (Duncan 1968; Nam *et al.* 1975; Treiman 1977; Featherman and Hauser 1978). But it is possible for the historical relationship among occupational groups to change, even if the status ordering of these groups remains the same. Such changes can have important implications for the structure of job ladders that has evolved in the modern bureaucratized organization. These implications can be illustrated through the study of the occupations involved in office work.

Office work occupations can broadly be characterized as either clerical or administrative, the latter category including managerial and executive positions. Although administrative jobs have always had higher status than clerical jobs, the social conception of what clerical work consisted of has shifted during the past century. The changing conception of clerical work was due to social acceptance of the idea that administrative work was something qualitatively distinct from clerical work. The developments that precipitated this change have had important effects on the structure of both clerical and administrative hierarchies.

The restriction of the term *clerical* to lower-level office work, a type of work qualitatively distinct from managerial, administrative, or executive work, is of comparatively recent origin. In the eighteenth, nine-

This chapter is an expanded version of a paper that was published in *Social Forces* (1987, 66:725–746) under the title "The Upgrading and Downgrading of Occupations: Status Redefinition vs. Deskilling as Alternative Theories of Change."

teenth, and twentieth centuries, the term had two meanings. It referred both to the function of office work and to a particular range of the office hierarchy, namely the lower part. But this range included all but the highest positions. In the nineteenth century, organizations were much smaller than today. But some organizations were large enough to have hierarchies, such as large banks, railroads, or the federal government. In such settings, the higher clerical positions could have responsibilities that today would be described as managerial or administrative in character (White 1948; Lockwood 1958; Braverman 1974). Routine tasks existed then as now and were performed by the lower clerks, though of course the tasks of recording and copying were only routine for those who could write, and a large portion of the population could not.[1] But the greater breadth of the clerical occupation and the correspondingly greater length of the clerical job ladder lifted the status of clerical work in general. The existence of administrative-level "clerical" jobs made the prospect of a career in the clerical ranks more attractive than today, even though actual opportunity depended on such factors as the vacancy structure and the number of eligible employees competing for these vacancies.

But the expansion of government, the development of larger bureaucracies, both public and private, and the quasi-professionalization of the occupation of management gradually led to a restructuring of clerical and administrative occupations. As a consequence, the term *clerk* today no longer refers to the same range of the office hierarchy that it once did. Once both routine office workers and middle management could be described as *clerks*, though they occupied positions of different rank. But in a modern position classification system, routine and managerial jobs are considered to be qualitatively different and classifiable into different occupations. The idea that a qualitative distinction exists between clerical and administrative work is a principal justification for placing them on separate job ladders.

CLERICAL HIERARCHIES IN THE FEDERAL GOVERNMENT BEFORE 1850

At the beginning of the Republic, the clerks of the federal civil service were officially divided into three ranks, "clerk," "principal clerk," and "chief clerk." Principal clerks presided over the clerical staffs

---

[1]The assessment of skill requirements must be a function of the skill levels of the population. The economist Alfred Marshall was aware of this relationship when he wrote in 1920 that "where education is universal, an occupation may fairly be classed as unskilled, though it requires a knowledge of reading and writing." (1920: 205).

of a single office, whereas chief clerks presided over the clerical staffs of an entire department (White 1948: 297). Chief clerks received about the same salary as principal clerks but had higher status and greater authority.[2]

Offices and departments were minuscule at the time in comparison to present-day government. The Department of the Treasury was the largest. In setting up the Treasury Department in 1778, Congress provided for the following employees: a treasurer, who had one clerk reporting to him, two chambers of accounts staffed by three commissioners in total, each commissioner having two clerks, an auditor, who had two clerks, and a comptroller, who also had two clerks. In all, the Washington office contained 6 "commissioned officers" and 11 clerks (U.S. Congress. House 1836b). By 1792 the central office of the treasury had grown to 90, whereas 570 employees worked in the field. Aside from deputy postmasters, there were only 120 other employees in the entire federal government in that year (White 1948: 255). The early U.S. presidents delegated their constitutional authority to appoint "inferior officers" (clerks) to the department secretaries. Nonetheless, the position of chief clerk was sufficiently important that department heads would often clear candidates for those positions with the president through the Jacksonian period (White 1954). Furthermore, the chief clerks of the War and State Departments, at least, were given responsibility to act as secretary in the secretary's absence.[3]

Accounts of the time stress the relatively low pay of clerical workers, and in particular, their own perception that they were inadequately paid (White 1948). From a contemporary perspective, their pay, although low in comparison to that of some of the higher "commissioned officers" of the civilian government, was high in relation to that of skilled labor. By 1801, chief clerks were making between $1700 and $1840, depending on the department. Clerks were paid between $700 and $800 in general. These figures compare with $1700 for the assistant postmaster general and $3000–$5000 for secretaries of departments. By way of comparison, the average daily wage for artisans in Philadelphia was only $1.64, whereas laborers made only $1.00 per day (U.S. Bureau of the Census 1975: 297–298).

As another indication of their status, the clerks at this time were referred to as *officers*, though subordinate ones. They had higher status

---

[2]The maximum pay for clerks at the time was $500, for principal and chief clerks, about $1000.

[3]In White's words, "they were supervisory-managerial officials, with only a very small number of immediate subordinates, to be sure, but with considerable responsibility for keeping papers in order and for expediting business" (White 1948: 309).

than the *employès* of government, such as the messengers or janitorial personnel (McMillan 1941: 4). This practice of referring to clerks as officers continued at least through the 1830s, and some clerical positions were described by the title *officer* into the 1920s. But the term *clerk* itself was a mark of a certain status. Clerks were distinguished from the mass of the population by their education; all competent clerks were literate, and some were even college graduates (White 1948: 313–315). As Lockwood (1958) has persuasively argued, it was their education and status as office workers that led them to use as their reference and comparison group their superiors, rather than manual workers.

The early government grew rapidly. This growth increased the complexity of work performed by the higher clerks. In the treasury department of 1778, for example, Congress provided for the following division of labor between clerks and commissioners:

> That the clerks of the chamber of accounts shall state [write off] the accounts, number and arrange the vouchers, examine the castings, and make the necessary copies, endorse, &c.
>
> That the commissioners shall carefully examine the authenticity of the vouchers, rejecting such as shall not appear good; compare them with the articles [items] to which they relate, and determine whether they support the charges; that they shall reduce such articles as are overcharged, and reject such as are improper.
>
> That the auditor shall receive the vouchers and accounts from the commissioners, and cause them to be examined by his clerk. He [the auditor] shall compare the several items with the vouchers, &c. (U.S. Congress. House 1836b: 4–5)

Until 1789, the commissioned officers apparently performed the "proper and essential" duties of their offices, whereas the clerks performed duties "of a purely formal and ministerial kind." However,

> From the passage of the Act of 1789, it appears to have become the policy of Congress, as the population of the country, and with it the business of the Departments, increased, to provide for this increase by augmenting the number of clerks, rather than the commissioned offices: the necessary effect of the increasing disproportion between which, has been a corresponding expansion of the duties of the former in amount and importance (U.S. Congress. House 1836b: 5).

Thus, as the business of government became more complicated, it fell to the clerks to prepare drafts and reports, to attend to general correspondence, and to assist commissioned officers in the more important correspondence. They also had to assist in the making of reports to Congress. They had to prepare forms for the collection of revenue, take care of general business, endorse, file and preserve papers, record all papers, keep the books and the accounts, and prepare "all tabular statements, documents and estimates required by Congress" (U.S. Congress. House 1836b).

The proliferation of work caused the clerical hierarchy to stretch. By 1818, the Treasury had six ranks of clerks. At the top was the chief clerk of the department, who performed a wide variety of duties. In the several bureaus of the Treasury, clerks were divided into a hierarchical classification. At the top of the scale was the chief clerk of the bureau, if there was one. Next came "clerks having charge of particular branches of the public service, with clerks subordinate to them." Third were "clerks having charge of separate branches of service, performing such without the aid of subordinate clerks." Fourth were "clerks employed in recording and keeping the books of the office." At the bottom of the clerical ladder were "clerks employed in copying only" (U.S. Congress. House 1818: 26a).

The Committee on Ways and Means went on to argue in 1836 that the current duties of clerks in the executive departments were

> of course much superior in amount, from the extension of the public business, and a great part superior in importance to the duties of the clerks, as defined by law when they were first employed, and to the duties as they are now generally understood to be indicated by the appellation of the office. To suppose that the present small number of heads, compared with the numerical size of their offices, can now, as they did in those days, adjust the accounts, keep the public books, prepare exhibits, or even conduct all the correspondence, would argue but a slight acquaintance with the course of the public business. They have besides this class of duties, a set still higher, of reading the communications addressed to them, conducting the more important correspondence, authenticating the business prepared by their subordinates, laying down general rules, expounding principles &c., &c. The performance of both descriptions would, it is clear, be physically impossible, and even with their acknowledged zeal in the public service, it is believed to be rarely, if by any, attempted. (U.S. Congress. House. 1936b: 7)[4]

Other evidence from the time supports the argument that higher clerical work was growing more complex. The Secretary of State reported in 1818 that he had eight clerks employed in the department. Of Daniel Brent, his chief clerk, he said:

> Through the chief clerk, all the directions of the Secretary are carried into effect. He assists in the correspondence of the office, under the orders of the head, and under the same orders, has the care and superintendence of every part of the department. (U.S. Congress. House 1818: 5).

---

[4]The House Committee went on to say that clerical duties in private industry were "inferior in variety and importance" to those in the government, with the closest similarity being found in the large banks (U.S. Congress. House 1836b: 8).

   In 1836, the secretary of state again reported to the House of Representatives on the duties of clerks in his department. The duties of Mr.
Dickens, the chief clerk, were such "in all respects as appertain to under
Secretary of State." His job was to "exercise an immediate superintendence over the duties of the respective bureaux and over those employed in them." (U.S. Congress. House 1836a: 1; see also U.S. Congress. Senate 1838). These duties must have increased in responsibility
because the clerical staff had increased in that time. Whereas one clerk in
1818 "copies and records the correspondence of the office with our own
and foreign ministers, and with foreign governments: (U.S. Congress.
House, 1818: 5), by 1836, three clerks performed the duties of the diplo-
matic bureau. Similarly, whereas one clerk took charge of correspondence with the consulates in 1818, in 1836 three clerks took care of the
work of the consular bureau.
   Similar developments occurred in the post office. In 1818 the chief
clerk of the post office

> makes out and arranges all the contracts; there are now between 800 and 900,
> for the mail's transport; keeps a register of the arrival and departure of
> various mails, and has the entire charge, under the direction of the
> postmaster general, of all correspondence relating to the mail establish-
> ments, including alternations of contracts, expedition of mails &c. &c. (U.S.
> Congress. House 1818: 48)

   Two clerks, one paid $1200, and one paid $1000, served as accountants. They "prepare the quarterly accounts of postmasters and contrac-
tors, correct the errors, notify postmasters of their errors," and conducted some occasional miscellaneous business (U.S. Congress. House
1818: 48).
   By 1836, the post office department had been subdivided into four
divisions. Assistant postmasters headed only two of the four. The chief
clerk, in addition to his duties as such, also served as head of the third
division. The fourth division was headed by another clerk who was
"denominated the accountant" and who supervised and directed the
work of 50 clerks under him. As the complexity of the post office grew,
the responsibilities of the higher clerks increased (U.S. Congress. Senate
1835).
   To take one final example, in 1851, Daniel Webster, then secretary
of state, wrote that

> I beg leave to add that all the clerks in this department ought to possess
> higher qualifications than those of mere penmen and copyists. In general,
> they should understand the modern languages, especially the French and
> Spanish; be persons of literary attainments, and should possess a good

knowledge of geography and statistics and the laws and history of their own country, and a quick capacity for learning. The clerk on claims should be a person of much political knowledge, especially well versed in national law, and competent to investigate questions of a judicial character. It is of great importance that the claims of American citizens against foreign governments, in behalf of which the interposition of this government is required, should be more thoroughly examined and more thoroughly understood than may be expected from the ex parte statements of the claimants, in as much as the honor of the government requires that its interposition be given in no case not apparently founded in law and justice. (U.S. Congress. Senate 1852b: 2)

STANDARD OF LIVING OF GOVERNMENT CLERKS

For a brief period, the rise in responsibilities of the higher clerks was accompanied by a rise in salaries. After 1795, Congress gave department heads a certain amount of discretion in the setting of salaries. Subsequent to this event, salaries for clerks rose from $500 to the $700–800 range. Principal clerks were generally paid $600 in the Treasury Department in 1789. In 1795, Congress raised the ceiling for principal clerks to $1000. Chief clerks were established at $600 and $800 in the War and State Departments in 1789. By 1801, the departmental chief clerks were paid between $1700 and $1840 (White 1948: 297–298). Prices also rose substantially between 1789 and 1800, though not as much as the salaries of chief clerks. The department heads were able to retain some control over salaries and maintained control thereafter.

. In 1818, Congress established five basic rates for clerks between $800 and $1600, with rates of $1700 and $2000 for chief clerks. These rates were officially maintained until 1836, though in fact some variation apparently existed at this time. Figure 3.1 shows the salary distribution of the 336 clerks in the federal government in 1835. The average salary for the group was $1119 per year, and the median salary was $1000 per year. These salaries had apparently varied little if at all during the preceding 15 years and were not to vary substantially until 1853.[5] The available documentary evidence reports that, in comparison to the stan-

[5]The Act of April 20, 1818, 3 Stat. 445 fixed the precise number of clerks to be employed in the various departments and their maximum rates of compensation. The statutory-roll method of appropriations was used until 1830. From then until 1853, Congress used the lump-sum method of making appropriations. But generally speaking, with slight adjustments, the pay rates set up in 1818 were adhered to until 1853 (3 Stat. 445, 4/20/1818; 5 Stat. 80, secs 43–44 7/2/1836; 10. Stat 189, sec 3 3/3/1853).

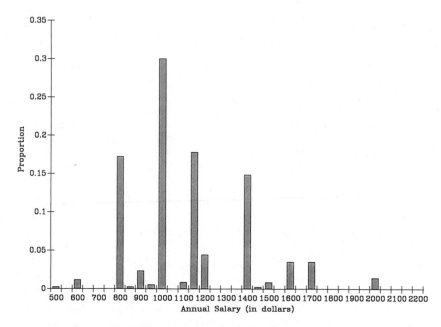

Figure 3.1 Salaries of clerical workers in 1835.

dard of living, the salaries of clerks were modest.[6] The postmaster general, in a report to the Congress in 1835, argued that salaries of "ordinary clerks" be set at $900, $1200, and $1500, instead of the $800, $1000, $1200 and $1400 that clerks in the post office were then paid.[7] He argued that this salary range would allow single men to live comfortably (at $900), and men with families to have "little more than the means of subsistence for themselves and families" (at $1500. U.S. Congress. Senate 1836b: 3).

However, consumer prices apparently dropped substantially from 1818, when the salary structure was set, until 1833 (David and Solar

[6]The postmaster general, for instance, argued that "probably a considerable majority of the clerks of this Department, are hopeless insolvents, and many of them are put to great straits even to subsist themselves and families on their present compensation." (U.S. Congress. Senate 1836b: 4). The House Ways and Means Committee, in considering the situation of the 175 clerks employed at salaries of $1000 or under in the 1830s, argued that "it requires but a slight knowledge of the expenses of living in Washington to be convinced that this sum is wholly inadequate for a family of ordinary size" (U.S. Congress. House, 1836b: 3).

[7]At that time, the chief clerk in the post office was paid $1700, three clerks were paid $1400, five were paid $1200, 23 were paid $1000, and 6 were paid $800 (U.S. Congress. Senate 1836b).

1977). On a scale where an 1860 price index is set at 100, the 1818 price index was 153. Between 1818 and 1833, the index dropped by roughly 50% to a level of 101. The Ways and Means Committee report indicates that prices rose in Washington between 1833 and 1836, and the David–Solar index confirms the trend. But in 1837, the peak of the rise, the index had only hit 115, still much below its 1818 level, while being 14% above the 1833 low for the period 1800–1840. It may be that status anxiety related to the rapid rise in the wages of unskilled labor at this time was also a cause of the intense concern for salary increases.[8] It should also be noted that an individual's satisfaction with his salary depends upon what he thinks is an appropriate salary and life-style for his position. Because British civil servants made three times what American civil servants did during the early 1800s (Finer 1952) and because they were a likely reference group, one would expect American clerks to believe that they were underpaid.

Congress responded to the clerks' appeals, but only by abolishing the bottom salary grade for clerks. The consumer price index began to fall after 1838, reaching a low of 89 in 1843. But even in 1836, some "frugal" clerks were apparently able to afford servants on their salaries.[9] Furthermore, the average salary of clerks in government was substantially higher than the average wages of artisans at the time.[10] On the other hand, clerical incomes were almost certainly not as high as the average of independent professionals such as physicians and lawyers.[11]

[8]On a scale where the price index in 1860 is set at 100, the money wage for unskilled labor in the United States jumped from 64 in 1833 to 107 in 1838, a rise of 67%. Thereafter, common labor wage rates dropped back substantially, though by 1850 they were still 28% above the 1833 level and 14% above the 1818 level (David and Solar 1977).

[9]One of the clerical employees of the Treasury Department reported that in 1836 "it has been my uniform practice to purchase with cash, and that I have not paid house-rent or pew-rent. My family has generally consisted of three grown persons, five children, and two servants; and as my children were taught at home, no expense for teaching has been incurred until last year; at present four of them attend school. . . ." (U.S. Congress. Senate 1836a: 355)

[10]The average daily wage rates of artisans in Philadelphia varied between $1.37 and $1.86 per day between 1818 and 1830 (U.S. Bureau of the Census 1975).

[11]Very little systematic evidence exists on the earnings of professionals at this time. Some documentary evidence for the time suggests that lawyers and engineers thought government service unattractive because they would have to take a pay cut. The head of the Office of the Solicitor of the Treasury department in 1836 noted that "all the other bureaux in the Treasury Department are allowed one clerk, with a salary of $1,700, while in this office, which ought to have at least one clerk who has been educated for the bar, and is capable of preparing the letters of minor importance which require legal information, no salary is provided higher than $1,150. The consequence is, as the services of no lawyer can be procured for this salary, that all these letters must be prepared by the head

Nonetheless, these positions were in demand. The postmaster general admitted in his report to Congress in 1835 that for each clerical position at the lowest salary level of $800, he had between one and two hundred applicants. He denigrated the quality of these applicants,[12] but his description of the types of men he was looking for suggests that he had rather lofty standards.[13]

In the middle 1850s, prices jumped by 10%, and clerks again pressured Congress to reorganize the salary structure (Baruch 1941a). Inflation coupled with stationary salary scales created a situation where the newer bureaus were paying higher salaries than the older ones (*Congressional Globe* 20: 825; 31st Cong., 2nd sess., 1851; *Congressional Globe* 20: 584; 31st Cong., 2nd sess., 1851). In 1854, Congress established four classes of clerks, to be paid annual salaries of $900, $1200, $1500, and $1800, respectively. It authorized bureaus to pay their chief clerk $2000, and departments to pay $2200 (Act of March 3, 1853, 10 Stat. 189: 209). The following year the Congress increased this salary schedule to $1200, $1400, $1600, $1800, $2000, and $2200, in response to complaints that the lowest salaries on the 1853 scale were inadequate (Baruch 1941a).

---

of the office, and occupy that time which, if devoted to legal examinations in reference to the more important cases under superintendence, would enable him to discharge the higher duties of his office in a manner more satisfactory to himself, and more useful to the public" (U.S. Congress, Senate 1836a: 21). This quotation suggests that the average lawyer earned considerably more than the average clerk, though it also indicated that the most responsible clerks may have earned salaries as high as those of some professionals.

[12]"They are almost exclusively young unmarried men—men in desperate circumstances, or men who are incompetent to make a living elsewhere, and seek for these appointments as a means of meager support to themselves and families." (U.S. Congress. Senate 1836b: 4).

[13]"When a citizen leaves his home in the States, and accepts a clerkship in the District of Columbia, as a permanent employment, he, in effect, surrenders all prospect of rising to the higher honors of his country,and even all hope of acquiring extensive wealth. . . . It seems but right that men of talents and great business qualifications, who voluntarily relinquish all high aspirations, and content themselves with the distinction which is to be gained within the walls of the Executive Departments, should be paid by their country a compensation so liberal that they will not be obliged to raise their children in ignorance and leave their families in want." (U.S. Congress. Senate 1836b, 4). The "leave" reference may refer to the question of whether they would be able to leave their families an inheritance after their death, an important issue because clerks did not have businesses or farms to pass on to their families. This issue comes up elsewhere in testimony as well. The postmaster general went on to note that these clerks could sometimes be promoted to chief clerk, but they were virtually never promoted any higher.

THE BEGINNING TRANSFORMATION OF HIGHER
CLERICAL WORK

As the business of each department grew too great for the departmental secretary and his few commissioned officers to keep track of it by
themselves, the higher clerks acquired greater autonomy over their own
particular domains, gradually becoming specialists in their areas by virtue of their on-the-job experience. But the process of organizational
differentiation initiated a process of occupational redefinition during the
course of the nineteenth century. Positions that had been considered
high *clerical* were redefined as *administrative* when the specialized domains of principal clerks evolved into formally defined divisions or bureaus. The principal clerk who headed the domain was frequently himself appointed to the position of bureau head or commissioner, and he
was given statutory authority over the work that he previously had
informal responsibility for (White 1954). For example, the clerk in charge
of patents in the State Department gave himself the title of "superintendent of patents" in the early nineteenth century. Congress formally
approved this title in 1830, changed the name of the job again to
commissioner in 1836, and made it a presidential appointment (White
1954: 535). Other specialized clerks began evolving into a professional
staff. As part of this process, the specialized clerks gradually assumed
titles to reflect their heightened responsibilities.

The newly appointed head of a newly recognized bureau, who was
formerly a principal clerk, eventually acquired his own chief clerk or
principal clerk (White 1954). The tasks of the new principal clerks and
chief clerks in the new bureau probably increased in complexity and
responsibility themselves as the young bureau grew in size and scope.
At some point, the positions of the new top principal clerks may have
been redefined themselves and perhaps given the title of "assistant
commissioner" or equivalent. During this transition period, employees
with similar titles could have quite different levels of responsibility and
pay. Government did not achieve a consistency in personnel terminology until after World War II, when position classification systems
reached maturity.

The 1850s rise in clerical salaries was the last for many decades.
Salaries for clerical workers in the established agencies were not officially raised again until 1923, and by then the status of clerical workers
was clearly on the decline. The 1850s was also the period during which
women began entering the clerical ranks of government. Women entered at the bottom of the clerical hierarchy in special positions described

as "female clerks." In 1864, Congress authorized a maximum salary for "female clerks" of $600 (13 Stat, 28, Mar. 14, 1864). This was raised the same year to $720 and then to $900 in 1866 (13 Stat. 160, June 25, 1864; 14 Stat. 207, July 23, 1866) but still was well below the salary levels authorized for the regular clerkships.[14] In 1876, the Congress authorized department heads to substitute women and "lower class" clerks for higher clerks when these replacements could do the job equally well (19 Stat. 169 8/15/1876; McMillan 1941: 4ff.). By 1900, women held 25% of the clerkships in Washington, though only 5% of positions in the field (Sageser 1935). The practice of paying women less for doing the same work as men was not officially ended until the passage of the Classification Act of 1923.[15]

Figure 3.2 shows the salary structure of the clerical work force in 1901, as compared with 1835. (U.S. CSC 1902). The average pay for government clerks at this time was about $1220, a 9% increase over its level in 1835. Prices in 1901 were 11% higher than in 1835, though they had fluctuated substantially during the interim period, particularly during the decade of the Civil War. Overall, though, the rate of pay for clerks had roughly kept pace with the cost of living. But because the real wages of blue-collar and other white-collar positions in the private sector had increased, the positions probably did not appear as attractive as they once had. Nonetheless, even with the influx of women into clerical positions, the average pay for clerks in the government was over twice what the average nonfarm employee earned in the nation. It was 21% higher than the average clerical worker's salary in manufacturing and steam railroads (U.S. Bureau of the Census 1975).

But our principal focus at present is on the highest clerks, those at the clerical–administrative boundary. In 1901, the highest paid clerks, at $1800 and above, were paid the same salaries as assistant chiefs of divisions. The majority of chiefs of divisions, excluding technical divisions, were paid $2000 or less. The average basic pay of officers in the military at this time was slightly over $2100, their average basic pay plus allowances being about $2500 (U.S. Bureau of the Census 1975). The average manager (excluding floor manager) in mercantile establishments in the central business district of Boston was paid $1500 (Kocka 1980: 77). The average physician was paid $1000–1500 (Cathell 1890, 1905, cited in Starr 1983). Elite clerical jobs in the government were certainly more attractive

---

[14]In 1870, department heads were authorized to pay women the same salary as men if they desired to. But the law was permissive, not mandatory.

[15]Agencies were, however, free to limit entrance examinations for positions to men (or to women) until the 1960s (U.S. CSC 1967).

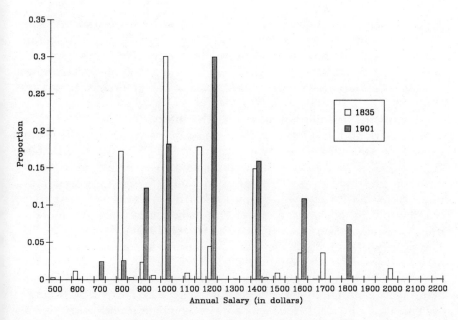

Figure 3.2 Salaries of clerical workers in 1835 and 1901.

than the average job in the nation at the turn of the century. Of course, most clerical jobs at the time paid much lower, though still respectable, salaries. This was to change, however, with the onset of inflation. Furthermore, the number of office positions with an "administrative" instead of a "clerical" title was gradually increasing. The proliferation of these administrative jobs gradually pushed the top clerical jobs farther from the peak of the government hierarchy. Eventually, these administrative jobs were organized on separate job ladders as well.

THE EMERGENCE OF ADMINISTRATION

At the turn of the century, bank clerks and other clerical workers were sometimes referred to, or referred to themselves, as professionals (Kirkland 1956: 179; Kocka 1980: 146 *ff.*).[16] However, most people made a distinction between the status of routine clerical workers and that of professionals or administrators, just as they made a distinction between the relative status of clerical and manual workers (Bloomfield 1915). But

---

[16]See Bills (1925) for a somewhat later demonstration of this point.

the higher end of the government clerical hierarchy still contained positions that clearly were administrative in nature. During the course of the twentieth century, however, these positions were reorganized and redefined as administrative, effectively pushing the clerical–administrative boundary downward with respect to the grade hierarchy as a whole.

During the first third of the twentieth century, the related positions of chief clerk and division chief (a descendant of principal clerk) were viewed as extensions of the lower clerical ladder. Chief clerks and often division chiefs as well were not yet viewed as technical, specialized positions and hence were distinguished from the growing number of professional positions (Willoughby 1927). They were classified, rather than patronage, positions, and were typically filled through promotion from lower clerical positions (Low 1900; Mayers 1922; Willoughby 1927). This pattern of promotion was viewed as normal and appropriate at the time (Mayers 1922; Willoughby 1927).

The first position classification system developed in the United States was instituted by the city of Chicago in 1908.[17] This classification system used the word *clerical* in both a hierarchical and a functional sense. In functional terms, clerical work meant office work. The Chicago CSC took the term *clerical service* to mean "positions . . . rendering . . . service in connection with general office work or management which does not require knowledge of any of the specialties included in other classes" (American Political Science Association 1913: 329ff.).[18]

In addition, the term had hierarchical connotations. Clerks were subordinate to individuals in "administrative" and "executive" positions. Administrators and executives were to be found in other services besides the clerical service. Those in charge of professional or technical services in Chicago exercised their executive function while keeping their status as scientists or professionals.[19] The administrative jobs in the "clerical" service were of the same rank as were administrative jobs in other services, as can be seen from the description of the highest grade in the clerical service:

> Grade VIII: Positions the duties of which are executive and administrative, involving responsibility for an entire department, either independently or directly under the head or heads of such department, or for an entire bureau.

[17]See Griffenhagen (1924) for a discussion of this effort.

[18]These specialties were 1. medical, 2. engineering, 3. (clerical), 4. police, 5. fire, 6. library, 7. inspection, 8. supervising (buildings, property, public charges), 9. skilled labor, 10. labor.

[19]The norm in the United States has been that the administrators of professionals are themselves professionals (Pear 1968; Freidson 1986).

[Examples:] Assistant city treasurer, deputy city collector, superintendent of special assessments, secretary (board of education). Salary $4020 and above. (American Political Science Association 1913: 330)

Nonetheless, they could still be described as administrative or executive in level, although clerical in function.

However, the changing attitude toward the nature of clerical work and the desire to systematize job descriptions were evident at the turn of the century. The CSC, in its 1902 report, observed that work of a high order of difficulty was sometimes assigned to positions called *clerical*. The CSC objected to the use of the title *clerk* for such technical positions. By way of illustration, the CSC singled out the case of a recent examination held for the position of medical clerk and translator. The position paid only $720 per year, which was a low clerical salary. But the examination for the position covered translation of French, German, Spanish and Italian as well as technical bibliographic work in medicine and zoology. The CSC viewed the use of the title *clerk* for this position as inappropriate and evidence of the need for a sound position classification system. Its position on this matter contrasts with Daniel Webster's apparently appropriate use of the word *clerk* to describe technical positions in the State Department 50 years earlier.

During the twentieth century, the classification schedules reveal a progressive narrowing of the use of the term *clerical*. Most of the uses referred to subordinate or routine office work; it was less frequently used to mean office work (including management) in general. In 1902, the CSC proposed a new classification of work in government into 11 categories, ranging from Grades A–K. This classification, which was never implemented but nonetheless reveals the use of job titles and assignment at the time, separated "executive work" from "executive clerical work," which was further separated from the work of "clerks" (U.S. CSC 1902: 175–176). But the classification placed the chief clerk as well as division chiefs in the executive class. The Keep Committee's proposed classification in 1907 distinguished the "subclerical grades," the "clerical grades," and the "supervisory grade." Chief clerks and division chiefs were classified in the supervisory grade. (Committee on Department Methods 1907). It proposed a classification of positions that separated clerical work into the categories of *under clerk, junior clerk, senior clerk,* and *chief clerk*. But still, distinctions were made between the work of the lower and higher clerks. The work of "under clerks" was "simple or routine," that of junior clerks was "of a routine character," and that of clerks was "more or less routine. . . ." The work of senior clerks was "largely supervisory or requiring the highest order of clerical

ability, involving much original thought, consideration and investigation."

The CSC's proposed 1902 classification also refrained from describing the work of clerks or senior clerks as merely "routine," a designation
it applied only to clerical assistants. But by the 1920s, clerical work in
general was described as routine. On 10/24/21, President Harding issued an executive order directing the Bureau of Efficiency to prescribe a
uniform system of ratings for all departments and requiring the heads of
the departments to put the system into effect. The order noted that there
should be both "standard ratings" and "special ratings." The order
indicated that clerical work was "routine" and suitable for "standard
ratings." "Professional, scientific, technical, administrative, or executive
work, or any other work involving for the most part original or constructive effort" was instead to be rated with "special ratings." The Bureau of
Efficiency observed that Harding's order

> represents a fundamental division of employees into two classes: Routine
> workers whose duties demand the exercise of comparatively little judgment
> or constructive effort, and workers occupying responsible administrative or
> technical positions. (U.S. Bureau of Efficiency 1922)

This restructuring of terminology was occurring at a time of declin-
ing status for lower-level clerical workers both in the government and in
the economy as a whole. Management was using scientific management
techniques to mechanize certain office operations (Parsons 1918; Leffingwell 1925; Nicholls *et al.* 1927). Women were moving into clerical positions in greater numbers, both in the government (U.S. Personnel Classification Board 1931; Saint 1931) and in the economy as a whole
(McMillan 1941; Bergmann 1986). Moreover, clerical salaries were falling
in comparison with blue-collar pay (National Industrial Conference
Board 1926). Government salaries were especially lagging.[20]

The proposed classification schedule of the Congressional Joint
Commission on the Reclassification of Salaries was published in 1920
and was the most extensive of its kind to date. It furnishes one of the last
clear examples of the use of the term *clerical* to refer both to the function
of office work and to the level at which the work was carried out. The
proposed classification of the committee divided the clerical services into
two groups, the "miscellaneous clerical service" and the "administrative and supervisory clerical service." The miscellaneous clerical

---

[20]Whereas the salary of the average government employee had increased $393 between
1893 and 1919, its purchasing power declined about 55% (U.S. CSC 1941b). This figure
includes employees other then clerks, but clerks were numerically dominant in the
government in these years.

service included positions ranging in title from "under clerk" to "principal clerk." The administrative and supervisory clerical service included positions from "head clerk" through "junior clerical administrator," "principal clerical administrator," "head clerical administrator," and "chief clerical administrator." The "special classes" in this "clerical" service included assistant bureau heads, bureau heads, administrative secretaries, and assistant secretaries of executive departments. In other words, very high administrative positions were described as part of the "clerical" service.

That the "clerical administrator" positions were important positions can be clearly seen through examinations of their job descriptions:

> *Principal Clerical Administrator:* Under direction—(1) to be responsible for the administration of the clerical and general business affairs of a bureau or office which requires a fairly large clerical organization, or which by reason of the complexity or the centralized control of its work entails in its business management considerable administrative responsibility, and to have administrative supervision over the clerical and subclerical or other employees thereof, or (2) to serve as assistant to the head of a bureau or office, or to a chief or head clerical administrator, with complete or partial administrative supervision over the personnel of the bureau or office, or (3) as the administrative head of a division or other unit, to direct, supervise, or to perform work entailing considerable administrative or substantive responsibility . . . formulating administrative procedure or action, arranging hours of labor, allotting tasks, and maintaining discipline, passing on administrative problems, administering appropriations, enforcing general regulations, directing the maintenance and protection of buildings or other property . . . .
> Qualifications: Training equivalent to that represented by graduation from high school, and preferably by graduation with a degree from an institution of recognized standing; not less than four years' successful experience in Government work in a responsible supervisory capacity; intimate knowledge of the structure of the Government, the laws and practices affecting the departmental service, the laws relating to appropriations, expenditures and accounting, and Civil Service laws and requirements; and administrative ability.

> *Head Clerical Administrator:* Under general direction—(1) to be responsible for the administration of the clerical affairs and the general business operations of a department, bureau, or independent establishment which requires a large clerical organization, . . . and to have general supervision over the clerical and subclerical or other employees of the department or establishment, or (2) as administrative assistant to the head of the department or large bureau, or (3) as the administrative head of a division or other unit, to direct work entailing broad administrative or substantive responsibility . . . .
> Qualifications: Training equivalent to that represented by graduation with a degree from an institution of recognized standing; not less than five years successful experience in Government work in an administrative or other responsible capacity . . . .

Chief Clerical Administrator: Subject to general administrative direction—(1) to be responsible for the administration of the clerical affairs and general business operations of one of the largest departments . . . .
Qualifications: Training equivalent to that represented by graduation with a degree from an institution of recognized standing; not less than six years' successful experience in Government work in an administrative or other responsible capacity . . . . (U.S. Congress. House 1920: Part II, 7–9)

The recommendations of the Congressional Joint Commission were not passed into law in unmodified form, however. In contrast to the proposed classification system of the Congressional Joint Commission, the language employed in the Classification Act of 1923 is much more "modern" in its treatment of clerical and administrative work. It organized clerical and administrative work into the same service and generally implied a certain continuity between the two tasks. However, it did not use the term *clerical* to describe middle- or higher-level grades. Instead, it described positions above the "principal clerical grade" as "administrative" or "executive" (U.S. Personnel Classification Board 1924). The position of chief clerk was used to illustrate the duties of some positions classified as CAF-7, the "assistant administrative grade" and CAF-9, the "full administrative grade," but the newer terminology was clearly on the advance. Above Grade CAF-9 was the "senior administrative grade," the "assistant chief administrative grade," the "chief administrative grade," the "executive grade" and the "special executive grade." In the increasingly dominant terminology, clerical positions were subordinate and routine in nature or involved low-level supervisory responsibilities. Middle-level administrators were no longer described as *clerical* in level or function.

The position of chief clerk itself, although an important one through the first third of the century, was also undergoing a process of transformation. When President Cleveland covered into the classified service the positions of chief clerk and division chief, department and bureau heads objected. Secretary of the Interior Cornelius N. Bliss argued that "these officers occupy confidential relations to the Secretary, and on their briefs or recommendations he is dependent, to a large extent, for the proper conduct of his office" (quoted in White 1958: 321). Benjamin Butterworth, commissioner of the Patent Office and a "long time advocate of civil service reform" (White 1958: 321), declared that "the [classification] rules should embrace in the main merely the clerical force, and certainly not those of the executive staff" (quoted in White 1958: 321). When these positions lost their "confidential" status, new confidential positions were authorized at higher levels. In 1889, McKinley issued revised civil service rules that gave each department head, assistant head, and bureau head who was appointed by the president with Senate confirmation two "confidential clerk" (but note the word *clerk* in the title) positions. These positions were placed outside of the classified service. They were later titled as *administrative assistant, assistant,* or *special assistant* (Commission of Organization of the Executive Branch of the Government 1955). They commanded higher salaries than chief clerks and began taking over some of the functions traditionally performed by the chief clerk.

The positions of chief clerk and division chief were eventually belittled as unworthy end points for a civil service career by reformers intent on extending the classification system to the very top of the executive branch (Willoughby 1927). Nonetheless, it is clear that even as late as the 1920s, these positions had relatively high rank in the bureaucracy. For example, in 1927 the State Department had only an undersecretary and three assistant secretaries above the chief clerk (U.S. Bureau of the Census 1927). In the office of the secretary of the treasury, there was an undersecretary, three assistant secretaries, an assistant to the secretary, two assistants to the undersecretary, two assistants to assistant secretaries, and a special assistant to an assistant secretary above the chief clerk, the disbursing clerk, and three division chiefs. In the comptroller's office, only the comptroller stood above the chief clerk and the division chiefs. The hierarchies of other bureaus were similar. The very listing of incumbents of chief clerk positions in the Official Registry of the U.S. Government attests to their status as responsible government positions. Nonetheless, these positions were becoming an anachronism as new titles, such as budget officer or personnel officer, came into existence in the 1920s and 1930s. The incumbents of these new positions, often the "assistants" or "confidential clerks" described before (Macmahon and Millet 1939), performed the functions formerly assigned to chief clerks. But their positions were considered fully administrative in nature and were titled accordingly.

The ambiguity in the positions of high clerks and lower managers extended beyond the government. Consider, for instance, the difficulties that the Taylor society, the institutional engine for the spread of scientific management, experienced in attempting to define what management consisted of. Before 1920, Taylorism's concern with "scientific management" was limited to the role of functional foreman on the factory floor and in the office.[21] It was not until 1921 that the Taylor society took up the question of the job of chief executive (Pearson 1945). H. S.

---

[21]The office foremen were designated as "clerks" by Taylor (1903).

Person, for a time the president of the Taylor society, proposed in the 1920s that the functions of direction, administration, and management be separated. By *direction*, he meant the determination of the most general policies. *Administration* referred to the setting of guidelines within which these policies were to be carried out. *Management* referred to the manipulation of facilities in the detailed conduct of operations. But Person wrote that

> among businessmen, and in government as well, all these words are used, but without uniformity of meaning. In one place administration, for instance, is given a meaning as I have defined it; in another place it is used to identify the functions of a chief clerk. (Person 1940: 66)

A check of the first edition of the *Dictionary of Occupational Titles* (U.S. Department of Labor 1939) also demonstrates the ambiguity of terminology during this period. The "office manager" is one who "supervises and directs clerical employees in the business office. . . ." The "chief clerk" "coordinates the clerical work of an establishment . . . may direct the work of several subordinate MANAGERS, OFFICE." In other words, a clerk directed the work of a manager. The lack of uniformity of meaning, mostly residual by the late 1930s, was based on a true social ambiguity. This ambiguity was ultimately resolved into a consistent social definition of managerial occupations as superordinate and involved with policymaking, and clerical occupations as involving structured work, with sometimes low-level supervisory responsibilities.

During the next two decades, the position of chief clerk did not so much drop in the hierarchy as disappear from the hierarchy. It had become an anachronism in a world where administrative-level work was performed by administrators, not clerks. By the middle 1950s, the position of chief clerk had disappeared from the civil service (U.S. CSC 1955b). By way of comparison, the position of division chief, which was roughly comparable to the chief clerk at the turn of the century, had been clearly elevated. The task force for the second Hoover Commission in fact proposed that chiefs of divisions, typically staffed then at GS-15 and higher, be included in its proposed "Senior Civil Service" (Commission on Organization of the Executive Branch of the Government 1955: 14ff.). The tasks of division chiefs had of course been radically transformed by the increased size and complexity of bureaus. But the same title was still appropriate, in part no doubt because it did not contain the adjective *clerical*.

The use of the word *clerical* to refer to the function of office work had also disappeared from position-classification terminology by the postwar period. In postwar terminology, there existed administrative, managerial, or executive work on the one hand, and clerical work on the other. Administrative work was that which

> involve[d] the exercise of analytical ability, judgment, discretion, personal responsibility and the application of a substantial body of knowledge of principles, concepts, and practices applicable to one or more fields of administration or management. (U.S. CSC 1976a: 4)

Clerical operations

> involve[ed] structured work in support of office, business, or fiscal operations; duties are performed in accordance with established policies, experience or working knowledge related to the tasks to be performed (U.S. CSC 1976a: 5).

The boundary between the two types of work had clearly shifted over the years, as the number of administrative jobs proliferated both in the government and in the private sector. Ironically, whereas once office work in general was referred to as the "clerical" sector or function, it became increasingly common for the term *administrative* to refer both to function and level, whereas the term *clerical* was reserved for routine office work.

SUMMARY OF PART I

In the eighteenth century, the work of government clerks extended from routine to middle-management levels. As the business of government become more complex, the work of clerks, and particularly the higher clerks, became still more responsible as the government shifted the ratio of clerks to "commissioned officers" in favor of the clerks. But sometime in the middle of the nineteenth century, the clerical–administrative boundary began a process of transformation.

The need for specialized work (e.g., accounting, correspondence with foreign ministers, preparation of exhibits, judicial investigations, oversight of patents, technical bibliographic work, etc.) led to the creation of new job duties before these jobs had social recognition as specialized occupations. Government clerks performed all these jobs at one time. But with growing social recognition for the specialized character of these tasks, the specialists claimed and were given new titles. During the transition, organizations did not all use titles in the same way. For example, some departments used a "chief clerk" to supervise personnel or the budget, whereas others would make use of a "personnel officer" or "budget officer" during the first third of the present century. Still others made use of an "administrative assistant" (Macmahon and Millet

1939; Mosher *et al.* 1950). But, gradually, the new occupations acquired more distinct social identities and were further differentiated from clerical work, where their origins lie. Today the tasks formerly done by higher clerks are done by employees called managers, administrators, or specialists of one kind or another.

The transformation of the boundary between clerical and administrative work was one of many changes taking place in a growing federal bureaucracy. As the grade structure of government expanded, the number of grades in both the clerical and administrative section of the hierarchy also increased in number. But even the higher jobs on clerical job ladders are now limited to routine work. More advanced clerical work is sometimes now classified on technical job ladders, which are descendants of the subprofessional service of the prewar era.[22] But, especially outside of highly technical fields such as engineering and the physical sciences, these positions also are concentrated in the lower levels of government. Nonroutine, responsible work is today almost entirely classified onto administrative or professional job ladders. As administration became a more well-defined occupation conceptually, the language of the maturing position classification system placed much more stress on the analytical, professional character of this work. The administrative and professional hierarchy gradually increased in length and accounted for an ever-larger proportion of the government work force. But even as position classification systems specified the character of professional and particularly administrative work with increased precision, the organizational status of these positions was becoming more diffuse. Any employee described as an administrator or professional in the first third of the century would necessarily have a job superior in rank, status, and pay to the great majority of white-collar workers. But by the 1980s, a low-level administrative position was very far down the totem pole. It is much more similar to a high clerical job in the present system than it is to an administrative position near the top of the hierarchy.

The separation of administrative and clerical work onto separate job ladders during the latter half of the twentieth century raises the question of how to characterize the boundary between them. The fact of a boundary suggests some qualitative distinction between the two types of work, as opposed to the quantitative distinctions made within the job ladders of the two tiers. The language used to describe the difference between clerical and administrative work highlights the supposed qualitative differences. Administrative work is nonroutine, responsible,

---

[22]See Appendix for details on this point.

and analytical in character, whereas clerical work is routine and structured. Positions within the ladders are then distinguished according to
whether they are more or less routine, more or less responsible, and so
forth. The qualitative distinctions between clerical and administrative
work that are found in the position classification standards should make
it easy to distinguish the type of work done by high clerks and low-level
administrators, if the differences truly are qualitative in nature. But
these distinctions are apparently difficult to make in practice.

The authors of the position classification standards recognized that
the theoretical distinctions between types of work are not sufficient to
specify a solution to the problem that the clerical–administrative boundary poses for classifiers. The position classification standards therefore
suggested a different standard for distinguishing positions at the top of
the lower tier from those at the bottom of the upper tier. This standard
concerned the mobility potential of the employees involved. Individuals
with high mobility potential should be assigned to the upper tier,
whereas those with low mobility potential should be assigned to the
lower tier. The issue of mobility is therefore inherent in the structure of
these ladders, at least in their practical, if not theoretical manifestation.[23]

The material of Part I, in short, has documented that a system of
bifurcated job ladders for administrative as well as professional work
presently exists in the federal civil service. The boundary between the
lower tier and the upper tier was quite ambiguous at earlier times and
retains an element of ambiguity even today. But, beyond suggesting
that mobility considerations as well as the content of the jobs themselves
were at work, Part I has not addressed the questions of where the model
or models for these ladders came from, or of what their implications
were for career mobility. Part II explores the development of recruitment
and promotion policies in the federal government and how conflicting
interpretations of these issues gradually led to the formation of a system
of tiered job ladders.

[23]See Appendix for a discussion of the standards for distinguishing between the higher
positions on lower-tier ladders and the lower positions on upper-tier ladders.

II
THE SHAPING OF RECRUITMENT AND PROMOTION POLICIES FOR WHITE-COLLAR JOBS

4

Early Personnel Management in the Federal Civil Service

Modern public personnel administration might be said to originate from the passage of the Civil Service Reform Act of 1883, or more generally from the management movement and from Taylor's work in the late nineteenth century, which together fueled the scientific management movement of the twentieth century (Person 1930–35). But these events have a history also. Officials of the American government had to deal with personnel problems from the beginning of the Republic. The early presidents, giving substantial weight to qualifications as well as to political views and class background ("community standing"), personally filled the top appointive positions of the government (Finer 1952). They delegated to department heads the job of filling clerical positions. Department heads in turn frequently relied on the recommendations of their chief clerks when making these appointments (White 1951: 129). There was no need to recruit for these jobs; the number of applicants was more than adequate. Once employed, the civil servants, with official sanction, enjoyed long tenure in office (White 1948: 513–515). During the Federalist and Jeffersonian years, some departments even had a rudimentary system of promotion (Fish 1905; White 1953). Thus, long before industrialists began organizing jobs into promotion lines at the turn of the twentieth century, at least some federal administrators had concluded that promotion was an efficient way to fill job vacancies.[1]

[1]"The expectation of promotion in civil as in military life is a great stimulus to virtuous exertion, while examples of unrewarded exertion, supported by talent and qualification, are proportionable discouragements. Where they do not produce resignations they leave

73

The introduction of the spoils system disrupted these policies, but even during the Jacksonian period, administrative procedures retained some continuity with the past.[2] Administrators often recognized the value of job-specific training and the need to retain some employees after a change in administration. These holdovers provided a source of knowledge for training the new employees who were rotated into office.[3] The proportion of employees able to keep their jobs during the height of the spoils era varied by agency and apparently by skill level. For example, in the New York assay office, where technical skills were needed, 27 of its 55 officers had been employed more than 10 years as of 1868. In contrast, only 5 of 282 had survived that long in the Office of the Treasurer in the Treasury Department, where technical skills were less important (Hoogenboom 1961).

Scholars have established that twentieth-century personnel reforms were sometimes forced on management by unions and sometimes started by managers to fight unionization (Jacoby 1983; Freeman and Medoff 1984). Similarly, workers had a hand in some nineteenth-century personnel reforms (U.S. Congress. Senate 1838a,b; Baruch 1941a). Employee efforts to secure changes in pay and personnel policies in both the 1830s and the 1850s corresponded to periods of price inflation. But their petitions reflected employee concern that salaries correspond with the difficulty and responsibility of the job. Employees of older bureaus were upset that their pay was no longer comparable with that of new bureaus. In both the 1830s and the 1850s, departmental heads agreed with their employees that clerical salaries were too low. House and Senate committees concluded that the classification of civil service positions was a matter "of primary importance" (U.S. Congress, House 1842; Congressional Globe 1851: 584).

Congress also showed interest in regulating promotion policies in the middle nineteenth century. In 1841, a committee of the House of Representatives proposed a system of examinations for promotion (U.S.

---

men dissatisfied,and a dissatisfied man seldom does his duty well"(Alexander Hamilton, quoted in White 1948: 310).

[2]It has long been established that Jackson did not make the "clean sweep" of federal office holders once thought. Eriksson (1927) estimated that during his tenure, he removed between 1/10 and 1/5 of all federal office holders for political reasons (also see Fish 1905: 125). The rate of replacement clearly grew during the next few decades.

[3]The holdovers tended to be clerks. Sageser (1935) maintained they were often "under-clerks" and were sometimes fired after their tutorial role was finished. White argued that employees in "the key positions of middle management" were also often retained (White 1953: 6), as were certain employees with valued technical skills (Fish 1905: 182; Van Riper 1958; Hoogenboom 1961).

CSC 1898; Goodnow 1900). Then in 1852, a committee of the Senate requested that the heads of the executive departments propose "some plan to provide for the examination of the qualifications of clerks and their promotion from one grade to another upon due regard to qualifications and service" (U.S. Congress. Senate 1852a: 1). A nonbinding Senate resolution suggested that when a clerical vacancy existed below the level of chief clerk

> a board shall be constituted by the head of the department in which the vacancy shall have occurred, to examine any candidates to fill the same, who may be sent before it by the head of the department, as well as to their condition of health and physical energy, as to their education, skill, and other qualifications for the duties of the place in question; and that no person shall be considered eligible to such appointment, who shall not produce to the head of the department, to be filed in its archives, a certificate of approval from such board of examination.
>
> That every vacancy, except in the chief clerkship or in a clerkship of the lowest class, shall be filled from the next inferior class in the same department, or bureau, by the individual who shall receive from a board constituted for his examination, in the same manner as prescribed in the foregoing paragraph, a certificate that he is fully qualified. But if no person in such inferior class receive such certificate, then such other person may be appointed as shall, by the direction of the head of the department, be sent before such board of examination, and receive therefrom the requisite certificate of qualification.
>
> That when such other person shall be so appointed without the previous presentment for examination of all the clerks of the class next inferior to that in which the vacancy is to be filled, the head of the department in which such appointment is made, shall cause to be entered fully on its records, the reasons for such procedure. (U.S. Congress. Senate 1852a: 1–2).

Other forces opposed these progressive concerns. Politicians favoring a spoils system naturally opposed systematic promotion policies. But some administrators also opposed the idea, though for a different reason. Although departmental heads generally were in favor of pay increases for their clerks (U.S. Congress. Senate 1938b), they viewed attempts to systematize the promotion process with more caution. Nineteenth-century managers, like their twentieth-century counterparts, feared a loss of their discretionary authority. In a letter to the Senate, the secretaries of the Treasury, Interior, War, Navy and the Postmaster General wrote that

> several of the undersigned entertain doubts in regard to the *practicability* or utility of the foregoing plan of preliminary examination and of promotion by regular gradation, [yet] they have, with some hesitation, concluded to unite in reporting it as worthy of trial, and more likely to accomplish the desired object than any other upon which all can agree. [emphasis theirs] (U.S. Congress. Senate 1852a: 2).

Daniel Webster, then secretary of state, was more straightforward in his opposition to the proposal. He wrote that

> he is not able to agree with the other heads of departments in the report which they have made to the Senate.
>
> In his opinion it is not expedient to establish any board for the examination of candidates either for original appointment or for promotion. The head of a department may always readily consult the more experienced clerks upon the fitness of new applicants, or the propriety of promotions. This is now always done in the department over which the undersigned has the honor to preside.
>
> The business of promotion always requires great consideration in this department, because the duties of the several bureaux are very various, and it is not always easy to make transfers from one line of occupation to another. (U.S. Congress. Senate 1852b: 1)

These early disputes about the merits of controls versus managerial discretion for making promotion decisions would recur during the twentieth century, also.

Policies for dealing with personnel issues such as pay and promotion were rudimentary compared with modern personnel systems.[4] No position classification system existed to order jobs into useful job ladders. The Act of March 3, 1853, 10 Stat. 209, provided that clerks in the Departments of Treasury, War, Navy, Interior, and the Post Office in Washington DC "shall be arranged into four classes," and in 1864, Congress authorized the position of "female clerk." However, as discussed earlier in this book, these classes did not constitute a system of position classification.

Congress left the job of classification to department heads and their chief clerks. Political, financial, and personal considerations, as well as technical difficulties in generating a systematic classification, guaranteed that classification would not be applied "scientifically." Thus the application of personnel policies was very uneven from a modern standpoint. The War Department experimented with primitive systems of efficiency ratings in 1887, before the era of scientific management (Graves 1948). But in other bureaus, employees had duties so nebulous that they were officially classified as having "no particular occupation" (Hoogenboom 1961: 3–4). The haphazard character of personnel management led the Keep Committee to report in 1907 that

> persons receiving the higher salaries may be found performing the simplest routine work, while others in the lowest grades are performing work of the most exacting character. Professional, technical and scientific work especially

[4]Much of the following material about grade systems is drawn from accounts by Betters (1931), U.S. Personnel Classification Board (1931), and Baruch (1941a).

is notoriously underpaid as compared with clerical work. (Committee on
Department Methods 1907)

It was not until the passage of the Classification Act of 1923 that the
government began to implement a systematic position classification
system.

The 1853 bill that classified Washington clerks into four grades also
required that new clerks be examined before appointment. The CSC
later commented in its first report that these examinations "were not
open to all persons apparently qualified, nor even to such persons belonging to the dominant party, but rather to such of the favorites of the
dominant faction of that party as members of Congress and great politicians recommended" (U.S. CSC 1884: 13). Nonetheless, like the previously mentioned developments, they show a continuity of concern
with personnel problems from the time of the Federalists through the
period of spoils to the present time. But the government could not
remedy these problems through systematic policies for many years.

THE ONSET OF REFORM

Several different factors triggered early reform developments. Some
were technical in nature, whereas others were cultural and political. The
continuing growth of government, and particularly the demands made
on the federal government during the Civil War, revealed shortcomings
in the existing administrative apparatus. Professionals reacting to the
perceived threat posed by increasingly powerful industrialists and the
feared development of "mass society" and an interventionist state provided a cultural force for change (Hofstadter 1955; Hoggenboom 1961;
Frederickson 1965; Wiebe 1967; McFarland 1975; Haskell 1977). The
American military and the British civil service provided models for organizing a civil service. Prominent scandals gave the spoils system bad
publicity and mobilized public opinion against it. These scandals provided Republicans with a weapon to use against the Democratic party.
All these developments fueled the strength of the reform movement.

The ideological message of reform legislation seemed plain enough.
But realizing this vision was another matter. The inability of the state to
implement early reform proposals revealed the tremendous administrative capacity necessary for such an operation—an administrative
capacity that did not yet exist. Operating officials, wishing to preserve
their authority, resisted efforts to centralize personnel management.
They also doubted the practicality of certain aspects of the reform pro-

gram. Their behavior combined with the limited administrative machinery available at the time to shape the practical effects of reform.

The brief life of America's first Civil Service Commission provided a model for later bureaucratic developments. The civil service rider to the sundry civil appropriations bill of 1871 gave U. S. Grant the authority to lay down "rules and regulations for the admission of persons into the civil service of the United States." He responded by establishing the first Civil Service Commission and appointing reformers to sit on it (Murphy 1942). Grant's Civil Service Commission self-consciously attempted to create a bureaucratic system designed to "best promote the efficiency" of the civil service. It proposed rules to accomplish this end, which were based on knowledge of conditions in the American civil service and further informed by study of the civil service systems in Britain and elsewhere (Murphy 1942). But it discovered that a systematic approach to personnel management required some form of position classification system. The commission therefore attempted to establish the groundwork for a classification system through proposed rules such as the following:

1. The commission proposed to distinguish positions according to their political responsibilities and along broad occupational categories. It saw three different types of federal employees: (1) higher officers who formulate the policy of the dominant party, (2) subordinate officers and clerks who carry out this policy, and (3) manual employees.

2. The Constitution governed the rules for appointing the highest officials of government. The commission recommended that the president use political criteria to fill other sensitive political positions.

3. Manual workers "were to be appointed at will." (Murphy 1942, quoting minutes of the Civil Service Commission, February 16, 1872, p. 124.) The commission recommended they be excluded from the rules because they were largely temporary employees.

4. The commission proposed to classify all "inferior officers in their several Departments throughout the country with reference to the character of the duties to be severally performed" (Murphy 1942, quoting minutes of the Civil Service Commission, October 18, 1971, p. 25).

5. The commission proposed to cluster positions in the civil service into "groups" for the purposes of filling vacancies.

6. Appointments would be made at the bottom level of the group,

through competitive examination. A "rule of three" would preserve some discretionary power for the appointing officer.
7. The commission proposed that all positions above the entry-level position in each group would be filled by promotion. First preference for the vacant jobs would go to individuals located in the same bureau as the vacancy. Insiders would compete on the basis of a competitive examination. Outsiders could be considered for a vacant position if no one in the service was found to be qualified.[5]

Grant approved the new rules in 1872. The commission had neither the time nor the resources to implement these rules, but it made a start. It developed a set of entrance and promotion exams for use both in the departmental and the field service (Sageser 1935: 27). By April of 1874, 2286 candidates for Washington jobs had been examined, and 1531 civil servants had taken promotion exams. Of the 2286 candidates for new positions, 717 had obtained jobs.[6]

But the effort of Grant's civil service commission generated heavy opposition from antireform elements in Congress. They eliminated the commission's budget in 1875 and thereby terminated the examination system. Congressmen opposed to the new rules argued that the existing system both served desirable political ends and was technically adequate. In contrast, they argued, the new system served undesirable political ends and, because of its expense and impracticality, was not technically sound.[7]

Significantly, nearly all the officers surveyed by Grant's Civil Service Commission specifically objected to the use of competitive examinations to control the promotion process, with arguments such as the following, made by the second comptroller of the Treasury.

> A clerk may become master of the business upon which he is engaged by devoting his entire energies to it for a series of years, and by reason of his experience and fidelity [come] to be almost invaluable to an office, and yet when examined on general subjects not be able to pass as good an examination as when he entered the service (U.S. Congress. Senate 1874, quoted in White 1858: 284).

[5]The commission considered using seniority as a qualification for promotion but rejected the idea (Murphy 1942: 288).
[6]The exams apparently were not easy to pass. Out of 1103 persons examined in Washington and New York for Treasury positions, 583 received failing grades. (Sageser 1935: Footnote 100).
[7]The establishment of an "evil" bureaucracy and the strengthening of the political power of an aristocratic class were often-repeated charges (Murphy 1947; Hoogenboom 1961).

The argument made by the first comptroller of the Treasury Department is similar.

> Promotions should depend upon the qualifications which a candidate has developed through the tests of practical experience . . . and no one outside of the Office . . . can be as well qualified to judge of his merits as the head of the Office in which he has served. (U.S. Congress. Senate 1874, quoted in White 1958: 284)

These objections, translated into contemporary terms, amounted to a claim that the proposed promotion examinations would not measure the abilities and skills that determined success in the new position as well as office superiors could. Administrators favored the management-prerogative method of promotion over any other.

The Civil Service Reform Act of 1883 contained some of the stipulations found in the rules of Grant's Civil Service Commission, but it excluded the systematic promotion controls favored by Grant's commission. Senator Pendleton, who introduced the reform bill, wanted agencies to fill vacancies above the lowest level in each group by promotion. He intended that fitness and seniority should jointly be the criteria for promotion, with 25% of the promotions based solely on merit. Senate Democrats worried that such a rule would delay their party's securing a proportional share of the public offices (Hoogenboom 1961). But they raised technical objections as well to support their case. They argued that on-the-job training did not always qualify an employee for higher positions in the same group. Hence, they concluded, all positions should be open to outsiders (Hoogenboom 1961: 241). Such an argument was clearly self-serving, but it anticipated later disputes about the same subject. Pendleton amended his bill to delete the requirement that appointments be limited to the lowest grade, and the measure passed. The merit system was thereby launched.

MERIT, THE MERIT SYSTEM, AND THE QUALIFICATIONS FOR OFFICE

The merit system gradually gained ascendancy as the only legitimate way to organize a bureaucratic personnel system. But the basis for this system, the concept of merit, lacked definition. The Pendleton Act contained only vague language calling for "open, competitive examinations for testing the fitness of applicants . . . fairly test the relative capacity and fitness . . . selections according to grade from among those graded highest." The CSC had to flesh out the practical definitions of fairness, capacity, and fitness.

The CSC's attempts at operationalization demonstrated how competing interests could use the ideology of merit to justify different interpretations of these terms. Furthermore, the CSC lacked the administrative capacity to implement the philosophy it continued to refine. In the early years, it spent most of its resources developing entrance examinations. Though the CSC tried, it could not effectively control promotion practices in the government. Even its control over the examination process left operating officials ample room to fill vacancies as they wished.

The two key qualities the CSC sought in job applicants were "good character" and "superior business capacity."[8] To determine whether a candidate had these qualities, it required him to fill out a detailed application and to take a test. The rules required the candidate to "set forth the facts as to his birth, age, residence, occupation, education, physical condition, and capacity for doing the public work." He was required to provide a residential and occupational history covering the 5 years prior to his application date. He had to document any criminal record, whether he "uses intoxicating drinks to excess," who had employed him during the previous 3 years, details about employment separations, and information about physical incapacities. Four people had to sign affidavits certifying the truthfulness of his statements (U.S. CSC 1884: 33–34).

The CSC acknowledged that its tests were imperfect selection tools. However, it believed that test scores would be "associated" with both character and business capacity, the two qualities it sought in applicants. It further believed that the examinations would "bring to the head of the registers" those who were "most competent" in what the public schools had taught. It valued book learning less than "attention to duty, and hence of patience, industry, good habits, and the command of the mental faculties." These traits, which were the true worth of an elementary-school education, showed an applicant's "promise of business capacity and ability to lead others."

[8]U.S. CSC 1885: 34. The association of merit with business was a key part of the ideological campaign to sell the idea. A principal argument for the merit system was that it would put the personnel affairs of government on a more businesslike footing (Godkin 1882: 292; U.S. CSC 1884: 15; 1885: 13; Keller 1977: 273). This argument shows the dual use of models as both sources of ideas and as rhetorical resources. For although the argument presumed the natural use of these tests by business (hence "businesslike"), the use of tests to screen applicants was not an adaptation of current business practices but rather an adaptation of earlier civil service practice both in the United States and abroad (U.S. CSC 1886: 33). In fact, one of the early criticisms against the idea was that business did not, in fact, recruit clerks through the use of tests. On the subject of character, see Bledstein (1976: 129ff.).

Now, if superiority shown in the schools or acquired there is not generally a test of the scholar's attention to duty, and hence of patience, industry,
good habits, and the command of the mental faculties, which promises business capacity and ability to lead others, and if faithful study in the schools
does not tend to increase these qualities, then indeed we have over-esti-
mated the good effects of our public-school system. If the best informed
mechanics and laborers are not generally the most trustworthy and successful; if, on the other hand, the uninstructed are just as successful in
business and just as useful to the community, there would seem to be little to
say in defense of universal taxation imposed for educating all the children in
the very subjects which the Civil Service Examinations cover. Though there
are many exceptions, yet as a rule the best scholars in our public schools are
the worthiest boys and girls, and are likely to make the best men and women
of business and the best citizens. There are bright rogues in school, but as a
rule the boys who most regularly and thoroughly learn and remember what
they are required to study are the boys who will certainly make the best
clerks, if not the best men of business. If bad habits are, as may be well
believed, more frequently than dullness the cause of little being learned in
the schools or remembered, the conclusion is inevitable that good scholars
are more moral and trustworthy than bad scholars. Consequently, the
schoolmaster's test is not a mere test of learning, but is indirectly a test of
character. (U.S. CSC 1886: 35)

This statement reflected a view, which was shared by many businessmen and educators, that schools disciplined the mental faculties as
they provided academic knowledge (Hapgood 1906; Kirkland 1956;
Kolensik 1958; Veysey 1965).

However, the CSC's praise for education was largely reserved for
elementary-school education. The CSC reported in its third annual report that diligent study in the "common school" was necessary for high
performance on the civil service examinations. But it argued that the
college educated should not and do not have any special advantage in
taking the tests.

It seems clear, therefore, that the college educated applicants have no real
advantage over those who have not been in college. Such subjects have been
selected and the questions have been so framed and marked as to make, in a
practical sense, the public school education of the country, united with good
character, the real test for securing appointments. . . . This is the answer to
the often repeated charge that the merit system of office gives a monopoly to
literary and college-bred men, and therefore favors an aristocracy. (U.S. CSC
1886: 65–66)

This charge was being reported in "journals hostile to the cause of
reform" (U.S. CSC 1886, 13), but it was being discussed and debated in
more sympathetic arenas as well. "The early reports of . . . National

Civil Service Reform League, as well as the periodical literature, are full of discussions of this possibility" (Van Riper 1958: 158).[9]

To a large extent, official praise for the common school education must be seen as politically motivated, an attempt to defuse charges that the CSC was violating the law's requirement that civil service tests be "practical" in character. However, the language of the Pendleton Act reflected social opinion on this matter. The opinion that education, and particularly higher education, did not prepare a young man for leadership was common in the 1880s and 1890s, in the business world (Veysey 1965), among government officials, and among the public at large (Hofstadter 1964: 181ff.).[10]

The CSC's operationalization of merit from the start attempted to incorporate the sometimes inconsistent values of fairness and efficiency. In a fair job competition, the most qualified candidate gets the job. However, when qualifications were linked so closely to educational attainment, then fairness in the eyes of the public also had to address the question whether the contest for the educational qualifications itself was fair. The college system at the time was seen as elitist. Much of the public denigrated the utility of a college education. They would have judged any system of recruitment that gave the college educated an advantage to be "unfair," and hence not a merit system.

In contrast, that part of the educational system that was most "democratic and American" was the common school system. It was open to all. Taxpayers supported the public schools with their money. Furthermore, it was generally accepted that a common school education was useful preparation for work. The public was more likely, therefore, to view tests based on common school education as "fair." Theodore Roosevelt, who was a civil service commissioner as well as a president, echoed public sentiment when he argued that "the merit system of

---

[9]It is interesting to note that the failure rate of those claiming college education was the same as those who had not (U.S. CSC 1886, 1887). College students apparently continued to have trouble with clerical examinations in later years as well. In the late 1930s, nearly half the college graduates taking clerical exams failed to pass the exam, let alone get a high enough score to obtain a job (Government Positions 1939).

[10]Andrew Carnegie's 1889 remarks on the subject are noteworthy: "While the college student has been learning a little about the barbarous and petty squabbles of a far-distant past, or trying to master languages which are dead, such knowledge as seems adapted for life upon another planet than this as far as business affairs are concerned, the future captain of industry is hotly engaged in the school of experience, obtaining the very knowledge required for his future triumphs. . . . College education as it exists is fatal to success in that domain." (quoted in Veysey 1965: 13–14)

making appointments is in its essence as democratic and American as the common school system itself" (quoted in Macy 1971: 16).

Government officials as well as elected politicians shared the public concern that civil service examinations might discriminate in favor the educated and work against the best interests of the service. When President Cleveland extended the merit system in 1896 to include chief clerks and chiefs of divisions in the departmental service, some departmental officials as well as politicians objected (White 1958: 319). Opponents asserted that these officials held confidential relations with bureau heads, and were rightly political offices, a position rejected by the Civil Service Commission.[11] At least one department head argued that the classification of these positions would lead to their being filled by "bright school boys" rather than by those who had acquired "sufficient practical experience" to do the job successfully.[12]

In 1899, McKinley exempted the highest positions in the classified civil service from the examination requirement. This exemption served the political purpose of making it easier for his administration to fill some of these positions with political appointees (Van Riper 1958: 177). The CSC argued for the wisdom of such a policy. Although the CSC's support may in part have been politically motivated, its defense of this policy tapped a sentiment concerning the nature of administrative work that continues to exist in the present day. It observed that the higher positions were "places of authority where discretion, a sense of justice, facility in arranging and dispatching business, capacity for discipline and for command are not only the most essential qualifications, but are the most difficult of all to be tested by examinations." (U.S. CSC 1886: 23). Fourteen years later, the CSC again took the same position.

> But examination for promotion must be confined to subjects which do not test the executive or administrative qualifications required in the position for which the examination is taken. If such qualifications predominate, a competitive examination is useless, because those qualifications are developed by experience and are best known to the appointing or promoting officer. Under existing conditions each department must adopt such a system as will most nearly meet its special requirements (U.S. CSC 1902: 23).

But though the CSC expressed reservations about the utility of entrance tests based on a college curriculum, it also showed some of the

---

[11]"The great bulk of the offices of the Government are purely administrative business offices. . . . There are properly very few of the many offices in the gift of the Government which are really political in character, after we pass below the highest, such as the members of the Cabinet and ministers to foreign countries" (U.S. CSC 1891: 15).
[12]Secretary of Agriculture James Wilson testifying before the Senate, quoted in White (1958: 321).

admiration for college education that progressive reformers later ampli-
fied. In its first annual report, the CSC, after reporting that only a common school education was required for entrance into the clerical grades,
went on to write that

> the best informed and most meritorious of those who enter it [the civil
> service] will be likely to win the higher prizes through promotion when once
> the merit system for admission shall be fairly established. And though the
> higher education is not necessary in order to gain admission to the public
> service, it will nevertheless prove its value in the mastery of the principles
> and methods of that service, and so gain higher consideration, and give
> increased power to those who possess it (U.S. CSC 1884: 21).

The connection between education and high office would thus emerge
out of the "revealed utility of the education, not the credentials, themselves" in the opinion of the CSC (U.S. CSC 1897: 18).

In the 1880s, the nation's universities had only begun their transformation to the modern, vocationally oriented institutions now standard
in this country (Veysey 1965). But the early civil service reformers already valued higher education as an asset for public service (Haskell
1977). They wanted the training of public servants to be a principal
university goal. These reformers dreamed of the creation of an administrative elite, trained in the social sciences, that would efficiently carry
out the state's role (typically limited, in their view) in national development (Fredrickson 1965: 209). In the period between 1865 and 1890,
universities such as Cornell and Harvard led the way toward a conceptualization of "public service as an academic goal" (Veysey 1965: 79; see
also Crick 1962; Sass 1982).

But even reformers could worry that college credentials not become
the sole basis for entry into high administrative jobs. Dorman Eaton, the
first Civil Service Commissioner and a university-educated lawyer long
active in the reform movement, wrote an influential history of British
civil service reforms. In his book, he wrote approvingly of the link that
civil service examinations established between education and admission
to the civil service. But repeatedly, he singled out common school education, not university education, as the proper basis for the link. In his
view, reliance on common school education could democratize the civil
service at the same time as it increased government efficiency. He disapproved of the then-current British practice of requiring a university degree for entry into high civil service positions (Eaton 1880: 235).

Later progressives were to object that Eaton's "excessive" concern
about democracy would, if acted upon, deny the United States the efficient administrative apparatus it needed. Thirty-four years after Eaton
wrote his book, Robert Moses criticized Eaton for not more fully endors-

ing the "aristocratic" linking of education with position. In his own history of the British civil service, Moses argued that

> in truth, Mr. Eaton's honest Americanism rather blinded him to the true inwardness of English civil service democracy. Mr. Eaton was able to carry home with him ideas of open competition and of fair promotion which were of enormous and lasting benefit to the American civil service; but the essential feature of an upper, highly-educated division and a lower, more mechanical second division—marking the definite appeal of the British service to the best scholars of British universities—seems to have made no real impression on Mr. Eaton, and to have borne no fruit in the early reforms which he helped to institute in the United States. Thus we have still in Washington a civil service which offers little attraction to the educated young university graduate (Moses 1914: 6–7).

On one side of this debate were those concerned that the college educated would unfairly monopolize the best positions in the civil service and block the advancement of deserving employees who lacked college credentials. On the other side, people like Moses believed that only a tiered personnel system, which reserved the best positions for college graduates, could create the powerful administrative apparatus that Progressives wanted for government. These conflicting views contributed to the shaping of civil service job ladders.

RECRUITMENT VERSUS PROMOTION IN THE FILLING OF VACANCIES

The CSC concentrated its early energies on control of recruitment, leaving the subject of promotion for later consideration (U.S. CSC 1884, 1885, 1886, 1887). Its principal means of control was the examination. It established a number of general examinations in one of four types: general ability exams, achievement exams, trades exams, and unassembled examinations (Van Riper 1958: 139). Appointing officials had to make most permanent appointments in the classified service from the civil service registers.[13] However, appointing officers could ask for special exams for a position, or for an exemption, or could fill a position temporarily, without resorting to the registers.[14] The CSC had the power to

---

[13]At the time, the classified service included only the lower-level white-collar positions in the departments in Washington.

[14]Presidents granted many of these exceptions for political reasons, sometimes over the protests of the CSC (Sageser 1935: 150ff.). In addition, the Congress included an apportionment rule in the Pendleton Act that gave people from underrepresented states preference in obtaining jobs. The Reform Act gave veterans preference in the examinations. Finally, nothing in the act required appointing officials to select women on the registers.

investigate illegal appointments, but its main weapons were publicity and presidential support (Van Riper 1958: 139).

The Pendleton bill would have required agencies to fill all vacancies above the lowest level through promotion. Because Congress deleted this requirement before passing the reform bill into law, the CSC consistently took the position that agency officials were free to decide when to use promotions to fill vacancies.[15] Nonetheless, the CSC was officially committed to applying the principle of merit to promotions as well as to entrance into the civil service in order to eliminate "importunate solicitations and coercive influence from the outside" and "prejudice, favoritism, or corruption on the part of the appointing offices" (U.S. CSC 1884: 28). But the record suggests that it was unsure about how to proceed. At first, it could not decide how much weight to give fitness, seniority and "well-tested fidelity" in promotion decisions (U.S. CSC 1884: 28). By 1902, it had concluded that fitness for office should be given preference and that seniority should only be considered when other more direct measures of qualifications are equal (U.S. CSC 1902: 24). But in practice, several agencies used seniority extensively in promotion decisions, the post office being the largest example (Stahl 1956: 156).[16]

The CSC was reluctant to institute any rigid procedures that would interfere too much with the discretion of appointing officers to make promotion decisions. It thought that appointing officers were generally familiar with the capabilities of those under consideration for promotion. It feared that mechanical procedures such as promotion examinations might not be an adequate substitute (U.S. CSC 1886: 54). Thus it saw its role sometimes as that of preventing abuse by selecting officials and probably more often as protecting selecting officials from political pressure exerted by higher officials.

Nevertheless, because the CSC was concerned about the lingering

---

Often, officials would not allow women to sit for civil service tests (Van Riper 1958: 101, 144, 194, 261).

[15]At least one observer commented in the 1920s that the CSC's position was "wholly indefensible from the standpoint of the interests of the personnel system as a whole," which would be better served by a positive promotion program (Mayers 1920: 236).

[16]This preference was at times stated formally. For example, the 1909 revised regulations for the Customs Service at New York provided "that promotions of clerks shall be made in the order of seniority of service in each class unless the nominating officer certifies that the person recommended for promotion, though not the senior, is by virtue of ability and efficiency best fitted for the position to be filled" (U.S. CSC 1909). In contrast, it is rare for modern promotion plans in the government to give much formal weight to seniority (see, e.g., U.S. CSC 1964b), though in practice it probably has more informal weight than the formal plans would suggest. See Abraham and Medoff (1985) for evidence to this effect from the private sector.

effects of the spoils system on promotions, it made some attempt to control promotions through examination. It justified its actions on the grounds that central control through the institutionalization of competitive examinations for promotion could leave to the administrative officer "his full right and responsibility" to promote whom he chose while being "protected" from partisan pressures and pleas for favoritism (U.S. CSC 1887: 87).[17]

The CSC was satisfied with the results of the competitive promotional examinations it set up for the New York Custom House in 1886. So it obtained authority from President Cleveland to institute promotional examinations throughout the departments, custom houses, and post offices (Sageser 1935; White 1958; U.S. CSC 1887: 70ff.). However, resistance from veterans (U.S. CSC 1888: 16ff.) and from agency officials caused the experiment in the War Department to fail and experiments in other departments to be stillborn (White 1958: 354).

In 1896, President Cleveland issued revised rules on the subject, calling for promotional examinations "as far as practical and useful" (White 1958: 355; Sageser 1935: 196). The order required agencies to base promotion decisions on the character, quantity, and quality of the work as well as on office habits and attendance. But the order imposed no time limit for establishing the new system. The CSC provided that until the regulations for each department had been approved, "promotions therein may be made from one class to another class which is in the same grade and from one grade to another grade upon any test of fitness not disapproved by the CSC which may be determined upon by the promoting officer" (U.S. CSC 1897: 17–18). In effect, the CSC's rule yielded most of the control over the promotion process to the individual departments.

But the new rules did contain one important conceptual advance. They included an examination requirement for any promotion "to a position in which, . . . there is not required the performance of the same class of work or the practice of the same mechanical trade" as in the original position. The practical test used by the CSC to distinguish work of the same class and work of a different class was whether the new position was filled through a different examination than the old position (U.S. CSC 1896: 63).

In general, the CSC allowed each agency to use any fitness test it chose, barring explicit action by the CSC to implement an examination

---

[17]"The first thing essential is a real liberty of choice on the part of the appointing officers to promote the most worthy. Then we can deal with prejudice and favoritism within the offices" (U.S. CSC 1884: 28).

(U.S. CSC 1896: 63). But in one case, that of promotion from subclerical to clerical positions, the CSC moved quickly to develop such an examination. Before 1896, subclerical positions were not part of the classified service, and this triggered a serious abuse. Many citizens used their political connections to obtain appointments to subclerical positions. They then obtained promotions into classified positions. This maneuver circumvented the examination process (U.S. CSC 1899: 102).[18] The CSC also gave the new exam a technical rationale, which foreshadowed arguments that others would later make in support of a tiered system of job ladders.

> There is a radical difference between the subordinate places of messenger, watchman, etc., and those of clerks and copyists, the difference extending to the qualifications required as well as to the duties to be performed, and the former places can not be relied upon or made an absolute dependence for filling all vacancies in the latter places. . . . Such a policy would result in deterioration of the higher grades. On the other hand, there are a few persons in these lower grades who by education and experience are fitted to occupy clerical positions; but the avenues of advancement open to them should not be made so wide as to permit the entrance of persons whose term of service has been too brief to give assurance of suitable experience, to give scope to improper influences, and to bring into the higher grades persons who are lacking in education, intellectual force, and capacity for promotion. . . . Persons who are trained to clerical duties do not as a rule render satisfactory service as skilled laborers, messengers, and watchmen. (U.S. CSC 1899: 104)

The CSC in effect argued that the distinction between a subclerical and a clerical position was qualitatively different from the distinction between the various levels of clerical work. Others would later claim that a similar qualitative distinction existed between higher clerical work and administrative work and would argue for a special institutional barrier to control movement across that line as well.

The requirement that those seeking a promotion into a different occupation had to pass a competitive examination was not important in a practical sense. The large number of vacancies in the clerical grades made the competitive examination a pass examination for all practical purposes. Many employees subsequently moved across this line.[19] Furthermore, the requirement that an employee had to take a qualifying examination when moving to an occupation falling under a different test

[18]Cleveland's order of 1896 prohibited the practice and brought the workers in these erroneously titled positions under the classification system (CSC 1909: 163).
[19]Mayers reported that those able to secure a clerical position through promotion from the subclerical grades were not as capable as those who moved into clerical positions from outside the service through competitive examinations (Mayers 1920: 250).

had little practical effect at higher levels either. Once an individual reached the clerical grades, he did not have to requalify for higher clerical and administrative jobs (Feldman 1931: 99). A similar situation existed for technical jobs. None of the bureau chiefs in 1926 with positions in the classified service had taken an examination "at any late stage in his career" (Macmahon 1926: 554). When examinations were given, they were noncompetitively administered to the individual nominated by an official for the promotion.

The net effect of these developments was that promotion decisions were almost completely under the control of agency heads, though "nominally under the [promotion] regulations promulgated" by the CSC. The CSC reported that the level of compliance varied substantially. In some departments, the regulations had been "entirely ignored," whereas in others there was "partial or nominal compliance." When promotion exams were used, they were often nothing more than a "mathematically expressed opinion" of supervisors concerning their clerks, in the form of an efficiency rating (U.S. CSC 1902: 22). In 1910, the CSC observed that systems of competitive examinations for promotion had been largely abandoned "apparently because of the belief that for such promotions the value of employees could be more accurately and fairly measured from daily observation of their actual work" (U.S. CSC 1910: 27).

Over time, the CSC gradually approved promotion plans for parts of the federal service. However, it generally did so only upon the invitation of the appropriate department head. By 1922, the Mint and Assay Service, the Customs Service, the Ordnance Department at Large, the Engineer Department at Large, Quartermaster Corps, the Military Academy, the Navy Yard Service, the Reclamation Service, the Indian Irrigation and Allotment service, St. Elizabeth's Hospital, the Lighthouse Service, and the Coast and Geodetic Survey had been covered by promotion regulations. But this left the bulk of the service without such plans (Mayers 1920: 242). Throughout the pre-World War II period, observers were to echo the CSC's 1902 judgment that no effective central control over promotions existed[20] and that agency practices were limited

[20]Lewis Meriam later wrote in 1938 that "the Civil Service Commission . . . only exercised its control if the administrative officer proposed to move the employee into another line for which he had never demonstrated his qualifications before the commission. Then it might refuse its approval, or order a noncompetitive examination requiring the employee to demonstrate his qualifications. Since most promotions are in the normal line of advancement, the referral of the case to the Civil Service Commission was ordinarily routine procedure, done by transmitting the necessary forms. . . . While the writer was in the classified civil service, dealing with personnel as an operating man, he had in

to the recording of personnel transactions, such as appointments and separations. One influential critic could write in 1931 that

> at present the Government's procedure seems clearly defective on this score. Everything is left to chance. There is no search for promising material; there is no systematized effort in the service as a whole to develop the powers latent in such candidates or to improve those who are held back through lack of qualifications. (Feldman 1931: 104).

SUMMARY

From the beginning of the Republic, federal administrators were concerned with the problems of personnel administration. During the Federalist years, civil service clerks generally enjoyed long tenure in office, and at least some administrators recognized the value of promotion as a way of motivating good performance. The personnel management system of the Federalists was disrupted but not completely destroyed by the introduction of the spoils system during the Jacksonian period.

When Congress established the civil service, it imposed a primitive grading system for clerks as a vehicle for salary administration. The agencies themselves, however, determined the duties of clerical workers in the various grades. Difficulties with salary administration during the inflationary periods of the 1830s and 1850s caused Congress, pressed by civil servants, to take up the question of position classification again. But although Congress raised salaries and instituted a new grading system for clerical positions in the 1850s, its actions did not constitute a modern position classification system. Congress also debated how to regulate promotion policies in the first half of the nineteenth century but did not reconcile competing demands for a system of promotion exams or for the status quo of unconstrained managerial discretion.

With the onset of the civil service reform movement, models for the organization of personnel management developed further. The first Civil Service Commission formulated a set of principles for personnel management, which it based on previous American and British experience. These principles addressed issues of classification, hiring, and promotion. The commission proposed a "rank-in-the-job" classification system, a system of competitive examination for appointment, and the use of promotion to fill all vacancies in each occupational group, though

---

several years only one case in which the commission did not approve promotion papers as a matter of routine" (p. 7; see also Willoughby 1927; Stewart 1929).

the groups themselves remained undefined. Similar principles were ex-
pounded by the Civil Service Commission that was established by the
Civil Service Reform Act of 1883. The CSC, however, was unsure of how
to put these principles into practice. Disagreements about the value of
common school versus college education, and of the relative value of an
examination system that would tightly control promotions, or a system
of loose control that would allow substantial managerial discretion, were
unresolved through the first 20 years of the merit system. In practice,
the CSC instituted entrance examinations for certain positions, left procedures for making promotions to the individual agencies, and made
virtually no progress toward systematizing positions into job ladders.

5

Progressivism and Public Personnel Administration

INTRODUCTION

The changing structure of government created personnel problems at the same time that big business was groping for new ways to manage personnel affairs. Ideological developments growing out of the professionalization and scientific management movements produced a strategy for addressing these problems that was supported by public sector unions as well as by many academics and civil service administrators. The eventual outcome of these developments was the implementation of a systematic position classification system for jobs in the federal civil service.

Position classification had potentially enormous implications for the structure of work careers. However, its precise effects would depend upon the form that the position classification system took. The institutionalization of any particular system and its effect on careers depended upon the answers that decision makers and their constituencies gave to questions such as the following: (1) What were the connections between the skill requirements of jobs that would justify a rational grouping of jobs into career ladders? (2) Could psychology place people into well-defined groupings based on their job aptitudes? (3) Could initial assignment be precise enough to justify employers raising the barriers between different job ladders to prevent promotions from giving rise to mismatches? Or would errors in job matching and low employee morale from reduced promotion chances outweigh the benefits of mobility barriers? Competing answers to these questions combined with political considerations and the constraints of a changing labor force to shape the development of job ladders in the civil service.

PROFESSIONALISM AND PUBLIC ADMINISTRATION

Occupational and organizational changes in the government and in American society at large during the years 1900 through 1920 fueled the development of what Wiebe has called the "bureaucratic orientation" of the new middle class (Wiebe 1967: 149). Concerned by the growth of what many Progressives thought was the crass commercialism of business, reformers looked to the development of professions as a solution to this problem. The professionalization of business and public administration figured prominently in their vision. They hoped to see a country ruled by experts who, through "immersion in the scientific method," would have "eradicated petty passions and narrow ambitions," "removed faults in reasoning," and raised the quality of leadership in America (Wiebe 1967: 161; Haber 1964; Johnson 1972; Haskell 1984). Progressive reformers foresaw the breakdown of the long-standing American belief that "there is an apparently inherent conflict between the democratic spirit and the employment of the capable man in the public service" (*New York Evening Post* editorial, *May 13, 1914*) Instead, rule by the capable would enhance the democratic potential of the American system of government.

One difficulty for this vision was that, at the time, the professions of business and public administration had no real social existence.[1] Instead, they had an ideological existence, based on the professional model provided by medicine and law. The obvious hope shared by reformers was that if public administration and the position of business executive could be given the form of professions, they would become socially established. Eventually, the formal knowledge base on which their work rested would catch up to give them intellectual legitimacy as well.[2]

[1] Aside from suggestions about limiting the power of legislatures compared with the executive branch, the science of public administration at the time did not amount to much more than the call for better trained personnel in government (Wilson 1901; Danner 1914; Wright 1918; also see American Political Science Association 1913: 304–305, Haber 1964: 107; Fitzpatrick 1914; Gaus, 1930: 8). Of all the positions that might be described as general administrative, only the occupation of city manager had even begun to take shape. But the early city managers were most often trained as engineers. Training in the profession of city manager was not available at the time (Karl 1963: 101). Thereafter, partly through borrowings from the scientific management movement, public administration began to take shape as a discipline in its own right (Waldo 1948; Haber 1964: 51 ff.; Merkle 1980).

[2] Woodrow Wilson wrote in 1887 that "it is a thing almost taken for granted among us, that the present movement called civil service reform must, after the accomplishment of its first purpose [the improvement of the quality of high civil servants], expand into efforts to

Thus, although it was unclear what these administrators should know, Progressives agreed about where these administrators should learn it. University training would make them professionals "of equal standing with law or medicine" (Weber 1919: 176). And they would have professional careers, by which was meant not simply extended work in a particular occupation but work that is complex, responsible, and increasingly rewarding over time (Claxton 1914; McClure 1914; Woodruff 1914).[3] Most reformers believed that theoretical training for administrators by itself was insufficient. They wanted future administrators to be given a combination of theoretical and practical training in the professional model, a training which the municipal research bureaus began to offer (Allen 1912; Mitchell 1914; Burritt 1914; Gilbertson 1914; Dewey 1914; Beard 1916; Weber 1919; Dahlberg 1966).[4]

A secondary theme underlying the movement for professionalizing the civil service was the value of liberal education for leadership positions. The idea that a college education gave an individual a perspective on the community necessary for leadership was an important element in Mugwump philosophy. It remained dominant at such institutions as Yale and Princeton, where humanists resisted the move toward vocational or utilitarian education, into the twentieth century (McFarland 1975: 36; Veysey 1965: 214). But even those as enthusiastic about the practical value of education as Francis Walker, second president of MIT, or Joseph Wharton, founder of the Wharton School at Penn, believed that liberal education provided important preparation for leadership positions (Fisher 1967: 62–63; Sass 1982: 20). Some Progressive reformers thought that a liberal arts education was sufficient preparation for government administrators and city managers by itself (James 1915; see also Hutchins 1938), but others did not share this opinion. The more common view was that aspiring administrators should acquire a specialized knowledge base along with a liberal education.[5]

---

improve, not the *personnel* only, but also the organization and methods of our government offices . . ." (Wilson 1887: 197; also see Goodnow 1900).

[3]Gaus (1949) later wrote that these pre-World War I discussions could not obtain the "sharpness of focus" on the objectives of these positions that would allow universities to develop a coherent professional program in administration. In his view, this goal was "more nearly possible" in 1949 (see also Mosher 1938; Waldo 1948).

[4]"There is but one answer—a training similar to that of the doctor. We must try out our public servants before we allow them to practice" (McCarthy 1914: 44; see also American Political Science Association 1913; Gray 1914).

[5]The relative importance of liberal and professional training for leadership positions are still live issues. One might only consider MITs recently expressed concern that its technically trained graduates too often ended up as subordinate employees of Princeton

The professional model was championed for lower-level white-collar occupations as well. The idea that one could have a life-long career as an employee of someone else, rather than pursue a career path that led to self-employment, became more acceptable.[6] Some thought that even positions as lowly as stenographer and bank clerk were professions (Kirkland 1956: 79; Kocka 1980: 146). Especially during World War I, industrial employers, who had once accepted high turnover as normal, even desirable, increasingly looked for ways to reduce turnover (Colvin 1919; Brissenden and Frankel 1922: 1; Jacoby 1983). Personnel specialists saw the transformation of jobs into careers as one way to keep workers from quitting their jobs.

But if employers were to transform jobs into careers, then getting "the right man for the right job" (Eilbirt 1959) necessarily becomes a more important concern. Many observers believed that it was a mistake to place a talented individual too low in the expanding hierarchies of business and government, just as it was a mistake to place an unqualified individual too high. Either mistake created a mismatch between an employee's capability and his or her job. Concern with mismatches naturally led these writers to favor tiered personnel systems that restricted promotions.

In the nineteenth century, many Americans believed that education beyond a certain point was worthless and sometimes even an impediment to success in the business world (Kirkland 1956: 85–87). But by the early twentieth century, opinion on this issue was changing. In the view of some, impediments to the success of a business were created not by hiring the college educated but by placing them in clerical jobs. They might lose their ambition or leave the company if not quickly promoted up the ladder (Taylor 1903; Hapgood 1906). At least one critic of educational mismatches recommended that the practice of promotion from

---

graduates. The solution was that "undergraduates . . . will be required to pursue more systematic study of the arts, humanities and social sciences" (Fiske 1987: 1). In the words of MIT's president, "A professional engineer can no longer be narrowly focused on technical interests. . . . He needs to understand cultural and human values." Or consider Felix Rohatyn, the well-known New York investment banker, who, in discussing the recent spate of indictments in the banking community, argued that "businesses should go back to basics in recruiting, should forget about the business schools and recruit the best young liberal arts students we can find" (Rohatyn 1987: 27).

[6]Compare Godkin's (1882: 290) discussion of the American mobility ethic in 1882, with the idea of career that developed among nineteenth-century professionals (Bledstein 1976: 111ff., 159ff.). By the early twentieth century, advocates of the "life career" principle were applying this principle to lower-level jobs also (Eliot 1910, discussed in Kocka 1980: 113).

within should be abolished, to prevent the poorly educated from advancing too far (Broadley 1927: 205). In this view, experience in lower-level jobs created a trained incapacity for higher work. Therefore, employers should fill vacancies through recruitment, not promotion.

Some personnel specialists also warned that the institutionalization of the organizational career could also produce undesirable mismatches between aptitude and job. They looked to psychology to prevent this problem from getting out of hand by finding ways to measure vocational aptitude. Success would allow schools to improve vocational guidance and employers to do a better job of recruitment. These changes, they thought, would increase overall social efficiency.

In the first 20 years of the present century, psychologists developed ability tests and investigated the relationship between test scores and job performance. Binet published his original intelligence scale in 1908. Whipple published his *Manual of Mental and Physical Tests* in 1910. By 1911, Munsterberg was researching the link between test scores and job performance (Baritz 1960). Some thought that research was uncovering the existence of qualitatively distinct groupings of jobs and corresponding groups of people best suited to work in these jobs. Whipple wrote in 1916 of his "conviction"

> that there is a tendency, even though not a clearly conscious tendency, for individuals to gravitate toward that type of occupation that is generally suited to their ability and inclinations; (2) that certain occupational levels are delimited by fairly definite boundaries over which some individuals may pass readily and others not at all; (3) that the application of mental tests may be expected to determine some of these boundaries and some of these individuals . . . (Whipple 1916: 194).

Whipple, however, was modest in his claims regarding the practical value of then-existing mental tests, in contrast with the "pysiognomic charlatans"that he criticized (Whipple 1916: 194).

The links between test scores and occupations revealed by the U.S. army tests in World War I accelerated their use (National Academy of Sciences 1921; Yerkes 1922; see also Harston 1928). By 1922, psychologists claimed success in designing tests for typists, stenographers, salesmen, clerical workers, and minor executives (Scott 1915; Thurstone 1919; Weber 1922; Kenegy and Yoakum 1925). Business executives, in particular, looked to psychological tests as a simple way of solving placement problems.

The thesis that people fell into qualitatively distinct groups based on measurable talents was controversial. Some interpreted the measured correlation between IQ and job status as proof that certain people were better suited for high-status jobs than others. They further concluded that jobs could be classified into a set of distinct groups, each with its own special intellectual requirements.[7] In this view, employers could use intelligence tests to match workers and jobs accurately (Yerkes 1922; Burtt 1926). Finally, some researchers (Bills 1923; Snow 1925; Bingham and Freyd 1926) warned that aptitude mismatches between worker and job could lead to higher quit rates.[8]

But one could also interpret psychological evidence as rebutting the thesis of sharp qualitative distinctions among jobs and among people. If sharp distinctions did not exist, then the use of IQ tests to slot people into narrowly drawn occupations did not make sense. The army test results of WWI and other studies showed not only that there was an ordering of average scores but also that test scores varied substantially within occupations. Perhaps the important message of these results was not that higher status occupations required a high IQ but rather that the scores of workers in jobs of widely different status were often similar. Studies looking for a link between intelligence and business success could not find one (Bingham 1924; Brandenberg 1925). As a consequence, several psychologists questioned the practical value of IQ tests. In particular, these critics contended that mental tests were not useful selection devices for higher-status occupations (Link 1923; Snow 1925; Watson 1927; Jenkins 1935; Baritz 1960; Vitele 1967). Most companies became disenchanted with tests during the years 1922–1925 and abandoned them. Although there was some revival of interest in the late 1920s, few firms used them by 1930 and then only for lower-level jobs such as typist, stenographer, and calculating-machine operator (U.S. PCB 1929: 280; Baritz 1960).[9]

The negative evidence notwithstanding, many still believed the ar-

[7]Burtt, for example, argued that "there are different kinds of industrial performance, each with a minimum intelligence requirement, and that a person tends finally to reach the highest level for which his intelligence qualifies him." (Burtt 1929: 273.) Viteles countered in his autobiography (Viteles 1967: 424) that his paper, "Tests in Industry" in 1921, "takes issue with what was then the prevailing common practice of placing almost exclusive reliance upon the measurement of general intelligence for assessing vocational aptitudes." See Beckham (1930) for a summary of several studies and Baritz (1960) for a comprehensive review of the issues from a more contemporary viewpoint.

[8]These views supported arguments such as Thurstone's to the effect that employers should attempt to recruit "persons only of moderate intelligence" for the lower positions (cited in White 1926: 299). See also Taylor (1903) and Hapgood (1906).

[9]Business did not like them because they failed to test the whole personality (Feldman 1928). The British Civil Service also found them to be too narrow. "These tests value only native intelligence, and for the civil servant we need native intelligence, it is true, but native intelligence is not enough; we want educated intelligence; so that these tests could only be supplementary to tests of attainment" (Leathes 1923: 359).

gument that both people and jobs fell into distinct aptitude groupings and that these groupings could form the basis of sound personnel policies. In 1935, the Commission of Inquiry on Public Service Personnel (CIPSP) justified its proposal to place administrative and clerical positions in separate services partly on the grounds that "psychologists and personnel experts have told the Commission that this grouping seems to conform also to the natural capacities and characteristics of human beings . . . this division seems to relate the kinds of work to be done to the kinds of persons best fitted to do them" (Commission of Inquiry on Public Service Personnel 1935: 26–27).[10]

THE CASE FOR THE LONG CAREER LINE

Although some Progressive reformers pushed for rule by the college bred and psychologists debated the usefulness of tests for job placement, operating officers in the civil service continued to stress the importance of practical experience at all levels of white-collar work. During World War I, for example, they were critical of the CSC for filling the registers with young men who had academic training but no experience (Van Riper 1958: 255).

Furthermore, writings toward the end of the Progressive era by those knowledgeable about public personnel matters show a concern that education not become a discriminatory tool working against the career opportunities of white-collar civil servants. Two books published by the Institute for Government Research, which later became a part of the Brookings Institution, demonstrate this concern.

Arthur W. Procter, who was a staff member for the Commission on Economy and Efficiency, the New York Bureau of Municipal Research, and the Institute of Government Research, wrote one of the first book-

---

[10]During hearings before the committee, Luther Gulick, a member of the commission, queried Professor Thurstone: "It has been suggested to us that in the work of government you can see a number of rather clearly defined kinds of work going on, with different kinds of men at work on those tasks. One kind is the professional work . . . . Another kind is the general, routine, clerical work. Another kind is purely manual, day laborers, and so on. Another is the general overhead supervision, direction, planning and control, which we call administrative work. Is there any foundation that you can see, in the study of human beings from the psychological standpoint, for such a classification of work?" Thurstone replied that "there seems to be no question but that the classification of men, these groups you mentioned, is based largely on different fundamental abilities with which they are endowed." He then went on to argue that there still were no psychological techniques that could easily measure these abilities, however (CIPSP 1934: 235ff.).

length treatments of public personnel administration in the United States. In his 1921 volume, he wrote that academic training in public administration might well be useful for higher civil servants, much as technical training is useful for scientists. He further argued that civil service commissions should establish "close contact" with educational institutions offering these courses and "do everything properly within their power to facilitate the placing of well-trained and well-qualified persons in public employment" (Procter 1921: 154–155). But, having argued this, he went on to qualify his statement, by writing that "it goes without saying that they [the graduates of educational institutions] should not jeopardize the opportunity of qualified persons who have not had special academic training" (Procter 1921: 151).[11]

Lewis Mayers's treatment of the federal service, also written under the auspices of the Institute for Government Research, showed even more concern about the potential harm that too much stress on education could do. In his view, education had more potential to create strata of employment within the federal service than any force other than political affiliation. Advanced educational requirements for higher-level jobs would reduce promotional opportunities for lower-level employees. Anticipating later developments, he wrote that this scenario was a possibility not only in "the technical branches of education; it presents itself in a more debatable way, in respect to general educational equipment. This phase of the problem presents itself particularly in connection with the filling of the higher nontechnical administrative posts" (Mayers 1922: 247). The value of such restrictions was thrown open to question by the wide variety of personnel practices then found in the business world, with some businesses drawing their executives "exclusively from the ranks of college graduates" whereas others filled "even the positions of highest responsibility" exclusively by promotion of those who had entered the organization at low levels (Mayers 1922: 252–253). The choice of strategy, in his view, had little relationship with business success.

The appropriate strategy depended upon the capabilities of the lower-level employees. Before World War I, he argued, the salaries for clerks in the federal government were so high compared with private salaries that many capable workers entered government at lower levels. But after the war, inflation and stagnant government salaries substan-

[11]He ended his chapter on promotions in a similar way. "As a final word, it may be well to stress again the fact that it is generally desirable to fill the higher positions in the civil service by promotion—in so far as they cannot be filled be reinstatement—rather than by recruiting from outside the service" (Procter 1921: 188).

tially reduced the attractiveness of government clerical jobs to the point where Mayers doubted that the government could continue to recruit as many higher-level administrators from the lower ranks. This argued in favor of recruiting those with more education at "a somewhat higher level" (Mayers 1922: 256).

But Mayers went on to argue that such an arrangement should not evolve into a tiered civil service on the British model, which would shut lower-level employees out of the competition for the best jobs. Instead, administrators should allow the lower-level employees whose job experience qualified them for better jobs to compete on an equal footing. But he recognized that, under existing circumstances, sometimes "the experience in the work of the lower grades in no wise furnishes such education and is in no wise equivalent to it" (Mayers 1922: 258–259). In these cases he recommended that

> the radical, and the only thoroughly satisfactory, solution of the difficulty is to be found, it is believed, not in lowering the educational standards fairly demanded by the needs of the service, but . . . so far as practicable those of the subordinate personnel who show sufficient promise should be provided with facilities, and with a certain allowance of time, for securing the advanced education needed for the posts in the natural line of promotion. (Mayers 1922: 264)

In effect, he proposed a porous tier structure, justified as much by the practical need to recruit qualified people from the outside as by qualitative distinctions in the work itself. Would-be barriers to advancement based on gaps in job progressions would be eroded through the provision of training for capable lower-level civil servants.

The report of the Congressional Joint Commission on Reclassification of Salaries was the first serious attempt to systematically and comprehensively delineate qualifications for positions and lines of promotion in the federal government.[12] Its methods were wholly derivative from previous classification efforts such as the 1903 city of Chicago classification, and its "rank in the job" duties classification philosophy was generally derivative of the scientific management, or efficiency, movement both in government and in private industry (U.S. House 1920, 146ff.; see also Weber 1919; Baruch 1941b; Eilbirt 1959). But its interpretation of the connection between jobs differs from the more "professional" perspective on the subject. In its view, the skill relationships

---

[12]The Keep Committee devised an earlier rudimentary classification system in 1907 that Roosevelt's Executive Order required agencies to put in place. But that order did not provide for an enforcement mechanism, and Congress did not provide the needed salary standardization. Consequently, the Keep Committee's classification system had little practical impact (U.S. CSC 1939b; Baruch 1941a).

between clerical and administrative positions were such a to justify job ladders that stretched from the bottom to the top of the service.

Between March 3, 1919, and March 12, 1920, the Congressional Joint Commission took a complete inventory of all positions in the departmental service in Washington and developed a proposed position classification system for these positions that filled an 884-page report. To analyze the questionnaires returned by the departments, the commission recruited a classification staff familiar both with the government and with personnel matters. The staff produced detailed organization charts from the questionnaires, charts that showed the relationships among all positions in the departmental service. It sorted positions into 44 "services" that "were defined more or less arbitrarily, the purpose being to set up a scaffolding across departmental lines that would aid in the erection of the classification"[13] After sorting positions into services, the staff sorted them again, this time into classes, and grouped the classes into occupational "series." The commission's definitions of these terms were as follows:

> A "position" is a specific office, employment, or job (whether occupied or vacant) calling for the performance of certain duties and the exercise of certain responsibilities by an individual.
>
> A "class" is a group of all positions which, regardless of their organization connection, or location, call for the performance of substantially similar duties or work and involve the exercise of responsibilities of like importance and therefore demand substantially the same qualifications on the part of incumbents, and are, for these reasons, subject to common treatment in the selection of qualified appointees and other employment processes, and that can be aptly described by the same title.
>
> Where a number of "classes" of positions are substantially similar as to the type of work involved and differ only in rank as determined by the importance of the duties, the degree of responsibility involved, and the amount of training and experience required, such "classes" constitute a "series" and each is given a title containing a common term descriptive of the type of work, with a modifying term indicative of the relative rank. (U.S. Congress. House 1920: 72–73)

The resulting classification "fully covered" the 107,000 positions under the jurisdiction of the commission.

---

[13]This motivation for the use of broad groupings followed that underlying the service designations in the first position classification system used in the United States, in the city of Chicago (Griffenhagen 1924). It can be contrasted with the use of services to group "as a unit all those positions which normally appeal to the same general type of mind of potential public employees" (Faught 1920: 49), a usage with clearer career connotations.

The commission made clear in its report that it supported a policy of promotion from within whenever possible.

> When vacancies in the higher classes are not filled by transfer or reinstatement, they [are to] be filled by promotion of properly qualified employees as determined by competitive civil service examination, and that ordinarily open competitive examinations for the filling of such vacancies be held only when three such eligibles cannot be secured from those already in the service. (U.S. Congress. House 1920: 124)

It took a position on the qualifications for advancement consistent with its support of a promote-from-within philosophy. It endorsed the principle that "proficiency increases with experience and industry in the work of the class," in contrast to those like Broadley, who argued that proficiency for higher-level work decreased with experience at a lower grade. Its position on educational qualifications was similar to that of Mayers, namely that experience could often substitute for education as a qualification for a job.[14]

In its report to the Congress, the Congressional Joint Commission arranged classes of positions according to their "principal lines of promotion."[15] Its representation of these "principal lines" represented an endorsement of the "long" rather than the "short" job ladder for occupations outside the scientific realm. The Congressional Joint Commission also recommended that departments define job qualifications broadly, to maximize the chance they could find a suitable employee to promote into the vacancy. Finally, it set as qualifications for positions "not those of the employee who has attained the maximum usefulness but those properly required of an employee at entrance." The qualifications were set at "the minimum to secure efficient service."

Two examples can show the implication of the commission's philosophy. The first, for personnel clerks and officers, was probably more normative than actual. Other sources indicate that personnel offices in departments were only rudimentary at the time and that the responsibilities were generally handled by the chief clerk or by an "appointment clerk" (Willoughby 1927: 109; White 1933: 155; Van Riper 1958: 149). Thus it may show what the commission thought would be an

---

[14]"In no case has the commission recommended that the possession of a degree or a certificate from an educational institution be made an absolute requirement" (U.S. Congress. House 1920: 77).

[15]"The lines of promotion listed are merely the main lines. They are neither exclusive nor inclusive. The Commission recommends a policy of the broadest avenues of promotion possible" (U.S. Congress. House 1920: 71). For more information on the use of "lines of promotion" at the time, see Telford (1924, 1925) or Meriam (1924).

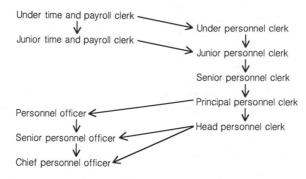

Figure 5.1. Principal lines of promotion for general personnel work, 1920.

"appropriate" promotion relationship among these jobs as personnel management became better developed.[16]

The arrows in Figure 5.1 indicate what the commission described as "principal lines of promotion." The commission saw a continuity in promotion lines from the bottom to the top of the system, a continuity that connected the clerical and the officer positions. Principal personnel clerks could either be promoted to personnel officer or to head personnel clerk. Head personnel clerks were not usually to be promoted to personnel officer. Instead, their usual advancement was either to senior personnel officer, or to chief personnel officer, the highest position in the hierarchy.

The second example concerns positions that were definitely in use at the time, namely the principal nonscientific clerical and administrative positions. The Congressional Joint Commission arranged them in the line of promotion shown in Figure 5.2. The descriptions of the top jobs on this hierarchy show they were administrative-level jobs. The chief clerical administrator was first in line under the assistant bureau head or assistant secretary and above the top of the classified service at that time.[17] Yet the promotion lines drawn by the Congressional Joint

[16]The commission wrote that "a few of the 1962 classes are made up of positions which are vacant. However, the titles and specification of these vacant classes have been permitted to stand because of their importance in understanding the various series of classes in the services." (U.S. Congress. House 1920: 172) Perhaps personnel was one such case.

[17]In particular, it included not only the positions of "division head" but also that of "administrative assistant," a title often used for the "confidential clerks" that McKinley permitted in 1898 (Commission on Organization of the Executive Branch of the Government 1955: 171–172). See Chapter 3 for detailed job descriptions.

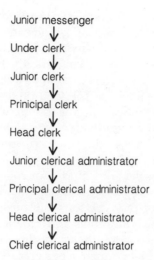

Figure 5.2. Principal lines of promotion for the miscellaneous clerical service and the Administrative and Supervisory Clerical Service, 1920.

Commission connected this position on an unbroken line with the lowliest white-collar jobs.

The commission made use of qualitative distinctions as well. It placed positions at the head clerk and higher level in a separate "service," called the "administrative and supervisory clerical service." It placed positions below that level in the "miscellaneous clerical service." The commission was ambiguous on the subject of whether the classification of classes into "services" was to have any career implications. It wrote that "a 'service' includes positions belonging to a given occupation, vocation, calling, profession, business, craft, trade, or group of trades—a general line of work." But at the same time, it referred to the groupings as "selected more or less arbitrarily to aid in the process of classification." This latter description suggests that promotion policy goals were not the basis for the service typology. The listed job qualifications as well as the principal lines of promotion the commission outlined supports this view.

The educational requirements (listed as "training equivalent to") in the line of promotion just described ranged from common school to collegiate. However, these requirements did not always articulate well with its "service" boundaries. The commission listed a high-school education as the "common qualification" for head clerk and for junior clerical administrator, the two lowest positions in the proposed administrative and supervisory clerical service. High-school graduation was also the qualification listed for principal clerk, the highest position in the miscellaneous clerical service. The educational qualification for principal clerical administrator was high school "and preferably" college graduation. For head and chief clerical administrators, it was "training equivalent to that represented by graduation with a degree" from a college. Thus the service boundaries did not correspond with educational credentials.

The absence of a special entry portal for college graduates into administrative work also supports the argument that the commission's services were not tiers of the type found in business and government today. In setting up these educational and experience requirements, the commission appeared to share the conviction expressed by agency heads back in the 1880s that young college graduates were not prepared to assume the responsibilities of even a high clerical position without substantial prior experience. Instead, the commission's job qualifications imply that young college graduates should begin their careers as lower-level clerks.

All positions in the miscellaneous clerical service above the rank of under clerk required previous experience. Senior clerks were required to have the equivalent of a high school education, and not less than three years experience in clerical work. Principal clerks required the equivalent of a high school diploma and two further years experience as senior clerk. Head clerks required two further years of experience in work "similar to that of principal clerk," or seven years clerical experience in all. Above these levels, the cumulative experience requirement is more difficult to calculate. Junior clerical administrators were to have three years experience in a supervisory clerical capacity. Principal clerical administrators were required to have four years work in a responsible supervisory capacity. Head clerical administrators and chief clerical administrators were to have more experience still.[18]

The Congressional Joint Commission's views on training were similar to those of Mayers, though perhaps not as far reaching. It argued that, because many government tasks had no counterpart in the private sector, the government should train its employees in-house. Some training

[18]In the personnel job ladder, the situation was similar: the personnel officer position, the lowest designated as an officer, required "three years of responsible clerical and personnel work."

should be done at the bureau level, whereas other training should be governmentwide. It contended that systematic training would increase the efficiency of government as it lengthened job ladders. Such a policy, in its view would also increase opportunity, as it converted "many of the 'blind alleys' now in the Federal service into highways to opportunities really worth while for those employees with sufficient energy and ambition to take advantage of them" (U.S. Congress. House 1920: 119).

The Congressional Joint Commission did not believe that all lower-level jobs could be linked through a principal line of promotion to high-level positions. It found fewer "long" job ladders in the professional and scientific areas, though it did identify some. For example, the copyist draftsman position required a high-school degree. The principal line of promotion from this position led to junior architectural draftsman. An employee could then be promoted to architectural draftsman, though the common requirements for this job were "training equivalent to that represented by graduation with a degree from an institution of recognized standing." Apparently the commission thought that able junior draftsmen could get such equivalent training in the government. In the biological sciences, however, laboratory aid positions and the like were not linked with scientific positions. In the actuarial service, head actuarial clerks did not enjoy a principal line of promotion to the position of associate actuary.[19]

The Congressional Joint Commission also specified "short" job ladders for the typing, stenographic, correspondence, and secretarial service, though the tiering in this case appeared to be justified on gender, rather than educational grounds. A stenographer or secretary would normally, in the commission's view, be promoted as high as senior private secretary. A typist or correspondence clerk would normally be promoted as high as "reviewer of correspondence." This position required a college degree (or equivalent experience) and contained supervisory responsibilities, but it was not connected in a normal promotion line to higher supervisory positions.

The commission considered but rejected the English model for the nonscientific service (White 1939: 310). Advisory opinion on the matter was probably not unanimous, however. The major advisers included E. O. Griffenhagen, the chief counsel for the commission, Charles Beard, Robert Moses, and Lewis Meriam (U.S. Congress. House 1920; White

---

[19]Scientific and professional job ladders did of course have their own internal hierarchies. The commission distinguished rungs on scientific job ladders with the adjectives *junior, assistant, associate,* and *senior,* with a *chief* at the top.

1939; Keating 1964). Moses, who wrote admiringly of the British civil service in his 1914 book on the subject, probably continued to favor the establishment of an administrative service dominated by the college educated. Beard was committed to the idea that the universities could uplift the federal service, too. But he believed that practical experience was important also and that "certainly, we shall be doing the public service a lasting injury if we attempt to make it more academic in character" (Beard 1916: 221). Years later, Griffenhagen would write that he opposed the creation of a special administrative corps (Griffenhagen and Associates 1937). Lewis Meriam also opposed the creation of a special administrative corps, both in 1920 and later in the 1930s when the issue reemerged.[20]

Finally, the work of the commission was substantially influenced by federal employees themselves, who had official representation on the commission through their union, the National Federation of Federal Employees (NFFE) (U.S. CSC 1941b). Employees organized the NFFE in 1917 because government had not granted pay increases during a period when private salaries were rising substantially (Johnson 1940; Spero 1948; Hollander 1968).[21] The union favored the establishment of a classification system because it wanted higher wages for its members as well as more equitable job assignments. It also apparently supported the establishment of training facilities and a policy of promotion from within, which it later argued were desirable because they "aid ambitious employees in preparing for promotions" (Johnson 1940: 38). The final report of the commission, in short, apparently conformed with the interests of federal white-collar employees.[22]

[20]Meriam "feared that a special form of selection and preparation for higher administration would stir up jealousies and lower morale; he believed that the professional and scientific services should be administered only by professional and scientific men" (White 1939: 310).

[21]From 1854 to 1915 the daily average wage increased by 137.4%, but the official wage scale did not change for government clerks. In the opinion of one Washington paper, the government "exhibits a remorseless disregard for their welfare which would bring down upon private employers the fierce denunciation of society" (quoted in Johnson 1940: 25). At least one author blamed the merit system for this state of affairs. Once Congress could not fill government jobs with patronage appointments, it had no particular interest in raising government salaries (Spero 1924).

[22]The NFFE also played a key role in gaining several salary increases in the years following the war and was a force behind the passage of the 1923 Classification Act and the Welch Act of 1928 (Van Riper 1958: 275, 302–303).

THE TRANSITION YEARS

In the postwar period, Progressive calls for college-bred professionals to direct the civil service grew fainter as Progressivism itself was pushed into the background, and the champions of a "new individualism" and economy in government gained control both of government and of public opinion (Hawley 1979: 52ff.). But the imagery of retrenchment notwithstanding, successive administrations increased the administrative capacity of the government throughout the decade. Service and monitoring agencies such as the Bureau of the Budget, the Personnel Classification Board, the General Supply Committee, and the Veteran's Bureau all began their existence during these years (White 1939; Karl 1963). Furthermore, as higher education expanded, college graduates were available for public service in greater numbers than ever before. However, at a time of private prosperity and a prevailing mood to economize on public expenditures, the federal bureaucracy looked much less attractive to graduates than did the corporate sector (O'Rourke 1930; Janowitz and Wright 1956; Sass 1982). The issue of whether personnel policies should be set up to create a college-bred administrative aristocracy in the federal government faded from attention and remained on the back burner until the 1930s.

The Classification Act of 1923 laid the basis for more systematic classification of federal positions, but it was hardly the comprehensive solution proposed by the Congressional Joint Commission. The fact of union representation on the advisory committees and subcommittees of the commission provoked Herbert Brown, who was the head of the Bureau of Efficiency and who already opposed the classification effort as an infringement on his domain (Spero 1948: 182). The opposition of Congressional Republicans, who saw the report of the Congressional Joint Commission as an effort to obtain unwarranted salary increases for government clerks, prevented any of the proposals of the commission from becoming law for 3 years.[23] These same forces also prevented the implementation of important parts of the 1923 Classification Act for much of the decade (U.S. Congress. House 1924; Van Riper 1958).

But though the Classification Act of 1923 was flawed in the view of

---

[23]In Smoot's view, the forces of modernity lay not with personnel management as interpreted by the Congressional Joint Commission but with other aspects of scientific management, which in his view were "making it possible to utilize low-paid clerical labor" through the introduction of "labor-saving devices." (quoted in Van Riper 1958: 278).

reformers, it provided a frame for the further development of white-collar internal labor markets in the federal service. It legitimized the principle that a position's pay be a function of its duties and responsibilities (see Baruch 1941a).[24] It provided a classification framework for applying this principle, mandated a uniform pay scale for positions in Washington, and, as a corollary, required agencies to give men and women equal pay in equal jobs.

The act also legitimized the idea that jobs in the American service belong in separate "services," based on qualitative differences in the character of work. It established a "professional and scientific service," which was separate from the "subprofessional service." All entry positions into the professional and scientific service required "training equivalent to that represented by graduation with a degree from an institution of recognized standing," according to the *Class Specifications for the Departmental Service* established by the Personnel Classification Board.[25] Positions in the subprofessional service, in contrast,

> perform work which is incident, subordinate, or preparatory to the work required of employees holding positions in the professional and scientific service, and which requires or involves professional, scientific, or technical training of any degree inferior to that represented by graduation from a college or university of recognized standing (U.S. Congress 1923: 6).

But although the Classification Act of 1923 created separate services for professional and subprofessional workers, it did not establish separate services for administrative and clerical workers. This failure to distinguish separate job ladders for these two forms of work reflected the prevailing uncertainty about the professional status of management described earlier in this book. Although the process of professionalization of management had begun in the nineteenth century, it had not progressed as quickly as the professionalization of more scientific work, and the value of college training for business jobs was in dispute. Lacking an American model to legitimize a separate administrative service, Congress chose not to innovate in this area.

Although the 1920s are not usually described as a "progressive" decade, both administrative and academic progress toward a "positive personnel system" occurred during these years. The spoils raids that occurred during the start of Harding's term were largely over by 1923,

---

[24]This principle is one basis of a "rank-in-the-job" system, as opposed to "rank-in-the-man" European systems, where an individual had a personal rank apart from his specific job assignment.

[25]In a separate act, Congress authorized the creation of a Foreign Service, and the CSC required applicants to have a college degree (U.S. CSC 1941b: 116–117).

and thereafter presidents continued to extend the merit system until it covered 80% of employees under Hoover. By the end of the decade, federal workers had secured three salary raises. The Personnel Classification Board made a survey of government jobs in the field and studied wage policies in both the federal government and private industry. The Civil Service Commission no longer had to depend upon temporary workers detailed from other departments for its work force and by the end of the decade had established its own research division.

The disciplines of public administration and business management became more academic in character during the 1920s, but social legitimacy was slow to arrive. By the end of the 1920s, the academic curriculum at the Training School for Public Service had grown to dominate the practical experience part of the curriculum (Graham 1941: 140ff.). The National Institute of Government Affairs, which succeeded the New York Bureau of Municipal Research, accepted only advanced graduate students for full-time apprenticeships after 1921. In the early 1930s, it further solidified its academic standing by affiliating with Columbia University (Graham 1941: 135ff.). Public administration was increasingly viewed as a part of political science and hence a subject to be taught at universities (Graham 1941: 142). Furthermore, the number of universities with training programs multiplied in the 1920s, reaching 24 by 1928 (Gaus 1930: Chapter 5; Graham 1941). The Harvard Business School was devoting itself to the training of general business administrators, and Wharton was trying to do the same, though without much success (Sass 1982).

But these developments did not signify the general acceptance of a profession of general administration. Public administration programs remained "paper affairs" at most universities (Gaus 1930: 11).[26] Most business schools still thought of general management in terms of the "scientific manager," that is, the floor manager, who was located at the lower end of the managerial hierarchy. Business school faculty emphasized specific skills that would make their increasingly middle-class graduates employable, rather than broader professional training for specifically executive or administrative roles (Sass 1982).

Some academics continued to stress the "moral" nature of work at the higher levels of management. Harlow Person, a former business dean and managing director of the Taylor Society after World War I, emphasized the distinction between management, which "characterizes the organization and procedure through which collective effort is ef-

[26]He went on to argue that "we shall probably have to seek in another direction, or through different arrangements, for the university contributions today."

fected," and administration, which "characterizes those considerations and decisions which establish the purposes which create the need for management and those broad governing policies under which the management proceeds." He went on to argue that "administration is largely a process of forming judgments" and can utilize only in a limited way "principles and laws determined by the scientific method of investigation" (Person 1924: 6; see also Haber 1964). In short, if Person was right about the nature of administration, it was not clear how it could be effectively taught in a professional school program.

Companies themselves believed that an individual required "intellect" and the right "personality" to be successful in business but were uncertain of any additional benefit from professional training for managers, particularly top managers (Bossard and Dewhurst 1931). A survey of Wharton graduates in 1930 revealed that those who had done poorly at Wharton were on the average more successful as businessmen than those who had done well. This finding supported contentions that business success did not require the mastery of a body of formal knowledge. This impression is reinforced by other survey findings. The graduates themselves reported that training in English was more important to their careers than training in specifically business subjects (Bossard and Dewhurst 1931).

The uncertainty as to whether effective administrative performance was a professional skill or a matter of moral perspective was one of the reasons why much academic research on personnel management continued to focus on the British civil service (Gibbon 1923; Blachly 1925; White 1926; Catherwood 1927; Lambie 1929; Walker 1935). Great Britain's use of a tiered personnel system that reserved the higher administrative positions for liberal arts graduates of Oxford and Cambridge provided a clear alternative to existing American practice. But perhaps the most visible concern of 1920s academic research was with the politically popular theme of reducing government expenditures, not with improving government efficiency through improvements in the organization of higher administration.[27] Academic research on public administration was generally done in some isolation from that of the governmental research bureaus, where staff members were under pressure to develop cordial relations with the government. Academics often crit-

---

[27]Gaus (1930: 68) reported that "this is due in part of course to the pressure for reducing the public charges resulting from the war period; it is also due to the absence in the last ten years of any significant public or civic movements or leadership." For a discussion on the compatibility or incompatibility of "economy" and "efficiency" as values, see Karl (1963).

icized bureau research as something less than serious, whereas bureau researchers viewed academics as remote and out of touch (Gaus 1930: 68; see also Hofstadter 1955: 213; Karl 1974: 227ff.).[28]

The ambiguity that continued to surround academic opinion about the best way to organize white-collar careers turns up in the two major treatises on public administration of the late 1920s, Leonard White's *Introduction to the Study of Public Administration* (1926) and F. W. Willoughby's *Principles of Public Administration* (1927). White discussed the British civil service system with evident admiration but concluded that whereas the British system has produced "a remarkable succession of administrators," it has "undoubtedly had a depressing influence . . .upon the abler second division men" (White 1926: 308–309). He appeared to pin his hopes for an American approach to the career service on psychology. Through the development of better testing programs, he hoped it would make possible a more rational assignment of workers to jobs in the first place.[29]

Willoughby supported efforts to professionalize the different specialties of the civil service as a way of increasing the attractiveness of the civil service to outsiders. He hoped to extend the professional mantle to cover all occupations that required specialized training, including some that were once thought clerical in character. He urged personnel specialists to examine occupations such as patent examiner, claims examiner, bookkeeper, accountant, statistician, and "specialists of all kinds" to see whether they should be "set up as a special class." The establishment of such a class, he wrote, would sharpen the occupational identities of these jobs, and help recruitment.

> The first requirement in seeking to give them such a status is that these positions should be carefully segregated, not only from the general clerical

[28]A special 1924 issue of the *Annals of the American Academy of Political and Social Science* indicates how low academic interest was in the question of staffing administrative positions. The issue, titled *Competency and Economy in Public Expenditures*, contains 18 papers that touch on the subject of the civil service. But none dealt with the staffing issue as if it were a problem of much intellectual interest. In contrast, the 1937 special volume of the *Annals*, *Improved Personnel in Government Service* (Gulick 1937), contains many papers on the development of "a professional public service," including three papers on the subject of administrators as professionals.

[29]White presented an organization table of the government by grade to show how the structure of government limited the number who could fill the top jobs of government to a small number. He then wrote that "an extremely significant classification of public positions would result from their tabulation according to the amount of 'native intelligence' and other qualities required for their performance," so that an optimal sorting could someday be worked out (White 1926: 299–300). He did not indicate how such a procedure would solve the motivation problem he perceived in the British service.

and labor positions, but also from each other. This done, there should then
be worked out a carefully graded class of such technical positions, together
with specifications and regulations prescribing the qualifications for entrance
into and advancement in such special services. (Willoughby 1927: 237)

For these technical jobs, as opposed to the clerical positions, Willoughby
proposed that the civil service take care to select only qualified individuals. He wanted the civil service to be "rigid" in its specification of
these job requirements, including the educational requirements (Willoughby 1927: 289, 292).

Willoughby thought that clerical positions, by contrast, did not lend
themselves to organization into professional-style careers because they
could not be professionalized. But he did not favor the establishment of
a clerical service that restricted the access of clerks to administrative
positions. Instead, he proposed that the government bring the higher
politically appointed administrative officers into the classified service so
that they could be *linked* with the clerical positions in long job ladders.
The government, he argued should

> establish them upon such a basis that merit will be the controlling factor in
> determining entrance into, and advancement in, the service . . . . At the
> present time what amounts to almost a dead line is drawn at the positions of
> chief clerk or chief of division . . . . Up to this point the government em-
> ployee may look upon his service as one in which he may hope for advance-
> ment as he shows merit. Beyond this lie the positions of the real directing
> heads of the services . . . the only ones offering a really effective incentive to
> persons to adopt the government service as a career. Remove this barrier;
> make it possible to pass as a matter of normal promotion from the position of
> chief of division to assistant chief of bureau, chief of bureau, and assistant
> secretary, and the government service at once becomes one offering a real
> career. (Willoughby 1927: 239)

He observed that agencies might occasionally find it necessary to
recruit from outside the ranks to a fill a high position, even with a strong
promote-from-within policy in place. However, in his view, this would
happen "only in exceptional cases, since the appointing power will
certainly prefer to select one whose qualifications and personal characteristics are definitely known rather than run the risk involved in holding an open competitive examination" (Willoughby 1927: 240).

Willoughby explicitly opposed the creation of a British-style administrative class in the United States. He saw certain advantages to the
British system, which filled all higher administrative positions with
"men of broad liberal education." However, the exclusionary character
of the system made it undemocratic, which was undesirable. He contended that a tiered system of the British type was ultimately also inefficient. He judged the potential harm to morale and job performance from

a tiered system to outweigh the benefit of direct college recruitment for administrative positions.[30]

After the passage of the Classification Act, the CSC showed increasing sensitivity to the question of how careers should be organized. It argued that the new position classification system would ease the task of finding qualified employees to fill higher level vacancies (U.S. CSC 1923: xlix). Almost yearly from 1923 onward, the CSC wrote in its annual report of the need for a better system of statistical records to make such a system workable. But its focus of attention, as reported in the *Annual Reports*, was on the scientific and professional jobs, not the clerical or administrative ones.

In 1924, it bragged at its level of success in filling scientific and professional vacancies through the merit system (U.S. CSC 1924: xlii). By 1926, it was communicating with heads of departments in colleges all over the country to interest seniors in government employment in scientific and professional positions (U.S. CSC 1926: xii ff.). By this time, the CSC was unsatisfied with its efforts to fill scientific, technical, and professional positions and thus was giving the announcements of examinations for these jobs the "widest possible publicity." Two years later, it again wrote about the need for cooperation with universities, this time in the development of tests for engineers. And the following year, once again, it reported that "the most notable advance in recruiting during the year was the establishment of closer relations with the standard colleges and universities in the effort to recruit junior technical, professional and scientific workers" (U.S. CSC 1929: 6). In 1930, it inaugurated a fact-finding study of the subsequent government careers of all persons who had entered the professional service since 1923 to determine how to improve career prospects and how to make the civil service more attractive to young scientists and engineers (O'Rourke 1930: 7–8).[31] In contrast, it made little effort to change personnel procedures for clerical and administrative positions. Its major effort in this regard was to study the worth of the high-school diploma and to establish what experience would qualify as "equivalent" to this educational credential (U.S. CSC 1923: xlii).

The position classification studies published by the government be-

---

[30]He also admired the Prussian system for its efficiency, but criticized its autocratic character.

[31]"In connection with our fact-finding study, we shall endeavor to discover why the highest quartile of the graduates of engineering schools do not care to enter the Government service . . . if conditions are disclosed which discourage the better graduates from entering the service, knowledge of the conditions will enable the departments to direct effort toward improving the situation."

tween the passage of the Classification Act of 1923 and the inauguration of Franklin D. Roosevelt show little change in the structure of clerical–administrative job ladders from that found in the 1920 report of the Congressional Joint Commission. The *Class Specifications for Positions in the Departmental Service*, published in 1924 by the Personnel Classification Board, made qualitative distinctions between administrative and clerical positions. But, like the system proposed by the Congressional Joint Commission, these distinctions did not articulate well with the educational system. In consequence, they did not constitute a two-tier job ladder system, in which college graduates entered the service at middle-grade levels into a separate tier closed off to clerical workers. The three lowest positions in the "administrative officer" group of the Personnel Classification Board's classification required only a high-school diploma, in addition to extensive prior clerical experience. No special entry portal existed for inexperienced young college graduates.[32]

The Personnel Classification Board's *Preliminary Class Specifications of Positions in the Field Service* was published 7 years later, in 1931. The major change in the educational qualifications required for clerical and administrative personnel concerned the more nearly universal requirement that clerks possess a high-school diploma. The percentage of persons 17 years old who were high-school graduates had risen continually from 6.3% in 1900 to 8.6% in 1920 to 16.3% in 1920 to 24.4% in 1925 to 28.8% in 1930 (U.S. Bureau of the Census 1975). Just as business was now requiring more education of its office workers in the 1920s than it had in the past, so the 1930 preliminary class specifications made greater educational demands on its prospective clerks. However, there was no corresponding inflation in the demand for college credentials for administrative positions; the administrative assistant positions still required high-school graduation only, plus previous experience.

Despite the debates regarding the usefulness or desirability of recognizing a profession of management or public administration, college enrollment steadily increased, as did enrollment in the business schools (Sass 1982: 164). Moreover, the increase in college enrollments was having an impact on recruitment policies. The perception that the colleges were attracting good students forced even recruiters skeptical of the value of a college education to recruit there. Thus, on the one hand, Bell found as late as 1940 that employers and hiring managers believed that some college was a minimum educational requirement for only 15% of

[32]The lowest position that required a "general collegiate education or equivalent practical training" was that of junior administrative officer (CAF-10), but this position also required extended experience to fill it.

the occupations falling into the occupation of "managers and officials" (Bell 1940). But,

> as the personnel manager of one of the largest banks said "It is useless for us to go to the high schools for good men, as we did fifteen years ago. All of the best high school graduates are now going to college, and we have to wait four years longer. (Bossard and Dewhurst 1931: 54; see also Emmer and Jeuck 1950: 554)

Sears, for example, started recruitment of managers directly from the colleges in 1928. By 1934 it was recruiting from colleges on a systematic basis (Emmer and Jeuck 1950: 554; cf. Bossard and Dewhurst 1931; Sass 1982). Many other companies, including Chrysler, Bethlehem Steel, Proctor and Gamble, and Western Electric, did the same (Graham 1935). By the later 1920s, more than 25% of all employees in higher white-collar jobs in the nation's economy had some college training, though only 1.1% of men over 20 held a college degree as of 1920 (Kocka 1980: 183). As more employers and managers themselves were college graduates, skepticism about the value of college naturally lessened (Meriam 1937b; Noyes 1945; Hawley 1979: 84). The increased supply of college manpower was in effect generating demand for this talent.

SUMMARY

The first third of the twentieth century witnessed major advances in the development of white-collar internal labor markets. The federal government as well as other public and private organizations accepted the principle that jobs should be ranked along a hierarchy according to their duties and paid according to their rank. That these hierarchies should be organized into job ladders and form the basis for careers was also widely accepted. However, academics and administrators lacked consensus on how to assign jobs to job ladders and on how high the barriers to mobility from one ladder to another should be. The disagreement was particularly acute in the case of administrative and clerical jobs, with some arguing that administration was a profession and others arguing it was an extension of clerical work. Accepting the legitimacy of professions, Congress mandated the separation of professional and subprofessional jobs into separate services, with the requirement of college graduation for professionals the principal basis for the separation. In contrast, despite calls for the professionalization of administration, position classifiers continued to emphasize the importance of prior clerical experience for access to the higher administrative positions. This requirement in effect demonstrated the lack of a mobility barrier in the hierarchy of office work, at least for males. In the 1920s, private sector employers began to recruit managers and administrators from the ranks of liberal arts graduates, though arguably this effort was a reaction to company perceptions about where the talent was, rather than a determination that college training *per se* was valuable for business. The federal government did not begin such an effort until the 1930s, an effort to be discussed in the next chapter.

6

The Development of a Tiered Personnel System in the Federal Government

INTRODUCTION

At the beginning of the 1930s, professions had developed to the point where personnel directors could use the professional/nonprofessional distinction as a legitimate organizing principle in the construction of job ladders. The distinction existed at two levels. First, the personnel office recognized a distinction between the job tasks of professionals and non-professionals. Second, this distinction justified the requirement that applicants for professional positions have the appropriate university-level degree. Beginning in the 1930s, the question of whether office work should be similarly organized was debated in a serious way within the federal government. Later, in the years following World War II, the Civil Service Commission, working with federal agencies, constructed a system of job ladders for office work that increasingly resembled the tiered structure the government had created in the 1920s for scientific work.

However, the boundary between clerical and administrative work did not achieve the same level of solidity as did the corresponding boundary on the scientific side. Academics, administrators, and workers never agreed about the existence of a clear qualitative basis for justifying the construction of a tiered personnel system for clerical and administrative work. Disagreements about the value of formal education, on-the-job training, and practical experience, and about the comparative quality of college graduates and of high-school-educated government clerks, also persisted. As this chapter will show, these disagreements

119

did not prevent the development of a tiered system for clerical and administrative work, which was largely in place by the 1960s. Recruitment pressures, the development of business schools and schools of public administration, the institutionalization of personnel management, the personnel practices of large private-sector firms, and gender stereotypes were, collectively, more than strong enough to separate the job ladders of clerks and administrators. Furthermore, despite continuing ambiguity about the nature of the clerical–administrative boundary, the evidence makes clear that federal administrators intended the bifurcation of clerical and administrative job ladders to have an impact on recruitment and promotion and hence on the careers of government civil servants.

HOW VACANCIES WERE TRADITIONALLY FILLED IN THE FEDERAL GOVERNMENT

The data needed for a comprehensive quantitative assessment of recruitment and promotion practices during the first 80 years of civil service operations under the Pendleton Act do not exist. However, observers of the civil service have reported their impressions and research findings at various times during the past century. We can piece these observations together to support some rough generalizations about personnel practices. First, even though the Civil Service Reform Act of 1883 did not require that agencies fill vacancies by promotion whenever possible, promotion was a frequently used personnel practice. Clerical positions in particular were generally filled through promotion, though female clerks were not allowed to advance very far in the system. Mayers reported that

> In the clerical service, . . . the general rule prior to the war [World War I] had been to recruit only at the lowest level, that of clerk, typist, or stenographer at entrance rates of $600 to $1000, and to regard those so entering, *or rather the men so entering, for the tradition has been against the advancement of women beyond fairly low levels,* as eligible through long service to the highest administrative positions of a permanent nonpolitical character; and generally speaking, to restrict selection for those positions to those already in the service, in the particular bureau or service in which the vacancy occurs. (Mayers 1922: 254; italics mine)[1]

Maurice Low (1900: 625), supporting this observation, wrote that the typical clerk began employment at $900, the trainee salary, and

[1]Willoughby (1927: 239) supported Mayers' observation.

almost surely would reach Class 3 or 4 after 10 years.[2] Although such a position may seem lowly, Grades 3 and 4 were roughly as high in the civil service of the day as administrative GS-11 or GS-12 positions today.[3]

This scenario only applied to employees who stuck it out in the federal service. It became increasingly common during the first 20 years of the century for employees to leave the government after a few years of employment. The voluntary turnover rates around the turn of the century in the federal civil service were about 3.5% per year, a figure much lower than for the economy as whole (Conyngton 1920). But this figure increased to the 6–7% range for 1905–1912 and then to the 8–10% range until 1916 before jumping to 17.5% in 1917 and roughly 35–40% during the war years (Brissendon 1929). No data on job tenure are available for these years. But simplifying assumptions based on available turnover data make possible some speculation on the subject. Although roughly one-half of employees entering the civil service remained there for 10 years at the turn of the century, the percentage remaining for 10 years probably dropped to about one-third around 1910. It dropped further, perhaps to about one-fifth, before the start of World War I, as government salary scales became increasingly uncompetitive with the private sector.[4] Separation rates came down again after the wartime disruption but not to their turn-of-the-century levels. In the second half of the 1920s, the separation rate averaged over 10% a year. In other words, during the first third of the century, it was common for employees to work in the government for a few years in order to obtain clerical experience and then to move to the private sector.

Although agencies usually used promotions to fill clerical vacancies, the proportion filled by promotion would depend on the number of vacancies, which in turn depended on the rates of growth and turnover.

---

[2]A 1939 recruiting manual also reported that government recruiting for clerical positions was limited to the lower grades (*Government Positions* 1939).

[3]Chapman noted in 1959 that seniority-based promotions are generally more common in the lower grades, where work is more routine and merit less important (Chapman 1959).

[4]These calculations are based on the assumption that all voluntary separations occurred during the first 10 years of the career and that roughly 50% of civil service employees had tenure less than 10 years at any point in time during these years. Because this period of time preceded the 1920 passage of the Civil Service Retirement Act, it appears that most older employees were either removed (involuntary discharge) or died in office. The assumptions just mentioned are roughly consistent with the data on size, accessions, and separations for this time, so the survival rates are probably in the right ball park. Regarding salary comparisons between the public and private sectors, data on clerks who voluntarily left the Agriculture department for the private sector during the 1919 fiscal year show that they on average received a 46% pay increase (Conyngton 1920).

Lewis Mayers reported that tremendous government growth during
World War I forced administrators to recruit heavily from the private
sector. Such growth spurts would generally also create tremendous promotional opportunity for existing employees. During World War II,
agencies promoted some employees so rapidly that the CSC used time-
in-grade restrictions to prevent possibly unqualified employees from
rising too far too fast (Kammerer 1951).

Even during normal times, however, administrators might sometimes conclude that they had to recruit from outside because they could
not find suitable talent in the ranks. Tuckerman's report about the filling
of vacancies in the Bureau of Standards during the late 1920s and early
1930s is illustrative. He wrote that

> by far the larger number of employees [for professional positions] are re-
> cruited from recent college graduates, with the hope that a sufficient number
> of them, of suitable quality, will remain with the service and occupy the
> positions in the higher grades made vacant by death or resignation. That this
> hope is not totally filled is shown by the fact that over 1/3 of the appoint-
> ments made were to fill vacancies in higher positions that could be filled by
> men already in the service. (Tuckerman 1932: 204)

Over the years, some observers have claimed that agency officials
frequently promoted the unqualified to fill important jobs, though objective evidence is hard to come by. Before 1920, when the retirement act
created a system of government pensions for retired civil servants, agencies sometimes kept older employees on the payroll even when health
problems interfered with their work. Through seniority-based promotions, these older employees might reach positions that were beyond
their capacity to handle (U.S. CSC 1898: 18–19). Even after 1920, though,
supporters of civil service reform condemned agencies for promoting
undeserving clerks to responsible jobs.[5]

Another way to fill a vacancy was to recruit an employee from a
different agency of the federal government. The ability of employees to
transfer from one job to another was variously easy or difficult depending upon the time in question. Before standardization of pay, salary
differentials between agencies made transfer an attractive option for
employees but a problem for the government as a whole. In 1901, the
CSC prohibited transfers by employees during the first 6 months of

[5]Stahl argued that as a result of an "overemphasis" on seniority, too often "the one-time
office boy has eventually become bureau chief or 'chief clerk.'" Sometimes these people
are good "but more often they are dismally unfit for top posts" (Stahl 1956: 144). See also
Tugwell's comments (in Schlesinger 1959: 534).

service in any position. In 1903, it restricted transfers to cases in which the agency claimed it could not fill the position in question by promotion (Van Riper 1958: 193). When these rules proved inadequate to deal with the problem, Congress, in 1906, required an employee to serve in one department for 3 years before he could be transferred to another. But the problem resurfaced during World War I, when Congress created new agencies that paid higher salaries than the existing agencies. Not bound by the 1906 statute, the new agencies were able to attract large numbers of transfers (U.S. CSC 1941b). Congress therefore extended the old law to the new agencies in 1917 and started a system of "bonuses" to raise the pay in the older agencies (Betters 1931: 33–34; U.S. CSC 1941b). The Classification Act of 1923 obviated the need for these regulations by standardizing salaries, but barriers to transfer remained (Feldman 1931: 153–154). Not until 1939, for example, was the rule rescinded that an employee's supervisor must approve his transfer (Van Riper 1958: 379).

From the turn of the century through the 1930s, the highest administrative classified positions were usually filled from within the ranks of the classified service. Mayers wrote in 1922 that

> a recent illustrative exception to this rule [of filling vacancies from within for clerical positions] was the filling of the position of Chief Clerk, Bureau of Education, by open competition. It is doubtful if there is another position of Chief Clerk of an established bureau in the federal service which has been filled other than by selection from within. (Mayers 1922: 254)

Mcmahon (1926) reported that of 54 bureau chiefs studied in 1926, 80% of the 32 classified positions had been filled by promotion.[6]

The Reform Act of 1883 left most civil service jobs, including all the important ones, outside the classified service. President Cleveland extended the classified service upwards in 1896, when he covered in the positions of chief clerk and division chief. Despite the controversy over Cleveland's action, no president ever reversed his order. However, McKinley, Cleveland's successor, exempted from examination two private secretary or "confidential clerk" positions for each bureau head, secretary, or assistant secretary of a department (Sageser 1935: 213–214; Van Riper 1958: 101, 216–217). Nonetheless, Macmahon and Millet reported that even these positions, typically classified as CAF-14 or CAF-15 in the 1930s, were often filled through "transfer or promotion"

---

[6]Macmahon and Millet (1939) further reported that, as of 1938, 11 of 62 bureau chiefs had no education past high school. This is notable because a large number of the bureaus were technical in nature and required scientific or professional heads. These 11 people presumably had moved through the clerical ranks to reach their positions.

from the ranks of the clerical, administrative, and fiscal service. A number of these officials had begun their careers as low-level government clerks (Macmahon and Millet 1939: 133).

Vacancies in the professional service were sometimes filled through promotion and sometimes not, depending upon the bureau or agency and its rate of growth. By World War I at least, the federal government did not generally fill highly technical positions from the ranks of subprofessional employees (Mayers 1922: 252). However, the practice was not unheard of. In the late 1920s in particular, many women were able to move into technical and professional jobs from subprofessional and clerical jobs, according to the CSC (U.S. CSC 1929: 12–13). The CSC also reported that official policy was to fill higher positions from the lower professional grades (U.S. CSC 1929). However, a large proportion of professional appointments were made to higher rungs on the professional ladder. In 1930, 60% of all scientific and professional appointments were made to P-1, 19% to P-2, 15% to P-3, 3% to P-4, 3% to P-5, and fewer than 1% to higher grades (Campbell 1932; see also Ordway 1942; Kingsley 1942: 9 ff.; Pfiffner 1946: 256 ff.).

An agency's willingness to recruit from outside the service depended upon how important previous government experience was for the job in question. Lewis Meriam, an officer in the Census Bureau, reported that government-specific experience was valuable even for many clerical jobs.

> What characterizes the good upper-filling clerks in an agency—and upon them rests in no small degree the routine efficiency of an office that handles a mass of papers—is their complete mastery of the particular filing system, their familiarity with the papers in the files, their knowledge of the people in the office, and their speed and accuracy. Speed and accuracy are moreover in part the product of knowledge and familiarity. A top file clerk from one agency is not interchangeable with a top file clerk from another. Every newcomer into a filing system has to learn that system and become familiar with the papers in it. (Meriam 1938: 64)[7]

Thus, it appears that promotion was a frequently used device to fill vacancies in the classified service, especially in the clerical, administrative, and fiscal service. The overall level of opportunity to advance to interesting jobs was limited ultimately by availability of good jobs. As in other organizations, most jobs were routine. Because of the scarcity of good jobs, "for the great mass of federal employees . . . there can be no prospect of even ultimate ascent to posts of even intermediate responsibility and importance (Mayers 1920: 235).

---

[7]He went on to say the same about stenographer–secretaries.

Specialized education was a definite asset for securing technical jobs, and a liberal arts degree probably increased a clerk's chances for advancement, though it is impossible to determine the extent to which this was so. It does appear that women were at a distinct disadvantage. Race was not an issue in white-collar promotion decisions because, before World War II, blacks were largely limited to manual jobs in the federal work force (Hayes 1941; Fair Employment Practice Committee 1945).

THE NEW DEAL AND THE PUSH FOR AN ADMINISTRATIVE CLASS

In 1922, a survey of 30 universities revealed that professors "stated definitely that they advised member of their classes not to enter Federal service" (O'Rourke 1930: 43). But by the early 1930s, universities were sending a significant proportion of their graduates into government service (Lambie 1935; U.S. CSC 1941a: 125–126; Graham 1941: 6). The reason for the heightened interest was due in part to the growth of opportunity in government (Fabricant 1952: 10, 14; U.S. Census 1975: 1102)[8] but mostly to the onset of the Great Depression. Private-sector jobs became hard to find, and government jobs had the reputation of being comparatively secure. Furthermore, the limited implementation of position classification buttressed claims that government could offer a career, not just a job, to university graduates. In light of these factors, it is not at all surprising that the university's interest in public service at this time would increase (Lambie 1932: 7–9; White 1934: 1–2; Mosher 1937).

Heightened academic interest in the federal service was shown in several ways. The Institute for Government Research and the Committee on Policy of the American Political Science Association each commissioned new studies of the British civil service at the start of the 1930s (Gaus 1931; Walker 1935: vii). In addition, university conferences on the subject of university training for the public service reappeared after a lapse of over a decade. The first of these was the Conference on University Training held at the University of Minnesota in July 1931, which was jointly sponsored by the Civil Service Commission and the University of

---

[8]In 1929, the service was 8% larger than its postwar trough but still only two-thirds the size of its wartime peak. Opportunities in state and local governments, in contrast, grew substantially during the 1920s. By 1930, government employees constituted 7.4% of the work force and roughly double that percentage of the white-collar work force (Fabricant 1952).

Minnesota. Conferences at the University of Chicago and at Princeton soon followed. Academics at these conferences championed the value of university training for government professionals. They also complained about the lack of reception the public and government had given to the idea that public administration was a science and urged people to get a new outlook on the subject.[9]

A final force sparking renewed interest in government administration and its appropriate ties to the university came from the New Deal administration of Franklin D. Roosevelt. Those committed to the development of general administration as a distinct profession found the New Deal to be the appropriate political climate for the expression of their views. The Social Science Research Council (SSRC) received the endorsement of Franklin Roosevelt to initiate a Commission of Inquiry on Public Service Personnel (CIPSP) (Karl 1963: 204).[10] The commission produced 12 different reports on the organization of the civil service. These included detailed studies of the American federal service, studies of European systems, a comprehensive bibliography of the literature on personnel up to that time, and the minutes of commission hearings in Washington, New York, Chicago, Minneapolis, St. Paul, Seattle, San Francisco, Berkeley, Palo Alto, Los Angeles, Richmond, and London.

The final report of the commission was a manifesto for the idea that administration was a distinct profession and should be treated as such. In its view, administration was not a secondary function of higher technical positions or an appendage to the political responsibilities of policy. Administrative jobs were especially not "a hazy terminus" for long-lasting clerks who gradually move higher and higher in the service by the sheer force of their seniority. Instead, in the commission's words:

> All complicated human organizations require correlation, planning, and the central direction, arrangement, and delegation of work. The sum of these is

[9]"One obstacle in the way of the new development is found in the fact that most men, and especially most political leaders, are not convinced that there is a science of public administration per se, just as many of them refuse to accept the judgments of economists and sociologists on governmental policy. For obvious reasons they must accept the conclusions of physicists, chemists, agricultural specialists, and even in most cases of lawyers and engineers, in their special fields, but every conclusion of a social scientists has its 'political' implications, which colors the reception of it by those whom it will affect" (Lambie 1932: 17).

[10]L. D. Coffman, the president of the University of Minnesota, was named the chairman of the commission. Louis Brownlow and Charles Merriam, along with Arthur Day and Ralph Budd, were commission members. The commission named Luther Gulick, the director of the Institute for Public Administration, as its director of research. Thus the people who later drafted Roosevelt's unsuccessful plan to reorganize the executive branch staffed the commission that proposed new personnel policies for the government.

administration. Administration is in itself a definable field of knowledge and experience. It possesses its own developing technology, peculiar experience, and extensive application for its mastery. (CIPSP 1935: 36)

The commission was critical of existing position classification schemes for their emphasis on the position instead of the career. In its view, the attempts of appointing officers to find workers to fit the "pigeonholes" of these systems obscured the importance of career development (CIPSP 1935: 5).[11] In making such an argument, the commission echoed the views of the Congressional Joint Commission on Reclassification of Salaries, which also had argued for a career system. But the Commission of Inquiry differed from the Congressional Joint Commission in its emphasis on a tiered system of job ladders for clerical–administrative as well as for professional work.

The commission's argument for the recognition of administration as a separate profession was part of a broader philosophy that emphasized qualitative distinctions between occupations and favored a personnel system that would reinforce these distinctions through management practices. The commission recommended that government divide civil service work into broad categories, specifically unskilled manual, skilled manual, clerical, clerical-executive, administrative, subprofessional, and professional (scientific). In its view, these "services" corresponded to "the natural capacities and characteristics of human beings." The Congressional Joint Commission on Reclassification of Salaries described its "services" as an "arbitrarily drawn" scaffolding to aid in the erection of a classification. In contrast, the CIPSP wanted to use services to "relate the kinds of work to be done to the kinds of persons best fitted to them" (CIPSP 1935: 26–27). Clearly, the CIPSP intended its services to have implications for civil service careers. The normal career would involve entry at the bottom of one of these services and progression through the service as far as a person's talents would take him.

The commission recommended that recruitment for these services be articulated with the educational system. In particular, this meant that agencies should routinely fill positions within the administrative class with college graduates "after general, but before special education"

[11]"When government desires to select men to enter its service and perform its work, it must decide at what stage it shall take them. Shall it wait until they are fully formed, after their special education and experience? When this is done, the vacant position can be carefully analyzed, determining the precise amount of technological training and the nature of experience required, and a competitive examination can be given to find a man who has reached precisely this point. This, in general, has been the American philosophy and policy of recruitment. It is a scheme of dividing most of the work of government into pigeonholes, and whenever one is vacant, finding a man ripe to fill it, in which niche he may be forgotten for the rest of his days" (CIPSP 1935: 38).

(CIPSP 1935: 39).[12] At the 1932 Minnesota conference on training, Leonard White had related a friend's advice that a liberal arts graduate desiring a career in government should first learn "to become a skilled stenographer," that is, to obtain a concrete skill that would get him started (White 1932). Under the commission's recommendation, such a graduate would instead, if successful on the entrance test, enter the government as an apprentice administrator and then progress to a prestigious position in government. Entrance tests for these positions would, following the British model, measure academic knowledge rather than either practical knowledge or native ability.[13] Because a young recruit for the administrative class would have no special qualifications for the position he would ultimately fill, he would have to acquire these skills through in-service training. Promotions, of course, would be based on merit.

The commission also proposed career services for other government jobs. Each service would have its own entry ports articulated with the educational system. The unskilled service would be recruited without regard to education, though entrants would normally have a grade-school education. Agencies would recruit mostly high-school graduates for the skilled and trades service but would require mastery of particular manual skills. The clerical service would be divided into two "series," again parallel to the British system. Employees for the "strictly clerical" service would be recruited after not less than 2 years of high school. High-school graduates would enter the "clerical–executive" service. Applicants for "strictly clerical" entry-level positions would take tests that primarily measured general intelligence. Entrance tests for the "clerical–executive" positions would draw primarily on the high-school curriculum. The professional and technical service would be recruited after professional training was complete but before the individual had acquired job experience.

The CIPSP showed a certain amount of sensitivity to concerns that a system modeled on British practice would be seen as castelike and undemocratic. It argued that such strong articulation with the educational system was not elitist because the American educational system was "universal" and itself meritocratic. Furthermore, it argued that the barriers between the proposed job ladders would not "be so far apart that the unusual employee may not pass from one to another on the basis of

---

[12]See also Friedrich's (1935) monograph that represented part of the commission's report.
[13]"Another American philosophy proposed to recruit grown men on the basis of their I.Q. or potential intelligence—as if one could run a railway train by harnessing an atom to it, merely because its potential energy is sufficient to pull it" (CIPSP 1935: 42).

further education or experience." But clearly, its use of the modifier *unusual* suggested that it did not see this route as the normal one into the higher services. Indeed, the commission itself did not speak unfavorably about the British "castelike" practices. Furthermore, staff reports expressed agreement with the view that clerical experience generally reduced one's capacity for administrative work and therefore that job ladders should have relatively impermeable boundaries.[14] The commission undoubtedly believed that the proposed system would reduce the number of cases in which clerks eventually obtained promotions to administrative positions in the American federal service.

Lucius Wilmerding, the assistant to the director of research for the CIPSP, did the best job of elaborating the commission's philosophy. In his *Government by Merit,* Monograph 12 of the series of reports released by the Commission, he wrote that

> 144. The clerical, administrative, and fiscal service of the federal classification . . . is not limited to one type of work, but contains all the general types from the simplest routine to the highest administrative. Yet in the federal classification the functional distinctions which exist between routine, clerical, executive, and administrative work are completely overlooked, or rather they are conceived to be hierarchical. This is extraordinary, for the difference between the ordinary administrator and the ordinary office boy must be apparent to the dullest perception. How much more apparent, then, should it be to a Congress able to tell a junior clerk from an assistant clerk, and to an administrative agency which can differentiate between an under property and supply clerk and an under storekeeper? Nevertheless the classifiers have been insensitive to the major distinctions. They have been like a singing master who, able to recognize all the half-tones, nay quarter-tones, of the chromatic scale, cannot tell a soprano from a bass voice. . . .

> 151. If classification is to be used as a tool for the reconstitution and reform of government, it must recognize the different *careers* which are possible in the civil service. Positions which are training posts for higher work must be kept apart from positions which are the culmination of lower work. Just as the careers of engineers and draftsmen are separated in the professional service, so should the different careers in the general service be separated.

> 153. The advantages of a proper classification are very great. In the first place, if posts are reserved in each career from the rank of apprentice to the highest possible substantive rank, the chances of inducing competent persons to enter will be greatly enhanced; in the second place, the separation of

[14]Wilmerding, the assistant to the director of research for the commission, argued that in the proposed system, promotions from one service to another "will, however, always be rare exceptions, for the hierarchical immobility of personnel is even greater than its departmental immobility; as a man gains in experience as a clerk, he rapidly loses transferability to superior hierarchies" as his mind is "dulled by routine and repetitive tasks" (Wilmerding 1935: 166, 177).

training posts in one career from substantive posts in another will clarify the
problem of recruitment versus promotion. (Wilmerding 1935: 58, 60–61)

The commission believed that the establishment of separate services
for what it believed were qualitatively distinct jobs would accomplish
several objectives. It would increase incentives for the "competent" to
enter government. It would reduce promotion rates for those with the
"wrong qualifications." Finally, the proposed reorganization would
clarify the training responsibilities of government and result, so the
commission thought, in a more capable civil service. To men such as
Merriam, Brownlow, and Gulick, who had linked in their minds the goal
of progress with expansion of the planning and administrative capacity
of government, such a reorganization was highly desirable.

The commission meant its proposed "administrative class" to include only the highest government positions. Wilmerding estimated
their number as perhaps 1000, exclusive of training positions. This
number would include administrative positions in scientific bureaus.
The commission's final report itself does not spell out precisely who
should get these top positions. But its discussion implies that the heads
of the technical and professional services would be subordinate to the
administrative service, as in England (see also Wilmerding 1935: 36).

Two years before the CIPSP issued its final report, Charles Merriam
had helped Leonard White gain the position of civil service commissioner. White demonstrated his support for the CIPSP's recommendations in his 1935 monograph, *Government Career Service*, and acknowledged his debt to the British model, which he had studied first-hand a
few years earlier. His plan for the creation of an administrative corps
was more detailed than that proposed in the final report of the CIPSP. In
contrast, he mentioned the other proposed services only in passing. His
proposed administrative corps would encompass the top administrative
positions, plus a set of training positions that would occupy the lower
rungs of the administrative job ladders. All positions in grades CAF-11
or higher would be included, plus the lower-graded trainee positions. In
all, he would have included about 2,500 current positions of government.

White construed administrative work more narrowly than did the
Commission of Inquiry. The report of the commission defined administration as consisting of the "correlation, planning and the central direction, arrangement, and delegation of work." White argued that "this
definition does not make the distinction between administrative work
and executive work which has long been established in the English Civil
Service. The essential point of the distinction is that between creative
and constructive work (administration) and the performance of current

operations (executive)." White proposed to exclude "the performance of current operations" from his administrative corps (White 1935a: 9).

White's formulation of the administrative corps also differed from the proposals of the CIPSP by its looser relationship between education and position. White wished to allow already-employed civil servants to compete for positions in the proposed administrative class.[15] New entrants, on the other hand, would be limited to college graduates under the age of 30. Insiders would be recruited through recommendations of a personnel officer made once a year. Outside applicants would take an examination that presumed a college education. Because White thought that tests could not accurately measure administrative ability, he proposed that the new corps rely heavily on the probation period as a selection device. These new entrants would spend a period of 5 years in training positions, a process that should weed out 150 of every 250 new entrants. He also would have allowed scientists and professionals to fill some administrative positions, which was already standard practice in the American system. The government would use in-service training, rotation of assignments, and other tools to prepare administrators for responsible positions.

Though White was a civil service commissioner, he did not have the authority to establish an administrative corps by himself. But he took what he thought was the first step by setting up an examination for the position of junior civil service examiner in 1934. He limited eligibility for the new examination to college graduates and encouraged agencies to fill positions from its register. He hoped thereby to create a "bridge" for liberal arts graduates that would take them in time to high administrative positions.

Other organizations, such as the League of Women Voters, the Civil Service Reform Association, and the American Political Science Association backed one form or other of the proposal for the creation of an administrative corps. So did many experts (CIPSP 1934: 198; Frederic 1935; Kingsley 1942).[16] White and W. W. Stockberger, who was considered to be the most effective personnel officer in the federal government, promoted the idea in a 1937 special issue of *The Annals of the American Academy of Political and Social Science* (Gulick 1937). The Public Administration Clearing House held a conference on the subject (Lam-

---

[15]Recruitment from the already-employed civil servants would be "irrespective of . . . educational background" (White 1935a: 41). Women would compete on equal terms with men but "subject to the right of the appointing officer to select either a man or woman as he prefers, under the terms of the civil service rules" (White 1935a: 39–40).

[16]Pfiffner argued in 1946 that "most American specialists in public administration are agreed that an American administrative class is desirable" (Pfiffner 1946: 14–15).

bie 1935). The President's Committee on Administrative Management endorsed elements of its plan (President's Committee on Administrative Management 1937; see also Reeves and David 1937).

But substantial opposition to the plan also existed, opposition that took various forms. For some, the principal issue was the work that these general administrators would do. Conservatives opposed expanding the power or functions of the state, no matter how it was organized. To the extent that the institution of a class of general administrators meant an expanded state, conservatives were opposed. In testimony before the commission, the president of the U.S. Chamber of Commerce argued that the way to bring about a career service in the government was to eliminate all jobs that did not involve strictly "governmental" functions. Government should then turn their tasks over to private industry. Finally, it should set up a career service for technicians who would write up specifications for goods and services that the government could have private industry provide (CIPSP 1934: 116).

Veterans opposed any plan that might do away with veteran preferences for jobs (see, e.g., Polenberg 1966). The leaders of the National Federation of Federal Employees (NFFE) expressed a mixed reaction. On the one hand, the union favored reforms that would increase the stature of the civil service and increase the role of merit at the expense of patronage in personnel decisions (e.g., *Federal Employee* 1935: 9–10, 31; Steward 1938: 1). But they opposed plans that might reduce the level of promotions for existing civil servants. In testimony before the CIPSP the head of the NFFE, Luther C. Steward, opposed the type of preferential treatment for young college graduates advocated by the CIPSP, arguing that college did not provide training comparable to that obtained on the job (CIPSP 1934).[17]

The frequent opposition of civil servants to stricter educational requirements for jobs has been characterized as self-serving by those favoring such change. For instance William Carpenter was to argue in 1952 that

> the most serious indictment of civil service employees stems from their opposition to increased educational requirements for public employment. . . .
> These people realize that they are denied opportunities for promotion when educational levels beyond which they have not progressed are set for civil service examinations. . . . They protest to civil service commissions, threaten litigation and otherwise exhibit an uncompromising opposition to all efforts to improve the civil service through greater requirements of formal education. Sometimes they succeed for a time in compelling the evaluation of experience with formal education. . . . The result is a general weakening of

[17]See also the argument of Vaux Owen, the vice president of the NFFE (Owen 1937: 15).

the government service to pave the way for the promotion of the unqualified. (Carpenter 1952: 49)

But others besides civil servants and veterans have argued that experience is a good substitute for education.

The most articulate statement of opposition to the CIPSP's proposals came from two people involved in the report of the Congressional Joint Commission on the Reclassification of Salaries 15 years earlier, E. O. Griffenhagen, who earlier had headed the research staff for the Congressional Joint Commission, and Lewis Meriam of the Brookings Institution. Griffenhagen stated his objections to the CIPSP's philosophy in a report (Griffenhagen and Associates 1937) to Harry Byrd, who later was a leader of the opposition to Roosevelt's reorganization plan (Polenberg 1966). He wrote in 1937 that

> much has been written recently, in glowing but vague terms, about what is represented as a new idea of a "career service." . . . Such proposals sound well when considered without reference to the practical problems in any government service. But the practical administrator sees that they fail to relate to the actual needs of the service at nearly every point. . . . True enough, the influx of recent college graduates, inducted at the high level of a fictitious "administrative" service . . . might well be pleased with the status thus accorded them, envisioning lifetime careers as members of a specially privileged class. But conditions would be different for the great bulk of the service. This would be composed in part of recent high school graduates brought in to recruit an equally fictitious "executive" service, comprised of positions involving requirements that they are for the most part in no way qualified to meet, and with but limited opportunities for advancement, after they have learned these jobs, to positions of higher responsibility and compensation, principally reserved for the more privileged group, *though these positions are merely higher in the same identical lines of work and are separated from their own by only imaginary lines of division.* It would also consist in part of elementary school graduates brought in to fill the lower grade positions (largely of kinds now ordinarily filled by high school graduates specially fitted to the duties), without any attempt to fit them to positions of different kinds according to their actual qualifications, condemned to a sort of perpetual peonage in subordinate positions, without opportunity or hope of reward by advancement to the higher levels, even in their own lines of work.
>   No, it is not in any such way that a career service can be established, at least under American ideals and American ideas of what constitutes either fair play or effective planning and organization for work to be done. (Griffenhagen and Associates 1937: 21–22; italics mine)

In short, Griffenhagen opposed the establishment of job ladders whose boundaries were based, not on qualitative distinctions in the type of work performed (which, despite the contention of the CIPSP, he denied existed) but on a desire by operating officials to control organizational mobility. He did not deny that quantitative distinctions existed in the work of administrators and clerks, but he thought that such quantitative distinctions existed all along the hierarchy from the bottom to the top. This justified the establishment of long job ladders that covered the entire range. In his own words, he argued that

> the lines of division of a true career service are vertical, providing the freest possible opportunity for advancement from the lowest position to the highest, instead of horizontal, dividing those in the service as between privileged and less-privileged classes . . . every possible encouragement should be provided for qualified eligibles to enter the service at whatever levels their qualifications merit and for employees to give their best efforts with a view to reward in the form of promotion to higher positions. As few barriers as possible should be left in the way of full opportunity for every employee to win advancement to any higher positions for which he can prove his qualifications in competition limited to employees in the service.
>
> Full application of these principles would call for absolute preference to employees in the service in filling higher positions, whenever there are any such in lower positions who are able and willing to demonstrate their qualifications competitively among themselves. (Griffenhagen and Associates 1937: 22–23)

Rather than have a formal entry position pegged to the educational system, Griffenhagen favored the possibility of entry at any level of the system, so long as "absolute preference" was given to qualified insiders.

Griffenhagen's argument was supported by Lewis Meriam of the Brookings Institution, who was perhaps a more visible figure to the reformers championing the proposed new structure for public personnel. In his testimony before the Commission (CIPSP 1934), in an article in the *Annals of the American Academy of Political and Social Science* (Meriam 1937b), in a set of lectures given at the University of Chicago (Meriam 1936), in an analysis of the Committee on American Management's proposals for reorganization of the civil service (Meriam 1937a), and in a book about his experiences in the government (Meriam 1938), Meriam argued against the idea of an administrative corps. He believed that the proposed reorganization overestimated the worth of a liberal arts college degree, underestimated the extent to which the high administrative jobs in government required technical and sometimes scientific skills, underestimated the level of administrative talent and interest possessed by many scientists and professionals, and underestimated the talent of many of the nation's high school graduates.[18]

---

[18]"Within recent months some leading educators and educational institutions have made statements or issued reports to the effect that the colleges and universities in America are not necessarily recruiting the best brains and the best ability and that some graduates of colleges and universities are inferior to persons who for one reason or another have not been to college. When university presidents and a leading educational research institu-

Lewis Meriam hardly opposed the imposition of educational requirements for positions where they were appropriate. Indeed, he believed that, because of the opposition of "some politicians and groups of citizens" to high educational requirements, the requirements were not given enough stress when the CSC advertised positions. As a result, many applied without the right type of skills and could not compete with the better qualified applicants (Meriam 1938: 85). However, he saw no point in raising educational requirements for positions that did not need them, in order to start a job ladder at that level (Meriam 1938: 330–331). Instead, he wanted the civil service organized so that educational requirements always corresponded to the needs of the position. He wanted a system that allowed capable employees to obtain more training and continue to advance.[19]

In his 1939 revised edition of his *Introduction to the Study of Public Administration,* Leonard White argued that two principal differences separated the two sides of the debate (White 1939). The first issue concerned whether general administration existed as a separate field of knowledge, that is, whether one could be a "general administrator *per se*" or whether one also needed intimate knowledge of the subject matter of the agency administered. The second disagreement concerned the effects of an administrative corps on the morale and career opportunities of employees in professional, scientific, or clerical positions. Those who favored a tiered system of personnel organization believed that the numbers of sufficiently qualified administrators in the civil service as presently structured was inadequate. They thought it was possible to identify managerial talent early in the career. They saw college graduates as an important source of this talent. Most importantly, they believed that the benefits of an administrative corps would outweigh its negative effect on morale and opportunity for other civil servants. Opponents disagreed. Commentators rarely phrased the issue in quantitative terms, but opinion clearly varied on the ideal ratio of admin-

---

tion make such statements they tend to give more confidence to administrators who have reached somewhat the same conclusions on the basis of their own observations. . . . Until the educational institutions have demonstrated that their methods of recruiting and training students produce a fairly consistently superior product, it is scarcely the part of wisdom for a democratic government to make higher education a prerequisite for classes of positions that do not require the knowledge and the skills that are obtained almost exclusively through such institutions" (Meriam 1938: 337). On the belief that few jobs existed in the U.S. civil service for "generalist" administrators, also see the testimony of Herbert Hoover before the commission (CIPSP 1934: 471).

[19]He was particularly concerned about the possibility that the new scheme might limit administrative opportunities for scientists and professionals (Meriam 1937a: 36–37).

istrators who worked their way through the ranks to administrators who entered government on a special track (cf. Friedrich 1935; Wilmerding 1935; White 1939; Baruch 1941b; Kingsley 1942; Pffifner 1946; Mosher, Kingsley, and Stahl 1950).

The proposals of the CIPSP were never implemented as proposed. Congress in 1938 defeated Roosevelt's reorganization plan, which contained some of the philosophy of the CIPSP report (Karl 1963; Polenberg 1966; Karl 1974).[20] A later Roosevelt commission, established to find the best way to organize middle- and higher-managerial positions in the government,[21] opposed separate administrative job ladders articulated with university education. Roosevelt's Committee on Civil Service Improvement (PCCSI) concluded in 1941 that the existing system of filling positions at these levels through competition among experienced civil servants was "fundamentally sound," though it could "usefully be made somewhat more systematic and widespread." In particular, the committee reported that "we do not recommend the formation of a specially organized administrative corps for which a special type of selection and training is proposed" (PCCSI 1941a: 57). Instead, it argued that vacancies for these positions should be filled by promotion or transfer and opposed the use of an open competitive examination (PCCSI 1941a: 60). The committee did, however, recommend that these positions be put into a separate "occupational group." This recommendation was not adopted immediately, but as we shall see, it did evolve over time.[22]

The creation of large numbers of veterans by the onset of World War II made any linkage of government careers and education even more unpopular. Veterans returning home from World War II viewed the federal government as a major source of opportunity and opposed any attempt by the CSC to expand opportunities for college graduates at their expense. In 1943 the CSC felt compelled to deny "published reports which have no factual foundation" that the CSC had set up standards for government jobs that would discriminate against veterans and

---

[20]All three members of the Roosevelt's Committee on Administrative Management, the author of his reorganization plan, were heavily involved in the work of the Committee of Inquiry on Public Service Personnel. Charles Merriam and Louis Brownlow were members of the committee, and Luther Gulick was the committee's director of research.

[21]Defined as those at Grades CAF-11 or P-4 or higher, which is the same grade range that would have fallen into White's proposed administrative corps.

[22]For a contrast between the "status quo" recommendations of the President's Committee on Civil Service Improvement and the recommendations of the Commission of Inquiry, see Wilmerding's testimony before the former (President's Committee on Civil Service Improvement 1941b).

others "who have not had college or university training" (U.S. CSC 1943).[23] Nonetheless, when Congress passed the Veteran's Preference Act of 1944, it included a stipulation that

> no minimum educational requirements will be prescribed in any civil service exam except for such scientific, technical or professional positions, the duties of which the Civil Service Commission deems cannot be performed by a person who does not have such education. (P.L. 359, 78th Cong. 58 Stat: 387)

The political unpopularity of the "administrative class" idea during the 1940s is also reflected in the failure of the first Hoover commission to recommend the creation of a senior executive service in its report on personnel management.[24]

THE MATURING BUREAUCRATIC LABOR MARKET

The postwar Civil Service Commission eventually succeeded in developing policies to recruit college graduates into administrative as well as professional positions. Its success was a result of the proliferation of middle-management jobs in government, the increased competition from the private sector for college graduates, and the growing acceptance of the view that administration had professional attributes and deserved its own job ladders. It accomplished this goal despite continuing political opposition to an administrative class and despite the opposition of veterans to any expansion in educational requirements for civil service jobs. But things had changed in one important respect.

The debates of the 1930s over the best way to structure administrative careers chiefly concerned a thousand or so positions at the top of the hierarchy. Leonard White assumed that about 40% of the administrative interns brought into the proposed administrative class would make their way to the top of the service in 5 years. But the tremendous expansion of middle-management positions and of collegiate education undercut any possibility that administrative job ladders could funnel most graduates to the top of the service. Entry-level administrative jobs

---

[23]It further reported that of the 1,600,000 placements it made in the federal civil service during the first 8 months of 1943, only 0.26% required college training (U.S. CSC 1943). These placements were not representative of positions in the federal service as a whole. In 1935, the CSC reported that 20% of its positions required special educational requirements (U.S. CSC 1935).

[24]It did, however, propose a list of reforms that were popular with civil service reformers in past decades (Commission on Organization of the Executive Branch of Government 1949; see also Moe 1982).

were no longer routes to the top. Rather, they were starting points for careers that typically would plateau at middle-management levels.[25]

In 1942, the CSC listed only four job ladders in the General Clerical and Administrative Group. One was for building managers, another was for factory managers, and a third was for the administrators of "eleemosynary" government institutions. The CSC grouped all other clerical and administrative staff into the fourth job ladder. Consequently, it located the great majority of administrative jobs on a ladder that covered the entire clerical–administrative grade range. After the war, however, the CSC, in collaboration with the maturing personnel offices of individual agencies, worked to complete the classification task that the now defunct Personnel Classification Board had begun (U.S. CSC 1946, 1948, 1949a).[26] By 1954, the number of job ladders in the general clerical and administrative group (now called the general administrative, clerical, and office services group) had grown from 4 to 57. But still only one of these job ladders (organization and methods examining) was restricted to administrative employees only.[27] Gradually, however, the CSC increasingly separated administrative and clerical employees into separate job ladders. In the process, the total number of job ladders identified by the CSC increased, from 370 in 1941 to 551 in 1957.

By 1957, 3 of the 64 job ladders in the general clerical and administrative group were exclusively administrative and accounted for 24% of journeymen-level administrators at the GS-12 level in this occupational group.[28] The other 76% were in mixed job ladders that included lower-level workers. After reaching a peak in the late 1950s or early 1960s, the number of white-collar job ladders in the federal government began to

[25]The use of the word *administrative*—the same word used for the proposed administrative class—to describe these middle-management jobs indicates a perception that their work was related to top-management activity. Bingham, for example, argued that administration had to do with both policymaking and operation. Middle-management is primarily involved in operations, but even "deputies and assistant administrators far down the line . . . shoulder some part of the policy-forming function" (Bingham 1939: 4).

[26]The Classification Act of 1949 required the agencies to classify their own positions in Grades GS-1 through GS-15 and gave the CSC the power to monitor these classifications and require corrections as it deemed necessary. For views of what position classification consisted of at the time, see Baruch (1941b) or Mosher *et al.* (1950).

[27]Most administrators were in the large catch-all "general administrative, clerical, and office services" job ladder. The Executive Development Agreement for participants in the Executive Development Program that was being planned by the CSC in 1953 listed 14 administrative occupations series in all occupational groups from which program participants might come. These included mixed occupational series that contained clerical employees at their lower levels (U.S. CSC 1953).

[28]GS-12 was chosen because it is unambiguously an administrative grade in the modern system. Calculations are based on tables in U.S. CSC (1957a).

shrink, perhaps in response to criticisms that the position classification system had become overly detailed (U.S. CSC 1959b; Keene 1960).[29] But the number of specifically administrative job ladders in the general clerical and administrative group continued to grow. By 1970, eight exclusively administrative jobs ladders in this group existed, accounting for 58% of GS-12 administrators. The structure of administrative job ladders remained stable in the 1970s. But differential rates of growth in the job ladders involved caused the proportion of GS-12 administrators in exclusively administrative job ladders to increase to 71% by the end of 1978. Further reorganization occurred thereafter, and by the end of 1983, 11 exclusively administrative careers existed in this occupational group. The proportion of GS-12 administrators in the general clerical and administrative group located in these exclusively administrative job ladders at the end of 1983 was 84% (U.S. OPM 1983). The process of differentiation between clerical and administrative job ladders thus was essentially completed during the time between the early 1940s and the present. By 1983, 140 exclusively administrative job ladders existed in all occupational groups in the federal civil service (U.S. OPM 1983).

During these years, agencies increased their efforts to identify administrative talent at the time of recruitment. They increasingly assigned these employees to "administrative trainee" grades, rather than clerical ones. In the 1930s, agencies that recruited college graduates who took the junior civil service examiner examination (the first test specifically designed for liberal arts BAs), placed them mostly in grade CAF-2, that is, "junior clerk." (White 1937a). This was three grades lower than the CAF grade equivalent to entry-level professional or scientific positions. Agencies gave these people no special training or special consideration for career advancement (Mandell 1953; Young 1956; Slesinger 1961).[30] The closest thing to an administrative intern program was conducted privately by the National Institute of Public Administration. By the early 1940s fewer than 300 individuals had finished the NIPA's program (Reining and Stromson 1942).

In the Depression years, it was easy to recruit college graduates into

---

[29]The CSC consolidated many clerical job ladders during this time. Consolidations reduced the total number of job ladders to 452 by 1970 and to 441 by 1983 (U.S. CSC 1941, 1957a, 1970c; U.S. OPM 1983).

[30]The Social Security Board was an exception to this generalization. It started a placement, training, and counseling program for these individuals, though of unknown effectiveness (U.S. CSC 1973c). A few other bureaus, including the army, the navy, the Foreign Service, the Forest Service, the Patent Office, the Bureau of Animal Industry, the Bureau of Public Roads, and the Children's Bureau had career systems at this time (Meriam 1937a).

lower-level clerical jobs. The job market was so bad that job seekers had few options. However, the job opportunities available during the war years and in the 1950s were much better. The federal government had little choice but to recruit graduates into higher grades, and, in the process, to differentiate administrative and clerical job ladders. As agencies raised the entry grade for graduates, they also began using two-grade promotions more frequently as well, from CAF-5 to CAF-7 to CAF-9 (Kammerer 1951). This practice brought the early steps of administrative careers into correspondence with the bottom three positions in the scientific and professional service. The Classification Act of 1949 defined grade GS-5 as the entry-level for college trained manpower. The CSC began recruiting college graduates with a year of graduate training into administrative positions at the GS-7 level. In 1958, Congress allowed the CSC to hire qualified college graduates at the GS-7 level as well.[31] Congress also restructured the top of the grade system, adding two grades in 1949 in order to increase top salaries and make government careers more attractive.

The CSC had introduced other initiatives to recruit college graduates in the late 1930s. In 1939, the CSC developed the Junior Professional Assistant Exam (U.S. CSC 1939). The following year, it subdivided this exam into a number of more specialized exams including the Junior Administrative Technician (JAT) Exam.[32] But World War II disrupted the development of these programs. The combination of reductions-in-force (RIFs) and veterans preference further hampered developments in the immediate postwar period. In 1947, for example, 3,000 passed the JAT, but only 13 were able to secure jobs (Slesinger 1961).

Because of this abysmal performance, the CSC changed the name of its initiative to the Junior Management Assistant (JMA) program. It also changed the content of the exam and made an effort to increase agency interest in the program (U.S. CSC 1953). The CSC did better with the JMA than it had with the JAT, but it still had problems making much headway. The previously mentioned problems, along with the low pass rate of this exam, tough competition, from the private sector, and government paranoia about "security risks" in the civil service chipped

[31]The higher level for starting managerial talent is also evidenced by Youmans's paper (1956) on the use of management internship programs in government. His data show that the average starting grade of those who participated in managerial internships since 1946 but who started working for the government in 1944–46 or before began their careers on average in Grades CAF-3 or CAF-4. Those who began their careers in government since 1950 began on the average in GS-5 or higher.

[32]Though see Olson and Pollock (1945) for other wartime efforts by the CSC to deal with administrative placement.

away at collegiate interest. It gradually became apparent that the JMA program was failing (David 1952; Macy 1954; Emmerich and Belsley 1954; Somers 1954; McClean 1954; Hattery 1955; Friedland 1955; Young 1956; Slesinger 1961; Pear 1968).

The CSC's solution to the recruitment problem was the Federal Service Entrance Examination (FSEE), a broad exam for filling positions in over 100 different job ladders. The FSEE was introduced with a major promotional program directed at the colleges and was immediately more successful than its predecessors (U.S. CSC 1955a; Young 1956; Stockard 1956; Reining 1956). In the first year, 30,375 applied and 17,572 took the exam, the largest number ever (Young 1956). In 1956, agencies hired over 5000 from the FSEE registers (Macy 1963). Between 1955 and 1959, 20,000 young people were brought into the government through these examinations (U.S. CSC 1958, 1959b). Even more were to use this route of entry in the early 1960s, when about 10,000 a year annually entered the government through this exam, a 100% increase over the middle 1950s (U.S. CSC 1963b; Stahl 1963; Macy 1963). Those selected were only a small fraction of applicants; over 1 million had applied to take the FSEE between 1955 and 1963 (Macy 1963; see also Pear 1968).

The CSC apparently hoped that the FSEE would not only regularize entry routes for college graduates into the service but also reduce the promotion rate of lower-level employees. The U.S. Civil Service Commissioner in 1955 stated that all 8,000–10,000 GS-5 vacancies in the coming year were "naturals" to fill from the FSEE. He urged personnel officers to fill as many of these vacancies from the FSEE registers as possible or otherwise "next year's [college] graduates will look elsewhere for career opportunities" (Young 1955). According to one source, the CSC hoped that the new exam would bring in 5000–7000 "college-caliber" recruits a year, as opposed to the 2500 brought in under the then-current system of college-level examinations (*Federal Employee*, August 1955). The program thus was expected to reduce internal promotions as it increased recruitment.[33]

The CSC's announcement of the new examination showed a continuing concern about possible resistance from veterans and federal employees to its recruitment drive. The CSC announced that applicants for the exam must be of "college caliber" rather than college graduates *per se*. The CSC emphasized that it would not deny those with experience

---

[33]Stahl commented in 1963 that "not all of these were of the fresh young college-graduate type, but the selection devices used were a pretty good barrier against mediocrity. Furthermore, the special advantage toward a higher level of entry given for high scholastic achievement has worked well" (Stahl 1963).

"equivalent" to a college education the opportunity to take the test (U.S. CSC 1955c). But it indicated repeatedly that it had to concentrate its recruitment efforts on the colleges, for example

> upon conclusion of a study of the results of efforts to recruit persons graduating each year from colleges and universities throughout the country, the Commission decided in the spring of 1955 to embark on an entirely new approach to this source of high caliber employees. A major objective of this new program is to provide the Federal service with greater numbers of college-caliber people for all types of programs at the entrance level. Such people constitute the primary source of talent which may be developed for future assignments to key positions. (U.S. CSC 1955c: 108)

The named source was the pool of college graduates, but qualified applicants were officially described only as being of "college caliber." Philip Young, the chairman of the Civil Service Commission, argued in a speech he made in 1955 that "40% of our high-school graduates" were also of college caliber. But the CSC apparently gave lower priority to this group. In the 1973 version of its autobiography, the CSC mentioned only college students as targets of its 1950s FSEE recruitment effort (U.S. CSC 1973c). The more visible recruitment efforts directed at high-school students were for filling clerical jobs (Beck 1960). Those interested in civil service careers were urged to take practical courses such as shorthand or stenography (Macy 1963; Harvey 1970).

Furthermore, the CSC downplayed the "career" aspects of clerical work. Discussions of the "career" aspect of the civil service in writings on the subject consistently focused on the problem of filling entry-level (GS-5) positions with "young college graduates" or "college-caliber" employees (U.S. CSC 1954, 1955c, 1956b, 1957c). When the subject of clerical work came up in such a context, it was to lament that college graduates once were forced to enter the civil service through the clerical ranks. The personnel developments of the 1950s were designed to correct this situation (Stockard 1956).[34]

The CSC did not rely solely on the FSEE to recruit management talent. It also started a program of Management Internships, which consisted of more difficult tests, oral interviews, and reference checks. In the first year, 42% of the 17,572 sitting for the FSEE took the management internship part of the exam. In 1963, 23,000 applied for the management intern program, 2500 passed, 700 reached the "eligible" regis-

---

[34]As late as 1949, the CSC wrote that "even for persons with a college or university education, stenography and typing skills often provide the best means of entering the federal service" (U.S. CSC 1949b: 55). Compare White's comments on the subject quoted earlier (Lambie 1932).

ter, and 300 were ultimately appointed (Pear 1968).[35] Meanwhile, in the universities, training programs for careers in public administration continued to multiply (Sweeney et al. 1958). These developments corresponded to increased recruitment efforts in private corporations and to continued academic efforts to perfect a "science of managing" (Noyes 1945; Knowlton 1948; Smiddy and Naum 1954; Litchfield 1956; Redlich 1957; Simon 1945/1957; Pollard 1965; Chandler 1977; Sass 1982).

Despite these developments, the professionalization of administration never attained the level of professionalization of engineering, accounting or other "public service organizational professions" (Larson 1977: 186). Consequently, the boundaries between administration and clerical–technical work were not as rigidly structured around particular educational credentials. Nonetheless, the trend was to rely more heavily on educational credentials for recruitment of managers and executives, both in the federal government and in the private sector (Granick, 1972). The splitting of clerical and administrative job ladders was at least the partial attainment of a goal sought after by personnel experts such as Mosher, Kingsley, and Stahl, the authors of the major textbook on public personnel administration at the time. They wrote in 1950 that it was important to maintain a

> clear distinction between clerical jobs, requiring certain manipulative skills and attitudes, and executive jobs, requiring superior training, imagination and ability, so that the latter are not automatically filled from the ranks of the former but are filled by men with the education, the capacity to deal in generalizations as well as with "things," and the gifts to lead and advance that ought to be required of all executives. (Mosher, Kingsley, and Stahl 1950: 161)[36]

Other writers hoped that the new college recruitment efforts would assist in the making of these clear distinctions. As Stockard argued, "a strict promotion-from-within" philosophy results in "persons of average ability" being "pushed along" past their capacities. Instead, the FSEE would expand the "trickle" of college caliber employees into government and "contribute to the common goal of maximum economy and efficiency in government operations" (Stockard 1956: 7,10).[37]

---

[35]The high ratio of applicants to openings was common in the 1970s also. See Shafritz et al. 1981.

[36]The writers went on to argue that more promotion from within is needed in the federal government, but their concern here was more with administrative careers than with passage across the clerical–administrative boundary.

[37]But when Stahl issued a revised version of his textbook on public personnel administration in 1962, he kept the complaint of earlier editions that the trend toward "a more satisfactory relationship between formal education and the requirements of the service"

During the 1950s, the CSC also elaborated scientific and professional job ladders. The Classification Act of 1949 collapsed the professional and subprofessional services into the general schedule, which in the minds of some tended to reduce the corporate identities of these two groups. But, at the job-ladder level, differentiation continued. The CSC increasingly systematized the separation by setting up parallel professional and subprofessional ("technical") series and extending the grade ceilings of the latter upward. This move was supposed to provide more opportunity for employees and "decrease(s) the tendency to shift talented technicians into professional jobs so they can be promoted, . . . [thereby] rupturing the dimensions of the type of job originally decided upon by jamming those without requisite qualifications into it" (Keene 1960: 24; see also U.S. CSC 1936b).

Thus, in both the professional and administrative realms, the evolving job ladders gradually created an upper and a lower tier of white-collar work. These developments in part reflected an evolution in the composition of government jobs. But the intellectual descendants of the Progressives would have viewed these developments as signs that personnel policies finally reflected the real distinction between lower-level and upper-level work. Supporters of a tiered personnel system would approve the developments to the extent that they kept all but the "exceptional" lower-level workers out of professional and administrative jobs and increased the proportion of these jobs filled by college graduates.

Meanwhile, those who desired a senior civil service had not given up on the issue. Although Democrats pushed for an administrative class in the 1930s, the Republican-organized second Hoover Commission did so in the 1950s (MacNeil and Metz 1956; Moe 1982). As envisioned by the Hoover Commission, the Senior Civil Service would ultimately encompass 3000 or more of the top positions in the government, including "administrative assistant secretaries and equivalent posts, bureau chiefs, assistant bureau chiefs, some division chiefs, heads of regional or district offices, heads of budget, personnel and other organic staff offices; deputy heads of policy staff offices and professional aides and assistants to important political executives" (Commission on Organization of the Executive Branch of Government 1955: 51–52).

The new version of the senior civil service differed in certain re-

---

was still "a far cry from the closely correlated system in England, for example, where the public service, in the 1912 description by the Royal Commission on the Civil Service, gathers 'the natural fruits of the educational system of the country in its various stages as they mature'" (Stahl 1962: 57).

spects from the earlier proposals. The Commission of Inquiry had proposed that recruits for administrative positions come from the ranks of college graduates. Leonard White would have established two tracks for recruitment: one for existing civil servants and the other for college graduates under the age of 30. By 1955, however, college graduates were not the elite group they had been in the 1930s. Furthermore, skepticism about the ability of operating officials to test for administrative talent with exams remained strong. Instead, the second Hoover Commission proposed to delay the selection process for senior civil servants for several years. Under its proposals, the government would only consider civil servants in GS-15 or higher who had more than 5 years of tenure as candidates for the Senior Civil Service.

Once again, partisans debated the idea. Again, proponents argued that the establishment of a senior civil service would improve talent at the top and would insulate the top civil service from politics, allowing it to function as a technical elite. Finally, they argued that by giving a "servicewide" orientation to top civil servants, it would increase their ability to rotate from one agency to another and thus increase their general administrative competence (White 1956; Paget 1957; Kestnbaum 1957). The justification for the idea was based in part upon the old dichotomy suggested by Goodnow between politics and administration and the idea that administration can best do its job when it remains "neutral" and unpoliticized.

This idea, however, which reached its fullest development in the reports of the Committee on Administrative Management (President's Committee on Administrative Management 1937; see also Gulick and Urwick 1937), was under attack by the middle 1950s (Kaufman 1956; Sayre 1958). A number of authors had argued that administrators must as a matter of course be involved in policymaking (Marx 1957; Appleby 1952), that administration was not a science with "universal principles" (Waldo 1948; Simon 1945/1957), and that bureaucracy was itself a form of political power (Selznick 1957). Thus some academics opposed the creation of such an administrative corps on the grounds that it overstressed neutrality and that it did not materially increase the prospects for recruiting better talent to top positions (Reimer 1956; Owen 1958). Civil servants also opposed the plan (Kaufman 1965; Pear 1968), as they typically opposed efforts to increase the educational requirements for civil service jobs (Carpenter 1952). Some congressmen objected to the "elitist" implications of a senior civil service and questioned the idea of neutrality at the top of the bureaucracy (Reimer 1956; Owen 1958; Pear 1968). Eisenhower supported the Hoover Commission recommendations, but Congress defeated his attempt to implement them (Pear 1968).

The proposal lay dormant until Carter successfully established the Senior Executive Service along similar lines in 1978 (Moe 1982).

The defeat of the Hoover Commission proposals illustrate the difference between the tiered personnel system desired in the 1930s and the tiered personnel system that developed in the postwar years. The upper tier implied by the FSEE and the evolving administrative job ladders encompassed much more than the elite positions of government. It combined the clerical–executive service envisioned by the CIPSP with its proposed administrative service.

The emerging administrative upper tier was not defined by absolute barriers to entry from below (see, e.g., U.S. CSC 1956c). Such barriers would have been difficult to enforce, for several reasons. First, there were no formal educational requirements for administrative positions. Second, the actual promotion decisions were made by thousands of managers who, no doubt, had differing views on the desirability of promoting clerical employees.[38] Finally, some claimed that inadequate government pay led to continued shortages of administrative manpower despite the numbers taking the FSEE exam (U.S. Congress. Senate 1957; Sweeney et al. 1958).

POSTWAR PROMOTION AND TRAINING POLICIES

The CSC developed additional tools besides entrance examinations and position classification for regulating the promotion process in years following the New Deal. At the end of the 1930s, the CSC attempted to institute a set of competitive promotional examinations. The agencies were to be given latitude to establish their own promotion lines and job requirements, though the CSC would retain the power of final review (Ordway 1938; CSC 1940). However, agencies resisted the idea of formalizing the promotion process to this extent, and Congress refused to authorize funds (Van Riper 1958). Wartime disruptions prevented the CSC from developing other initiatives until the late 1940s (Kammerer 1951; U.S. CSC 1957b).

After the war, the approach of the CSC to the subject of promotions shifted. In the past, the CSC had direct control over agency promotion and could review agency recommendations before the promotion decision. But this control in practice amounted to nothing; agency decision were virtually never challenged (Meriam 1938). After the war, the CSC,

[38]Many of these administrators themselves had started as clerks (Warner et al. 1963; see also U.S. CSC 1956a).

apparently recognizing the impossibility of controlling promotion decisions directly, relinquished this authority to the agencies. Instead it attempted to increase its control over promotion procedures. The 1950 Federal Employees Promotion Policy, established at the urging of the first Hoover Commission, required each agency to establish a promotion program, but the guidelines were very general (U.S. CSC 1950).[39] The guidelines required only that promoted employees meet the minimum qualifications established by the CSC for the new position (U.S. CSC 1957b, 1959c; Curran 1961). The CSC urged agencies to consider filling entry-level administrative and professional jobs through internal promotions from lower levels as well as from external sources, but it exercised little positive control over their decision. In its suggested worksheet for determining the number of career recruits needed, it instructed each agency to "decide" the percentage of entrance-level vacancies to be filled internally and from this and other figures determine its recruiting needs (U.S. CSC 1956c). Each agency could determine its own percentage.

During the 1950s, dissatisfaction with the way that promotions were being handled in the federal government grew both in the ranks of federal employees and in the Congress. The CSC was concerned about promotions, too. Its own study showed that, too often, supervisors considered only one person when deciding to fill a slot. This pattern suggested that they were not giving due consideration to all employees qualified for the job.[40] Employee unions were dissatisfied because they perceived many instances of "personal patronage" in promotion decisions in the middle 1950s, in which promotions were going to friends of the appointing officer (Curran 1961; Harvey 1970; see also U.S. CSC 1959c). Also employees feared that the Eisenhower administration was politicizing personnel policy.[41] In response to the growing pressure for reform and to head off the restrictive legislation introduced into the

---

[39]The standards were "(1) Consult employees on appropriate aspects of the program; (2) State the policy in writing and make it available to all employees; (3) Provide for broad areas of selection and consider individuals outside the organization to assure selection of the best qualified; (4) Assist employees to develop themselves for promotion; (5) Use realistic qualifications requirements; (6) Apply the same standards for selection systematically and equitably to all interested employees who meet the minimum standards; and (7) Provide for release in all cases of employees selected for promotion" (U.S. CSC 1950b).

[40]The study showed that this occurred in 50% of the promotion decisions (U.S. CSC 1956a,b; Curran 1961).

[41]See the remarks of Senator Johnston in the Congressional Record (Congressional Record 1957: 4748).

Senate by Senator Johnston, the CSC inaugurated the Merit Promotion Policy of 1958 (Harvey 1970).[42]

The 1958 Merit Promotion Policy tightened the procedural constraints on agency promotion policies. Under the 1950 rules, agencies were required to promote only those who met the minimum qualifications for the new position. But 1958 rules further required agencies to promote from the group of "best-qualified" candidates. The rules directed agencies to keep records of promotion actions, which were subject to review by the commission, and to follow the guidelines described in the new rules.[43] Although these rules restricted to some extent the discretion of agency officials, they did not materially affect the right of the official to decide whether to fill a position through promotion or through recruitment (*Federal Employee* 1958: 15). Indeed, the CSC intended these rules to provide more discretion than would the alternative plan contained in the Johnston bill (Harvey 1970).[44] Nonetheless some agency administrators still viewed such policy initiatives as hampering managerial decision making (Shafritz 1973; Rosenbloom 1977; see also U.S. CSC 1968c; President's Reorganization Project 1977).

The organization of formal training in the government, which began during the Taft administration in the Patent Office, the Forest Service, and the Bureau of Standards (U.S. CSC 1973c), also evolved significantly during the 1950s. The CSC had taken control over the management internship programs run by the National Institute of Public Affairs at the end of the war and continued to administer them throughout the 1950s. However, they reached only a small proportion of the white-collar workers, and by the middle 1950s, they were largely recruiting from those entering government at the GS-5 level. Civil service personnel officers, academics, and some administrators had believed for years that training was a key aspect of the development of manpower and the creation of a career civil service (Mayers 1922; Feldman 1931; CIPSP 1935; Friedrich 1935; Frederic 1935; Lambie 1935; Brooks 1938; Civil Service

---

[42]Union involvement was such that an attorney for the NFFE wrote the bill introduced by Johnston (Curran 1961).

[43]The guidelines required that (1) areas of consideration be as broad as possible, (2) qualification standards be at least equal to competitive standards, (3) evaluation methods be reasonable, valid, and applied fairly, (4) selection be made from among the best qualified, (5) those selected be promptly released from their former positions, (6) agencies consult employees in the development and implementation of plans, (7) agencies make information about the plans readily available to employees (U.S. CSC 1958: 47–48; 1959c; see also Nigro and Nigro 1976).

[44]Most agency plans in fact used very general language that tended to mirror the CSC directives (U.S. CSC 1964b).

Assembly 1941; Felser 1947; Mosher *et al.* 1950). However, legislators in Congress had traditionally been more concerned with the costs of training than with its possible benefits (Harvey 1970; Macy 1971). Congressional skeptics of training programs argued that employees should get their own training because they were the ones who got the career benefit (David 1952; *Federal Employee* 1956). As time passed, however, new Congressmen themselves were better educated and more likely to be sympathetic of the need for training. Wartime experiences with training contributed to the shift in Congressional sentiment on the subject (Meriam 1937b; Kammerer 1951; DePhillips *et al.* 1960; Van Riper 1958).[45]

Gradually, the view that government-specific training was necessary in a professional civil service prevailed. Eisenhower expressed support for the idea (Macy 1956), and Congress enacted the Government Employees Training Act in 1959. The new law provided for funds for out-of-service training for employees, whenever agency administrators determined that such training was in the interest of the agency. In the interests of efficiency, it directed that the government not provide training for employees to fill a job whenever available candidates already had the requisite skills. The budget for training government employees steadily increased during the 1960s and 1970s, until more than 1/3 of government employees were involved in a formal training program in any given year (U.S. CSC 1973c).[46]

THE MATURE BUREAUCRATIC LABOR MARKET

By the 1960s and 1970s, personnel systems of the federal government had reached a point of comparative maturity. Personnel efforts had moved steadily away from the prewar emphasis on police functions toward a positive management function (Mosher 1968, 1971). Echoing the 1930s, supporters of "rank-in-the-man" European-style civil service systems and writers criticized position classification systems and bureaucratic procedures as a "restraining leash" on what should be a "fluid and adaptive" organization (Mosher 1971: 58; see also Fisher 1945; Shafritz 1973; Nigro and Nigro 1976; President's Reorganization Project 1977).[47] The trend toward positive personnel management was a prin-

[45]On the effects World War II had on personnel developments in general, see Baron *et al.* 1986.
[46]See Nigro and Nigro (1976) for further details about government training programs. For a critical view of the way the programs have been organized, see Wynia (1972) and Shafritz *et al.* (1981).
[47]For a defense of American-style position classification, see Stahl (1968).

cipal force propelling passage of the Reform Act of 1978. This law created a new Office of Personnel Management in 1978 to deal with personnel management and relegated the "negative" policing functions to a
separate agency, the Merit Systems Protection Board (Campbell 1978).

However, despite the criticisms of position classification, it remained an important personnel tool in government, as in business. By
the 1960s and 1970s, personnel offices had organized the white-collar
work force into distinct job ladders. These job ladders were divided up
into a set of occupational groups. They were further divided into two
overlapping tiers, with clerical and technical jobs on the lower tier and
administrative and professionals jobs on the upper one. In the classification system of the CSC, "professional" jobs involved work based on "a
field of science or learning characteristically acquired through education
or training pertinent to the specialized field." "Administrative" jobs, on
the other hand, involved "the application of substantial body of knowledge of principles, concepts, and practices applicable to one or more
fields of administration or management" (U.S. CSC 1976a: 4). The bottom grades were typically reserved for clerical jobs. Middle grades were
reserved for higher clerical and technical jobs and for trainee-level jobs
in administrative and professional job ladders (see Table 6.1).

The boundary between clerical and administrative jobs was not created through legislation mandating a European-style service. Instead, it
grew from the gradual professionalization of administration, the large-
scale expansion of the university system, and the pragmatic need for
recruitment strategies to lure college graduates into the civil service. The
routine development of position-classification guidelines by the CSC
and their application by the agencies institutionalized the boundary in
government. This process grouped jobs onto job ladders with unequal
job ceilings, and labeled these ladders as professional, administrative,
technical, or clerical, in agreement with common usage. A government
task force in the 1970s urged an even more formal separation of the
lower and upper tier, though the proposal was not adopted.[48]

The job ladders of the administrative tier did not correspond to the
1930s vision of an administrative class. The administrative and professional tiers now included jobs that were well below the levels of respon-

[48]The Job Evaluation and Pay Review Task Force of the CSC recommended in 1972 that the
government establish broad horizontal strata to separate professional and administrative
from lower-level workers. Members of the AFL-CIO advisory council expressed objections on the grounds that "separate systems for professionals would serve to segregate
subprofessionals—many of whom have higher qualifications or technical competence
than full professionals—from the professional ranks to which they could not aspire"
(U.S. CSC 1972: 130).

Table 6.1
Definition of PATCO Categories

Professsional occupations are those that require knowledge in a field of science or learning characteristically acquired through education or training equivalent to a bachelor's or higher degree with major study in or pertinent to the specialized field, as distinguished from general education. The work of a professional occupation requires the exercise of discretion, judgment, and personal responsibility for the application of an organized body of knowledge that is constantly studied to make new discoveries and interpretations and to improve the data, materials, and methods. These occupations follow a two-grade interval pattern.

Administrative occupations are those that involve the exercise of analytical ability, judgment, discretion, personal responsibility, and the application of a substantial body of knowledge of prinicples, concepts, and practices applicable to one or more fields of administration or management. Although these positions do not require specialized educational majors, they do involve the type of skills (analytical, research, writing, judgment) typically gained through a college-level general education or through progressively responsible experience. Occupations in this group typically follow a two-grade interval pattern.

Technical occupations are those that involve work typically associated with, and supportive of, a professional or administrative field, which is nonroutine in nature; such occupations involve extensive practical knowledge, gained through on-the-job experience and/or specific training less than that represented by college graduation. Work in these occupations may involve substantial elements of the work of the professional or administrative field but requires less than full competence in the field involved. Occupational series in this group typically follow a one-grade interval pattern.

Clerical occupations are those that involve structured work in support of office, business, or fiscal operations; duties are performed in accordance with established policies, experience, or working knowledge related to the tasks to be performed.

Other occupations are those that cannot be related to the previously mentioned professional, administrative, technical, or clerical groups.

sibility and power envisioned for jobs in the administrative class. This can be seen by a brief consideration of the proposed lower boundary for the administrative class. The 1935 proposal of the Commission of Inquiry on Public Service Personnel would have placed this boundary at Grade 11, exclusive of trainee grades, which was where the lowest high-level administrative positions were then located. The 1955 proposals of the Hoover Commission placed it at Grade 15. The Senior Executive Service started in 1978 is located predominantly in the "supergrades" of GS-16 through GS-18.[49] In real terms, the clerical–administrative and the subprofessional–professional boundaries moved lower down the hierarchy over the years.

[49]Technically, these employees are not considered part of the general schedule (U.S. OPM 1983).

Agencies have filled entry jobs on administrative job ladders through an examination system that the government has continually refined in the face of technical developments and especially discrimination suits.[50] Educational requirements to sit for upper-tier examinations generally existed, but they were looser for administrative job ladders than for professional ones. The government provided in-service training so that employees could do their present jobs better or qualify for higher-graded jobs. A set of formalized procedures governed the promotion process. Although the job ladder continued to be the "most natural line of promotion," the CSC and later OPM encouraged agencies to widen their search for talent whenever practical. Job ladders were guides for managerial decision making, but they did not control these decisions.

GENDER AND RACIAL INEQUALITY AND THE STRUCTURE OF JOB LADDERS

It has been argued in the past (cf. Carpenter 1952) that a principal force preventing a closer articulation of education and career is opposition from civil service employees themselves, who wished to gain promotions even if they are not educationally qualified for the new job. In the federal civil service, the opposition of employees and veterans did not prevent the construction of a two-tier job ladder structure, though this opposition arguably reduced the extent to which education came to serve as a formal barrier between the sectors. Those sharing Carpenter's view would see the formalization that has occurred as progress and might argue that further professionalization would represent still more progress toward a universalistic, technically efficient, bureaucratic labor market. But this view is distorted in at least one important respect. The "discovery" of substantial racial and gender inequality in organizational labor markets has represented the most serious challenge to the proposition that a tiered personnel system was a technically rational way of organizing careers.

Although the civil service system of the federal government has in certain formal respects been a "merit" system since the 1880s, merit has not translated into equality for women and minorities during its first 100 years. From their first entry into white-collar office jobs as "female clerks" around 1850, women disproportionately occupied the inferior ranks of government as they did in the labor force at large.[51] But al-

[50]Thus, the FSEE exam was replaced by the PACE exam, which itself was then replaced (see, e.g., Downing 1981; Shafritz et al. 1981; Hays and Kearney 1982).
[51]Their first employment in the government was in postal positions, which began before

though they found it difficult to obtain the better jobs, they gradually filled the bulk of the clerical jobs, and their overall share of white-collar jobs increased over time (Saint 1931; Fair Employment Practice Committee 1945).[52] In 1903, women held 7.5% of civil service positions (Van Riper 1958). By 1954, their representation in white-collar jobs had reached 34% (not counting the postal service). It reached 41% by 1969, 42% by 1976, and 46% by 1983.

Figure 6.1 shows the relative distribution of women and men in the lowest civil service grades during the last 30 years.[53] In 1954, when 62% of all white-collar jobs were located in Grades 1–6, 90% of all female employees were working at this level, as compared with only 42% of male employees. Between 1954 and 1983, the proportion of jobs located in the bottom six grades dropped from 62% to 36%, and the proportion of all women located there also dropped, dipping to 59% by 1983. But the proportion of men in these lowest grades was dropping, too; by 1983 only 17% of all male employees were in the lowest six white-collar grades of the civil service.

Figure 6.2 shows another view of the disparity between the positions of women and men in the civil service. It shows the percentage of employees in Grades 1–6 who were women and the percentage in Grades 11 and higher who were women, along with the percentage of women in the white-collar service in each of these years. Figure 6.2 makes clear that, whereas women have made some gains relative to men, especially during the years between 1970 and 1983, they were still predominantly working in the lower grades. In 1954, women held 64% of lower-level (GS 1-6) white-collar positions in the federal government but only 4% of positions at grades GS-11 and higher. During the years between 1954 and 1983, the proportion of men in these positions continued to drop, so that by 1983, 75% of these lower-level positions were held by women. Women did, however, make noticeable strides in gaining higher-level positions. Their representation in positions at GS-11 or higher increased from 4% to 1954 to 7% in 1970 and to 19% by 1983.[54] In

---

1800. They also gained blue-collar jobs at the Philadelphia mint, the Bureau of Engraving and Printing, and the Government Printing Office at a relatively early date (McMillin 1941).

[52]The proportion of women did not grow monotonically, however. There were temporary fallbacks after the world wars and during the depression of the 1930s.

[53]The figure excludes employees in the postal service (U.S. CSC 1954, 1961, 1970c; U.S. OPM 1983).

[54]Statistics for 1983 include the Senior Executive Service, which came into existence in 1978. Statistics for all periods exclude the postal service. If attention is limited to the supergrades, including the Senior Executive Service, the statistics show that women improved their representation at the highest levels as well. They held 1% of these

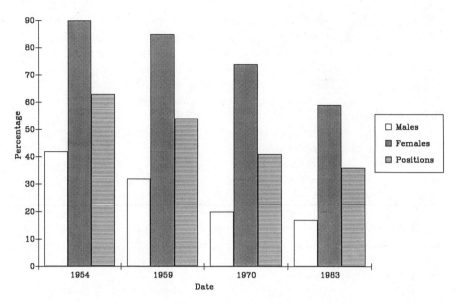

Figure 6.1. Percentage of women, men, and total positions in Grades 1–6, by date.

short, women were able to improve their representation in managerial and professional positions in the government, as they have in the labor market as a whole (England and Farkas 1986; Bergmann 1986). But the feminization of clerical positions intensified during this period, and the disparity between the positions of women and men, although it diminished somewhat in the 1970s, remained strong.

Along with women, blacks have also traditionally been relegated to the lower positions of government. They were prohibited from federal employment until 1865 (Rosenbloom 1971). When they began entering the civil service, they were disproportionately located in the blue-collar jobs in government; in 1938, 90% of blacks were in the craft and custodial service of the federal government (Hayes 1941; Fair Employment Practices Committee 1945). Like women, blacks as a group were able to increase their share of government jobs and particularly of government white-collar jobs during World War II. By 1944, 36% of blacks were in one of the three white-collar services, a big change from 1938 (Kammerer 1951). Despite the temporary fallback in their position after the war ended, they accounted for 15% of all workers by 1967 (U.S.

positions in 1970 and 6% in 1983, though they are far from achieving equality at that level.

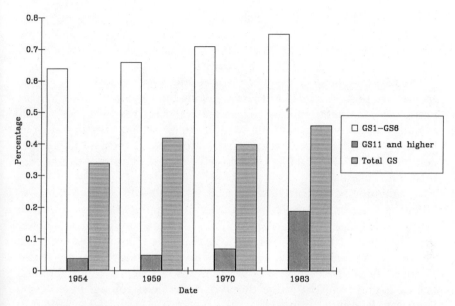

Figure 6.2 Percentage of employees at low and high grades who were women.

Commission on Civil Rights 1970: 68) and 11% of all general schedule white-collar workers. However, blacks, like women, were still heavily concentrated in the lower grades, accounting for 20% of all federal employees in GS 1-6 in 1970 (U.S. CSC 1971).

The Ramspeak Act of 1940 made discrimination against blacks in federal employment illegal. The CSC prohibited federal agencies from discriminating against women in hiring in 1962, a prohibition reinforced by Executive Order 11375 in 1967 (U.S. CSC 1967; U.S. 1968d). But an official nondiscrimination policy would not by itself change the traditional imbalance in the positions of white men, women, and minorities. At the same time, the developing tiered personnel structure imposed an administrative barrier to their advancement. The tiered structure made it easier for management to recruit young university graduates to fill entry-level administrative and professional positions, instead of looking in the ranks for suitable talent.

Collins has argued that the clerical–administrative boundary is "noncontroversial" because it is based not so much on educational requirements but rather "quite blatantly on the ascriptive quality of sex" (Collins 1979). The analysis presented here suggests that his argument is an oversimplification of events. Even before the present structure of tiers developed, women held subordinate clerical jobs, and agencies kept blacks out of the white-collar sector altogether. Furthermore, the tiered structure of white-collar jobs ladders began to emerge well before these groups made concerted efforts to improve their labor market status. The clerical–administrative distinction is largely based on educational requirements, in the sense that educational expansion and the spread of a professional culture have justified its development. Changes in the labor market for young college graduates further fueled its institutionalization. Nonetheless, in a world where formal structures such as job ladders do not necessarily constrain behavior, the possibility that gender and racial inequality contributed to the solidarity of this barrier must be considered.

Personnel specialists have formalized white-collar jobs ladders in large- and medium-sized organizations throughout the economy. But despite this formalization, white-collar careers are not completely determined by these structures. For, although job ladders imply the existence of both quantitative and qualitative differences among jobs, these differences do not necessarily amount to much in practical terms. In practice, a manager might judge the skill differences among a set of job ladders to be unimportant and often transfer workers from one ladder to another. His or her decision to fill vacancies by promotion within the ladder, by transfer from a different ladder, or by recruitment would depend upon the managers's perception of the needs and the available talent. The regulations would of course limit discretion when highly specific educational prerequisites were involved. They would also require that certain formal procedures be followed in reaching a decision. But in the end, managerial discretion plays an important role in determining how strictly job ladder boundaries are observed.

Similar issues pertain to the level of permeability between the lower tier and the upper tier, particularly on the administrative side of the occupational distribution. So long as personnel rules did not make specific educational preparation a formal requirement for administrative jobs, promotion from the lower-tier was a viable option. The amount of promotion would depend in large part upon the use operating officials made of their discretionary authority. Qualitative differences between the skill requirements for administrative jobs and the skills possessed by lower-level workers would matter also. But, as we saw earlier in this book, these qualitative distinctions were fuzzier in practice than the language of job classifications would suggest.

A gap existed between the ideologically clarity of tier distinctions and the difficulties of finding this clarity in day-to-day practice. Because of this gap, the disproportionate presence of women and minorities is an important factor in the development of tier boundaries. At the boundaries between tiers, it is difficult to distinguish the work of the lower-tier worker and the upper-tier trainee. In other words, the principle of rank in the job, which dictates that rank and status be a function of job duties, tends to break down near these boundaries.

At these points, the major distinction must often by the "mobility potential" of the worker. The widespread perception that women did not make good managers (Macy 1971; Wallace 1976) would lead managers to view them as less promotable. The association of many types of clerical work with "women's work" might have reinforced managerial perception that a woman's clerical experience was not good preparation for promotion. We can hypothesize that this implicit rank-in-the-man/woman system, which necessarily operates where tier boundaries overlap, would lead to a greater *de facto* separation between the lower and the upper tier. The higher concentration of nonwhite workers in the lower tier might further reinforce this separation, for similar reasons.

In short, the forces of racial and sexual discrimination did not create the tiers. Nonetheless, the disproportionate presence of women and minorities in lower white-collar jobs arguably reinforced tendencies supporting professionalization and increased the perception that clerical work and administrative or managerial work were qualitatively distinct. In a world in which only white men worked at office jobs, the clerical–administrative distinction would still have developed, but the boundary might have been weaker. Instead, the racial and sexual imbalance probably increased its empirical importance.

Ultimately, the effects of job-ladder structure on employee mobility must be addressed through the statistical analysis of personnel data. The following chapters do this and, in the process, address four questions about the connection between structure and outcomes. The first question concerns the extent to which job mobility is confined to narrowly drawn job ladders. This is the subject of the next chapter. The second question asks how high is the barrier between the lower and the upper tier in the federal government. The third question addresses the impact of equal employment opportunity programs on this barrier. Questions 2 and 3 are the subject of Chapter 8. Finally, Chapter 9 raises the question of the overall impact of job ladder structure on advancement rates up the civil service hierarchy for women and minorities.

III
JOB LADDERS AND CAREER OUTCOMES

How Constraining Are White-Collar Job Ladders?

Horizontal and Vertical Mobility in the Federal Government

INTRODUCTION

Job ladders are an administrative tool for efficiently filling vacancies, for compensating incumbents in a rational way, and for attracting high-quality recruits by the promise of career advancement. But the relationship between job ladders and actual job mobility is somewhat problematic. Forces tending to constrain mobility within these ladders are countered by other forces that tend to weaken their effect. The uncertain relationship between job ladders and job mobility was recognized by the Congressional Joint Commission, which observed that the promotion lines it identified were only the "principal" ones. Telford wrote in 1925 that "a number of serious difficulties are encountered in indicating lines of promotion, and this part of classification has not been highly developed" (Telford 1925: 45; see also Baruch 1941b). The connection between job ladders and mobility is still ambiguous. Thus, although the U.S.

This chapter is an expanded version of a paper that was published in *Administrative Science Quarterly* (1987, 32:422–444) under the title "Horizontal and Vertical Mobility in Organizations."

Office of Personnel Management (OPM) describes the several hundred occupational series of the white-collar work force as "steps in the most natural line of promotion" (U.S. OPM 1981), the federal personnel manual urges managers to reach out beyond the narrow base of consideration defined by organization and job ladder. Operating officials, of course, have a certain amount of discretion in this matter, so long as the procedures they follow are consistent with federal guidelines. Before examining the implications of the bureaucratic labor market for gender and racial inequality, therefore, it is important to better understand the role of job ladders in shaping personnel decisions.

The formal job ladders defined by the position classification system imply a career trajectory starting at the bottom of a ladder and moving up its rungs. These implied career trajectories can be distinguished from the career trajectories that an organization's employees actually experience. Ideal-typical conceptions of internal labor markets may posit as an essential property of a true internal labor market (ILM) a congruence between implied and realized trajectories or equivalently between formal structure and behavioral structure (Althauser and Kalleberg 1981). But the implied and realized trajectories will typically not be completely congruent even in highly bureaucratized organizations. If we take the connection between implied and realized trajectories as problematic, two questions arise: first, to what extent is actual mobility consistent with job ladders, and second, does any divergence between implied and realized trajectories follow a recognizable pattern.

This chapter explores how the organizational and occupational structure of the federal bureaucracy constrains job mobility. Observers have described the civil service as a career service since the passage of the Civil Service Reform Act in 1883. However, most of the emphasis on career development in the civil service has focused on the upper grades, where administrative and professional job ladders are located.[1] Thus, this chapter first focuses attention on the way that vacancies are filled in Grades 12 and higher, a range numerically dominated by administrative and professional jobs. It then broadens its focus to all the grades of the civil service hierarchy.

---

[1]Macy, the former head of the U.S. Civil Service Commission, wrote in his book that the work experiences of clerical workers in the government could only "euphemistically" be called careers because of the lack of a career orientation and the relatively high turnover (Macy 1971).

THE RELATIONSHIP BETWEEN IMPLIED AND REALIZED CAREER TRAJECTORIES

Jobs in bureaucratized organizations are, at least in a formal sense, products of the organization's position classification system, which describes the tasks to be performed in each job. The position classification system describes the skill requirements for different positions and provides guidelines for assigning jobs a rank or grade based on their level of difficulty, responsibility, and requirements. The job's rank is a major determinant of the pay of the employee holding that job. Finally, the position classification system typically groups jobs onto job ladders, which contain jobs in the same line of work but with differing levels of skill and responsibility. These job ladders define natural lines of promotion. In an ideal-typical ILM, workers would be hired into the bottom level of a job ladder and work their way up the ladder while they gained more skill through on-the-job training and experience. Job ladders differ in their extent and shape. Some job ladders end at relatively low grades, whereas others reach the top of the organization. On one ladder, jobs may be distributed so as to allow easy movement from Level 2 to Level 3. On another, the number of positions at Level 2 may be so much greater than at Level 3 that advancement is difficult (cf. Stewman and Konda 1983). Job ladders thus structure an employee's mobility chances.

Job ladders have organizational as well as occupational boundaries. These organizational boundaries are of two types. Organizations have legally defined boundaries that separate them from their environments. Medium-sized and large organizations are typically divided into a number of divisions as well. Although these intra- and interorganizational boundaries are not primarily instruments of personnel policy, they have clear implications for mobility. The boundary between an organization and its external environment has received much attention in the literature on ILMs (Althauser and Kalleberg 1981). But intraorganizational boundaries (which shall be referred to generically as divisional boundaries) can also play an important role. In some cases, divisional boundaries are explicitly taken into account in personnel rules. In certain blue-collar jobs in unionized firms, for instance, divisional boundaries (e.g., plant boundaries) are in the formulas used to determine seniority, which affects promotions or transfers (Roos and Reskin 1984; Abraham and Medoff 1985). Even when such boundaries play no formal role, they still may channel job mobility.

Along with the grade structure, occupational and divisional boundaries carve up an organization's work force into groups of workers who are more or less eligible to fill any particular vacancy. Differential eligibility arises partly because of differences in the skill requirements of job ladders and partly because of the absence of perfect information in an organization, which makes some workers better known than others to the official filling the vacancy. But skill differences between job ladders are not necessarily so large that they cause officials to disqualify those outside the job-ladder from consideration. Similarly, information deficiencies are not necessarily so great that they preclude consideration of divisional outsiders.

The permeability of occupational and organizational boundaries depends on a set of contingencies (cf. Doeringer and Piore 1971; Williamson 1975; Pfeffer and Cohen 1984). These contingencies can be classified as one of four types: (a) skills-based contingencies, (b) information-based contingencies, (c) contingencies due to the particular configuration of positions in an organization, and (d) contingencies arising from the institutionalization of formal structure. Some of these contingencies tend to increase the level of congruence between implied and realized career trajectories. Others tend to create divergence between formal and behavioral structure but do so in systematic ways that will be elaborated next.

Contingencies That Create Congruence between Implied and Realized Career Trajectories

1. Task Idiosyncrasy

The existence of task idiosyncrasy was one of the principal reasons why large companies organized jobs into ILMs, according to some scholars (Doeringer and Piore 1971; Williamson 1975). These scholars have argued that job ladders provide an orderly sequence of training experiences, as well as incentives that reduce employee turnover. Job ladders ostensibly allow an organization to obtain a well-trained work force at a minimum cost. Although most accounts of the subject stress the extent to which technology varies from one organization to another, it is important to recognize that technology frequently also differs in the various divisions and levels of a single organization as well (Scott 1981). Thus, the task idiosyncrasies that a worker learns by experience may apply more to work in his own division than elsewhere in the organization, where similar functions may be carried out with different procedures.

2. The Effects of Imperfect Information within Organizations

Some conceptions of ILMs rely heavily on the argument that ILMs are rational responses to situations where uncertainty is high and opportunism by one of the contracting parties is a potential problem (Williamson 1975). Internal promotion systems reduce the level of employee opportunism in two ways. First, by giving firms a chance to monitor an employee's performance over time, they provide a more accurate measure of his or her performance. Second, by loosely tying promotion to performance, they create disincentives for employees to behave opportunistically. Williamson argued that if markets could perform these experience-rating functions equally well, port-of-entry restrictions would be unnecessary. But markets cannot do this well, because firms cannot or will not communicate ratings adequately.

If information transfer were perfect within organizations, then it would be efficient for career ladders to span entire firms or at least that portion of the firm located in a particular geographic area. However, a substantial amount of research has documented the extent to which organizations are "loosely coupled" (Weick 1976). Information impactedness can occur within organizations, too. Operating officials generally know their own employees better than those in another division. Although officials can consult the personnel files of applicants from other divisions, these files are no substitute for first-hand experience. An old saying in government, "they pass the queen of spades"—the worst card in the game of hearts—underlines the danger of recruiting an unknown from a different organizational location to fill a vacancy (Meriam 1937a). Therefore, a supervisor in one part of a large organization may be unwilling to spread his or her search too widely for fear of being taken advantage of by an opportunistic employee or supervisor of another division. This reluctance should be especially common in the administrative and professional grades, where job performance is more difficult to evaluate (Halaby 1978).

Employee movement will also be affected by the absence of perfect information. Employees are more likely to know about vacancies within their own division than in other divisions because these vacancies are more likely to be posted there or otherwise communicated to employees. This structuring of information can have official standing in the personnel system of the organization. For example, in the federal government, the requirement that promotion plans make use of a "minimum area of consideration" allows selecting officials to restrict information about jobs to certain sections of the organization. This minimum area must be determined so that it "keeps the area of search within the limits of administrative efficiency" (U.S. Office of Personnel Management 1973: 11). Because selecting officials are required to consider applications from otherwise qualified employees outside the minimum area of consideration, social networks can play an important part in obtaining new jobs (Granovetter 1981). But these networks are imperfect communications media and do not make up for the informational advantage of divisional insiders.

At the extreme, task idiosyncrasy at the occupational and organizational levels and the effects of imperfect information would completely channel mobility along organizationally and occupationally defined job ladders. As we shall see, other considerations create structured divergence between this extreme case and real-world conditions. Nevertheless, if job ladders have any technical justification at all, if task idiosyncrasy at the divisional level exists, and if organizational boundaries serve as informational barriers to even a moderate extent, one might expect the following hypotheses to be valid:

> *Hypothesis 1:* An incumbent on a job ladder will have a higher probability of filling a vacancy on the same job ladder than an individual whose job is not on the same job ladder. Those on the same job ladder and in the same division as the vacancy (i.e., those on the divisional job ladder) will be especially advantaged.
> *Hypothesis 2:* When a vacancy is not filled from within the job ladder, an individual in a more closely related occupation has a higher probability of filling the vacancy than someone in a less closely related occupation.
> *Hypothesis 3:* When a vacancy is not filled from within the job ladder, an individual in the same division as the vacancy will have a greater probability of filling it than someone from a different division.

Contingencies That Structure Divergence between Implied and Realized Career Trajectories

If job ladders were too broad, they would not efficiently identify the group of best-qualified employees for a given vacancy. If they were too narrow, they would introduce largely artificial skill distinctions between jobs and impede rather than facilitate the process of matching workers and vacancies. "Technically perfect" job ladders would strike a balance between these two extremes. But even if technically perfect job ladders existed, real careers would still cross occupational and divisional boundaries. Employees might acquire new skills or demonstrate that they had skills not anticipated by management. Management might not find anyone within the division appropriate to fill a particular vacancy and be forced to look outside. In reality, of course, job ladders are not simply the realization of a technically optimal classification of jobs. Cultural conceptions of appropriate occupational distinctions and of the extent to which skill requirements are formally linked with particular educational credentials often influence the construction of job ladders. These considerations can make some job-ladder boundaries relatively permeable to entry, whereas others are relatively impermeable, creating divergence between implied and realized career trajectories. This divergence should be patterned, however, by grade, by position type, by the number of positions to be filled, and by the number of employees eligible to fill them on the formal job ladder.

1. Divergence That Varies with the Number of Eligibles

Tournament models of organizational mobility (Rosenbaum 1984) treat promotion decisions as tournaments, in which a number of individuals compete for the chance to fill a single vacancy. All other things being equal, the probability of any single employee being chosen varies inversely with the number of individuals in competition for the position. Conversely, when individuals in competition to fill a vacancy are grouped by major characteristics of their jobs in relation to the vacancy to be filled (for instance, by whether or not they are on the same job ladder as the vacancy, whether or not they are in the same division as the vacancy, etc.), then, *ceteris paribus*, the probability of filling a vacancy from a given source should vary directly with the number of individuals located at that source. McFadden (1981) has formalized this principle in his mathematical models of sequential choice. It leads to the following hypothesis:

Hypothesis 4: The probability of filling a vacancy from a particular source increases or decreases as the number of individuals available from that source increases or decreases. In particular, the smaller the population of eligible employees within the job ladder, the more likely it is that an operating official will look elsewhere to fill a vacancy.

2. Divergence That Varies with the Number of Vacancies

During a short period of time, multiple vacancies may arise in a particular job ladder. The availability of multiple vacancies should increase the probability that any given individual in the job ladder is promoted, but it may also increase the probability that the selecting official will look outside the job ladder to fill each successive vacancy as he or she exhausts the queue of sufficiently qualified eligible people in the divisional job ladder. This leads to the following hypothesis:

> *Hypothesis 5:* The greater the number of vacancies to be filled in a job ladder in a given period of time, the greater the probability that a selecting official will look outside the job ladder to fill each successive vacancy.

3. Divergence That Varies with Grade

Divergence that varies with grade is the result of four organizational effects: (a) the pyramidal shape of organizations, (b) job-ladder ceilings, (c) cross-functional job assignments, and (d) increased ambiguity about performance at the higher levels of an organization.

Pyramidal Shape. Organizations tend to be pyramidal in shape. The number of jobs located at the higher grades is generally smaller than the number of jobs located at lower grades, though the exact shape varies from one organization to another (Stewman and Konda 1983). Consequently, the number of employees eligible to compete for a higher graded vacancy is generally smaller than the number who could compete for lower graded vacancies. Organizations have an incentive to broaden the "area of consideration" at higher grades in order to maintain a reasonable probability of finding a satisfactory candidate, because the number of potential candidates within a given organizational area would diminish at higher grades. This principle is sometimes given official standing in personnel systems. For example, the *Federal Personnel Manual* stipulates that

> the minimum area should be determined so that it–(a) includes a sufficient supply of eligible employees to produce enough highly qualified candidates (generally at least three) for promotion considerations. (U.S. Office of Personnel Management 1973: 10)
>
> Generally, the minimum area of consideration should be broadened as grades increase and the number of eligible candidates decrease. Highly skilled and policy-making jobs, for example, should have broader areas of consideration than low-level and routine jobs. For key types and levels of positions, the minimum area of consideration normally should be a major

organizational component (such as a command, bureau, or service) if not the entire agency. (U.S. Office of Personnel Management 1973: 9–10)

Consequently, both occupational and divisional boundary crossing would be expected to increase at higher grades to compensate for the reduction in the number of potentially eligible employees within any given area (e.g., job ladder, division) at the higher grades.

Job-ladder Ceilings. White-collar job ladders typically have ceilings that are lower than the highest grade found in the organization. The existence of these ceilings has given rise to the concept of the dead-end job at the top of a job ladder, from which further movement is difficult. But individuals at the top of a job ladder have an incentive to compete more vigorously for higher graded vacancies in other job ladders, in order to continue their advancement. Some of these individuals may be perceived by top management to be potential leaders who should continue to be promoted. Because they can no longer be promoted within their old job ladder, they must be moved to a new one. This source of boundary crossing should be greater at levels of the organization where job ceilings are most abundant. The grades near the top of clerical ladders are one such location, whereas the grades near the top of the organization are another.

Cross-Functional Job Assignments. Personnel specialists have often argued that high-level jobs are best filled by individuals with broad training and experience. This background presumably gives them the perspective necessary for intelligent decision making, which is the principal activity of higher-level positions in organizations. Educators have used this argument to justify the inclusion of liberal arts courses in the curriculum of professional and technical schools (Veysey 1965; Fisher 1967; Sass 1982). Some private businesses provide cross-functional job assignments in order to give those destined for high-level jobs the broader perspective that comes from hands-on familiarity with different aspects of the organization (Shaeffer 1972). A similar arrangement has been suggested for managers in the federal government (Committee for Economic Development 1964; Presidential Task Force on Career Advancement 1967). A policy or practice of cross-functional job assignment is, in effect, a concession that job ladders alone are not always sufficient tools for training.

One would expect such cross-functional movement, that is, the crossing of divisional and occupational boundaries, to occur more frequently at higher grade levels, where those targeted as candidates for leadership positions are more concentrated. A variant of this argument would hold that several different career routes may provide roughly equivalent training for the higher positions in an organization, leading to more boundary crossing at higher levels of the organization.

Increased Performance Ambiguity. Organization theorists who take an anarchistic perspective on organizational structure (Pinfield 1986) have argued that the goals of organizations are frequently problematic, technologies are frequently ambiguous, and the performance of organizational personnel is often difficult to assess (Cohen, March, and Olsen 1972; March and Olsen 1976). Ouchi (1980) developed this insight by arguing that organizational structures sometimes adapt to the level of performance ambiguity and goal incongruence found there. In his view, bureaucratic structures are efficient when both performance ambiguity and goal incongruence are moderately high (Ouchi 1980: 135). But in situations where opportunism is low and performance ambiguity is high, the clan form of organization, which relies heavily on socialization to create internal controls, is more efficient. Ouchi and Jaeger (1978) argued that a clan makes use of nonspecialized career paths to familiarize employees with its norms, values, and culture and thereby increase the level of goal congruence between the individual and the organization. In the terminology of this chapter, nonspecialized career paths correspond to the crossing of intraorganizational boundaries.

Ouchi described such forms of control as characteristics of organizations, not of parts of organizations. But clearly, performance ambiguity and opportunism can vary within an organization. Performance ambiguity should be greatest at the highest levels of an organization (Ouchi and Maguire 1975; Simpson 1985). Also, the employees in the higher positions of an organization are more likely than others to have high job satisfaction and to identify with the organization's goals (Locke 1976; Shepard 1977; Larson 1977), which should reduce their tendency to engage in opportunistic behavior. Thus characteristics of clanlike organization and, in particular, nonspecialized career paths (boundary crossing) should be more prevalent at higher levels than at lower levels of an organization. But if this mechanism were the primary force driving boundary crossing at higher levels, it would restrict movement from the outside world into the organization at higher levels as well.

All four of these considerations about the effects of grade lead to the following hypothesis:

> *Hypothesis 6:* Selecting officials will be more likely to select individuals outside the job ladder to fill a vacancy at a higher grade than

at a lower grade, with the exception of entry positions on the job ladder.

If all of the grade effect comes from the pyramidal shape of organizations, however, Hypothesis 6 would be a side effect of the relationship between the probability of filling a vacancy from a given source and the number of eligible individuals located at that source (Hypothesis 4).

4. Divergence That Varies with Position Type

Pfeffer and Cohen (1984: 556) argued that the presence of personnel departments ensures that "normatively sanctioned, institutionalized practices are implemented in the organization . . . [and] provides an internal constituency that would be interested in having an ILM as a professional sanctioned practice." They further argued that the presence of a personnel department should increase promotion from within and limit the hiring of outsiders to entry positions. However, as Meyer and Rowan (1977) observed, the presence of formal structure in an organization, to the extent that it serves only legitimation functions, may be decoupled from the ongoing activities of the organization itself. It has been argued in the past that the civil service classification was cumbersome and not responsive to the needs of the bureaucracy (Shafritz 1973). Consequently, although personnel departments may affect the empirical trajectories of employees, they may also propagate structures that in some cases are largely ignored.

The extent to which job-ladder boundaries are ignored by selecting officials may depend on the type of job. High-level jobs in the federal government are typically classified as either administrative or professional. Professional jobs require specialized training, whereas training for administrative jobs can be more general. Despite these differences, the institutionalization of personnel systems has caused job ladders in the two types of positions to look very similar. One might therefore expect that the implied and realized career trajectories will be more congruent for professional job ladders than for administrative ones. This leads to the following hypothesis:

Hypothesis 7: Selecting officials will more frequently reach across occupational boundaries to fill an administrative vacancy than a professional vacancy.

An elaboration of the same argument would suggest that clerical job ladders may be particularly permeable to mobility. At job levels where job tasks are most routine, a worker does not need much training to do a job in a different job ladder. Therefore, the crossing of occupational boundaries may be more common (see, e.g., Butler 1954). After a detailed examination of data for upper-tier positions, this chapter will focus on clerical job ladders as well.

RESEARCH PROCEDURE AND FINDINGS

The hypotheses just discussed are best tested with data representing a complete population of an organization. Such data would allow an accurate count of vacancies and a count of the eligibility pools defined by organizational and occupational boundaries. Such data were available for one agency of the federal government. Therefore, this chapter uses the agency data to explore the hypotheses discussed before. Later, we will look more generally at the relationship between the structure of job ladders and job mobility for a more representative sample of government workers.

The first analysis reported here focuses on the pattern of vacancy filling during the years 1975–1978 for the Washington offices of four bureaus of this agency. All four of these bureaus had substantial field staffs as well. But because geographic transfers were relatively uncommon, it was important to take the geographic location of both vacancies and employees into account. The Washington offices were by far the largest and are the subject of this study.

Each bureau contained a number of organizational divisions. The division was used as the level of analysis for studying intraorganizational boundaries, whereas the job ladder, or occupational series, was used to define occupational boundaries. Positions at Grades 12 through 18 in these four belonged to many different occupational series, including social science series, economist series, equal opportunity series, personnel management series, position classification series, miscellaneous administration series, administrative officer series, program analysis series, computer specialist series, financial administration series, accounting series, mathematical statistician series, and many others. These occupational series clustered into occupational groups that embrace "generally several series of classes of positions in associated or related occupations, professions, or activities, within the [general] schedule" (U.S. Office of Personnel Management 1981: 4). The U.S. Office of Personnel Management described almost all of these job ladders as professional or administrative, with the exception of one job ladder in Bureau 4 that was classified as technical. Some of the occupational series listed in the *Handbook of Occupational Groups* are rather general and were further elaborated in bureau personnel records. These elaborations divided certain larger series, in particular, Series 301, the "general clerical and administrative series," into a number of subseries. The elaborated classification employed by the bureaus was used to further refine the definition of the job ladder.

The data analyzed here come from year-end personnel files for each bureau for the years 1974 through 1978. Such information does not allow one to identify the presence of vacancies directly. However, when an individual moves to a new position or enters the organization to fill a position, one can infer that a vacancy was filled.[2] By following the movement of existing employees and the arrival of new ones, one can keep track of the vacancies that were filled. Thus, with 1974 as a baseline, the data permit the identification of vacancy filling for 4 years. The Washington office of Bureau 1 filled 779 vacancies in grades GS-12 or above during 1975 through 1978. The other three bureaus filled 320, 452, and 474 vacancies, respectively.

Job vacancies were classified according to the job ladder, the organizational division, the grade, and the year in which they were filled. Cases in the data file consisted of all unique combinations of these four variables in which one or more positions were filled during 1975–1978. If multiple positions were filled in a given combination of job ladder, division, grade, and year, the combination was included in the data file as many times as the number of vacancies filled there. The people who filled these vacancies came from one of eight sources, either from within or outside the bureau.

Within the bureau, vacancies were filled either from the division where the vacancy was located or from other divisions. Potentially eligible employees in the same division as the vacancy were either (1) employees on the same job ladder and in the same division as the vacancy, that is, on the divisional job ladder; (2) employees on a different job ladder in the same occupational group as the vacancy; or (3) employees on a job ladder outside the occupational group of the vacancy. Those in a different division than the vacancy were either (1) employees on the same job ladder as the vacancy, though in a different division; (2) employees on a different job ladder but in the same occupational group as

---

[2]These data allow one to study the filling of vacancies, not their creation or elimination. Vacancies that are created but not filled are thus unobservable. Nor, in this analysis, can one distinguish upgradings from the filling of vacancies. In effect, then, an upgrading must be viewed as a two-part action: the creation of a virtual vacancy and the filling of that vacancy with an employee who has been handling its tasks from a lower graded job (see, e.g., Howell and Elledge 1971).

the vacancy; or (3) employees on a job ladder outside the occupational group of the vacancy.

Sources outside the bureau were either (1) people who entered the bureau with prior government service, who could have transferred, had been reinstated, or who entered the civil service with credit for military service; or (2) people who entered the bureau with no previous government service. Reinstatements have a special status and are not easily compared with the other categories in this study. Unfortunately, it was not possible to separate them from transfers in these data.

Vacancies filled from within the divisional job ladder would typically involve promoting an employee one grade. The employee's grade would change, but his or her division and job ladder would not. Employees could also fill a vacancy on a different job ladder or in a different division from their own either by moving up a grade or by moving laterally, without changing grades.[3] Although the 8 sources just described could be expanded to 14 by distinguishing employees at the same grade as the vacancy from those one grade lower, this distinction would be operationally cumbersome and is not made here. Nonetheless, lateral moves from outside the divisional job ladder were frequent and were counted along with boundary-crossing promotions in the analysis.

The study of organizational boundary crossing to fill vacancies is complicated by the phenomenon of mass transfers. In a reorganization, a number of individuals can be transferred across divisional lines. This transfer can be thought of as the simultaneous creation and destruction of a group of positions. A few such mass transfers occurred in the four bureaus during 1974–1978. This movement is qualitatively distinct from the normal process of vacancy filling and was excluded from consideration in these analyses.

Table 7.1 shows the number of vacancies filled from each source, broken down by grade. Table 7.2 shows the number of vacancies filled from each source, broken down by the type of vacancy (administrative, professional, or technical) for each bureau. Both tables also show the percentage of positions filled from the divisional job ladder, the percentage of positions filled from the same division as the vacancy that was filled, and the percentage filled from within the bureau's current work force. Although more rigorous analyses of these data will be presented later, the tabulations shown in Tables 7.1 and 7.2 by themselves shed light on the accuracy of several of the hypotheses under examination here.

---

[3]Grade demotions were comparatively rare during the years studied and were not included in the analyses presented here.

Table 7.1
Number of Vacancies Filled from Each Source for Each Bureau by Grade

| Grade | Sources inside the bureau | | | | | | | | Outside | | |
| | Same division | | | Different division | | | | | | | |
	Same ladder	Same occupational group	Other occupational group	Total same division	Same ladder	Same occupational group	Other occupational group	Total from inside	Reinstatements transfers, etc.	New hires	Grand total
					Bureau 1						
12	107[a] 42%	16	47	170 67%	14	5	6	195 77%	22	35	252
13	78 20%	25	46	149 62%	16	3	18	186 77%	25	29	240
14	36 25%	15	31	82 57%	9	1	9	101 70%	30	12	143
15	16 16%	11	22	49 48%	11	3	12	75 72%	14	14	103
16	3 16%	2	4	9 47%	2	1	2	14 73%	4	1	19
17	3 21%	2	2	7 50%	4	0	0	11 78%	0	3	14
18	2[b]	0	1	3	3	0	0	6	0	2	8
Totals	245 31%	71	153	469 60%	59	13	47	588 75%	95	96	779

(continued)

Table 7.1
(Continued)

Bureau 2

| | Sources inside the bureau | | | | | | | | Outside | | |
| | Same division | | | | Different division | | | | | | |
Grade	Same ladder	Same occupational group	Other occupational group	Total same division	Same ladder	Same occupational group	Other occupational group	Total from inside	Reinstatements transfers, etc.	New hires	Grand total
12	56 43%	8	7	71 55%	7	1	0	79 61%	18	32	129
13	24 24%	3	9	36 36%	18	3	2	59 58%	14	28	101
14	4 12%	4	1	9 27%	6	1	1	17 51%	5	11	33
15	4 10%	5	2	11 28%	4	0	2	17 42%	7	16	40
16	1 7%	1	3	5 36%	0	0	2	7 50%	5	2	14
17	0	0	0	0	0	0	0	0	0	0	0
18	0	0	0	0	0	0	0	0	0	3	3
Totals	89 28%	21	22	132 41%	35	5	7	179 56%	49	92	320

Bureau 3

12	173 73%	4	9	186 78%	15	0	2	203 85%	8	26	237
13	100 72%	5	2	107 78%	6	1	2	116 84%	4	18	138
14	34 71%	1	2	37 77%	3	0	0	40 83%	1	7	48
15	9 47%	0	3	12 63%	1	0	1	14 73%	1	4	19
16	6	0	0	6	0	0	0	6	0	0	6
17	—1	0	0	—1	1	0	0	—2	0	0	2
18	—1	0	0	—1	1	0	0	—2	0	0	2
Totals	324 72%	10	16	350 77%	27	1	5	383 85%	14	55	452

Bureau 4

12	52 35%	3	18	73 50%	2	0	2	77 52%	30	40	147
13	51 28%	4	19	74 40%	5	2	5	86 46%	50	47	183

(continued)

Table 7.1
(*Continued*)

Grade	Sources inside the bureau								Outside		Grand Total
	Same division				Different division						
	Same ladder	Same occupational group	Other occupational group	Total same division	Same ladder	Same occupational group	Other occupational group	Total from inside	Reinstatements transfers, etc.	New hires	
14	7 10%	1	12	20 30%	1	0	1	22 32%	26	19	67
15	5 9%	2	3	10 18%	3	1	2	16 28%	19	21	56
16	0 0%	0	0	0 0%	0	0	1	1 8%	6	5	12
17	3	0	0	3	0	0	0	3	2	2	7
18	1	0	0	0	0	0	0	0	1	1	2
Totals	118 25%	10	52	180 38%	11	3	11	205 43%	134	135	474

[a]Percentage of the total vacancies at this grade level that were filled from this source.
[b]Percentages not reported when the total (base) is smaller than 10.

Number of Vacancies Filled from Each Source for Each Bureau by Type of Vacancy

Type of vacancy	Sources inside the bureau — Same division				Different division			Total from inside	Outside — Reinstatements transfers, etc.	New hires	Grand total
	Same ladder	Same occupational group	Other occupational group	Total same division	Same ladder	Same occupational group	Other occupational group				
Bureau 1											
Administrative	27 23%	25	25	77 66%	11	2	3	93 80%	4	19	116
Professional	218 33%	46	128	392 59%	48	11	44	495 74%	91	77	663
Bureau 2											
Administrative	64 30%	15	15	94 43%	20	5	3	122 57%	31	58	211
Professional	25 23%	6	7	38 35%	15	0	4	57 52%	18	34	109
Bureau 3											
Administrative	86 67%	3	10	99 77%	15	0	2	116 89%	2	11	129
Professional	238 74%	7	6	251 78%	12	1	3	267 82%	12	44	323
Bureau 4											
Administrative	73 20%	9	44	126 35%	11	3	9	149 41%	102	112	363
Professional	12 22%	1	5	18 33%	0	0	2	20 36%	20	15	55
Technical	33 59%	0	3	36 64%	0	0	0	36 64%	12	8	56

Bureau officials filled a large number of vacancies, in fact a majority in three of the four bureaus, from outside the divisional job ladder. Boundary crossing, that is, the selection of individuals from different job ladders or divisions as the vacancy to be filled or the selection of individuals from outside the bureau to fill a vacancy, was therefore common in these bureaus. Bureau 3, which had a highly technical mission, is the only one of the four bureaus in which relatively little boundary crossing occurred. A large proportion of vacancies in all four bureaus were filled from outside the bureau: 25%, 44%, 15%, and 57%, respectively, at all grade levels. Individuals with no prior government service filled 12%, 29%, 12%, and 28%, respectively, of the total number of vacancies filled. Taken together, these findings show clear discrepancies between implied and realized career trajectories in these bureaus.

Despite these discrepancies, however, personnel decisions were hardly random. The official job-ladder structure did constrain the process of filling vacancies. In all four bureaus, the divisional job ladder was used more frequently than any of the other internal sources. When one takes into account that four of the other five internal sources encompass multiple job ladders, it would appear that in all four bureaus individuals on the divisional job ladder stood a better chance of filling a vacancy on that job ladder than did other employees. New hires were as common a source for vacancy filling as were incumbents on the divisional job ladder in two of the bureaus, but it must be remembered that the pool of potential new hires is vast compared with the pool of incumbents on the divisional job ladder. Furthermore, Bureau 3, which had the most highly technical mission and thus arguably the greatest level of task idiosyncrasy, had the lowest level of boundary crossing. Hypothesis 1, which predicts that task idiosyncrasy and limits on organizational information will constrain movement along divisional job ladders, is therefore supported by the data.

The boundary crossing that did occur was structured in the hypothesized ways. The proportion of positions filled from within the divisional job ladder decreased from Grades 12 through 15 in all four bureaus. In Bureau 1, 42% of all placements in Grade 12 were from the divisional job ladder, but only 16% of the placements in Grade 15 were from the divisional job ladder. In Bureau 2, the comparable figures were 43% and 10%, in Bureau 3, 73% and 47%, and in Bureau 4, 35% and 9%. Selecting officials were also more likely to reach across divisional boundaries at higher grade levels. Finally, the proportion of vacancies filled from outside the bureau itself tended to rise as the grade of the vacancy increased. It is possible that the proportion filled from within the divisional job ladder leveled off or even increased in Grades 16 through 18, but the sample size is too small to be sure of this.

As can be seen from Table 7.2, selecting officials showed some tendency to recruit more heavily from the job ladder to fill professional as compared with administrative vacancies, but the tendency is not strong. For Bureau 1, Bureau 2, Bureau 3, and Bureau 4, 23%, 30%, 67%, and 20%, respectively, of administrative vacancies were filled from the divisional job ladder, compared with 33%, 23%, 74%, and 22% for professional vacancies. Although divisional job ladders are more constraining for filling professional vacancies in three of the four bureaus, the data hardly provide strong confirmation of the hypothesis. These statistics, along with the others shown in Table 7.2, suggest that officials were almost as likely to reach across occupational and divisional boundaries to fill a professional vacancy as they were to fill an administrative one. This outcome was contrary to expectations.

MULTINOMIAL LOGIT MODEL

The descriptive findings just discussed reveal important aspects of the process of vacancy filling in the four bureaus. However, a more complex analysis is required to adequately address the validity of the set of hypotheses proposed here. A multinomial logit analysis of the pattern of vacancy filling was therefore performed for the data from each of the four bureaus. An appropriate set of independent variables was used to detect structured divergence between implied and realized career trajectories. These variables were defined as follows: "Administrative" was defined as 1 if the position of the vacancy was in an administrative job ladder, and 0 if in a professional job ladder. "Grade" was measured as the general schedule grade of the vacancy to be filled. "Number of vacancies filled" (the count of the number of positions filled that year from all internal sources) was included to control for the possibility that the filling of many vacancies in a given year would exhaust the queue in the divisional job ladder and increase the probability of boundary crossing. "ln(number eligible for vacancy)" was measured as the natural logarithm of the number of individuals eligible to move from each source. For the divisional job ladder, it equals the natural log of the number of individuals one grade lower in the job ladder in the previous year. For the other five categories, it equals the natural log of the number of individuals who were at the same grade or one grade lower in the previous year. When no individuals were eligible to move from a given source, the value zero [$= \log(1)$] was assigned to the eligibility variable for that source.

Two coefficients were used to specify the effect of grade on divisional and occupational boundary crossing. The first coefficient contrasted selections from the divisional job ladder with other sources, whereas the second contrasted selections from the same organizational division with selections from outside the division. Two coefficients were also used to specify the effect of the type of vacancy (professional, administrative, or technical). One contrasted the same job ladder (in or out of the division) with other sources, whereas the second contrasted the same division with other divisions. Slightly different specifications for grade and for type of position were employed because the hypotheses are different. Hypothesis 6, which addresses the relationship between grade and boundary crossing, pertains specifically to the divisional job ladder. In contrast, Hypothesis 7, which addresses differences in the filling of professional and administrative vacancies, concerns the permeability of the occupation (not just the divisional job ladder) to entrance from other occupations. These same specification for number of vacancies filled was used as for grade for Bureaus 2, 3, and 4. A more complicated specification was used for Bureau 1 because it fit better. A separate coefficient was used for each of the six eligibility variables. Because eligibility variables could not be specified for sources outside of the bureau, the multinomial logit analysis was limited to the six internal sources. Finally, multiple contrasts were employed for calendar time, in order to control for its effects.

The term *eligible* is used here in a loose sense. Not all individuals at a particular source (as defined before) would be serious candidates to fill a given vacancy, although the number of serious candidates would generally grow with the number of individuals located at each source. The ratio of serious candidates to eligible individuals might vary, however, depending upon the source. The multinomial logit model takes this possibility into account. The parameter values of the eligibility variables measure the likelihood that individuals in a particular source tend to be serious candidates for a vacancy. The smaller the parameter, the more slowly the probability of selecting from a given source would grow with the number of individuals there. At the extreme, if the coefficient were zero, the probability of selecting from a given source would not increase at all as the number of eligible individuals from a given source increased.

A natural prediction regarding the eligibility coefficients is that they should be smaller for sources outside the divisional job ladder than for the divisional job ladder itself. Also, they should be smaller for sources outside the division than for sources inside the division. There are two reasons for expecting this hypothesis to hold. First, the proportion of employees who are considered serious candidates by selecting officials should be higher on the divisional job ladder of the vacancy than at other sources. Second, the selecting official is presumably more familiar with potential candidates in his or her division than with outsiders; insiders would, in effect, appear to be relatively more distinct from each other to the selecting official. This prediction can be treated as an elaboration of Hypothesis 4 and provides another way for this hypothesis to account for the relationship between grade and boundary crossing predicted by Hypothesis 6. If the number of eligible employees from the divisional job ladder and from an alternative source decrease in equal proportion, but the coefficient for the divisional job ladder is larger than the coefficient for the alternative source, the effect of the reductions would be to increase the probability of a selection from the alternative source, relative to selection from the divisional job ladder.

With the definition used here for the number of eligible employees, the eligibility variables have the same form as inclusive value variables in a sequential nested (two-level) multinomial logit model (Hensher and Johnson 1981). In the form used here, all parameters to be estimated at the lower level of the model (in this case, all individual-level parameters) are set to zero. The setting of all parameters at the lower level to zero causes all eligible individuals to be treated as equivalent in the model. A natural extension of this model would be to estimate parameters that distinguish these individuals by race, sex, education, tenure, and so forth, but this extension is left to another time.[4]

Table 7.3, which shows the average number of employees eligible to fill a vacancy from each of the six internal sources, gives a picture of how these eligible employees were distributed. The number eligible to fill a position varied substantially across the six sources. Not surprisingly, the largest number of eligible employees was always in the "different division, other occupational group" location. The number of eligible individuals in the divisional job ladder was generally smaller than the number in other sources. Bureau 3, which had by far the highest number of placements from within the divisional job ladder, is a partial exception to this generalization. There, the average number of eligible

---

[4]For the coefficient to be given its economic interpretation as a coefficient of inclusive value, it would need to lie between 0 and 1 (McFadden 1981). Although the estimated coefficients to be reported in Table 7.4 are not uniformly between 0 and 1, a 95% confidence interval around each estimate includes all or a portion of this interval.

Table 7.3
Average Number of Employees Eligible to Fill a Vacancy by Grade

Grade	Same division			Different division		
	Same ladder	Same occupational group	Other occupational group	Same ladder	Same occupational group	Other occupational group
			Bureau 1			
12	3	9	35	21	52	192
13	7	15	43	28	71	300
14	12	13	29	35	104	235
15	7	11	21	23	60	154
16	6	3	9	11	19	76
17	2	1	2	4	6	11
18	1	1	1	3	3	4
			Bureau 2			
12	3	3	21	6	7	83
13	2	4	21	9	9	98
14	3	4	18	7	9	77
15	1	4	9	3	9	51
16	1	2	8	1	4	25
17	—	—	—	—	—	—
18	—	—				

Bureau 3

12	12	20	62	30	23	181
13	18	4	58	46	21	147
14	19	3	37	50	8	99
15	18	3	14	23	3	71
16	16	4	6	5	1	36
17	4	0	0	1	0	1
18	2	1	0	1	0	1

Bureau 4

12	4	2	17	3	12	100
13	4	5	26	5	22	140
14	7	4	22	4	15	109
15	2	2	7	5	10	50
16	3	0	3	0	0	23
17	1	0	0	8	0	1
18	—	—	—	—	—	—

employees in the divisional job ladder was both large in contrast to the other three bureaus and large compared with the number of eligible employees in other sources in Bureau 3.[5] Only tentative conclusions about the pattern of vacancy filling could be drawn from Tables 7.1 and 7.2 because the statistics presented there did not control for the number of individuals eligible to fill a vacancy from the different sources. The multinomial logit models, which control for the number eligible at each source, remedy this shortcoming.

Tables 7.1 and 7.2 showed that, although boundary crossing was quite common, vacancies were more often filled from the divisional job ladder than from any other single source. But Table 7.4, which contains the results of the multinomial logit analysis, shows that the more subtle predictions of Hypothesis 2, which also concerns the strength of occupational boundaries, were not confirmed by the results. The models show that when the number of eligible individuals and number of positions to be filled is controlled, there is no consistent ordering of the predicted probabilities of choosing an individual from the same occupational group (but different job ladder) in the same division as compared with a different occupational group in the same division. Similarly, there is no consistent ordering of the predicted probabilities of choosing someone from the same occupational group (but different job ladder) in a different division as compared with a different occupational group in a different division. These results are similar for all four bureaus.[6] This result calls into question the extent to which the occupational groups employed in the federal civil service accurately group the job ladders found in these four bureaus according to skill.

Hypothesis 3, in contrast, is supported by the results, with a qualification. Twelve contrasts are available to examine the constraining effect of divisional boundaries on mobility. One can contrast the probability of selecting an individual from the same job ladder inside or outside of the division, from the same occupational group but different job ladder inside or outside of the division, or from a different occupational group inside or outside of the division. When the independent variables are

---

[5]This outcome is possible because cases in the analysis were limited to job ladders in which vacancies were filled during the period under examination. If no vacancies were filled in a particular job ladder during the period of time under study, the job ladder would not be included as a case. Hence, it would not influence the average in the "same division, same job ladder" column of Table 7.3.

[6]These results can be most easily viewed by setting the number of vacancies to be filled at 1 or 2 (the most common values by far), then by choosing a value for the number of eligible individuals (the same for both sources), and finally by summing the product of the variable value and the associated coefficient for all relevant variables.

Table 7.4
Multinomial Logit Model of Vacancy Filling (Internal Sources Only)

Variable[a]	Same division			Different division		
	Same ladder	Same occupational group	Other occupational group	Same ladder	Same occupational group	Other occupational group
	Bureau 1 (N = 588 vacancies filled)					
Constant	—	-10.45[b] (.0000)	-9.30 (.0000)	-12.00 (.0000)	-15.74 (.0000)	-15.42 (.0000)
Grade	-0.55 (.0000)	—	—	—	—	—
Grade	-0.17[c] (.080)	-0.17 (.080)	-0.17 (.080)	—	—	—
Administrative	-0.51 (.038)	—	—	-0.51 (.038)	—	—
Administrative	0.16 (.67)	0.16 (.67)	0.16 (.67)	—	—	—
Number of vacancies filled	—	0.10 (.0034)	0.19 (.0000)	—	0.10 (.0034)	0.19 (.0000)
Number of vacancies filled	-0.023 (.48)	-0.023 (.48)	-0.023 (.48)	—	—	—
ln(number eligible for vacancy)	0.77 (.0000)	0.86 (.0000)	0.30 (.018)	0.60 (.0000)	0.92 (.12)	0.79 (.035)

(continued)

Table 7.4
(Continued)

	Same division			Different division		
Variable[a]	Same ladder	Same occupational group	Other occupational group	Same ladder	Same occupational group	Other occupational group
		Bureau 2 (N = 179 vacancies filled)				
Constant	—	-12.83 (.0002)	-10.93 (.0027)	-16.64 (.0004)	-20.80 (.47)	-13.38 (.094)
Grade	-0.78 (.0012)	—	—	—	—	—
Grade	-0.29 (.048)	-0.29 (.048)	-0.29 (.048)	—	—	—
Administrative	0.011 (.98)	—	—	0.011 (.98)	—	—
Administrative	0.48 (.32)	0.48 (.32)	0.48 (.32)	—	—	—
Number of vacancies filled	-0.36 (.44)	—	—	—	—	—
Number of vacancies filled	-0.38 (.48)	-0.38 (.48)	-0.38 (.48)	—	—	—
ln(number eligible for vacancy)	1.51 (.0002)	1.51 (.0000)	0.16 (.59)	1.09 (.0001)	1.25 (.90)	-1.02 (.37)
		Bureau 3 (N = 383 vacancies filled)				
Constant	—	-0.48 (.90)	-0.38 (.93)	-7.82 (.040)	-10.93 (.53)	-9.48 (.31)
Grade	0.055	—	—	—	—	—

Grade	−0.47 (.19)	−0.47 (.19)	−0.47 (.19)	—	—	—
Administrative	0.23 (.68)	—	—	0.23 (.68)	—	—
Administrative	−1.29 (.03)	−1.29 (.03)	−1.29 (.03)	—	—	—
Number of vacancies filled	0.016 (.76)	—	—	—	—	—
Number of vacancies filled	−0.086 (.12)	−0.086 (.12)	−0.086 (.12)	—	—	—
ln(number eligible for vacancy)	0.93 (.0000)	0.052 (.90)	−0.097 (.76)	0.61 (.0067)	0.56 (.93)	0.30 (.85)

Bureau 4 ($N = 205$ vacancies filled)

Constant	—	−9.01 (.0029)	−9.28 (.0066)	−9.25 (.039)	−12.89 (.19)	−8.80 (.21)
Grade	−0.48 (.032)	—	—	—	—	—
Grade	−0.089 (.79)	−0.089 (.79)	−0.089 (.79)	—	—	—
Administrative	−0.29 (.50)	—	—	−0.29 (.50)	—	—
Administrative	−0.91 (.41)	−0.91 (.41)	−0.91 (.41)	—	—	—
Number of vacancies filled	−0.17 (.17)	—	—	—	—	—
Number of vacancies filled	0.39 (.35)	0.39 (.35)	0.39 (.35)	—	—	—
ln(number eligible for vacancy)	0.75 (.0031)	0.75 (.10)	1.00 (.0004)	1.30 (.033)	1.48 (.53)	0.31 (.72)

[a] Models also include controls for calendar time (not shown).
[b] P-values are in parentheses.
[c] Identical parameter values in any row were constrained to be equal.

fixed at reasonable values, all 12 contrasts are in the expected direction for filling vacancies at grade 12.[7] But when the grade of the vacancy is fixed at 16, some reversals occur. Divisional boundaries may be more controlling in the filling of lower-graded vacancies than higher-graded ones.

Hypothesis 4 in its original form received strong support from the analysis. The probability of selecting someone from a particular source increased as the number of eligible individuals there increased and decreased as the number of eligible individuals decreased. These effects were highly significant for sources close to a given vacancy (divisional job ladder, same occupational group/same division, same job ladder/other division). However, the elaboration of this hypothesis to the effect that the coefficients for the number of eligible individuals would be larger for the divisional job ladder than for other sources is not supported by the results. Also, these results do not confirm the speculation that individuals in the same division would appear more distinct to the selecting official than those outside the division. The sample size and particularly the number of selections from the more distant sources may be too small for a definitive test of the elaboration of Hypothesis 4.

Hypothesis 5 proposed that an exhaustion-of-the-queue effect would increase the probability that a selecting official would look outside the divisional job ladder to fill vacancies as the number of vacancies to be filled in a given year increased. This hypothesis received strong support from the results for Bureau 1 but little support elsewhere. There may have been too few instances in the other bureaus of multiple vacancies in divisional job ladders in the same year to allow an adequate test of this hypothesis. Upgrading, which probably accounts for some of the job changes reported here, may also have diluted this effect. When a supervisor upgrades an employee's position, he or she in effect creates and immediately fills a higher-level vacancy but only because an employee on the divisional job ladder is qualified for and indeed is doing higher-level work. Because the creation of these virtual vacancies depends on the existence of qualified employees to fill them, an exhaustion-of-the-queue effect would never occur in these cases.

Hypothesis 6 is supported by the analysis. The grade coefficients show that, in three of the four bureaus, selecting officials were signifi-

---

[7]The number of eligible individuals was fixed at values of 5–30 for comparisons across divisional boundaries of the same occupation/different job ladder source and at values of 10–40 for comparisons of the other occupational group source within and outside the division of the vacancy. The number of eligible individuals was fixed in the range of 2–10 for comparisons of the same job-ladder source within and outside the division.

cantly more likely to select an individual from outside the divisional job ladder to fill higher-graded positions than lower-graded ones. In Bureau 1, there was an additional tendency to go outside the division of the vacancy to fill it at higher grade levels, as can be seen by the second grade coefficient. The signs of the second grade coefficients for the other three bureaus were in the same direction as for Bureau 1, but these other coefficients were not statistically significant.

It should be noted that this grade effect persisted even when the number of eligible individuals was controlled. If the configuration of eligible individuals by itself had been sufficient to explain the relationship between grade and the pattern of vacancy filling, then the other justifications presented for Hypothesis 6 would have been undercut. But the statistical significance of the grade coefficients in Table 7.4 suggests that other factors in addition to the shape of an organization produce a relationship between the grade of a vacancy and boundary crossing to fill that vacancy.

Finally, Hypothesis 7 was supported by the results for Bureau 1 but not elsewhere. In three of the four bureaus, selecting officials were about as likely to reach across occupational boundaries to fill professional positions as they were to fill administrative ones. The uneven support for Hypothesis 7 may be a result of the different professional occupations found in the four bureaus.

DISCUSSION

An ideal-type view of ILMs might assume that job ladders completely control job mobility. At least for these four bureaus, this view is too simple. Empirical trajectories are not completely congruent with formal job ladders. Mobility was not solely within divisional boundaries. But the existence of boundary crossing does not make boundaries meaningless. Generally speaking, employees on the same job ladder and in the same division as a vacancy were more likely than others to get the job. Their advantage did not preclude outsiders from also filling vacancies, but insiders nonetheless had an advantage.

The boundary crossing found in these four bureaus was patterned in predictable ways. I argued that the divergence between implied and realized career trajectories should be structured by grade, by type of job, by the number of eligibles from a given source, and by the number of vacancies to be filled within a given divisional job ladder. Two of these predictions were realized, whereas two were not.

The configuration of potentially eligible employees for filling a position constrained the choices made by selecting officials. The perhaps surprisingly high level of boundary crossing into a divisional job ladder from other parts of an organization can be explained in part by the large number of outsiders relative to insiders who could compete for a particular vacancy. Overall, the results suggest that the greater the number of eligible individuals from any particular source, the greater the probability that an individual would be selected from that source. Although the results did not consistently uncover the postulated exhaustion-of-the-queue effect, they did not contradict the hypothesis either. I would still predict that further research would demonstrate its existence.

A significant relationship between boundary crossing and grade was uncovered in these data, as hypothesized. The statistical results disprove the argument that boundary crossing at higher grade levels is due to the desire of top managers to socialize upwardly mobile individuals into the organizational culture, because so many individuals were brought into the organization at high grade levels from outside the bureau. The results also are inconsistent with the hypothesis that the relationship between the grade of the vacancy and boundary crossing is due entirely to the smaller number of eligible individuals in the divisional job ladder at higher grade levels. Three possible explanations remain viable: (1) alternative career paths to higher-level positions provide training of equivalent value; (2) cross-functional job assignments become more important at higher levels; and (3) upwardly mobile individuals who reach the ceiling of their job ladder compete more energetically for positions in other job ladders.

I expected to find substantial boundary crossing to fill administrative positions. The technical desirability of cross-functional job assignments, coupled with the likelihood that narrow administrative job ladders were produced as much by the institutionalization of formal personnel systems as by technical considerations, supported this expectation. But the extent of boundary crossing to fill professional positions was rather surprising. To some extent, this boundary crossing may represent the fact that above a certain level in an organization, a professional's duties are largely administrative. Thus professionals may move from formally professional to formally administrative jobs and back, all the while doing essentially administrative work. In addition, most of the professionals in these bureaus are social science, mathematics and statistics, or accounting and budgetary professionals, and it may be that the boundary crossing observed with these data is more common for these professionals than for others. Finally, although the earlier discussion in this chapter stressed the extent to which institutional forces would differentiate administrative job ladders beyond the point required by training considerations, it may be that these same institutional forces also have created unnecessarily narrow professional job ladders as well.

One should keep in mind that the bureaus studied here are not a random sample of bureaus in the federal government. Nonetheless, they show similar importance of divisional job ladders and of divisional boundaries, along with similar effects of grade and the size of the eligibility pool. These similarities suggest that the major findings can be generalized to other settings. However, other results, particularly the amount of boundary crossing to fill professional relative to administrative jobs, may differ in other organizations, especially if substantively different professional positions were to be found there.

EXTENSIONS TO THE ENTIRE CIVIL SERVICE

As I noted earlier, it was not possible to perform this type of analysis for the employees of other government agencies because personnel data for their entire work forces were not available. However, it was possible to perform rough checks on these answers with data from a 1% sample of employees in the federal government as a whole, taken from the Central Personnel Data File of federal government.[8] These data were used to compute a list of all grade promotions that employees in the 1% sample experienced during the years 1972 through 1977. Grade promotions were then divided into those that occurred in the same job ladder and those that involved a change in job ladder. These tabulations speak only to the question of occupational boundaries. They cannot make use of the detailed controls for number of vacancies and number of positions found in the bureau analyses. Nonetheless, the pattern they reveal is in general agreement with the results found for the Washington offices of the four bureaus (see Table 7.5).

The governmentwide data showed that promotion often occurred within the same job ladder but that job ladders did not rigidly channel job mobility. Job-ladder changing was probably less common in the administrative–professional range in the government at large than in the four bureaus. But still, 15.7% of grade promotions at Grades 11 and higher involved a job ladder shift. This 15.7% figure is certainly an

---

[8]These data were collected by Taylor and Grandjean (1977). See Taylor (1979) and Grandjean (1981) for other analyses of these data.

Table 7.5

Percentage of Promoted Employees Who Changed Job Ladders by Grade and PATCO Status

	Grade																
	1	2	3	4	5	6	7	8	9	10	11	12	13	14	15	16	17
Percentage who changed job ladders	41 (46)[b]	33 (568)	47 (1206)	46 (1176)	25 (1249)	28 (419)	15 (1051)	26 (134)	12 (908)	27 (75)	14 (678)	16 (445)	18 (217)	18 (101)	36 (22)	* (*)	* (*)
Percentage changing job ladder from:																	
Professional	*[c] (*)	* (*)	* (*)	* (*)	8 (102)	* (*)	4 (263)	0 (8)	8 (278)	* (*)	9 (276)	13 (200)	13 (99)	8 (51)	33 (9)	* (*)	* (*)
Administrative	* (*)	* (*)	* (*)	0 (9)	9 (222)	* (*)	11 (377)	50 (10)	31 (402)	4 (28)	13 (298)	15 (209)	17 (99)	25 (40)	30 (10)	* (*)	* (*)
Technical	*	14	18	13	14	18	17	18	23	32	22	50	*	*	*	*	*
(percentage changing PATCO)[d]	(*)	75 (28)	73 (61)	57 (164)	71 (316)	75 (136)	72 (206)	83 (67)	96 (114)	100 (25)	82 (51)	100 (10)	(*)	(*)	(*)	(*)	(*)
Clerical	33	33	57	68	47	38	32	55	29	*	*	*	*	*	*	*	*
(percentage changing PATCO)	33 (27)	42 (303)	56 (799)	56 (573)	75 (247)	92 (103)	100 (47)	100 (11)	100 (7)	(*)	(*)	(*)	(*)	(*)	(*)	(*)	(*)

[a] Sample is all individuals who received a grade promotion between 1972 and June 1977. The last recorded status of each individual was compared with the first recorded status during the years 1972–77.
[b] Base for each percentage is in parentheses.
[c] A "*" is shown if the base is less than 5 cases.
[d] The percentage of technical and clerical workers changing PATCO status is computed as a percentage of the number who change job ladder.

undercount of the prevalence of job ladder shifts because Table 7.5 does not count job ladder shifts within the same grade. What is important to focus on, however, is that job ladder boundaries do matter, though they are not impassable.

The governmentwide data confirm expectations that the rate of crossing would increase near the top of the administrative–professional job ladders.[9] They also showed that administrators generally do change job ladders somewhat more often than professionals, though the difference is not great. Whereas 15.5% of administrators at Grades 11 and higher changed job ladders, 11.1% of professionals did so.[10] Third, Table 7.5 shows that job-ladder shifts were less common for administrative and professional trainees (in Grades 5, 7 and 9) than for employees on the higher rungs of upper-tier job ladders.

Finally, Table 7.5 allows us to examine the constraining effect of job ladders at the lower grades. The data make clear that, even more so than professional and administrative careers, clerical careers did not typically unfold within a single job ladder. Promotions routinely took clerical workers out of their old job ladders and into new ones. The second row of figures for clerical and technical jobs shows the percentage of cases in which the change in job ladder involved a change to a new PATCO status. Jobs in the PATCO classification were classified as either professional, administrative, technical, clerical, other, or mixed clerical–technical–administrative job ladders. For clerical workers in particular, a change of PATCO status might represent an increase in opportunity for future grade mobility. Even at the lower grades, a fairly high proportion of job ladder changes led to a change in PATCO status as well. At the middle grades, where administrative and professional trainee jobs as well as clerical and technical jobs were located, the proportion of job ladder shifts to a new PATCO status increased even more. This proportion eventually reached 100% at grade levels above the job ceilings of the lower-tier job ladders. Unlike the results for the four bureaus, these results do not tell how likely it was that officials would choose clerical workers to fill vacancies in nonclerical job ladders. But they do underscore the connection between promotion and job-ladder change in a personnel system where job ladders are tiered.

---

[9]When attention is limited to promotions out of Grades 11 and higher (which corresponds with filling vacancies in Grades 12 and higher), the Mantel-Haenszel test of no association versus a linear association between grade and the prevalence of job-ladder shifts rejects the null hypothesis at the 0.01 level.

[10]Such a difference is statistically significant at the 0.02 level.

CONCLUSION

Job-ladder boundaries do constrain mobility, but they are partially porous as well. Grade promotions near job-ladder ceilings and grade promotions on clerical job ladders, in particular, often brought the employee to a new job ladder. At the very lowest grades, the high level of job-ladder switching suggests that job-specific skills were so easily mastered that officials had no reason to avoid the switching of workers from one clerical job ladder to another. At higher grades in the both the lower-tier and the upper-tier, job-ladder shifts were an increasingly necessary aspect of grade promotion because of job-ceiling effects. Once one reached the top of one's job ladder, one could only gain a promotion by moving to a new job ladder. Such a promotion would then enhance opportunity for future grade promotion.

The porousness of job-ladder boundaries at the lowest grades may not have serious career implications for clerical workers. But the question of job-ladder mobility near tier boundaries is linked with a central issue in the development of the bureaucratic labor market in the federal government during the twentieth century. Should job ladders should be organized into separate tiers, and if they are so organized, how much movement between tiers should operating officials permit? The results presented in this chapter show only that such mobility was possible. Important questions remain to be answered. What proportion of entry-level vacancies were filled through promotion of lower-tier workers? Which lower-tier workers were able to get such promotions? What impact did the structure of job ladders have on gender or racial differences in promotion rates? These questions are the subjects of the next two chapters.

8

Equal Employment Opportunity and the Bridging of Job Ladders

EQUAL EMPLOYMENT OPPORTUNITY AND ITS IMPLICATIONS FOR MOBILITY

Many personnel practices of public and private organizations have come under legal scrutiny for their potential discriminatory impact in recent years. Discriminatory practices in testing, in recruitment, in the provision of training opportunities, and in promotion practices have all been the subject of litigation (Wallace 1976; O'Farrell and Harlan 1984; Burstein 1985). Scholars have done several studies of the impact of the equal employment opportunity movement (EEO) on gender and racial inequality (Butler and Heckman 1977; Lazear 1979; Northrup and Larson 1979; Beller 1980, 1982b; Welch 1981; Borjas 1982; Abbott and Smith 1984; Leonard 1984; Smith and Welch 1984a; Burstein 1985; Smith and Welch 1986). The overall impact of EEO is still a matter of dispute. But policies that benefited women and minorities held the promise of widening the mobility bridge between the lower and the upper tier, even if these policies did not eliminate the tier boundaries that had formed. The reason for the connection between EEO and the structure of job ladders is obvious. Women and blacks were overrepresented in precisely the occupations that now form a recognizable lower white-collar tier in bureaucratized organizations.

One of the goals of the EEO effort in the federal civil service was the expansion of promotional opportunities for lower-level employees (U.S. CSC 1976a,b; Rosenbloom 1977). The CSC diagnosed the overrepresentation of women and minorities at lower levels of the government as a

This chapter is an expanded version of a paper that was published in the *American Journal of Sociology* (1987, 93:119–140) under the title "The Professionalization of Administrative and Equal Employment Opportunity in the U.S. Federal Government."

correctable flaw in an otherwise fundamentally sound personnel system. The solution proposed by presidents, the CSC, and Congress was to stipulate that promotion policies must more effectively implement the merit system. This policy was supposed to aid deserving lower-level employees, particularly those who were victims of past discrimination, to advance.

One formulation of the problems of women and minorities in government derives from the philosophy of the "representative bureaucracy" (Kingsley 1944; Krislov 1967; Mosher 1968). One version of this philosophy holds that each level of the bureaucracy should contain all major social groups in proportions equal to their share of the population and that the government should achieve this goal by allocation, if necessary. The federal government rejected this formulation of the problem and solution. Instead, the CSC consistently took the position during the 1960s and 1970s that representation in this sense was desirable but only if it could be realized through the normal operation of a properly functioning merit system (Rosenbloom 1977; U.S. Comptroller General 1977).

The development of upward mobility programs in the federal government began in the late 1960s but did not seriously proliferate until the early 1970s. In 1966, the CSC initiated the Maximum Utilization of Skills and Training (MUST) Program "to improve the federal work force's efficiency by redesigning jobs . . . to best use employee's skills and training" (U.S. Comptroller General 1975a: 1). Upward mobility, as a specific set of programs, was not an official policy of the federal government until 1969, when President Nixon issued Executive Order 11478. This order reflected the CSC's earlier diagnosis that the plight of women and minorities was a correctable flaw in an otherwise sound personnel system. It essentially ordered agencies to correct this flaw by fully using employees' skills, by providing maximum opportunities for advancement, by providing sufficient resources to administer their programs, and by periodically evaluating program effectiveness. Program guidelines were first promulgated to federal agencies in 1970 (U.S. Comptroller General 1975: 37).

The Equal Employment Opportunity Act of 1972 was designed to help women and minorities. However, the government rejected a quota system approach as incompatible with a merit system.[1] The General

---

[1] A quota approach of course had its supporters, and even some government agencies were confused about official policy on equal employment opportunity. On social conflict over the goals of EEO, see Glazer 1978 and Burstein 1985. For a discussion of government confusion, see U.S. Comptroller General 1977.

Accounting Office gave the Equal Employment Opportunity Act of 1972
an interpretation consistent with a merit system philosophy when it
argued that

> by law, the government's upward mobility program is for all federal em-
> ployees. This means that the program should be nondiscriminatory and
> available to all. The Civil Service Commission stresses, however, that the
> greatest opportunity for impact is in the lower grade levels. Therefore, it
> defines upward mobility as a systematic Federal management effort to focus
> personnel policy and practice on developing and implementing specific ca-
> reer opportunities for lower-level employees in positions or occupational
> series which do not enable them to realize their full work potential. Female
> and minority employees will inevitably benefit most from upward mobility
> programs. (U.S. Comptroller General 1975a: 2)

Early efforts to implement upward mobility programs were spo-
radic (U.S. Commission on Civil Rights 1970; U.S. Congress. House
1972; Rosenbloom 1977). The Equal Employment Opportunity Act of
1972 required agencies to increase their EEO efforts, and the CSC was
given the power to monitor these activities. The CSC issued communications to agencies to guide them in their development of EEO programs
(U.S. CSC 1970, 1973a, 1974a, 1976b). The General Accounting Office
evaluated agency upward mobility plans in 19 departments and agencies in 1973. It found no significant programs at all in 10 agencies and
inadequately staffed programs in the other 9 (U.S. Comptroller General
1975). The director of the Civil Service Commission responded that early
efforts had been less effective than hoped for, in part because of their
newness. He went on to argue that

> as a result of our published guidance and follow-up visits with program
> officials, agencies have made significant progress in planning and admin-
> istering upward mobility programs. Our review of 1974 and 1975 plans
> shows marked improvement in agency planning efforts, particularly in their
> attention to the integration of upward mobility with other actions designed
> to overcome problems relating to equal employment opportunity. (U.S.
> Comptroller General 1975a: 38)

At the end of 1973, approximately 10,000 federal employees were
participating in upward mobility programs in over 1000 agency plans.
Governmentwide allocations for EEO increased from about $56 million
in Fiscal Year 1972 to approximately $169 million for Fiscal Year 1976
(U.S. Comptroller General 1977). About $46 million was spent on up-
ward mobility programs in Fiscal Year 1975 (U.S. Comptroller General
1975a).[2] In one agency examined in some detail, the number of em-

[2]These expenditure statistics are only estimates. Actual expenditures are not known.

ployees participating in upward mobility programs increased by more than an order of magnitude from 1971 to 1976 (DiPrete and Soule 1986).

Agency upward mobility programs contained elements such as the following:

1. The development of EEO goals and plans to achieve them.
2. The identification of underutilized talent.
3. The identification of target positions that these lower-level employees might be eligible for.
4. The creation of bridge positions that would make it easier for them to move from lower-tier to upper-tier positions.
5. The use of on-the-job and classroom training (both in the government and in academic settings) to prepare able lower-level employees for promotion.
6. The counseling of participants and potential participants by supervisors.
7. The provision of EEO training for managers and supervisors to increase their cooperation in the effort.
8. The establishment of prizes to grant recognition to managers and supervisors for their EEO efforts.
9. The establishment of an EEO complaint and investigation process.
10. Recruitment efforts to increase the representation of women and minorities at specific grade levels and in specific job ladders.
11. The performance of studies to determine time-in-grade differentials by minority group and sex.
12. The performance of studies to evaluate EEO efforts.

The upward mobility program was the product of political pressure from women, minorities, and their supporters for greater employment opportunity for members of these groups. But the effort also had clear implications for the further development of the structure of job ladders as well. An upper tier of professional positions had been in existence since the 1920s. The development of an upper tier of administrative job ladders represented a policy to increase the inflow of college graduates into administrative jobs and consequently to reduce the promotion rate of clerical workers. But the EEO effort contained an admission that agencies had overlooked qualified lower-level workers when filling entry positions on upper-tier job ladders. This admission represented an implicit, if perhaps temporary, repudiation of policies that separated white-collar job ladders into separate tiers in the first place. If EEO programs could be successful, they would in effect rebut the claim that the imposition of tier boundaries represented progress toward a more efficient and equitable personnel system.

Many of the upward mobility programs were essentially symbolic in character. EEO seminars, posters, and other publicity efforts arguably fall into this category. However, some of these programs had the potential to affect the structure of job ladders in the government. These "structural" (as opposed to "consciousness raising") programs involved the creation of bridge positions between job ladders and the creation of training programs.

One such strategy has been called a "train-then-place" strategy. It consisted of training lower-tier employees to make them competitive for target positions on upper-tier job ladders. A second strategy is the "bridge" strategy. It consisted of moving program participants into bridge positions that would give them the qualifying experience to move to an upper-tier job ladder. A third strategy is the "place-then-train" strategy. It consisted of moving a program participant from a lower-tier to an upper-tier job ladder at a trainee level. The agency would then train the employee to perform the duties required for positions in the new job ladder (Granville Corporation 1981).

As we have seen, the organization of professional and office work was asymmetric in the period from the 1920s through the 1940s. During that time, the government divided professional and subprofessional jobs into separate services but used a single service for all clerical and administrative jobs. In the postwar period, a superficial symmetry in the organization of professional and administrative work has evolved. Nonetheless, for reasons that have already been discussed, the professional barriers separating office work were not as well developed as those separating work in the more established professional and scientific fields. Consequently, one might expect agencies to make greater efforts to move lower-level employees into administrative rather than professional positions.

According to the CSC, administrative positions in particular were "excellent candidates as target positions for upward mobility programs" for two reasons: "(1) they did not necessarily require formal academic training in a speciality, in contrast to professional positions, and (2) administrative job ladders, like professional job ladders, spanned the entire upper grade range of the general schedule" (U.S. CSC 1976b: iii). Because of the decentralized nature of the government's EEO effort (over 1,000 separate plans were in existence by 1973), it is not possible to catalog the target positions of upward mobility programs with precision. But available evidence suggests that personnel practices in filling entry-level administrative positions should have been more responsive to the upward mobility efforts than practices regarding the filling of professional vacancies.

In summary, four expectations concerning the outcomes of the upwardly mobility program are justified:

1. The levels of promotion from lower-tier to upper-tier job ladders should have been greater for administrative than for professional positions both before and after the implementation of upward mobility programs.
2. If the upward mobility programs had an effect on promotion rates, the effect should have been greatest at the peak of the effort, namely 1973 and thereafter.
3. The upward mobility programs should have had a greater impact on personnel decisions affecting administrative positions than on personnel decisions affecting professional positions.
4. Women and minorities as groups should have benefitted from upward mobility programs because they were overrepresented at lower grade levels.

THE EXTENT OF MOBILITY FROM THE LOWER TO THE UPPER TIER

Government personnel data were used to compare the number of new hires and the number of promotions from lower-tier to upper-tier job ladders during the years 1962–1977. The analyses made use of personnel data for white-collar workers in the general schedule in the 15 largest agencies of the federal government (excluding the post office).[3] Together, these agencies accounted for slightly over 90% of the white-collar federal work force, excluding postal employees. These data were drawn from the 1% sample of civilian government workers from the CPDF used in Chapter 7, combined with personnel transactions for the same individuals extracted from the Federal Personnel Statistics Program (FPSP) for the years 1962–1972. Some personnel transactions for employees in the FPSP and the CPDF are missing, particularly in the earlier years. Therefore, the number of documented accessions and status promotions in personnel files is an undercount of the actual number of such events for sample employees. However, the observed ratio of

[3]These agencies consisted of the Departments of Agriculture, Commerce, Defense, Justice, Labor, Health, Education and Welfare, Housing and Urban Development, Interior, State, Transportation, and the Treasury. In addition, the Environmental Protection Agency, the General Services Administration, the National Aeronautical and Space Administration, and the Veterans Administration were included.

one type of event to the other was apparently unaffected in any material way by the presence of missing transactions. The present analysis relies only on these ratios.[4]

The CSC used the term *occupational series* to refer to job ladders in the government. Personnel agencies of the federal government had traditionally described the jobs in an occupational series as defining a "line of promotion."[5] In the early 1970s the CSC began classifying occupational series into four principal categories (the "PATCO" designation). The CSC classified upper-tier job ladders as either professional or administrative. Professional jobs required specialized skills obtained in a college or university degree program. The CSC described administrative jobs as involving "college-caliber" duties during the 1950s and 1960s. In the 1970s, it wrote that administrative jobs required skills "typically gained through a college-level general education, or through progressively responsible experience" (U.S. CSC 1976a: 5).[6] Entry-level positions in administrative and professional series typically spanned Grades 5, 7, and 9, which the CSC described as "trainee" or "developmental" positions. The level at which an individual entered depended upon his or her qualifications. The CSC described administrative and professional job ladders as "two-grade interval series." Employees typically advanced two grades at a time through the trainee grades and one grade at a time after they reached Grade 11.

Lower-tier job ladders consisted of technical jobs and clerical jobs. Technical jobs "involve work typically associated with, and supportive of a professional or administrative field, which is nonroutine in nature . . . involving extensive practical knowledge, gained through on-the-job experience and/or specific training less than that represented by college graduation" (U.S. CSC 1976a: 5). Clerical work involved "structured work" where the duties were "performed in accordance with established policies, experience, or working knowledge" (U.S. CSC 1976a: 5). These definitions suggest that technical work is more substantive and less routine than is clerical work. Technical positions had a somewhat higher average grade than did clerical positions. But the difference between the two was not always clear-cut, and the grade ranges of the two types of positions overlapped. The average salary of clerical workers in 1976 was $12,237 (or $9956 if postal clerks were excluded), which is near the $13,708 average for technical workers. Both figures are

---

[4]See the first appendix to this chapter for details.
[5]It was a "usual line of promotion" in 1931 (U.S. PCB 1931), and a "most natural line of promotion" in the 1970s and 1980s (U.S. OPM 1981).
[6]See Table 6.1 for complete definitions of the PATCO categories.

far below the average salaries for professional ($23,187) and administrative ($21,240) workers (U.S. CSC 1976a). The CSC described both technical and clerical job ladders as "one-grade-interval" job ladders because employees typically advanced one grade at a time on these ladders.

In addition, the CSC used "mixed" job ladders to classify jobs that it could not classify more precisely. These mixed job ladders spanned the entire grade range. "General clerical and administrative" or "general accounting, clerical, and assistant" are examples. The CSC labeled positions at Grades 1–6 on mixed job ladders as clerical, positions at Grades 7–10 as technical, and positions at Grades 11 and higher as administrative. However, the agencies themselves had the freedom to divide positions on these mixed job ladders into more narrowly drawn ladders.

During the years covered by the personnel data available for analysis, the job ladder structure of the federal civil service was continually evolving. Some of these new ladders had differentiated from old ones, whereas others were a combination of two or more older ladders. This study relied on the 1970s PATCO classification to designate the status of a job ladder. Job ladders used in the 1960s that could not unambiguously be assigned a designation as professional or administrative were excluded from the analysis, to avoid misclassification.

From 1960 to the middle 1970s, the number of administrators and professionals in the government grew substantially. The number of employees on exclusively administrative job ladders nearly doubled from 160,000 to 312,000. The number of employees on professional job ladders increased by nearly 50%, from 206,000 to 306,000 (U.S. CSC 1960, 1976a). Vacancies on these ladders could be filled in two ways: through recruitment of an outsider or through what might be termed a status promotion. A status promotion as defined here consists in the movement of an employee from a lower-tier job ladder to an upper-tier one. This move may or may not involve a grade promotion, the usual meaning of the word *promotion* in personnel literature. Movement from a lower-tier to an upper-tier job ladder had the obvious advantage of placing an individual on a job ladder where his or her "most natural line of promotion" included higher graded positions. These status promotions could be further distinguished by the source of the promoted employee:

1. Clerical job ladders defined as such in the 1970s PATCO system. Virtually all of these ladders had been in existence since 1962 or before.
2. Technical job ladders defined as such in the 1970s PATCO sys-

tem. Some of these technical ladders had existed throughout the years since 1962, and some were of more recent origin.
3. Mixed job ladders. All mixed job ladders existed throughout the years 1962–1977. However, it is difficult to establish the status of workers on the lower grades of these series, even though the government conventionally classifies those in Grades 1–6 as clerical and those in Grades 7–10 as technical. Some employees in Grades 1–10 on mixed job ladders may have been newly hired by their agencies as administrative trainees.[7] To avoid counting any job ladder switches by such individuals as status promotions, attention was limited to employees in this group who had worked in the civil service for more than 3 years. Such employees moving to entry-level grades in administrative job ladders were more likely to be clerks or technicians. Agencies would probably have promoted those hired into clearly administrative jobs on mixed job ladders out of this grade range comparatively quickly.[8]
4. Other job ladders.[9] These were sometimes skilled manual workers (especially in the Department of Defense). Sometimes they were clerical or technical job ladders that no longer existed by the 1970s. These positions were grouped with technical job ladders to form the "technical and other" category that is presented in the tables. This grouping was used because both the technical and the "other" group were changing in composition over time, and because some positions shifted from the "other" category into the technical category during this time.

Table 8.1 compares the two strategies of filling entry-level vacancies by new hires or by status promotions on job ladders that were professional or exclusively administrative (i.e., excluding the mixed job ladders) during 1962–1977.[10] Table 8.1 shows separate statistics for the DOD and the other 14 agencies. This was done for several reasons. The DOD was nearly as large as the other agencies combined. Furthermore,

---

[7]Because of this ambiguity, vacancies in mixed job ladders were not included in the present analysis. I did count certain employees who moved from mixed job ladders to administrative ones as status promotions, using the rule described in the text.

[8]The second appendix to this chapter further discusses the validity of this assumption.

[9]The use of *other* here is not equivalent to the *other* PATCO group, which consists of security and student trainee positions.

[10]Vacancies can also be filled by reinstatement or by transfer from another agency or from another upper-tier job ladder. These sources of vacancy filling were not of particular interest for present purposes, and were excluded.

Table 8.1

A Comparison of New Hires and Status Promotions into Entry-Grade Positions
(GS-5, GS-7, and GS-9)

	Administrative job ladders				
	1962–1965	1966–1968	1969–1972	1973–1977	Total
Fourteen agencies					
New hires	51	61	112	192	416
Promotions (P)	30	38	61	196	325
Promotions (C)	30	42	65	196	333
Percentage promotions (P)	37.0	38.4	35.3	50.5	43.9
Percentage promotions (C)	37.0	40.8	36.7	50.5	44.5
Department of Defense					
New hires	48	70	53	90	261
Promotions (P)	67	99	77	170	413
Promotions (C)	78	110	91	171	450
Percentage promotions (P)	58.3	58.6	59.2	65.4	61.3
Percentage promotions (C)	61.9	61.1	63.2	65.5	63.3
Professional job ladders					
Fourteen agencies					
New hires	162	130	84	202	578
Promotions	18	15	19	39	91
Percentage promotions	10.0	10.1	18.4	16.4	13.6
Department of Defense					
New hires	88	99	69	152	408
Promotions	25	15	12	12	64
Percentage promotions	22.1	13.2	14.8	7.3	13.6

Note. The counts in rows labeled "(P)" (for probable) do not include as promotions movements into administrative career lines that are probably artifacts of a reorganization of career lines. Rows labeled "(C)" (for conservative) include these movements. Only administrative job ladders were affected. Most of the cases involved were in the Department of Defense. See text for further details.

the Vietnam War disrupted its work force more than those of other agencies (Grandjean 1981). Finally, its job ladders were not as stable during the time period covered here. Table 8.1 contains a "conservative" and a "probable" estimate of the proportion of status promotions into administrative job ladders. The difference between the two depends upon how one treats certain job shifts that were arguably artificial, a consequence of the restructuring of job ladders involved during the years preceding 1973.[11]

It is apparent from Table 8.1 that managers responsible for filling vacancies drew heavily on existing personnel to fill entry-level administrative positions. When attention is limited to vacancies filled either by new hire or by status promotion (i.e., excluding reinstatements, temporary employment, etc.), Table 8.1 shows that the 14 agencies filled more than 40% of the vacancies by status promotions, whereas the DOD filled over 60% by status promotions. Furthermore, a significant change occurred in the pattern of filling vacancies in the 14 agencies in the 1970s. The proportion of vacancies filled through status promotion in the years 1972–1977, when the upward mobility effort had increased substantially, was more than 10 percentage points higher than previously. In the Defense Department, a trend in the same direction also existed, though it was more modest.[12] To summarize, then, it was commonplace throughout the 1960s and 1970s for government agencies to fill entry-level administrative positions by promotion from lower-tier job ladders.[13]

In contrast to the way agencies filled administrative positions, Table 8.1 shows that professional positions were almost always filled from outside the government. These results are consistent with expectations. Furthermore, the use of status promotions into professional positions in the government does not show a consistent response to the implementation of upward mobility programs.[14]

---

[11]Only administrative ladders were affected by this ambiguity.

[12]The DOD was also more heavily affected by job-ladder reorganization. If one counts all questionable job shifts caused by job-ladder reorganization as status promotions, no significant time trend exists in Table 8.1. If one excludes these changes as artificial, which is the more reasonable course, the DOD looks similar to the other agencies.

[13]The larger yearly counts in the later years than the earlier years in Table 8.1 is due to two factors besides the substantial rate of increase in employment in administrative and professional job positions during these years. First, vacancies in 1960s job ladders that could not unambiguously be assigned a designation as administrative or professional (based on 1970s PATCO codes) were excluded from the analysis. Second, only "documented" actions were counted, and the rate of missing personnel transactions was higher in earlier years than in later ones (see the first appendix to this chapter for a discussion of the implications of missing personnel transactions.) The goal of the analysis was to compare ways of filling vacancies in unambiguously administrative or professional positions, not to accurately determine the overall rate of vacancy filling in the government in these years. Therefore shortfalls in the counts were acceptable so long as they did not materially affect the ratio between promotions and new hires.

[14]The observed percentage of status promotions for professional job ladders is actually a liberal estimate. It includes student trainees, who constituted a quarter of the promotions in the DOD and a third in the 14 agencies.

Table 8.2
A Comparison of New Hires and Status Promotions into Entry-Grade Positions (GS-5, GS-7, and GS-9) in Administrative Job Ladders, by Origin Status

	1962–1965	1966–1968	1969–1972	1973–1977	Total
Fourteen agencies					
New hires	51	61	112	192	416
Clerical	5	12	17	67	105
Technical/other[a]	21	17	26	66	130
Mixed[b]	4	13	22	63	102
Total actions	81	103	177	388	753
Percentage new hires	63.0	59.2	63.3	49.5	55.5
Department of Defense					
New hires	48	70	53	90	261
Clerical	13	17	10	31	71
Technical/other	37	59	35	58	189
Mixed	28	34	46	82	190
Total actions	126	180	141	261	711
Percentage new hires	38.1	38.9	36.8	34.5	36.7

[a]Includes skilled manual and other occupations.
[b]Status promotions from mixed job ladders include only employees with more than three years tenure.

Table 8.2 breaks down status promotions into administrative positions according to whether they originated in clerical, technical, or mixed job ladders.[15] It shows that all three sources were regularly used to fill administrative vacancies in the 1970s. The increased use of status promotions to fill vacancies was due to the increased rate of status promotions from the clerical and mixed job ladders.

The peak in the use of status promotions to fill administrative vacancies occurred when the upward mobility effort was greatest. In order to determine whether the observed trend persisted in the presence of controls, I used logistic regression to model how administrative vacancies were filled. I modeled personnel practices in the DOD and the 14 agencies separately, for the reasons stated before. The following variables were included in the analysis:

1. *Time.* Time was measured in two ways, as a polynomial in calendar year, and through the time period groupings used in Table 8.1.

[15]The conservative coding is used here.

2. *Occupation.* Major group of the position (as defined by the federal government) was used for the occupational groups with the largest number of positions filled. Because the occupational composition of the DOD differed substantially from the 14 agencies, it was not practical to use the same set of occupational controls for both samples.
3. *The agency where the vacancy was located.* Dummy variables for the larger agencies were included in the analysis of the 14 agencies. The rationale for including agency is that different agencies might have had different levels of commitment to identifying and training lower-level employees for promotion.
4. The grade of the vacancy (Grade).
5. The location of the vacancy (Washington, DC versus the regions) (WASH, DC).
6. Change in the size of the agency between year $t - 1$ and t, where t was the year the vacancy was filled (ΔSize).
7. The change in the relative pay of federal-sector to private-sector jobs at the GS-11 equivalent level between years $t - 2$ and $t - 1$ and between years $t - 1$ and t, where t is the year the vacancy was filled (ΔPay($t - 1$) and ΔPay(t)). The pay index was constructed from data found in the *Statistical Abstracts of the United States* and from Belman (1968), Rosow (1970), and the Advisory Committee on Federal Pay (1979).
8. Change in the unemployment rate between years $t - 2$ and $t - 1$ and between years $t - 1$ and t (ΔUnem($t - 1$) and ΔUnem(t)).

The rationale for including the variables measuring size, pay, and unemployment deserves comment. Convincing arguments can be made to the effect that changes in size and changes in the relative attractiveness of public to private jobs should affect personnel practices. But these arguments can be used to support findings in either direction.

Consider the net effect of a change in organizational size first. When an organization grows, the number of vacancies grows, whereas the number of qualified on-board employees to fill them does not accelerate as rapidly. This fact should have a negative effect on the proportion of vacancies filled from within. However, an expanding organization might be unable or unwilling to expand recruitment efforts rapidly enough to keep up with demand and instead might reach further down the queue of available insiders to fill the expanding number of vacancies. Too little is known about organizational responsiveness to growth to make a clear prediction about the net effect of growth on the probability of filling a position from within.

The net effect of a change in the relative attractiveness of jobs in the public sector to jobs in the private sector is not clear-cut either. The more attractive government jobs became, the more outsiders would want them. The quality and size of the outside pool of contestants would grow, and an organization might be attracted to such talent. At the same time, the turnover rate of government employees would be expected to decrease, and therefore the quality of the inside pool would also increase. The two effects have opposite signs. We might expect, however, that an organization such as a federal agency, which has a career personnel system in place, should favor insiders over outsiders when it finds insiders to be competent for the job. An organization that favored insiders should respond more strongly to changes in the quality of the internal work force than to changes in the quality of external applicants. The crucial issue, of course, is an agency's perception of the quality of its in-place work force.

Table 8.3 shows all coefficients for the models in which time was measured through the period dummy variables. For a second model, in which time was measured continuously, only the linear time coefficient is shown for each result. The "conservative" coding was used for the 14 agencies, whereas both the "conservative" and the "probable" codings were used for the DOD because the choice of coding had a larger effect on the trend for the DOD sample.

Despite the presence of control variables, the time variables are still significant and show that the level of status promotions rose as the upward mobility effort grew. Period effects for the 14 agencies and the DOD, using the "probable" coding, are jointly significant at the 0.026 level.[16] When the "conservative" DOD coding is used, the joint significance level is 0.088. For models using the linear time trend, time is significant at the 0.003 level when the "probable" DOD coding was used and is significant at the 0.01 level when the "conservative" DOD coding was used. The data also support the more specific hypothesis that the rate of promotions was greater during the later EEO period than the early EEO period. When the "conservative" coding for the DOD is used along with the 14 agencies, the difference in the level of status promotions between the 1969–1972 and 1973–1977 period is significant at the 0.029 level. When the "probable" coding was used, the significance level is 0.007. Quadratic and cubic time variables were not significant for either the 14 agencies or the DOD, for either the conservative or the probable coding. However, the DOD results using the time period dummy variables suggest that the proportion of status promotions rose

[16]Pearson's p-lambda test was used for all joint tests reported in this paragraph.

during the Vietnam buildup.[17] It fell thereafter before rising again after the passage of the EEO Act of 1972.

Although personnel practices in the DOD apparently responded to the Vietnam War buildup, organizational growth *per se* had no significant effect on the ratio of status promotions to new hires, either in the DOD or in the 14 agencies. A measure of the rate of change in the number of vacancies to be filled (instead of change in the size of the agency) might have shown a more clear-cut effect on the proportion of these vacancies filled internally.

The presence of the pay and unemployment-change variables attenuated the effect of the time variables, though the time trend remained significant, as documented before. When government jobs become more attractive, whether because government pay rose or because jobs in general became harder to find, status promotions rose. The estimates suggest that the improvement in the quality of insiders competing for positions increased promotions more than the improvement in the quality of competition from the outside increased new hires. Such an effect is consistent with a practice of recruiting from within whenever an organization finds the available talent there to be sufficient. As I noted before, such a practice is to be expected in any organization that claims to have a career personnel system in place. This effect does not, of course, demonstrate that government agencies always did a good job of assessing the talent of available insiders. Controlling for this effect, promotions were more common in the EEO period than previously, which suggests that EEO increased agency use of organizational insiders independently of shifts in market conditions.

The results of Table 8.3 also show an interesting pattern of variation by agency. Overall, status promotions were more common in the Departments of Transportation, the Interior, Agriculture, and in the Department of Health, Education, and Welfare than they were in the other 9 agencies. We have already noted that the DOD also made extensive use of status promotions to fill vacancies. Although the data do not allow a definitive interpretation, the agency coefficients are broadly consistent with the hypothesis that agencies with the greatest amount of in-house training of intermediate level employees were most likely to fill these positions with insiders. Agencies that made less use of in-house training would instead tend to hire outsiders instead of promoting insiders.

To evaluate this hypothesis, I computed the proportion of total

[17]The hypothesis of equality between the 1962–1965 period and the 1966–1968 period in the DOD is rejected at the 0.10 level for the "probable" coding.

Table 8.3
Coefficients from a Logistic Regression Analysis of the Probability of Filling an Entry-Grade (GS-5, 7, or 9) Administrative Vacancy through Status Promotion (as Opposed to New Hire)

	14 agencies (C)		DOD (C)		DOD (P)	
	Coefficient[a]	P-value[b]	Coefficient[a]	P-value[b]	Coefficient[a]	P-value[b]
Constant	-1.40	(0.006)	-1.84	(0.000)	-1.77	(0.000)
Grade	0.22	(0.000)	0.39	(0.000)	0.37	(0.000)
Wash, DC	0.22	(0.45)	0.22	(0.73)	0.32	(0.63)
Agriculture	0.83	(0.03)	—	—	—	—
HEW	0.76	(0.05)	—	—	—	—
Treasury	0.12	(0.70)	—	—	—	—
Interior	1.27	(0.002)	—	—	—	—
Transportation	1.73	(0.01)	—	—	—	—
Veterans administration	0.60	(0.13)	—	—	—	—
Justice	0.61	(0.23) (0.007)	—	—	—	—
Social science	-0.95	—	—	—	—	—
Personnel	—	(0.88)	-0.45	(0.24)	-0.34	(0.38)
General administration	0.05	—	-0.54	(0.07)	-0.37	(0.23)
Accounting	—	—	0.51	(0.30)	0.68	(0.17)

	(1)		(2)		(3)	
Information/arts	—		−1.17	(0.007)	−1.21	(0.007)
Business/industry	−0.40	(0.16)	−0.15	(0.61)	−0.15	(0.61)
Training	—		−0.93	(0.016)	−0.72	(0.07)
Investigating	−1.85	(0.000)	—		—	
Supply	—		0.52	(0.10)	0.68	(0.04)
Transport	−4.16	(0.000)	—		—	
ΔSize	−5.4E-5	(0.76)	−2.08E-6	(0.41)	−2.13E-6	(0.41)
ΔPay ($t − 1$)	−3.71	(0.40)	−8.83	(0.03)	−10.7	(0.01)
ΔPay (t)	−7.53	(0.05)	−3.25	(0.35)	−4.13	(0.24)
ΔUnemployed ($t − 1$)	0.58	(0.01)	0.30	(0.24)	0.37	(0.15)
ΔUnemployed (t)	0.33	(0.05)	0.08	(0.66)	0.033	(0.86)
1962–1965	−0.69	(0.03)	−0.29	(0.31)	−0.51	(0.08)
1966–1968	−0.31	(0.28)	0.30	(0.41)	0.19	(0.61)
1969–1972[c]	−0.44	(0.15)	−0.63	(0.03)	−0.84	(0.006)
Year[d]	0.066	(0.007)	0.031	(0.19)	0.048	(0.05)
Observations	752		711		674	

[a] A positive coefficient means a higher probability of filling a vacancy through status promotion. To illustrate, a coefficient of +0.5 for a dummy variable would imply an increase in the probability of promoting a lower-level employee instead of hiring an outsider from 0.2 to 0.29, i.e. 9 percentage points.

[b] P-values (two-tailed) are in parentheses.

[c] 1973–1977 is the omitted category for the model in which time was measured with four time-period dummy variables.

[d] The "year" variable is a linear representation of time, and was used in a separate estimation. Other coefficients are not shown for the model that used the "year" variable.

Table 8.4
A Comparison of the Level of Education[a] of Employees Moving into Entry-Level
(GS-5 through GS-9) Administrative and Professional Positions, by Source

Administrative positions	N	Percentage high school[b] or less	Percentage some post-high school	Percentage 4 years[c] college
14 Agencies				
New hires	338	16.6	19.5	63.9
Clerical	96	28.1	52.1	18.8
Technical/other	122	22.1	41.0	36.9
Mixed	91	37.4	54.9	7.7
Department of Defense				
New hires	188	12.2	16.5	71.3
Clerical	56	37.5	42.9	19.6
Technical/other	155	39.4	49.7	11.0
Mixed	145	51.7	42.1	6.2
Professional positions				
14 Agencies				
New hires	405	2.0	3.5	94.6
Clerical	3	0.0	0.0	100.0
Technical/other	71	2.8	16.9	80.3
Mixed	2	0.0	50.0	50.0
Department of Defense				
New hires	266	0.7	5.3	94.0
Clerical	5	40.0	20.0	40.0
Technical/other	46	6.5	21.7	71.7
Mixed	1	100.0	0.0	0.0

[a]Education only available for individuals who were still employed in the federal government during the period 1972–1977.
[b]Percentage with no more than a high school education.
[c]Percentage with at least 4 years of college education.

man-hours that GS 9–12 employees spent in training in Fiscal Year 1973, the year for which such data were available (U.S. CSC 1974b: Appendix B). This grade level was chosen because positions at this level are mostly located at the lower end of administrative or professional job ladders, which are generally the targets of upward mobility programs. The four departments that (after controlling for other factors) had the highest level of status promotions outside the DOD, namely Agriculture, Interior, HEW, and Transportation, each trained more hours on average than did the other agencies for which such data were available.[18] The DOD trained more than 9 of the 12 other agencies for which we have information. Thus the data are broadly consistent with our hypothesis.

However, it is also clear that such an explanation could not be completely responsible for the observed pattern of coefficients. Transportation probably spent much of its training budget on air traffic controllers, who were more likely to be hired from outside (note the negative coefficient in Table 8.3). Also, Justice trained more than any other agency did, but its coefficient, although positive, was not significantly different from zero.[19] A complete explanation for agency differences would be multidimensional in character, involving occupational composition, commitment to training, and political environment. The available data do not allow a definitive decomposition of these effects.

Table 8.4 shows that a large (though not overwhelming) majority of new hires had finished 4 years of college or more. The new hires generally fit the description of the people the CSC had hoped to recruit for upper-tier jobs when it started the FSEE program in 1955. In contrast, a high proportion of employees moving to administrative job ladders from the lower tier had never been to college. A clear majority did not have a college degree. The data cannot establish whether the employees who moved to administrative job ladders from lower-tier positions had received special training as part of upward mobility programs. But the group of promoted employees evidently had convinced agency officials that their experience was a valid substitute for a university education.

SEX AND RACE COMPOSITION OF NEW HIRES AND PROMOTEES

As noted at the start of this chapter, civil rights groups lobbied for upward mobility programs because of the disproportionate numbers of women and minority members in lower-tier jobs. Tables 8.5 and 8.6 show that status promotions were a key vehicle of opportunity for wom-

---

[18]No data were available for the EPA or State. The average employee (GS 9–12) hours spent in training for Fiscal Year 1973 were as follows—Agriculture: 31.35, Commerce: 29.96, DOD: 33.83, HEW: 31.02, HUD: 12.73, Interior: 30.19, Justice: 78.82, Labor: 14.07, Transportation: 62.10, Treasury: 34.28, GSA: 27.28, NASA: 22.88, VA: 18.55.

[19]The coefficient for Transportation becomes significantly negative if the occupational controls are removed. The coefficient for Justice is still not significantly different from 0, despite the negative coefficient on investigation in Table 8.4. It should be noted that other agencies besides Justice employed workers in investigation.

Table 8.5
A Comparison of New Hires and Status Promotions into Entry-Grade (GS-5 through GS-9) Positions in Administrative Career Lines, by Sex

	1962–1965	1966–1968	1969–1972	1973–1977	Total
Fourteen agencies					
New hires					
Males	48	38	104	140	330
Females	3	23	8	51	85
Percentage female	5.9	37.7	7.1	26.7	25.8
Promotions					
Males	21	21	30	74	146
Females	9	21	35	123	188
Percentage female	30.0	50.0	46.2	62.4	56.3
Total					
Males	69	59	134	214	476
Females	12	44	43	174	273
Percentage female	14.8	42.7	24.3	44.9	36.5
Department of Defense					
New hires					
Males	42	54	40	72	208
Females	5	16	13	18	52
Percentage female	11.6	20.6	25.0	21.4	20.0
Promotions					
Males	51	62	62	82	257
Females	27	48	29	89	193
Percentage female	34.6	43.6	31.9	52.1	42.9
Total					
Males	93	116	102	154	465
Females	32	64	42	107	245
Percentage female	25.6	35.6	29.2	41.0	34.5

en and for minorities. Their representation among those moving from the lower to the upper tier was always greater than among the new hires.[20] Moreover, despite the rise in the proportion of new hires who were women, the proportion of promotees who were women in 1973–1977 was still twice as high as the proportion of new hires who were women. A similar pattern existed for minorities. Women and minorities benefitted by increased representation in the two types of entry-level administrative employees (new hires and promotees), but they also ben-

[20]The hypothesis that the association between sex and promotion is 0 is rejected ($G^{**}2=132$ with 1 d.f.), and the hypothesis that the association between race and promotion is 0 is also rejected ($G^{**}2=22$ with 1 d.f.).

Table 8.6
A Comparison of New Hires and Status Promotions into Entry-Grade (GS-5 through GS-9) Positions in Administrative Career Lines, by Race

	1962–65	1966–68	1969–72	1973–77	Total
	Fourteen agencies				
New hires					
Nonwhites	1	2	6	20	29
Whites	28	38	84	158	308
Percentage nonwhites	3.5	5.0	6.7	11.2	8.6
Promotions					
Nonwhites	1	4	15	37	57
Whites	22	30	43	144	239
Percentage nonwhites	4.4	11.8	25.9	20.4	19.3
Total					
Nonwhites	2	6	21	57	86
Whites	50	68	127	302	547
Percentage nonwhites	0	5.9	12.2	16.3	11.5
	Department of Defense				
New hires					
Nonwhites	1	1	3	8	13
Whites	35	41	36	77	189
Percentage nonwhites	2.8	2.4	7.7	9.4	6.4
Promotions					
Nonwhites	9	10	9	29	57
Whites	47	74	66	142	329
Percentage nonwhites	16.1	11.9	12.0	17.0	14.8
Total					
Nonwhites	10	11	12	37	70
Whites	82	115	102	219	518
Percentage nonwhites	10.9	8.7	10.5	14.4	11.9

Note. Information on race is not available for employees who left the government before 1973. These employees are therefore excluded from the above table. Nonwhite category includes only blacks and Hispanics.

efitted indirectly from the agencies' increased use of promotions to fill vacancies. A shift toward greater use of promotions favored lower-level civil servants over outside workers, and women and minorities were more heavily represented in the former group. Women and minorities had a smaller share of both new hires and promotions in the DOD than in the 14 agencies. Nonetheless, the DOD's greater use of status promotions allowed DOD women and minorities to gain about the same share of entry-level administrative jobs as their counterparts elsewhere in government.

Table 8.5 also shows that the position of women began improving in the federal government during the late 1960s. Although the focus here is not specifically on recruitment, it should be noted that EEO efforts on behalf of women predated the upward mobility programs. Agencies were prohibited from specifying a sex preference when filling government jobs in 1962, and Executive Order 11375 reaffirmed the official policy prohibiting discrimination against women in the federal civil service in 1967. Partially as a result of such policies, the proportion of new hires from FSEE registers who were women increased from 15% in 1961 to 33% in 1967 (U.S. CSC 1968b).

MORE EVIDENCE ON THE EFFECTIVENESS OF THE BRIDGING STRATEGY

The evidence presented so far in this chapter only extends through 1977. Furthermore, the data do not allow an identification of the individuals who participated in officially designated upward mobility programs and who either were or were not successful in moving to the upper tier. However, some evidence on the effectiveness of specifically designed upward mobility programs does exist. In 1980, OPM commissioned the Granville Corporation to study upward mobility programs in nine different agencies.[21] One purpose of this study was to determine whether upward mobility programs had succeeded in moving workers from lower-tier to upper-tier job ladders. Another purpose was to determine which particular upward mobility program was the most successful. The study also measured subsequent advancement by those who gained upper-tier jobs because of their program participation.

In the Granville study, researchers selected for study a random sample of 407 employees who had participated in upward mobility programs at some time between 1973 and January 1, 1980, in one of the nine agencies. These employees generally fit the description of lower-level employees who were not "fast-tracking" through their organizations. Fifty-eight percent were in clerical job ladders, and another 27% were in technical job ladders before the start of their participation in upward mobility programs. Eighty percent of these employees were in Grades 4 through 7 prior to program entry. Fifty-three percent of the target posi-

---

[21]Participating agencies consisted of the Department of Agriculture, the National Institute of Health, the National Oceanic and Atmosphere Administration, the Bureau of the Census, the Federal Aviation Administration, the National Aeronautics and Space Administration, the Central Intelligence Agency, the Veterans Administration, and the Defense Mapping Agency.

tions for this group were in professional or administrative job ladders, and only 8% of the target positions were clerical. Of the remaining positions, 27% were described as technical, though these may have been located at Grades 7–10 on mixed job ladders because such positions were officially counted as technical by OPM (see U.S. OPM 1983).[22] The relative proportion of professional to administrative target positions varied substantially by agency however, with the CIA at one extreme, where all target positions were professional, to the Agriculture Department at the other, where only 17% were professional.[23] The target positions were largely (82%) located in the trainee grades of 5, 7, and 9, as expected. Seventy percent of the program participants were female, and 40% were minority group members. Entry into the upward mobility program was competitive in 89% of the cases. Roughly half of the program participants were trained for 1 year or less, with another third receiving 2 or 3 years of training.

As measured by the Granville study, the training programs were extremely successful in obtaining promotions to job ladders that offered opportunity for further advancement. In 70% of the cases in the study, a "place-then-train" strategy was used, in 10% a "bridge" strategy was used, whereas in 20% a "train-then-place" strategy was employed. As of October 1981, the rates of success for the "train-then-place" strategy was 69%, whereas 95% of the "bridge" and 98% of the "place-then-train" participants had been successfully placed in their target positions. Furthermore, these employees were able to continue moving beyond the attainment of their target positions. Seventy percent of employees who had achieved their target positions at least a year before the Granville study was conducted had received at least one grade promotion since achieving that position. An even higher 82% of those who had achieved their target position more than 3 years before the Granville study had received at least two grade promotions since that time. As a consequence, whereas 58% of program participants had been in clerical job ladders before their entry into the program, only 8.2% were in clerical positions at the time of the Granville study. Thirty-two percent were in administrative positions, 24% were in professional positions, and 23% in technical positions as of October 1981. Before participation, the medi-

[22]Similarly, the target jobs that were clerical may have been at Grades 5 or 6 on mixed job ladders.

[23]Because of this variability, one cannot easily generalize from this sample to the proportion of target positions that were professional in the civil service as a whole. As the analysis described before indicated, status promotions to professional positions filled a much smaller proportion of professional vacancies in the trainee grades than did status promotions to administrative positions.

an grade of participants was 5.6, with only 4.6% in Grades GS-9 and above. By October, 1981, the median grade of participants was 8.9, with 61% in Grades GS-9 and above and 34% in Grades GS-11 or above. In other words, one-third of the participants had reached journeyman-level administrative or professional positions by the early 1980s.

Finally, interviews conducted with program participants at the end of 1982 found them in general agreement that their careers had benefited from participation in the upward mobility programs. The methodology of the Granville study does not allow an assessment of whether lower-level employees in general believed that selection for participation was handled fairly.[24] But clearly, the overwhelming majority of program participants apparently thought so.[25] Researchers asked 23 supervisors in six of the nine agencies for their opinion of the program participants and their sense of what other supervisors believed. Only 9 of the 23 thought that most government supervisors would not willingly allocate an upward mobility position at the present time. Over 50% of the polled supervisors thought that the number of supervisors willing to allocate such positions had increased in the years between 1979 and late 1982, when the interviews were conducted. Thus, even during the initial years of a highly conservative presidency, when EEO was not in vogue in Washington, the accomplishments of program participants were apparently improving the reputation of the upward mobility program.

These results should not be taken as proof that the upward mobility programs were a complete success. As in the early years (when the GAO reported management resistance to the implementation of upward mobility programs [U.S. Comptroller General 1975a]), more than half the supervisors in 1982 reported that lack of acceptance of the program by managers was still a barrier to its implementation. More than one-third said that too few positions were allocated under the program. Clearly, the number of positions allocated would critically affect the number of promotions the program could produce. The evidence presented earlier in the chapter, however, shows that by the middle 1970s a substantial proportion of entry-level positions in administrative job ladders were filled by promotion from lower-tier job ladders. Professional vacancies were predominantly filled by outsiders. However, the Granville study raises the question whether the proportion of professional vacancies filled by status promotion increased in the later 1970s.

---

[24]What is needed for an accurate assessment of perceived fairness is a polling of those who were not selected for participation as well as those who were.
[25]But even among this group, a few thought there was some preselection of program participants.

DISCUSSION

The evidence presented in this chapter suggests that EEO programs were somewhat successful in bridging job ladders for selected lower-tier employees in the federal government. It further supports the hypothesis that the proportion of entry-level administrative positions filled by promotion increased during the middle 1970s. One might imagine that if two job ladders were bridged, they become one job ladder. But the bridging of the lower and upper tiers in the federal government was not accompanied by a unification of lower- and upper-tier job ladders. EEO did not eliminate the tiered personnel system, not did it attempt to do so.

The EEO effort had unfolded within a culture that accepts the professional model for higher-level work. It further accepts the idea that administrative and clerical work lay in separate occupations. Most of all, employers accept the desirability of recruiting a large portion of their management talent from the ranks of college graduates. Labor market forces require that they be recruited at higher grade levels than lower-level workers. Pragmatic and cultural considerations dictate that these higher entry positions anchor separate upper-tier job ladders. Consequently, even as EEO programs to move selected individuals across the tier boundary proliferated, the CSC and later OPM continued the business of completing the differentiation of clerical and administrative job ladders begun in the 1940s.[26]

The technical justification for drawing a line at a particular point in the hierarchy and arguing that jobs below the line are qualitatively different from jobs above the line is often weak. But some occupations have a professional identity in society. This identity provides a justification for excluding lower-level work from their job ladders. By convention, backed sometimes by law and often by social pressure from organized professions, professional hierarchies make their professional character as unambiguous as possible. The articulation of these ladders with the educational system is clearly stated; positions on professional job ladders require a university degree and sometimes a license. Finally, professional and subprofessional positions do not coexist on the same job ladder.

Administrative work has not been fully professionalized in American society. But by the postwar years a professional culture had firmly entrenched itself in the administrative sector as well. Along with the

[26]For example, in 1979, OPM divided the largest mixed job ladder (301) into a merged clerical–technical job ladder and a separate administrative job ladder (U.S. OPM 1981).

growth of the higher educational system, this fact probably made the bifurcation of clerical and administrative job ladders unstoppable. The desire of the government to compete with private industry for these college graduates led it to form separate administrative job ladders to attract them and to decrease the number of clerical workers who were promoted into administrative jobs.

Job analysis can make a valid claim to being scientific in character. But this claim notwithstanding, the job ladders it produces are influenced by conventional views regarding the character of work, specifically its sex type and the educational credentials needed to perform it (see, e.g., Berg 1970; Wallace 1976; Collins 1979; Miller *et al.* 1980; Bielby and Baron 1986). Sometimes job ladders are occupationally homogeneous. Sometimes job ladders contain both blue-collar and lower management jobs (Baron *et al.* 1986). But regardless of the precise placement of the boundary, bureaucratized firms usually use a system of tiers to provide college graduates with a separate entry route into management or professional positions.

In principle, one could organize office work into one long hierarchy and simply recruit college graduates into the system at higher grade levels, to reflect their greater training. However, three considerations suggest that this strategy was unlikely to develop. First, job analysis tends to follow occupational distinctions, at least in a general way. The fact that administrative and clerical work have developed separate identifies leads to institutionalized expectations that they be organized on separate job ladders. Second, separate job ladders were more in keeping with the professional model and arguably made administrative jobs more attractive to potential college recruits.

Finally, the bifurcation of job ladders eased employee pressure on management to favor insiders for promotions to entry-level administrative positions. It enables managers to more easily distinguish between those they consider promotable and those they do not. They can more easily justify hiring from the outside at entry levels of the higher occupational series instead of promoting more from within, because entry-level hiring at GS-5, 7, and 9 has been institutionalized. So long as they are able to maintain flexibility, they can promote across job ladder boundaries when the need arises and not do it when they think it more important to hire from outside.

By way of comparison, a semipermeable boundary was also established around the Senior Executive Service when it was brought into existence by the Civil Service Reform Act of 1978. The personnel structures that defined the Senior Executive Service were intended to have occupational, mobility, and pay implications. The employees located on the Senior Executive Service, along with the Executive Schedule presidential appointees, were considered the "executives" of government. Employees at this level (along with personnel at the "midlevel" grades of 13 through 15) were eligible for performance bonuses. The law required agencies to fill a group of positions vulnerable to political abuse (e.g., Internal Revenue Service auditors) with career civil servants.[27] It further restricted the total number of political appointments in the Senior Executive Service to 10% of the total.[28] Finally, the law's creators hoped that a Senior Executive Service would produce more organizational mobility for top civil servants, which would make them more effective as executives.

Thus, it is clear that controlled mobility across boundaries can represent a management policy for realizing objectives. Such policies can arise through a set of relatively precise actions, such as the passage of the 1978 Reform Act, or it can evolve slowly, as in the case of the boundary between clerical and administrative positions.[29] The semipermeable quality of both boundaries is a response (whether formal or informal) to competing forces or concerns. For the Senior Executive Service, these forces are the conflict between the political and administrative character of the bureaucracy. In the case of the clerical–administrative boundary, the desire of managers to bring in talent from the colleges conflicts with *de facto* acceptance by operating officials of the proposition that collegiate training is not needed for all administrative jobs. It also clashes with political pressure for promoting women and minorities.

It would appear from the discussion so far that only the administrative boundaries were problematic. In contrast, the division of the scientific hierarchy into professional and subprofessional appears much more objective. Work that calls for the level of "formal knowledge" (Friedson 1986) represented by a college degree is classified onto a professional job ladder. Work that instead requires "less than full competence" and training "less than that represented by college graduation" is classified on technical, that is, subprofessional job ladders. The mobility implication of this classification philosophy follows directly: Little

---

[27]These restricted positions amounted to 45% of the total SES.

[28]In other words, 700 of the 7000 positions in the Senior Executive Service at the end of 1983 could be filled by outsiders. Before the passage of the Civil Service Reform Act of 1978, Congress set no clear limit on the proportion of high bureaucratic positions that the administration could fill with political appointees (Campbell 1978).

[29]Of course, the 1978 Reform Act was shaped by a history of conflict about the validity of the Senior Executive Service. The consequences of its establishment will also evolve over time (cf. Heclo 1984).

crossover from nonprofessional to professional job ladders occurs because of the barrier raised by the educational requirement for professional jobs.

But even in this case, the structure of job ladders can be shaped by policy goals regarding mobility. The CSC was worried in the 1950s about a managerial "tendency" to "shift talented technicians into professional jobs so that they can be promoted" (Keene 1960). This practice changed the character of the professional jobs, in the view of the CSC, because the new incumbents did not have the requisite educational qualifications for their jobs. If the character of the work performed was the sole basis for making decisions about job ladders and mobility policy, the solution to this state of affairs would have been to more actively monitor this tendency. But the CSC decided instead to extend the grade ceilings of certain technical series upwards (Keene 1960).

This development was particularly noticeable in the physical and engineering sciences (U.S. CSC 1954, 1976a).[30] For example, the largest subprofessional job ladder in the engineering group in 1957 was the "engineering aid" job ladder. In 1957, the median grade for this job ladder was 5, and 95% of all positions on this ladder were located in Grades 7 and below. Only 0.2% of the positions were located at Grades 11 and higher. In contrast, incumbents on the professional "general engineering" job ladder had a median grade of 12, and 89% of the incumbents were at grades 11 or above. By 1983, the general engineering job ladder had roughly the same grade distribution, the median grade now being 13 instead of 12, and the proportion at Grade 11 or higher was now 95%. But the engineering aid job ladder, which later was renamed as the "engineering technician" job ladder, had been upgraded to the point that Grade 9 was now the median. By 1983, 35% of the jobs it contained were located at grades 11 or higher. The electronics technician, which did not exist as a job ladder in the 1950s had a median grade of 11 and 38% of its positions at grade 12 or higher in 1983. Thus, whereas in the 1950s there was virtually no overlap in the grade ranges of the engineering aid job ladder and the engineer job ladder, by the 1980s there was a substantial overlap.

The changing nature of these technical job ladders may have reduced mobility from the subprofessional to the professional tier.[31] But the classification of subprofessional jobs at such high grade levels raises the question of why such positions are described as subprofessional,

---

[30]These job ladders also happen to be predominantly male.
[31]No data exist to provide an answer to this question.

when their work is classified at a level equivalent to other work that is described as professional or college caliber in character.[32] The right answer is that implied by Keene in 1960. High-graded positions on subprofessional job ladders provide mobility opportunities for technicians (in this case to enable the government to pay them a market wage), and they allow agencies more control of personnel decisions. But the strategies for achieving management goals are different for the professional and the administrative cases. The government expanded the subprofessional–professional overlap to include more grades, whereas the level of boundary crossing was kept relatively low. For some subprofessional jobs, such as engineering technician or communications specialist, the overlap is broad. For others, such as biological technician, nursing assistant, or educational assistant, the overlap is narrower. The size of the overlap apparently depends on market conditions. The clerical–administrative grade overlap is narrower than the subprofessional–professional overlap, but management allows more employees to cross the former boundary.

CONCLUSION

This chapter has focused on the filling of entry-level positions on administrative and professional job ladders. In order to fully interpret the results presented here, however, one must consider the implications of job ladders for subsequent success. At one time, supporters of an administrative class for the United States hoped to establish separate administrative job ladders and to use these ladders to lead high-quality college graduates to the top positions in government. But by the 1970s, most employees at trainee grades of administrative job ladders were not in training for supergrade positions at the top of the hierarchy. Instead, they were trainees for positions at low- or middle-management levels. Large numbers of both the new hires and the promoted employees lacked the college degree that proponents of an administrative class once viewed as an important prerequisite for responsible administrative work. In contrast, less than 1% of the employees in the supergrades of

---

[32]The *Handbook of Occupational Groups and Series of Classes* (U.S. OPM 1981:78) makes quite clear that these technical positions are considered less than professional. For example, the engineering technician position (65-802) is said to require "primarily application of a practical knowledge. . . . The positions do not require professional knowledges [sic] and abilities . . . and therefore do not require training equivalent . . . to a bachelor's degree."

the government lacked a college degree in 1970–1971 (Heclo 1984). The changes in the government hierarchy have substantially downgraded the status of entry-level administrative and professional jobs, which are much farther from the top of the hierarchy than they once were. Nonetheless, it is still the case that opportunity for advancement on an administrative or professional job ladder is much greater than on a clerical or technical job ladder. For ambitious lower-tier workers, these trainee-level jobs are still the salient goal.

But lower-level employees who succeed in getting an administrative or professional job usually want to advance further still. Their ability to progress at a good pace depends not only on how shielded they are from outside competition but also on their competition with co-workers who are located on the same job ladder. In the tournament conceptualization of career movement (Rosenbaum 1984), the job ladder defines the players but not the outcome. Those who lose a round of the tournament are disadvantaged in subsequent play, if they are allowed to stay in the advancement game at all. Especially in administrative job ladders and especially after the onset of a successful EEO program, the occupants of lower-rung positions can exhibit substantial heterogeneity. Some are older employees, frequently women, who have attained a status promotion from a lower-tier position, whereas others are much younger employees, who typically have college or postgraduate degrees. To the extent that the promotees are disadvantaged compared with younger college graduates in subsequent tournaments, then their opportunity for further movement is restricted. The net advantage of their status promotion may be small.

Furthermore, the shift from the lower to the upper tier is only one of many contingencies that affected the overall distribution of women and minorities in the federal government. We have learned so far that job ladders do structure mobility but that mobility from one job ladder to another was not uncommon in the federal government. We have also learned that women and minorities were disproportionately found in the lower levels of the federal government, though their positions were gradually improving. But important issues remain to be addressed. These include (1) an overall comparison of the advancement patterns of women, minorities, and white males, (2) an assessment of how job-ladder structure affects both grade promotions and status promotions from the lower to the upper tier, and (3) the extent to which gender and racial differences in promotion rates can be explained in terms of the existing structure of job ladders in the federal civil service. These issues are the subject of the next chapter.

APPENDIX 1. MISSING DATA

The machine-readable data file of the CSC was intended to be complete for all targeted employees, which consisted of 10% of civilian employees for the period 1962–1972 and all employees for later years. However, later analysis has demonstrated that some transactions went unreported, particularly in the earlier years of operation (Nenni 1984). It is sometimes possible to determine whether a transaction is missing from the data base by examining the structure of an individual's file. Each individual in the data base had a background record of personal information and a set of transaction records. Every time an employment-related event (hiring, promotion, demotion, occupation change, agency change, resignation etc.) occurred, the file was supposed to contain a record of the transaction, which not only detailed the nature of the transaction but also provided detailed information about the employee's employment status (grade, occupation, agency, etc.) at that time. By comparing adjacent records for a given employee, it is possible to infer that an undocumented event has occurred when a data field (e.g., occupation) has a new value but when the nature of action code describes a different change (e.g., resignation).

By making a comparison of adjacent records, it is possible to fill in many missed status promotions, though one cannot be sure of their precise timing. This process does not work as well in establishing the status an employee had when first hired. One can determine what an individual's present status is but not what his or her status was at the time of hiring. Also, because the government service date is adjusted to reflect military service, one cannot determine initial hiring date precisely.

Depending upon the pattern of missing information, observed trends could be a function of missing data rather than substantive change. Fortunately, OPM recently conducted a study of missing transactions for the major nature of action codes in the data (Nenni 1984). The OPM analysis allows us to obtain a general sense of the pattern of missing information.[33] In order to increase our confidence in trend results from the analysis, I limited the analysis to what I called *documented* status promotions and accessions. I defined a documented accession as one accompanied by a nature of action code describing the action as a

[33]Nenni also showed that the personnel information that was recorded in the computerized data base was generally accurate.

Table 8.7

Percentage of Missing Events, by Nature of Action Code and Adjustment for the
Missing Transactions[a]

Nature of action code	1962–1972	1973–1976	1977–1980[b]
702 Promotion	24.44	20.90	14.97
	(19.5–29.4)[c]	(16.1–25.7)	(10.6–19.4)
721 Reassignment	19.38	32.94	19.66
	(13.3–25.4)	(27.4–38.5)	(14.4–24.9)
All competitive new hires	21.43	14.13	4.03
	(15.0–29.9)	(9.9–18.3)	(1.5–6.6)

Uncorrected and Corrected Tables of the Use of New Hires and Status
Promotions to Fill Entry Grade (GS-5 through GS-9) Positions
in Administrative Career Lines

Fourteen agencies				
Uncorrected table			Corrected table	
1962–1972	1973–1977		1962–1972	1973–1977
225	193	New hires	286	225
115	212	Promotions	201	290
59.2	47.7	% New Hires	58.8	43.6

Department of Defense				
Uncorrected table			Corrected table	
1962–1972	1973–1977		1962–1972	1973–1977
171	90	New hires	218	105
297	180	Promotions	383	243
36.5	33.3	% New Hires	36.2	30.2

[a]Note that the listed percentages of missing transactions strictly apply to all actions with the given
nature of action codes, not just the subset that we have analyzed (namely those for Grades 5–9).
[b]I used the 1973–1976 missing rates for the first half of 1977 as well.
[c]95% confidence intervals.

career or career-conditional appointment.[34] I defined a documented status promotion as a change in occupational series from a lower-tier to an upper-tier job ladder that was documented as a grade promotion or a reassignment. A reassignment was a job-ladder shift without a grade promotion. Thus the counts for both status promotions and accessions in the tables accompanying this chapter are undercounts of the true totals for sample members. But Table 8.7 shows that the rates of missing data for promotions and reassignments are similar to the rates of missing data for new hires. Thus, whereas the data problems are troublesome, they probably do not invalidate the trend analysis presented in this chapter. When adjustments in the observed counts of new hires and status promotions are made for the proportions of missing data found in the Nenni analysis, the corrected figures still show that a greater proportion of entry administrative positions were filled from internal sources during the 1973–1977 period than previously.

APPENDIX 2. THE STATUS OF WORKERS IN MIXED JOB LADDERS

As noted in the text, mixed job ladders spanned the clerical, technical, and administrative levels. The Office of Personnel Management defines workers in Grades 1–6 on mixed job ladders as being in clerical positions, workers in Grades 7–10 on mixed job ladders as being in technical positions, and workers in Grades 11 and higher as being in administrative positions. However, this designation may sometimes be only a matter of convention. Individual agencies might divide these mixed job ladders into more refined ladders and differentiate between lower- and upper-tier workers in the crucial region between Grades 5 and 10 (see, e.g., DiPrete and Soule 1986).

In order to avoid counting as a status promotion instances where an individual began his or her career as an administrative trainee on a mixed job ladder and then switched to an administrative ladder, such switches were only counted as status promotions if the individual in question had already been with the government for the 3 years required to obtain career status. If such employees were actually advancing through the ranks at the normal rate for trainees, they would presum-

---

[34]Career appointments could occur under CSC recruiting authority for direct hire. Typically, an individual was hired with career-conditional status and was given career status after 3 years. Reinstatements and term of temporary appointments were ignored in the present analysis.

ably have advanced beyond Grade 9 by the time they acquired career status. Their slow pace through the middle grades suggests that their agencies considered their jobs to be clerical or technical in nature.

To check this assumption, I compared the educational attainment of administrative new hires with the educational attainment of employees who obtained status promotions. Because the government did not begin collecting educational information until 1973, this information is not available for anyone who left the government before that time. Nonetheless, the data in Table 8.4 make clear that employees moving from mixed job ladders to administrative ladders had even less education on average than did workers moving from clerical job ladders. Hence the decision to count these moves from mixed to administrative job ladders as status promotions appears valid.

9

The Determinants of Advancement on White-Collar Job Ladders

INTRODUCTION

Although the status of minority workers continues to lag behind that of whites, women have received at least as much attention in recent years. The pay gap between men's and women's jobs remains large despite some improvement during the 1980s (Bergman 1986). Several studies have suggested that women's promotion rates lag behind men's as well (Wolf and Fligstein 1979; Rosenfeld 1980; Marini 1980). The fate of women in the labor market is strongly tied to the structure of occupations and job ladders. Female job ladders offer lower pay and have lower ceilings than the job ladders that men work on.

However, segregation is not the only problem a group may face in the job market. Several factors can be responsible for group inequality. A group may have lower average human capital. It may get a lower average return on its human capital because of job segregation or discrimination. Its members may do more part-time work or have some other status that inhibits advancement. It may get less than its share of promotions to job ladders that offer opportunity for career growth. This chapter addresses the question whether promotion rates for white males, females, and minorities were unequal in the federal government in the middle 1970s. It identifies where the inequality was greatest.

This chapter is an expanded version of a paper, which I coauthored with Whitman T. Soule, that was published in the *American Sociological Review* 1988, 53: 26–40) under the title "Gender and Promotion in Segmented Job Ladder Systems."

Finally, it shows how a model combining structural opportunity, human capital, and other relevant statuses can explain group differences in promotion rates. Its focus is primarily on gender inequality, because, as will become clear, gender differences in promotion rates were greater than racial ones.

JOB SEGREGATION AND CAREER ADVANCEMENT

Theories of sex segregation have gained prominence in recent years as the inadequacies of human capital explanations for gender inequality have become apparent (England 1982; Corcoran *et al.* 1984; Bergmann 1986). Researchers have confirmed that high levels of sex segregation persist in the American economy despite efforts to end discrimination against women (Beller 1982a; Bielby and Baron 1984). Because of the civil rights and women's movements, personnel rules in bureaucratized organizations now forbid discriminatory behavior (Burstein 1985). But segregation by job ladder still has the potential to retard career advancement. In the white-collar work force of bureaucratized organizations, segregation by sex is greater than segregation by race (Albelda 1986).

The sex-segregation approach to the question of gender differences in career advancement assumes that unequal initial placement combined with mobility barriers to subsequent advancement are principal causes of gender inequality. In order to address the adequacy of this approach, however, it is necessary to embed this potential source of inequality in a broader model of the promotion process. Gender differences in advancement can be attributed to a number of factors, including the following: (1) gender differences in levels of, or rates of return to, human capital, (2) gender differences in distribution across job ladders; what is usually referred to as sex segregation, (3) gender differences in preferred organizational statuses other than rank and the job ladder of one's job, (4) unequal rates of mobility from job ladders with limited opportunity to those with greater opportunity, and (5) gender differences that persist when human capital and organizational location are controlled. Although segregation by minority status is not as great as segregation by gender, the same factors could in principle produce racial differences in advancement, also.

The probability of advancement up a job ladder by any of its incumbents depends on the level of opportunity available for such advancement. Measures such as the percentage female or whether a job is in the upper or lower tier are associated with the room for advancement on a given job ladder, but neither measure is perfect. A better measure would be based on the ratio of vacancies to the number of competitors. Although such detailed information is almost never available, a good substitute is the multiple grade ratio (MGR, Stewman and Konda 1983), which is based on the ratio of workers at one level of a hierarchy to those at higher levels. The MGR has usually been applied to organizations as a whole, but it can be modified to apply to individual job ladders.

Aside from one's rank or location on a job ladder, an employee's advancement rate can be affected by the character of his or her employment relationship with the organization. For example, part-time employees would not be expected to advance as rapidly as full-time employees, perhaps because they acquire on-the-job training at a lower rate, or perhaps because their progress is hampered by the formal personnel procedures of the firm. Other types of "irregular" employment relationships exist as well. Civil service systems frequently vest a large portion of white-collar employees with a form of tenure, although also employing "irregular" employees as well, that is, those not tenured or on a "tenure track."[1] These irregulars may work part-time, or they may have a temporary or otherwise "untenured" though indefinite full-time job. Although grade advancement for irregular employees is not impossible, it is probably slower than for regular employees.

Although tenure status and job ladder would generally have powerful effects on advancement, any obstacles they may present can be overcome if the organization allows employees to change these statuses. The frequency of job-ladder shifts probably varies from one organization to another, as do other characteristics of job ladders (see, e.g., Baron *et al.* 1986). For employees in organizations with partially permeable ladders, the probability of a shift arguably depends on two factors: an employee's opportunity for further advancement on the current job ladder and transferability of skills from one ladder to another.

Low job-ladder ceilings are a principal reason why employees would want to shift ladders. Consequently, it is not unreasonable to hypothesize a negative relationship between opportunity on one's job ladder and the probability of job-ladder shifts. But this relationship describes only employee preferences. The ability of a given employee to realize his or her preferences depends upon management's evaluation of his or her qualifications for other jobs. This judgment is in part a function of the personal characteristics of the employee. But it also depends upon the jobs in question.

---

[1]In the federal civil service, this is called "career conditional" status, which normally converts to career status after 3 years. When the term *tenured* is used in this chapter, it will include both career and career conditional status.

In some types of work, job-ladder boundaries may correspond to substantial differences in skill requirements. These differences may be reinforced by educational or licensing requirements. But despite the efforts that have gone into the construction of job ladders, there is little evidence that personnel management has succeeded in creating a system where skill distances between adjacent job ladders are in any sense equidistant. Sometimes these job ladders correspond more to conventional distinctions between jobs than to major skill differences. Although relatively little is known about the skill differences among job ladders, some reasonable guesses can be made. Job-ladder shifts are probably more common for clerical jobs than for administrative or technical ones, and more common for administrative or technical jobs than for professional ones.

The most important type of job-ladder shift involves a change from a job ladder with a low ceiling to one with a high ceiling. As we have seen, the boundary between the lower and the upper tier in the federal civil service was partially porous during the 1970s, at least for administrative jobs. Although Chapter 8 did not determine the probability that lower-tier workers would advance to upper-tier administrative and professional jobs, the results suggest that it was easier to move from clerical to administrative positions than to move from subprofessional to professional ones because the credential barrier was lower in the former case.

Promotion rates depend heavily on an organization's shape and demographic composition. But an individual's chances for promotion will also depend on the management practices that handicap employees in organizational promotion "tournaments" (Rosenbaum 1979). As we noted earlier, organizations will generally favor tenured or tenure-track employees for promotions. The effects of education will generally be strongest on the process of initial assignment. Otherwise, education will generally be a more important factor in job-ladder switches than in movement up the rungs of a single ladder. Past performance will also shape a supervisor's appraisal of promotion potential. The advantages that allowed an employee to move rapidly to his or her present position will generally continue to benefit him or her in the future. In contrast, a current supervisor may interpret an employee's slow progress in the past as indicating limited future potential (On the subject of age-graded mobility, also see Spilerman 1977; Kaufmann and Spilerman 1982). An employee's particular route to his or her present position may also be related to further advancement. Managers have sometimes viewed certain types of clerical experiences as "disqualifying" an employee for further advancement (Kanter 1977). Today, such attitudes have the potential to harm women more than men and minorities more than whites.

THE LOCATION OF GENDER- AND RACE-SPECIFIC BOTTLENECKS

Gender or race differences in advancement rates need not be uniform throughout the organizational hierarchy. On the contrary, the segmented character of job-ladder systems suggests that such uniformity is unlikely. Stewman and Konda (1983) have shown how an organization's shape and the seniority distribution of its employees can create promotion bottlenecks in certain grades. It is possible that race- and especially gender-specific bottlenecks exist as well. In the middle-grade range, lower- and upper-tier job ladders overlap. But women, and to a lesser extent minorities, are more likely to be found on lower-tier job ladders. Near the tier boundary, therefore, a randomly selected woman or minority worker should have a lower promotion rate than a randomly selected white male because the selected person is more likely to be working on a lower-tier job ladder. At the lowest grades, in contrast, all job ladders have relatively low ceilings. One would not expect job-ladder placement to matter as much there. Similarly, one would expect job ladder placement to matter less in the higher grades than in the middle ones.

Group differences net of the structural opportunity offered by the job ladder can exist because of the association between gender or race and other resources or liabilities for promotion. These factors can also vary by grade level. At high grades, group differences may indicate management resistance to promoting the relatively few women workers found there to still more responsible positions.[2] Some researchers have found that informal networks help with promotion by teaching an employee the right way to act, by arranging sponsorship for promotion, and by other forms of peer support. Because men and women often have their own networks, women may be at a disadvantage at organizational levels where males dominate (Lorber 1979; Miller and Garrison 1982; Roos and Reskin 1984). Minorities could suffer for similar reasons. At low grades, net gender differences may indicate management preference for the relatively few men who work in female-dominated job ladders. At the middle grades, mobility for employees located near the grade ceiling of lower-tier job ladders occurs primarily through their ability to secure access to upper-tier jobs. Further mobility for administrative or professional trainees shows their success in passing through apprenticeship to achieve administrative or professional journeymen

---

[2]President's Commission on the Status of Women 1963; see also Macy 1971, p. 85. A similar finding has been reported for the private sector also (see, e.g., Wallace 1976).

status. The transition from the female-dominated job world to the male-dominated job world may be the area where discrimination and other disadvantages faced by women are most evident.

But disadvantages such as these do not guarantee that women or minority workers will do worse than white males at all levels of the hierarchy. Workers from disadvantaged groups who have reached high organizational levels have shown that they can overcome gender- or race-specific disadvantages. Furthermore, equal employment opportunity programs can partially or fully offset any disadvantages a worker faces because of gender or race. The precise character of gender differences in promotion rates must be assessed through empirical analysis.

DATA AND ANALYTIC STRATEGY

Personnel data for a 1% sample of the careers of white-collar employees of the federal government between 1962 and 1977 were used to examine gender and racial differences in promotion rates in a government where women and minorities were generally in inferior positions (Taylor 1978; Grandjean 1981). Three distinct grade promotion analyses were conducted. They covered the following ranges: (1) Grade promotions in the lower grades (GS1–GS4). Jobs at this level are clerical or technical, and most workers are female. (2) Grade promotions in the middle grades (GS5–GS10). Here higher clerical and technical positions as well as professional and administrative trainee positions can be found. (3) Grade promotions in the upper grades (GS11 and higher). These jobs are mostly professional and administrative. They lie above the trainee grades.

In each of these analyses, the dependent variable measured whether a promotion of one or more grades occurred within 2 years of each first entry into a grade, to be described as the origin grade or position. All first entries occurred during the period between January 1972 and June 1975. The study focused on general schedule white-collar employees,which includes most white-collar employees outside the postal service.[3] Although 2 years is a short time compared with a whole career,

[3]Note that this analytic strategy, which was used for the grade promotion analyses reported here, dictated that the base sample be limited to employees who entered grades in the time period under analysis. This sample is not representative of the total population of workers in these grades because individuals who rarely changed grades are underrepresented. In a similar way, a sample of formerly employed individuals who became unemployed in a particular range of time could be used to study the factors that affect the

it is sufficiently long for a respectable proportion of employees to attain grade promotions and thus is appropriate for an analysis of the type performed here.[4]

Promotion probabilities were specified as a function of the structural opportunity inherent in an employee's position and of individual-level factors pertinent to the personnel policies and practices that structure promotion tournaments. The following variables were used to accomplish this:

Ascribed Characteristics

1. "Female" was measured as 1 if female and 0 if male.
2. "Minority" status was measured as 1 if nonwhite and 0 if white.

Education, Military Service, and Work Experience

3. "Education" was measured by years of schooling and by a dummy variable indicating whether the employee had a bachelor's degree.
4. "Veterans" status was included, along with an interaction between veteran's status and employment in the Department of Defense (Veteran*DOD).
5. Two measures of the rapidity of career progress prior to reaching current grade were used. Estimated pregovernment work experience ("pregovernment work experience") was defined as age minus length of government service until the time of reaching the origin grade minus years of education minus 5. Govern-

---

rate of reemployment. But such a sample would not represent a random sample of people who were employed during the period under study.

[4]For technical reasons, we used a 25-month risk period. The analysis presented in this chapter used as the sample all instances of first entry into a grade during the period described before. Analyses in which the sample was restricted to employees who did not leave the government during the risk period, or to an employee's first entry into an origin grade during these 3.5 years were also performed. They gave substantially similar results. Promotions were measured through transactions posted to the computerized Central Personnel Data File (CPDF), the source of the data analyzed here. A check of the physical personnel files for a sample of employees showed that 20% of all transactions specifically reporting a grade promotion were missing from the CPDF, apparently at random (Nenni 1984). However, virtually all employees received an administrative pay increase each year. The transaction record for this event reported the employee's current grade, as would any other transaction record (reclassification, transfer, separation, temporary leave, and so forth) posted to an individual's personnel file. Therefore, although it was not always possible to determine the precise month of a grade promotion, it was possible to determine with acceptable accuracy whether a grade promotion occurred at some time during a 25-month interval.

ment service ("government service") was defined as the number of years of service prior to attaining the origin grade. Thus an individual's age at reaching the origin grade is equal to 5 + education + estimated pregovernment work experience + government service. The separate coefficients for education, pregovernment work experience, and government service allow us to distinguish the effects of each period on an employee's promotion chances.

Early Government Experience

6. A dummy variable indicating whether the employee had begun his or her career in an "irregular" status, that is, in a temporary job, term job, or part-time job ("first government job irregular"). When appropriate, a dummy variable indicating whether the employee had begun his or her career in a lower-tier job (to be defined later) was also included ("first government job lower-tier").[5]

Structural Opportunity Associated with an Employee's Source Position

7. In the middle 1970s, white-collar jobs in the federal government were divided into approximately 450 separate job ladders. As I reported earlier, these job ladders were officially called "occupational series." They defined "steps in the most natural line of promotion" (U.S. OPM 1981). For each job ladder, the "multiple grade ratio" (MGR) for each grade was computed from data found in the 1976 edition of *Occupations of Federal White-Collar Workers* (U.S. CSC 1976a). Stewman and Konda's (1983) formula was modified to be job-ladder specific:

$$\text{MGR}_{li} = \sum_{j=i}^{K} \frac{n_{lj}}{n_{li}}$$

where l is the job ladder, i is the source grade, K is the top grade in the system (GS18), and n_{lj} is the number of employees located in grade j in ladder l in 1976.[6] This ladder-specific multiple

---

[5]Because both of these variables could only be measured with personnel data for 1962 and after, they undercount irregular and lower-tier origins for employees who entered the government before that time.

[6]In certain cases, the ladder-specific multiple grade ratio computed to an unreasonably large value. Because we did not expect its effect on outcomes to be linear over such a

grade ratio cannot perfectly predict the ratio of vacancies to competitors in any given promotion tournament. The ratio of vacancies to competitors is also a function of the turnover rate, growth, recruitment patterns, job-ladder shifts, and heterogeneity in the shape of job ladders by agency or region. Nonetheless, we expected the ladder-specific multiple grade ratio to have an effect on outcomes.

8. The "proportion female in the job ladder" in 1976 (U.S. Civil Service Commission 1976a) was included as an indicator of the extent to which a job ladder was sex-segregated.

Opportunities for Promotion Linked to Citizenship Status and Other Measures of an Employee's Position

9. The origin grade.
10. Region and agency of the origin grade. These variables, although important, are not of compelling theoretical interest. They are not reported in the tables, to conserve space.
11. A dummy variable indicating whether the origin position was irregular (temporary, term, or part-time) (irregular status).
12. The PATCO designation of a job, which indicates whether it is in the lower or the upper tier and the type of job ladder within each tier.
13. A dummy variable indicating any recorded "temporary leaves" of absence from the government during the 2-year risk period for promotion.

Variables Measuring Gender Differences in the Effects of Human Capital

14. Interactions between sex and years of education, possession of a college degree, years of pregovernment work experience, and years of government service were included in the models.

Table 9.1 presents means and standard deviations for selected human capital and structural variables for men and women in each of the three grade ranges in the samples under analysis in this chapter.[7] At all three ranges, women had less education than men, though the difference was greatest in the middle grades, where the upper tier and the lower tier overlap. At the lowest and middle grades, it is perhaps sur-

range, the measure of MGR actually employed in the analysis was minimum (MGR_{li}, 20). The value 20 was chosen after investigation of the distribution of the scores and their effects on the probability of promotion.

[7] Note that these means and standard deviations are not for all employees in the grade ranges indicated but only those first entering grades in the period under study.

Table 9.1

Means and Standard Deviations of Selected Human Capital and Structural Variables, by Sex and Origin Grade[a]

Variable	Grades 1–4		Grades 5–10		Grades 11–16	
	Male	Female	Male	Female	Male	Female
Years of Education	13.0	12.7***	14.4	13.4***	15.8	15.5*
	(1.8)	(1.4)	(2.2)	(1.7)	(2.4)	(2.5)
BA or more	0.097	0.052**	0.44	0.18**	0.66	0.60*
Pregovernment work experience	6.6	9.3***	6.9	9.6***	6.2	6.3
	(8.4)	(10.0)	(7.7)	(9.4)	(7.3)	(7.5)
Years of government service	3.5	2.6***	7.4	8.6***	12.1	12.1
	(3.9)	(3.4)	(7.2)	(7.2)	(8.6)	(9.3)
Proportion female in job ladder	0.42	0.80***	0.25	0.67***	0.14	0.32***
Multiple grade ratio	7.2	4.9***	6.6	2.8***	1.7	1.8
	(7.0)	(6.2)	(6.6)	(4.0)	(2.0)	(1.7)
Irregular status	0.37	0.24***	0.10	0.050***	0.025	0.031
N	1024	3145	2529	2308	2170	286

[a]Standard deviations are in parentheses.
* = difference of means significant at the 0.05 level.
** = difference of means significant at the 0.01 level.
*** = difference of means significant at the 0.001 level.

prising to find that a greater percentage of women than men had full tenure (i.e., career or career conditional status). In general, the percentage of employees "with irregular status" is much lower in the higher grades than in the lower ones. At all three levels, women were more likely to work in female-dominated job ladders than were men. The average percentage female of women's job ladders ranged from a high of 79% in the lower grades to 31% in the higher ones. Men also were more likely to work in female-dominated job ladders in the lower grades than in the higher ones, but at all grade levels the average percentage female for men was lower than for women.

Table 9.1 also shows that average multiple grade ratio was higher for women working in the lower grades than in the middle or higher grades. The average MGR for men, in contrast, was nearly as high in the middle grades as in the lower grades. The job ladders of women offered lower opportunity for advancement on average than did the job ladders of men in the middle grades, where men were more likely to be on upper-tier ladders than were women. But even in the lower grades of the federal government, the MGR for men was much higher than for women. This reflected their greater tendency to work on technical ladders, which had higher grade ceilings than the clerical ladders where women worked. In the higher grades, however, women had the same level of structural opportunity for promotion as men, even though their job ladders were more heavily female. The percentage female of one's job ladder may be correlated with opportunity overall, but the correlation is hardly perfect.

THE STRUCTURE OF PROMOTION IN LOWER GRADES

As Table 9.2 shows, women's zero-order promotion chances were equal to men's in the lower grades. Nonwhite workers had the same promotion rates as whites. However, when controls were entered, both women and minority workers had a net disadvantage. Education had only a slight effect on advancement in the lower grades. Length of service mattered more; although the average length of service in the lower grades was relatively short, those who had been there longer had lower promotion rates. Irregular status also clearly hurt one's chances for advancement, as hypothesized. Interactions between gender and education or experience were not a factor.

The ladder-specific multiple grade ratio had a positive and significant effect on promotion probabilities. It did not completely account for structural opportunity, however, because it is not a direct measure of the ratio of vacancies to competitors in each promotion tournament. It should also be noted that job ladders did not constrain mobility very much in the lower levels of government. Table 7.5 showed that 14% of promotions from technical jobs and a majority of promotions from clerical jobs took the employee out of his or her old job ladder into a new one. At levels where job-ladder boundaries, particularly clerical boundaries, were not very meaningful, the multiple grade ratio could not be expected to have strong predictive value. For this reason, the coefficient for technical jobs, which generally had higher grade ceilings than clerical jobs, was strongly positive.

Contrary to the usual expectations, the proportion female in the job ladder actually had a strong positive effect on advancement in the lower grades. This finding suggests that some structural force was creating vacancies in female-dominated job ladders at a greater rate than in male-dominated job ladders, net of what would be expected from the shape of these job ladders (as measured by the ladder-specific multiple grade ratio). If turnover rates for women were greater than for men, turnover could provide such a force. But gender differences in turnover rates from these grades were very small. We believe that the proportion

Table 9.2
Logistic Regression Coefficients for Grade Promotion from Grades 1–4

Coefficient	1	2	3	4	Mean/SD
Female	0.059	−0.064	−0.39	−0.40	0.76
	(0.4)	(0.5)	(0.0005)	(0.0005)	
Minority	−0.054	−0.035	−0.038	−0.16	0.28
	(0.4)	(0.6)	(0.6)	(0.05)	
Education (years)		0.023	0.039	0.062	12.8
		(0.4)	(0.2)	(0.04)	(1.5)
BA or more		−0.063	−0.019	−0.10	0.061
		(0.7)	(0.9)	(0.6)	
Veteran		−0.31	−0.29	−0.27	0.19
		(0.005)	(0.01)	(0.03)	
Veteran*DOD		0.16	0.25	0.36	0.052
		(0.3)	(0.1)	(0.06)	
Pregovernment work			−0.0030	−0.0016	8.6
experience			(0.4)	(0.7)	(9.7)
First government job			−0.40	−0.039	0.39
irregular			(0.0000)	(0.7)	
Years of government service			−0.043	−0.038	2.87
			(0.0001)	(0.0007)	(3.6)
Temporary leave			−0.034	−0.013	0.15
			(0.7)	(0.9)	
Grade 2			0.73	0.76	0.20
			(0.0002)	(0.0004)	
Grade 3			0.17	0.19	0.36
			(0.4)	(0.4)	
Grade 4			−0.27	0.36	0.41
			(0.2)	(0.1)	
Proportion female in job			0.75	1.24	0.71
ladder			(0.0000)	(0.0000)	(0.28)
Multiple grade ratio				0.019	5.5
				(0.02)	(6.5)
Irregular status				−0.69	0.26
				(0.0000)	
Technical				0.76	0.11
				(0.0000)	
Other				0.25	0.15
				(0.05)	

Note. N = 3950, proportion promoted (*P*) = .52. *N*, means and standard deviations apply to fourth-column sample. Listwise deletion of missing values was used. *P*-values and (in the last column) standard deviations are in parentheses

The following coefficients were included in Column 4 models in all tables, but are not reported because of space considerations: intercept, Department of Defense, Agriculture, Commerce, General Services Administration, Health, Education and Welfare, Interior, Justice, Transportation, Treasury, Veterans Administration, and location of job (District of Columbia, eastern region, southern region, or western region). In addition to these variables, interactions of government service were included in Column 5 models. Column 5 was only reported when at least one of the interaction coefficients was significant at the 0.05 level. A main-effect/interaction pair of coefficients was reported in Column 5 only if the interaction was significant at the 0.05 level.

female was associated with higher rates of upward mobility at the very bottom grades because of a positive association between the proportion female of a job ladder and the size of the net outflow from this ladder to other ladders. Many of the ladders with high-proportion female workers had very low ceilings even for clerical job ladders. High outflow rates allowed workers on these ladders to continue advancing even after they reached the top of the ladder. In short, the ladder-specific MGR understated the promotional opportunities for such employees. But because the ceiling on their job ladders was so low, their additional movement would still be in the clerical ranks. For example, further analysis showed that employees in such heavily female job ladders as clerk–typist or stenographer had significantly higher promotion rates in the Grade 1–4 range, when other factors (including, importantly, the MGR), were controlled. Summary data showed that 97% of all clerk–typists were in Grades 1–4, and 98% of stenographers were in Grades 1–5 (U.S. CSC 1976a). Further advancement for such employees would require that they move to clerical ladders such as secretary, where 92% of the positions were in Grades 5 and above. New outflow from ladders such as typist or stenographer would then create room for advancement by workers in the bottom grades in these low-ceiling ladders. The net advantage for employees in female-dominated job ladders was not insignificant; controlling for other factors, employees who would have a 0.4 probability of a grade promotion in 2 years would have a 0.49 probability if they were instead situated in a job ladder whose proportion female was 0.3 higher.

But the greater opportunity for advancement in female-dominated job ladders, net of other factors, should not obscure the net disadvantage of female employees compared with males. Under situations in which a man had a 2-year promotion probability of 0.5, a comparable women would have a predicted rate of only 0.4.[8] The minority disadvantage was much smaller.

THE STRUCTURE OF PROMOTION IN MIDDLE GRADES

In contrast to the zero-order equality in the promotion rates of women and men located in the lower grades, the overall promotion rate of women in the middle grades was much lower than that of men. The lower advancement rate for women also contrasts with the equal rate of

---

[8]The female coefficient was significantly negative in analyses restricted to organizational survivors as well. This is no surprise, because their turnover rates were similar to those of males.

Table 9.3
Logistic Regression Coefficients for Grade Promotion from Grades 5–10

Coefficient	1	2	3	4	5	Mean/SD
Female	−0.65	−0.47	0.0047	−0.20	0.55	0.51
	(0.0000)	(0.0000)	(0.96)	(0.08)	(0.4)	
Minority	−0.049	0.012	−0.025	−0.013	−0.0052	0.20
	(0.5)	(0.9)	(0.8)	(0.9)	(0.96)	
Education		0.057	−0.0080	0.0054	a	14.0
(years)		(0.04)	(0.8)	(0.9)		(2.0)
BA or more		0.91	0.64	0.39	a	0.33
		(0.0000)	(0.0000)	(0.009)		
Veteran		0.0061	0.21	0.16	0.23	0.33
		(0.9)	(0.04)	(0.2)	(0.05)	
Veteran*DOD		−0.39	−0.33	−0.0054	0.025	0.11
		(0.0005)	(0.009)	(0.97)	(0.9)	
Pregovernment			−0.031	−0.025	a	8.2
work			(0.0000)	(0.0000)		(8.8)
experience						
First			−0.25	−0.045	−0.037	0.22
government			(0.002)	(0.6)	(0.7)	
job irregular						
First			−0.032	0.057	0.031	0.54
government			(0.7)	(0.6)	(0.8)	
job lower tier						
Years of			−0.056	−0.044	−0.066	7.7
government			(0.0000)	(0.0000)	(0.0000)	(7.1)
service						
Temporary			−0.33	−0.25	−0.24	0.11
leave			(0.003)	(0.03)	(0.04)	
Grade 6			0.14	0.059	0.060	0.13
			(0.2)	(0.6)	(0.6)	
Grade 7			0.29	0.16	0.14	0.25
			(0.002)	(0.1)	(0.2)	
Grade 8			−0.070	−0.26	−0.25	0.043
			(0.7)	(0.2)	(0.2)	
Grade 9			−0.14	−0.25	−0.25	0.21
			(0.2)	(0.05)	(0.06)	
Grade 10			−0.44	−0.85	−0.79	0.022
			(0.09)	(0.002)	(0.004)	
Proportion			−0.81	−0.27	−0.29	0.45
female in job			(0.0000)	(0.2)	(0.2)	(0.34)
ladder						
Multiple grade				0.074	0.072	4.8
ratio				(0.0000)	(0.0000)	(6.0)
Irregular status				−0.43	−0.46	0.072
				(0.008)	(0.005)	

Table 9.3
(Continued)

Coefficient	1	2	3	4	5	Mean/SD
Technical				0.11	0.14	0.24
				(0.5)	(0.3)	
Professional				0.10	0.10	0.13
				(0.7)	(0.6)	
Administrative				0.29	0.30	0.19
				(0.1)	(0.1)	
Mixed				0.084	0.083	0.18
				(0.5)	(0.5)	
Other				−0.57	−0.55	0.08
				(0.02)	(0.02)	
Female * yrs government service					0.038 (0.002)	4.3 (6.6)

Note: $N = 4114$, $P = .45$
[a]See notes at bottom of Table 9.2.

minorities and whites, once gender is controlled. Although one-half of all males in grades 5–10 were able to obtain a grade promotion in 2 years, only about one-third of females were able to do so.[9] However, the gender differences are largely explainable by the individual and organizational variables entered into the model in Columns 3 and 4 of Table 9.3. Furthermore, when gender was controlled, minority workers had the same promotion rates as whites.

Women in the middle grades had less education than men (see Table 9.1). Although education had little effect on mobility in the lower grades, it had a strong positive association with promotion in the middle grades. This association remained even when organizational position was controlled. One reason that possession of a bachelor's degree continued to be significant in the presence of organizational controls is that

[9]In 1977, the General Accounting Office reported a promotion analysis for the period May 1973 to February 1977. Their results showed that women were obtaining a larger proportion of promotions at "midlevel" grades (which they defined as the range GS-7 to GS-13) than their share of jobs in this range (U.S. Comptroller General 1977). Their finding, which may appear to be inconsistent with the one reported here, is explainable by their inclusion of three higher grades and exclusion of the two lowest ones in our middle-grade analysis. Grade promotions are less frequent at the top of their midlevel range than at the bottom, and women are disproportionately located at the bottom of this range. Furthermore, the GAO's range excludes employees on lower-tier job ladders in Grades 5 and 6, which have lower promotion rates than employees on upper-tier job ladders and which are disproportionately women. The GAO did not control for grade or any other factors in its analysis.

it eased the transition from the lower to the upper tier. This issue will be addressed in more detail later in the chapter.

Women's job ladders held lower prospects for advancement than men's at the middle levels, and this difference also explained part of the zero-order gender difference. The multiple grade ratio had a strong effect on job mobility at middle-grade levels, where a smaller proportion of grade promotions involved job-ladder shifts (20%) than in the lower grades (44%). The differences in opportunity offered by lower-tier and upper-tier jobs or between female-dominated and male-dominated job ladders was adequately captured by the MGR. Neither the ladder's PAT-CO status nor the proportion female in the job ladder was significant when this variable was included.

Table 9.1 showed that the MGR for women dropped rather substantially from the lower to the middle grades. The reason for this drop was the tendency for women to be located on job ladders that had a ceiling in the middle grades. This slowdown can be demonstrated with the estimated coefficients. We computed predicted 2-year promotion probabilities for a set of hypothetical employees. Each was a white female, with 13 years of education, who was not a veteran, who had 8 years of pregovernment work experience, and who worked on a job ladder that was 80% female.[10] They were located in Grades GS-2 through GS-9, one to a grade. We assumed that the higher-graded employees had progressively more government seniority.[11] The predicted probability of promotion within 2 years of first entering a grade drops steadily from 0.73 to 0.59, 0.46, 0.35, 0.35, 0.36, 0.26, and 0.23, as she moved from Grades GS-2 to Grade GS-10. The predicted rate did not drop to zero near the job ladder ceiling because, as we will see later in this chapter, employees could move from their old ladder to a new one with a higher ceiling.

As in the lower grades, tenured employees at middle levels had higher promotion rates than irregular employees, though a lower proportion of workers at the middle levels were irregular. Employees who did not take a temporary leave during the risk period were also advantaged. Length of government service again had a strong negative effect on promotion rates, as did years of pregovernment work experience.

---

[10]Percentage female rather than the MGR was used to simplify the computations.

[11]We assumed 1.5, 3, 4.5, 6, 8, 10, 12, and 14 years of seniority for Grades 2, 3, 4, 5, 6, 7, 8, and 9, respectively. These assumptions are consistent with the mean values presented in Table 9.1. Column 3 coefficients from Tables 9.2 and 9.3 were used. The intercepts were −0.38 for the lower grade and 0.73 for the middle-grade analysis.

THE STRUCTURE OF PROMOTION IN HIGHER GRADES

Compared with women in the lower or middle grades, the relatively few women who made it to the higher grades were similar to men, both in their attributes (see Table 9.1) and in their chances for promotion. Their chances were similar even though they worked on job ladders with a significantly higher proportion female than did male workers. As we noted earlier, this fact was not associated with lowered structural opportunity, and so women were not disadvantaged in promotion tournaments at these levels of the civil service. But to repeat, relatively few women had reached these levels in the middle 1970s.

Employees who began their careers on lower-tier job ladders were not at a net disadvantage in upper-level promotion tournaments. However, these employees would generally have had longer government service, and length of service had a strong negative effect on future promotion rates. If women more often began their government careers in the lower tier, they would have a higher average seniority. This would be expected to disadvantage them relative to men. But Table 9.1 shows that high-graded women actually had the same average seniority as men. Origin position in government thus had no effect on group differences in promotion rates.

Like women, minority workers were rarer in the higher grades than in the lower ones. But the minority workers who had made it to the upper grade range in the middle 1970s enjoyed the same promotion rates as whites. At one time, discrimination hurt the careers of educated blacks the most (Farley 1985). But by the middle 1970s, a relatively small group of the best minority workers were able to compete on roughly equal terms with their white co-workers (Table 9.4).

In summary then, the grade promotion analyses reveal that women had difficulty advancing in the lower and middle grades. These difficulties were due in part to gender differences in education, but organizational location was an important determinant of promotion rates. In the lower grades, no zero-order differences existed between the promotion rates of women and men, though detailed controls for education, organizational tenure status, and structural position revealed that women did somewhat worse in promotion tournaments than comparable men. Minorities also suffered a modest net disadvantage in the lower grades. In the middle grades, a strong zero-order gender difference existed, a difference largely due to job ladder and education. All groups had similar promotion rates in the higher grades, though women and minority workers were underrepresented at these levels. In short, the

Table 9.4
Logistic Regression Coefficients for Grade Promotion from Grades 11–17[a]

Coefficient	1	2	3	4	Mean/SD
Female	0.18	0.077	0.12	−0.0021	0.12
	(0.2)	(0.6)	(0.5)	(0.99)	
Minority	0.12	0.14	0.17	0.11	0.097
	(0.4)	(0.4)	(0.3)	(0.6)	
Education (years)		0.058	0.057	0.046	15.8
		(0.08)	(0.2)	(0.3)	(2.3)
BA or more		0.34	−0.22	0.018	0.66
		(0.05)	(0.3)	(0.9)	
Veteran		−0.11	0.53	0.27	0.55
		(0.3)	(0.0001)	(0.08)	
Veteran*DOD		−0.51	−0.68	−0.015	0.17
		(0.0009)	(0.0001)	(.96)	
Pregovernment work experience			−0.047	−0.046	6.2
			(0.0000)	(0.0000)	(7.4)
First government job, irregular			0.19	0.10	0.16
			(0.2)	(0.5)	
First government job, lower-tier			−0.37	−0.28	0.13
			(0.04)	(0.2)	
Years of government service			−0.095	−0.079	11.9
			(0.0000)	(0.0000)	(8.6)
Temporary leave			−0.44	−0.26	0.068
			(0.05)	(0.3)	
Grade 12			−0.53	−0.49	0.32
			(0.0000)	(0.0006)	
Grade 13			−1.08	−1.06	0.20
			(0.0000)	(0.0000)	
Grade 14			−1.74	−1.91	0.10
			(0.0000)	(0.0000)	
Grade 15			−2.52	−3.29	0.035
			(0.0000)	(0.0000)	
Grade 16			−0.64	−1.05	0.0057
			(.4)	(0.2)	
Proportion female in job ladder			0.15	0.25	0.16
			(.7)	(0.5)	(0.18)
Multiple grade ratio				0.089	1.7
				(0.003)	(2.0)
Professional				−0.18	0.43
				(0.2)	

Note. $N = 2112$, $P = .25$; No promotions in the sample occurred for GS-17 employees or irregular employees, who were omitted from the analysis.
[a]See notes at bottom of Table 9.2.

structure of job ladders in the federal service concentrated gender differences in advancement in a relatively narrow band of grades. This band spanned the boundary between the lower and upper tier of white-collar jobs.

CHANGE OF TIER, CHANGE OF TENURE

The results of Tables 9.2, 9.3, and 9.4 make clear that opportunity for promotion depends on both one's job ladder and on one's tenure status in the organization. Employees in the trainee grades of upper-tier job ladders had higher rates of promotion than comparably graded lower-tier workers. Employees with career or career-conditional status were promoted more rapidly than employees without such status. But neither one's job ladder nor one's tenure status is fixed. Both can change over time. Because such changes are an important mechanism behind upward mobility, it is important to look for gender or racial differences in the rates at which workers changed these statuses. We therefore performed two additional analyses. The first determined the probability of short-term promotion from lower-tier to upper-tier job ladders. The second determined the probability of promotion from temporary, term, or part-time to career or career conditional status, which might be called a tenure promotion. Both analyses used the same set of variables as the grade promotion analyses.

The base population for the tenure promotion analysis was all employees who had irregular status in the period January 1972 through June 1975. The base population for the analysis of promotions from the lower-tier to the upper-tier population was all clerical and technical employees. The Office of Personnel Management defines employees in mixed occupational series in Grades 1–6 as clerical and in Grades 7–10 as technical (U.S. OPM 1983), but some of these may actually have been moved through the ranks at the same rate as administrative trainees by their agencies. We therefore limited the definition of lower-tier workers in mixed job ladders to employees in Grades 1–4, plus those in Grades 5 or 6 who already had served more than 3 years in the federal civil service, and thus could not have been newly hired administrative trainees. The upper-tier destination positions were defined to include all exclusively administrative and professional job ladders. Due to the ambiguous status of positions on mixed job ladders in the middle grades (which by official convention would be classified as technical, not administrative positions in any case), they were excluded from the definition of the upper tier.[12]

Table 9.5 shows that approximately 8% of the lower-tier workers were able to obtain promotions to professional or exclusively administrative job ladders during a 2-year period of time. Although 8% is not a large figure, 2 years is not a long period of time, either. Furthermore, the rate of mobility to the upper tier was higher for lower-tier employees located in higher grades, as can be seen by the size of the grade coefficient in Table 9.5. Earlier in this chapter we described the estimated rate of movement for a set of hypothetical lower-level female employees. If we use the coefficient from Table 9.5 to compute the predicted probability that our hypothetical employees would shift from the lower tier to a professional or exclusively administrative job ladder in a 2-year period as a function of her grade, the results for Grades 5 through 9 would be 0.08, 0.09, 0.10, 0.11, and 0.13, respectively. In addition, as we noted before, employees could shift to mixed job ladders, which also would offer prospects for further advancement, if not necessarily at the same rate as positions on the two-grade interval administrative or professional job ladders. In short, the boundary between the lower and the upper tier was partially permeable during these years in the federal civil service.

However, the boundary was not so permeable as to make job ladders meaningless. As we have already seen, the rate of grade promotion at middle levels clearly depended on the character of one's job ladder (see Table 9.3) and slowed down near job-ladder ceilings. Thus the observed rate of promotion from the lower to the upper tier did not eliminate the disadvantage of low job ceilings. Furthermore, it did not eliminate the group disadvantage women experienced because they were concentrated in lower-tier jobs (see the first column of Table 9.3). Finally, Table 9.5 shows that women were at a significant zero-order disadvantage in obtaining status promotions from the lower to the upper tier. This advantage could not be explained by the introduction of

---

[12]The ambiguous character of mixed job ladders is demonstrated by the 1979 split of the mixed job ladder 301, "general clerical and administrative," into two job ladders: 301, "miscellaneous administration and programs," which was defined as an administrative job ladder, and 303, "miscellaneous clerk and assistant," which was defined as a mixed clerical–technical job ladder. In 1976, 28,000 employees on job ladder 301 were located in Grade 5 and 17,000 in Grade 7. In 1983, 1,926 employees were located in GS-5 on job ladder 301, now an exclusively administrative job ladder. In addition, 14,474 were located in GS-5 on 303. 2,827 were located in GS-7 on 301 and 8,765 in GS-7 on 303. It would appear that most of the positions in Grades 5–8 of 301 in the years preceding its division were in fact considered to be clerical–technical jobs.

Table 9.5

Logistic Regression Coefficients for Promotions from Lower to Upper Tier and from Temporary to Career or Career-Conditional Status

Coefficient	Change of tier			Change of tenure	
	1	4	5	1	4
Female	−0.53	−0.66	−2.07	0.40	−0.21
	(0.0000)	(0.0000)	(0.07)	(0.0001)	(0.2)
Minority	0.051	−0.025	−0.025	0.23	0.30
	(0.6)	(0.8)	(0.8)	(0.07)	(0.05)
Education (years)		0.043	a		−0.042
		(0.3)			(0.4)
BA or more		0.97	a		0.0035
		(0.0000)			(0.99)
Veteran		0.075	0.14		0.21
		(0.7)	(0.4)		(0.3)
Veteran*DOD		0.063	0.17		−0.19
		(0.8)	(0.5)		(0.6)
Pregovernment work experience		−0.019	a		−0.0040
		(0.001)			(0.6)
Years of government service		−0.043	−0.069		−0.017
		(0.0000)	(0.0000)		(0.2)
Temporary leave		−0.85	−0.86		−0.66
		(0.0001)	(0.0001)		(0.0002)
Grade		0.21	0.21		0.052
		(0.0000)	(0.0000)		(0.2)
Proportion female in job ladder		1.24	1.11		1.10
		(0.0001)	(0.0005)		(0.002)
Multiple grade ratio		−0.042	−0.043		−0.025
		(0.002)	(0.002)		(0.02)
Irregular status		−0.065	−0.044		
		(0.7)	(0.8)		
Technical		−0.11	0.14		−0.23
		(0.6)	(0.5)		(0.4)
Mixed		1.1	1.02		−0.40
		(0.0000)	(0.0000)		(0.03)
Female * years government service		0.043			
		(0.0007)			

Note. For promotion from lower to upper tier, $N = 6457$, $P = 0.081$; for change of tenure promotions, $N = 1398$, $P = 0.52$.
^aSee notes at the bottom of Table 9.2.

control variables. Even when education, grade, type of job ladder, the proportion female in the job ladder, and the multiple grade ratio were controlled, women had significantly lower probabilities of shifting from lower-tier to upper-tier job ladders than did men. Minorities, in contrast, did as well as whites.

But whereas women were at a significant disadvantage in gaining status promotions, employees who worked on job ladders with a high proportion female were actually at an advantage, when other factors were controlled. The advantage was not huge (a 0.3 increase in proportion female lifted the predicted probability of promotion in a 2-year period from 0.10 to 0.14), but it was highly significant. This association occurred because shifts from lower-tier to upper-tier positions were rare from technical jobs in engineering and the physical sciences, where few women worked. They were comparatively frequent in technical jobs in law (claims examiners of various sorts) where women were found in much greater numbers. When controls were entered for a select set of occupational groups, the coefficient for proportion female became small and statistically insignificant.[13]

It should be pointed out, though, that employees in the male-dominated technical positions in engineering and the physical sciences had relatively high grade ceilings compared with most lower-tier jobs. The average salary of engineer technicians was $17,402 in 1976 (U.S. CSC 1976a), whereas physical science technicians made an average of $14,766, compared with the $13,708 average for technicians generally, and the $9,976 average for clerical workers outside the postal service. The greater opportunity for grade advancement in these jobs than in most lower-tier positions offset the disadvantage of a lower net rate of promotion to upper-tier job ladders.

In sum, the employees who found it easiest to shift from the lower to the upper tier were male and worked in the higher grades of the lower tier.[14] They had a college degree,[15] and relatively short government careers to date. They did office work, as opposed to scientific work, and (judging from the sign of the MGR coefficient) had nearly reached the

[13]The addition of these occupational controls did not materially affect the gender coefficient ($b = -0.60$, $p = 0.0001$).

[14]Because promotions from the lower tier to the upper tier were comparatively rare (though not impossible) in the lowest grades of the lower tier, we performed another analysis that restricted the sample to lower-tier employees in Grades 4 and higher. The results still showed women to have a highly significant ($b = 0.56$, $p = 0.002$) disadvantage in obtaining promotions to the upper tier.

[15]Ten percent of lower-tier employees in Grades 4 and higher had a college degree.

limit for advancement offered by their current job ladder. To put it another way, the lower-tier employees who found it easiest to make the switch were those who were most similar (in age, education, and gender) to those newly hired into upper-tier job ladders. Because men were at a significant advantage in gaining promotions from the lower to the upper tier, their share of status promotions was disproportionate to their representation in the lower-tier population. Although 68% of the base population was female, women obtained only about 57% of the promotions.

Rates of tenure promotion were much higher than rates of promotion from the lower to the upper tier. Table 9.5 shows that over 50% of the irregular employees were able to change their tenure status during a 2-year period of time. Women had a substantial zero-order advantage in making this switch, but this difference disappeared in the presence of controls. Minorities also had an advantage, which persisted in the presence of controls. As hypothesized, irregular status was an important entry route into clerical, female-dominated job ladders. Although irregular employees had difficulty achieving grade promotions compared to tenured employees, they found it comparatively easy to make the transition to tenured status. Moreover, as Tables 9.2 and 9.3 show, they suffered no significant handicap once this transition had been made, if compared with similarly situated workers who entered the government with career or career-conditional (tenured) status.

GENDER AND RACIAL DIFFERENCES IN INITIAL ASSIGNMENT

We argued at the start of this chapter that two contingencies affected an individual's access to the more desirable jobs in an organization. The first concerned initial placement, whereas the second concerned the ability of an employee to move through the ranks. The analyses described so far have shown that women in particular had considerable difficulties in moving out of the lower ranks of government. In certain cases, these difficulties could be attributed entirely to their organizational status or human capital attributes. The female handicap in the bottom grades or in moving to the upper tier remained even when educational qualifications, organizational location, and other important characteristics were controlled. Their structural disadvantage was compounded by their tendency to enter the civil service at lower grades than men did. Figure 9.1 shows the grade distribution by gender for all accessions during the period from 1972 through June 1977, while

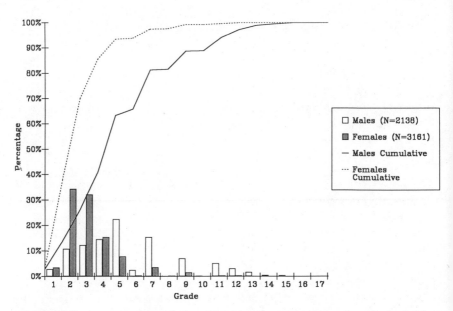

Figure 9.1 Percentage and cumulative percentage of accessions at each grade, by gender, 1972–1977.

Figure 9.2 shows the grade distribution only for employees with college degrees who entered with career or career-conditional status.[16] About one-third of the newly hired women with college degrees entered the government in Grades 1–4, where positions are located on lower-tier job ladders. In contrast, only 8% of men with college degrees entered at such a low level in the hierarchy. These gender differences in initial assignment play an important role in determining the ultimate level these workers will reach (Grandjean 1981; Rosenbaum 1984).[17]

Figures 9.3 and 9.4 show the grade distribution of accessions for nonwhites in general and for those with a bachelor's degree entering with career or career-conditional status. These figures show that non-

[16]Reinstatements, reemployment, transfers in, and return to duty are excluded from Figures 9.1 through 9.4.
[17]Women's difficulties in gaining positions of equal rank as those of men were due in part to the veterans preference system. This system favored men, because 98% of veterans in the middle 1970s were male. In 1976, for example, 19% of employees scoring in an eligible range on the PACE (Professional and Administrative Careers Examination) were veterans, but 29% of the new hires were veterans. Women constituted 41% of those scoring in the eligible range but obtained only 31% of the jobs (Campbell 1978; see also Downing 1981).

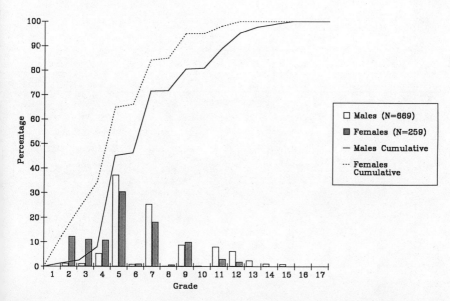

Figure 9.2 Percentage and cumulative percentage of accessions at each grade for college graduates, by gender, 1972–1977: career and career-conditional appointments only.

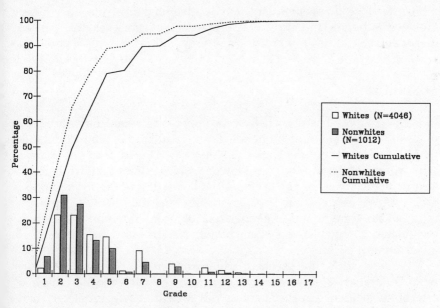

Figure 9.3 Percentage and cumulative percentage of accessions at each grade, by race.

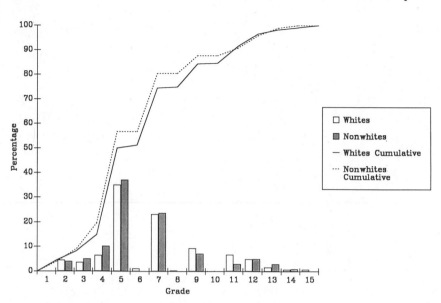

Figure 9.4 Percentage and cumulative percentage of accessions at each grade for college graduates, by race, 1972–1977: career and career-conditional appointments only.

whites as a group were somewhat disadvantaged relative to whites. However, the racial disadvantage was not as great as the gender disadvantage.

SUMMARY

This chapter has shown how promotion rates are influenced by one's job ladder and more generally by the structure of job ladders that make up the civil service hierarchy. It also has allowed us to understand why women and minorities have lower average grades than white men. Group inequality is not due to across-the-board differences in promotion rates or to sex-segregation *per se*. Inequality is instead due to differences in initial assignment and to gender-specific promotion bottlenecks that are related to the tiered system of job ladders used by the federal government.

Women who had reached administrative or professional journeymen levels (5% of women in the current analysis) enjoyed the same rate of subsequent advancement as did men. But women clearly had difficulty reaching journeymen levels. These difficulties are of three distinct types. First, women tended to enter the federal hierarchy at lower levels than men. Even in a sex-neutral promotion system, such differentials would tend to persist over time. Second, women tended to advance in the crucial middle grades at lower rates than men. Most of this difference was due to the concentration of women in female-dominated lower-tier job ladders, which offered relatively little opportunity for advancement. Third, although it was not impossible to obtain promotions from lower-tier to upper-tier job ladders, it was harder for women to do so than for men, even when other factors were controlled.

In contrast to the experience of women, minority workers enjoyed rates of promotion that were very similar to white rates. Their entry grades lagged somewhat behind whites, but the racial gap in initial assignment was smaller than the gender gap. Minority workers have found federal, state, and local government to be a comparatively congenial environment for their push to gain equal employment opportunity (Farley 1984). They clearly had not achieved racial parity in the federal government of the 1970s. But they were no longer victims of blatant discrimination either, at least in the competition for promotions.

10

Conclusion

Structures and Outcomes in Bureaucratic Labor Markets

JOB LADDERS AND JOB MOBILITY

In creating the most systematic conceptual scheme for studying labor market segmentation since Doeringer and Piore (1971), Althauser and Kalleberg (1981) argued that job security, prospects for advancement, and job control were the three foundations for a typology of labor markets. In their view, an internal labor market (ILM) was best defined as "a cluster of jobs, regardless of occupational titles, or employing organizations, that have three basic structural features: (a) a job ladder, with (b) entry only at the bottom, and (c) movement up this ladder, which is associated with a progressive development of knowledge and skill" (p. 130). The four possible pairings of type of control with prospects for advancement produced four different categories of labor market structures: (a) firm internal labor markets (FILM), which are internal labor markets controlled by firms, (b) occupational internal labor markets, which are internal labor markets controlled by occupational incumbents, (c) firm labor markets (FLM) or jobs with firm-specific security but without advancement prospects, and (d) occupational labor markets or jobs with occupational security but without advancement prospects. In describing internal labor markets and occupational labor markets further, they argued that "some holders of FLM jobs originally enter FILM job ladders but either level off or for other reasons do not progress all the way up the ladder" (p. 135). The jobs these workers have, which exist at

259

many levels and "parallel" firm internal labor market and occupational internal labor market job ladders, constitute the firm or occupational labor market.

Michael Piore observed that internal labor markets could be divided into an upper and a lower tier (Piore 1975). Althauser and Kalleberg accepted the validity of Piore's observation. But they did not see much use for the tier distinction in developing a typology of market segments. In their view, the differences between the upper and lower tiers was best described in terms of "broad occupational categories (e.g., professional, managerial" and "job characteristics (e.g., routine or repetitive work, autonomy)." But, they continued, the upper and lower tiers did not differ in "such structural relations as ladders or limited entry ports" because job ladders and job security are found in both tiers. Thus they developed a typology that emphasized advancement prospects, job security, and control, and downplayed the tier distinctions proposed by Piore.

For Althauser and Kalleberg, the distinctions between a firm or occupational internal labor market, a firm or occupational labor market, or a secondary labor market provided the basis for characterizing a job's advancement potential. But the results presented in this volume suggest that the tiered structure of bureaucratic labor markets is an important additional factor affecting the advancement potential of jobs. Many jobs offer restricted prospects for further advancement, even though they lie on job ladders. Among this group are the jobs on the highest rungs of job ladders. Jobs at the top of an organization offer no prospects for further advancement, by definition. Of course, the level of rewards provided by these jobs is such that no one ever refers to them as "dead-end" positions.[1] But workers who have reached the top of the lower-tier are often in the same boat with workers whose jobs are not located on ladders at all. To move higher, they must get jobs on new job ladders that have higher ceilings. Because the necessary next step in their careers does not lie in the "most natural line of promotion" a job ladder, this step is often difficult. To succeed, they must win a competition with workers who are in the normal channel for filling the target jobs, that is, young college graduates. If they fail in this competition, they still have job security but only the job security of a dead-end job.

Althauser and Kalleberg argued that "In firm internal labor markets, limited entry ports are a deliberate firm policy designed to support promotion from within" (p. 130). But, as we have seen, entry ports do

---

[1]Individuals fortunate enough to have reached the top may wonder what worlds are left for them to conquer, but their concerns are outside the scope of this book.

more than this. At the very bottom of an organization, entry jobs are filled by organizational outsiders. However, entry ports of upper-tier job ladders are almost never at the bottom of an organization. Many organizational insiders rank below the grade of these jobs and would like to move into them. Whether they can easily do so depends on a firm's personnel policies. The skill requirements a firm establishes for jobs, the level of training it offers, and the way it evaluates employee talents can all make a difference. A firm can use entry ports to enhance the promotion prospects of workers on the upper-tier job ladders. It can also use them to restrict the promotion prospects of lower-tier workers. In short, when a firm establishes entry ports, it makes policies that affect careers at both lower and higher grades.

Tier boundaries and the personnel policies that give them meaning affect the structure of group inequality as well as the career chances of individual workers. In the white-collar sector, the existence of tier boundaries is a major reason why sex segregation has such a strong effect on the earnings and career attainment of women. Tiers, in short, are a structural feature of labor markets. In addition to indexing occupational standing or the quality of work, they affect job mobility, too.

THE EMPIRICAL IMPACT OF BUREAUCRATIC LABOR MARKETS

The work career is often viewed as a kind of sporting event, particularly in the middle-class, self-oriented culture of the United States (Bellah *et al.* 1985). For many workers, a portion of this contest is played out within the relatively structured arena of a bureaucratized organization. In real sporting events, the final standing matters, but other measures of success matter, too. A major-league baseball player would like his team to win the world series and would like to win the MVP award for himself. But he is pleased by the high salary he makes even when neither he nor his team has a great year. The situation in organizational tournaments is similar.

The prize structure in bureaucratized organizations has changed during the past 50 years. Once anyone with the title of administrator could count on one or two hands the number of his superiors. He could look to the large number of inferior positions in the organization as a measure of his success. Today, a low-ranking administrator or professional in a large organization can no longer count the number of jobs that outrank his or hers very easily. If he or she had an historical sense, he or she would recognize that his or her position is much closer to the middle of the hierarchy than professional or administrative positions used to be. The higher positions on clerical ladders have been even more sharply devalued compared with higher clerical positions in the past.

But career rewards are not measured simply by relative standing. Although only one player can win a tournament no matter what its size, the total reward package can still grow. The expansion in the number of professional and administrative jobs and the changed shape of the grade hierarchy represent a net increase in rewards and potential job satisfaction for workers. Even though the average professional or administrative job ranks lower than its counterpart 50 years ago, it is still desirable to ambitious clerical and technical workers. A low-ranking administrative or professional job is the important next step in career advancement for the elite workers on the lower tier. Their ability to make the transition depends on the structure of job ladders.

Despite the porous character of job-ladder boundaries, job ladders are a major determinant of advancement in the civil service. Generally speaking, the more opportunity in one's job ladder, the more rapidly one advances, especially in the middle and upper grades. But a lot of job mobility takes place across job-ladder boundaries. Job-ladder shifts frequently accompany grade promotions throughout clerical job ladders. Near the ceiling of lower-tier ladders, grade promotions are impossible without a job-ladder shift. Job-ladder shifts also tend to rise in the higher grades of upper-tier job ladders as well.

At one time, it was normal for young recruits to the nonscientific positions to enter the service at low grade levels and then gradually work their way upwards. The better workers could advance quite far up the hierarchy. Even chiefs of nontechnical bureaus typically had started their careers as lower-level clerks. It is probable that the institutionalization of a separate entry route for college graduates in the 1950s, coupled with the development of separate administrative job ladders in the name of professionalism, restricted promotions from clerical to administrative jobs. In the 1970s the equal employment opportunity movement at least temporarily stalled any further heightening of the mobility barrier between the two tiers. However, the formal differentiation of clerical and administrative positions continued.[2] EEO did not dismantle the tiers. Instead, it facilitated movement across the still-in-place boundary.

If the wall between the lower tier and the upper tier had been

---

[2]As noted earlier, the largest remaining mixed job ladder was divided into an administrative and a clerical–technical job ladder in 1979, even as upward mobility efforts to create bridge positions from lower- to upper-tier job ladders were intensifying (U.S. OPM 1981).

impenetrable, mobility for clerical workers within the civil service would have ended somewhere between Grades 5 and 10, depending upon an employee's particular job ladder. Instead, some employees were able to continue their advancement by moving to the upper tier. But competition from young college graduates entering the service slowed down advancement rates for lower-tier workers as they approached the ceilings of their job ladders. Promotion to the upper tier, in short, was not an automatic event. Even those who made it across the boundary were not home free. Employees who took too long to make this passage saw future promotions come more slowly for them than for the young college graduates who worked alongside them.

Because job-ladder shifts are less routine than advancement along the job ladder, management discretion inevitably plays a greater role in allowing or preventing them. Nonetheless, it is probably not surprising to learn that the employees chosen by management to make the shift to the upper tier were those who most resembled the group of new hires into upper-tier jobs. Lower-tier employees who had a college degree, who had relatively little work experience (whether in the government or elsewhere), and who were male had a significant advantage. It also helped to work in jobs where the natural progression would be to move to the administrative, as opposed to the professional side of the upper-tier. Employees in the mostly male subprofessional scientific jobs found it more difficult to move to professional positions because of the more stringent educational requirement. However, these employees had less need to make such a switch. Gradual changes in personnel policies had lengthened their job ladders to the point where they could reach respectable grade levels without moving to the upper tier.

Because women and minorities held a disproportionate share of lower-tier jobs, they benefited from the expansion of the mobility bridge between clerical and administrative jobs. But in many other respects, women continued to have trouble in the bureaucratic labor market of the federal government. Women as well as minorities disproportionately started their government careers in the lower tier. The imbalance in initial placements made it all but impossible for them to achieve parity. The structure of job ladders contributed further to gender inequality, and, to a lesser extent racial inequality, by creating group differences in advancement rates. Only in the higher grades were gender differences absent. The results suggest that only the best women can hold their own against men under conditions where overt discrimination is absent but group-specific disadvantages persist. For most women, segregation by job ladder compounded the difficulties they already faced in a competitive labor market.

GENERALIZING FROM A CASE STUDY

The research reported in this volume has largely dealt with the case of the federal civil service. One might legitimately ask how representative it is of the work force in general. Clearly the federal government differs from other employers in the crucial respect that it need not be concerned with making a profit. Thus market forces need not shape its actions in the same way that they would shape the actions of other employers. Furthermore, it might legitimately be argued that the federal bureaucracy is more susceptible to political pressures than private bureaucracies because it is more visible to political scrutiny.

Although these considerations are certainly valid, they do not change the fact that the organization of the federal work force has more similarities to the organization of other medium-sized and large employers than differences. First, the separation of job ladders into an upper and a lower tier is commonplace in American companies. Second, formalized personnel policies are also common. Third, sex segregation is a pervasive phenomenon in American firms. Fourth, the findings on the mobility process in the federal government are generally consistent with available findings from other case studies of organizational mobility (Halaby 1978; Rosenbaum 1984; Baron et al. 1986).

Any such similarities of course cannot justify the generalization of the particular estimates found here to a national sample. But that is not really the point. The advantage of focusing on a case study is its value in identifying the major elements underlying organizational inequality. A case study methodology allowed a more detailed examination of the development of personnel structures in a highly visible bureaucracy that both reflects and influences personnel trends in the nation at large. It also allowed a more detailed look at the impact of such a system for promotion rates. Many studies have demonstrated that women do not achieve the same rate of career growth either in status or income as do men (Wolf and Fligstein 1979; Rosenfeld 1980; Marini 1980). But studies based on national samples cannot easily pinpoint the reasons for these differences. This study has shown that organizational data can disentangle the multiple processes that potentially affect the advancement of women and minorities. The estimated rates from this study obviously cannot be applied to the nation at large. But similar mechanisms no doubt have affected and continue to affect female workers throughout the economy.

Other organizations will differ in how they structure entry ports, in how broadly or narrowly they define job ladders, in the porousness of tier boundaries, or in their efforts to recruit and promote minorities and women (Baron *et al.* 1986; O'Farrell and Harlan 1984). Clearly, more research is needed on the extent to which such factors vary by firms. It is through the accumulation of research findings that all the pieces of the puzzle ultimately fall into place.

THE PROFESSIONAL CHARACTER OF UPPER-TIER WORK

Repeatedly, justifications for the development of an upper tier in the federal service involved the concept of profession. Scholars have always had a hard time characterizing the professions. Eliot Freidson recently concluded that the difficulties are inescapable because the term has not had a precise technical meaning. In his words, professions are "changing historic concepts with particularistic roots in those industrial nations that are strongly influenced by Anglo-American institutions" (p. 32). In short, profession is a "folk concept" (Becker 1970). The conception of profession that derives from this view is primarily historical, not technical. Moreover, occupations looking for public acceptance of their claim to professional status have often had difficulty getting this acceptance. Some claims are never satisfactorily resolved, which leads to the problems of definition that scholars wrestle with.

The professional character of administrative and managerial jobs is an especially sticky point (Ehrenreich and Ehrenreich 1977a,b; Gouldner 1979; Freidson 1984, 1986). Freidson's proposed resolution of this dispute is based on the concept of "formal knowledge," defined as the subjects of research and teaching in the modern university. Professions, he argued, "are occupations for which [higher] education is a prerequisite to employment in particular positions" (p. 59). Starting with this definition, he argued that some managers are professionals, "namely, those managers and administrators for whose jobs specific educational credentials are required" (p. 60).

Freidson's solution, which relies on official conceptions of profession, is useful for many purposes. But it is too black and white to adequately characterize the different career paths leading to administrative and professional jobs in government. The role of formal knowledge in administration depends on the criteria one uses to assess this role. The job descriptions in position classification manuals, the formal educational requirements, the actual mobility patterns, the characteristics of elite practitioners all lead to answers, but these answers are not consistent.

Repeatedly, the position classification standards refer to the requirement that administrative employees understand "the principles of management," or "administrative principles," or possess "specialized knowledge" of one or another branch of administration. Such "principles" have a claim to being the formal knowledge that Freidson writes about.

But these requirements do not lead to easy distinctions in practice. The administrative and professional hierarchies in government are now extremely long, and the work on them is extremely varied. An administrative or professional employee near the bottom of the upper tier does work that is much more like the work of lower-tier employees than like the work that top-level personnel do. The argument that this employee's work is nonetheless qualitatively similar to what his distant superiors do, and qualitatively different from what his lower-level co-workers do, is shaky at best. The system relies therefore on a combination of differences in work tasks and differences in mobility policy to justify the boundaries between administrative and lower-level work.

The system's tolerance for the ambiguity of this boundary is reflected in its recruitment and promotion practices. Strictly speaking, the college degree is not required for the typical administrative job ladder. Nonetheless, personnel policies have evolved to favor the college educated, while not completely shutting out those who lack college. But the system recruits college graduates at levels that those without college reach only after many years of work. The higher the grade, the more difficult it is for those without college to compete. At the top grades of the administrative hierarchy, the number of such individuals becomes vanishingly small. Whether or not a degree is "required" to get to top managerial positions in a formal sense, it is clearly a practical requirement. Furthermore, it is the only way to gain access to the system at high enough levels at an early enough age to make it to the top before one's time runs out.

Boundary problems have occupied the attention of social scientists for many years. They are inherently problematic in theoretical work on social structure. When a scholar proposes a conceptual framework for understanding a particular phenomenon, the framework frequently relies upon classification for much of its power. The classification differentiates among social entities that, the theory claims, have different interests, values, capabilities, or other characteristics. The attributes and relationships among these entities are used to explain empirical phenomena. But because the conceptual framework must (if it is to be useful) be a simplification of social reality, it is inevitable that some entities will be harder to classify than others.

The gray zone around the boundaries of a typology's classes may or may not be a matter of theoretical interest. The size of this gray zone may be small enough to be inconsequential. A larger gray zone may represent an inadequacy of the underlying conceptual framework. Instead, the zone may highlight theoretical puzzles, whose solution would contribute to the advancement of theory. For example, a major boundary problem of twentieth-century sociology is the status of the middle-class vis-à-vis the class struggle theories of Marxism (see, e.g., Parkin 1979). Some contend that the difficulty of fitting the middle class into Marxian class categories shows the inadequacy of Marxian theory for postindustrial societies (Dahrendorf 1959; Bell 1973). Others argue that the behavior of those in a "contradictory class location" under situations of system crisis is an inadequately understood problem of major social and theoretical interest (Wright 1985).

The professional status of occupations such as managers or administrators is also a boundary problem. If it made no difference how social scientists classified these jobs, one would have to agree that this boundary problem is not very important. But the way social actors handle boundary issues often does make a difference. For example, the attempts of semiprofessionals to gain professional status may have an impact on their rewards and the cost of their services to others. For another example, the extent to which senior professionals think of themselves primarily as managers or as professionals may affect how much they try to control their professional subordinates.

The analyses of this book have demonstrated that the boundary between the lower and the upper tier is not a problem that can be addressed in purely occupational terms. Mobility issues play a key role. Furthermore, the gray zone around this boundary is not a problem to be cleared up through analysis, Rather, it is an essential part of the structure. It arises from attempts to impose qualitative distinctions on long hierarchies, where quantitative distinctions are, in a technical sense, more appropriate. The attempts to convert quantitative distinctions into qualitative ones is not simply a misunderstanding on the part of the personnel profession. It is basically a response to the structure of the educational system and to the social power of professions.

The combination of these factors produces a gray zone between the lower and the upper tiers. This zone reflects the ambiguity involved in classifying work as either professional or subprofessional, and as either administrative or clerical, near the boundary between these pairs of occupations. It also serves as a control device to regulate job mobility. The ability of management to recruit outsiders into a range of upper-tier grades gives it flexibility in filling job vacancies. The ability to extend lower-tier job ladders into regions of overlap with upper-tier ladders allows management to reward lower-tier employees at competitive rates, while controlling movement across the boundary. The ability of management to broaden this overlap for certain technical jobs allows it to respond to market conditions, while maintaining the "integrity" of professional jobs. The control capabilities of the promotion process on upper-tier ladders allows management to bring lower-tier workers across the artificial boundary separating clerical from administrative work, while reserving almost all top jobs for the college-educated. The structure of job ladders is not the product of a managerial master plan. But, at least in certain respects, it has been responsive to managerial needs.

IMPLICATIONS FOR POLICY

The economic model of organizational labor markets has conceptualized job ladders as rationally developed strategies for optimizing the process of matching workers and jobs. Clearly, efficiency considerations have played a role in their development. But for this model to be the whole story, two conditions must be met. First, detailed, accurate knowledge about the skill requirements for jobs must exist to allow jobs to be rationally organized onto job ladders. Second, the events affecting the development of organizational labor markets must consist of little more than managerial decisions to maximize productivity per dollar of labor cost in the face of market constraints.

However, these two conditions are never met in the real world. The following considerations suggest that a technically optimal arrangement of jobs on job ladders is an unattainable goal:

1. Job analysis cannot provide objective knowledge about the best way to link jobs together. The results of job analyses are based on a mixture of facts and opinion about the job linkages that "make sense." Some opinions are idiosyncratic, but others can claim a certain amount of social legitimacy because they are supported by social actors. Personnel managers, the professions, unions, or organizations representing disadvantaged groups are prime examples of such actors. The views of such groups provide the menu of alternatives from which job ladders emerge.
2. There is no guarantee that these options include the technically optimal one. Furthermore, it is difficult to objectively determine which of the possible solutions is technically preferable at any given point in time.
3. The productivity outcomes of the different solutions are typically

too hard to measure and too similar for a definitive answer to emerge out of any evaluation of the comparative performance of alternative forms of organization.

4. The labor market and the technology underlying it change too rapidly for experimentation to identify small advantages of one form of organization over others.

These considerations do not preclude the possibility that personnel practices may in certain respects become more efficient over time. However, they do not support the Panglossian conclusion that the arrangements in place at any given point in history are optimally efficient, either. Furthermore, they suggest that, whereas theories of technical incrementalism may identify one important dimension of change, these theories are only part of the story. Doeringer and Piore (1971) recognized the inadequacy of a purely technical explanation for the structure of job ladders when they argued that internal labor markets were a product of both technical forces tied to the costs of job training and of custom.

Customary forces were clearly involved in the shaping of federal job ladders. The mobility interests of government clerks, patronage policies, the American practice of promoting scientists into administrative jobs, or the demands by veterans for preferential treatment are all customary forces. These forces may have prevented an even more rigidly tiered system of job ladders from developing. But custom is not sufficiently descriptive of all the nontechnical determinants of the structure of job ladders. Indeed, the division of causality into the *technical* and the *customary* oversimplifies the picture. The image this dichotomy conveys is of a technical engine fighting against the frictions of tradition. But the forces propelling the development of labor market tiers were not uniformly technical, and the forces working to reverse this direction were not simply customary.

Other research has persuasively argued that many jobs do not require the level of education their incumbents frequently have (Berg 1970). Personnel officers do not have the luxury of working out exact skill requirements and ideal training programs for jobs in isolation from history. Government had to react to the expansion of higher education, to the power of the professions, and to the growth of the welfare state. These developments were as much institutional as technical in character, yet they had a major effect on the structure of job ladders.

On the other side, the challenge to the tiered personnel system mounted by the equal employment opportunity movement was not a customary force retarding the march of progress. First, this force was not old. Although working women and blacks traditionally held less desirable jobs, they did not mount a serious assault on this system until relatively recently. Organizations began changing their recruitment policies during a time when young white males still had a strong stake in promotions from clerical jobs. They were the source of much customary opposition. As the barriers between the tiers grew, the gender and racial composition of the lower tier increased. Finally, it was these groups that had the major stake in crossing the increasingly institutionalized boundary between the tiers.

It took the newly acquired political strength of women and minorities to force from business and government an official acknowledgment that the separation of the lower and the upper tiers had gone too far (Wallace 1976; Northrup and Larson 1979; O'Farrell and Harlan 1984; Burstein 1985). The modifications that have resulted from this movement cannot be dismissed as the drag of customary forces on a technically oriented management. A stronger case can be made that management efforts to keep women out of traditionally male jobs was the real customary force shaping personnel arrangements. Both sides have provided technical as well as political justifications for their positions. In essence, the conflict has revealed the political character of arrangements that in tranquil times are routinely accepted as a product of competitive markets.

The limitations of market models that claim to explain the structure of job ladders are a subset of the problems that monocausal explanations often face. Their shortcomings (and for that matter, their strengths) can best be understood if we inquire into the theoretical purpose of such models. It is useful to do that in the context of a distinction often made in the social sciences, that between theories and metatheories (cf. Wagner and Berger 1985).

Theories are models that purport to explain empirical phenomena. Metatheories such as rational choice, symbolic interactionism or Marxism are ways of looking at empirical phenomena. As theoretical perspectives, they can be applied to a variety of phenomena but do not generate the kinds of testable propositions that can be refuted by data. Warner and Berger have suggested the term *unit theories* to describe the applications of metatheories to particular phenomena. Unit theories derive their perspective from the metatheory they draw upon, but their closer ties to empirical phenomena allow them in principle to be tested and refuted by data.

Metatheories are inherent in the scientific fabric of the social sciences. They provide a fertile source of increasingly powerful accounts of the social world. However, the link between theory and metatheory also has a downside. These linkages too often result in theories that try to overplay the hand of the theoretical perspective, so to speak, and introduce simplification at the price of distortion. The paradigm for scientific inquiry suggests that such an overextension would lead to both false and falsifiable predictions. The falsification of these predictions would provide a self-correcting solution to the problem and a motor for further progress. However, social science has learned that theories that may in principle be falsifiable are in practice not easily falsifiable. Too often the data do not allow a definitive resolution of theoretical disputes.

The most salient example of this is the unequal attainment of women and men in the labor market. Evidence for this inequality is interpreted by supporters of market models to mean that market forces are producing these gender differences, which therefore must somehow contribute to overall efficiency. To supporters of institutional theories, the evidence proves the existence of institutional barriers to female advancement, which create social inefficiency as well as social injustice. Thus, even as evidence accumulates, both sides conclude that their theory is supported, even though their interpretations of the evidence are inconsistent.

One can, of course, attribute these inconsistencies to ideological differences, and they certainly do play a role. But more can said about the disagreement than this. The intellectual conflict also derives from the complicated relationship between theories and metatheories in the social sciences. There is a natural tendency for some scholars to be more committed to the advancement of a particular theoretical perspective than they are to the explanation of any particular empirical phenomenon. For example, the value of a particular research project might lie primarily in its demonstration that a certain metatheory can be usefully applied to an empirical phenomenon that others had thought lie outside its domain. A researcher's interest in greater understanding of the particular phenomenon under study may be secondary to this metatheoretical agenda. Alan Cicourel's (1974) phenomenological study of Argentinian fertility, a subject normally considered to be explainable by demographic theories, or Gary Becker's (1973) economic theory of marriage, a subject once thought to be explainable by love and romance, are examples of studies with a metatheoretical as well as a theoretical agenda.

Research tied to a particular metatheory can accomplish both theoretical and metatheoretical ends, and both purposes can have a scientific payoff. The metatheoretically driven theory may explain certain aspects of a phenomenon better than previous attempts. It may provide building blocks out of which better theories of the phenomenon could be constructed. And it may affect the way scholars think about a whole class of problems and thereby have impact far beyond its specific empirical focus. But the two enterprises of developing theories and of developing metatheories are not completely compatible. There is always the danger that interpretations of theoretical work that is strongly tied a particular metatheory will succumb to what I have termed the *metatheoretical fallacy*.

The metatheoretical fallacy occurs when scholars confuse metatheories and theories. A consequence of this fallacy is the claim that a straightforward application of a metatheory can completely account for a particular phenomenon, instead of providing insights into only one aspect of it. For example, when Becker wrote two articles (1973, 1974) on a theory of marriage, his papers might more appropriately have been called "The Value of a Rational Choice Perspective for Understanding Certain Aspects of Behavior Relating to Marriage, Child Bearing, and Divorce." To many scholars, his work established the value of rational choice as a tool for studying family dynamics. But those under the spell of the metatheoretical fallacy might interpret Becker's work to mean that a comprehensive theory of family dynamics can be derived from economic considerations alone. Such an interpretation can lead to erroneous conclusions. Instead of understanding that economic calculations are involved in the decision to divorce, some might erroneously conclude that divorce is a form of economic behavior. A similar misinterpretation might follow from research titled "A Romantic Theory of Marriage," or more appropriately, "The Value of a Romantic Perspective for Understanding Certain Aspects of Behavior Relating to Marriage, Child Bearing and Divorce."

Either of these metatheoretically derived efforts must be distinguished from attempts to work out a theory of divorce *per se*. Such a theory would likely be less elegant and less parsimonious than straightforward derivations from rational choice or romantic metatheories. The value of the trade-off must be based upon judgments by the scholarly community about how worthwhile it is to generate a comprehensive and accurate "theory of divorce" and whether this goal is worth the loss of the parsimony and elegance possessed by rational choice or romantic theories of divorce.

Science is ultimately in the business of accounting for the real world, not developing elegance for its own sake, or justifying certain value orientations, or rationalizing the material interests of certain groups. Nonetheless, it is clear that neither the scholarly nor the social community judges all questions to be equally worthy of scientific inquiry. The metatheoretical fallacy is of little concern when the phenomena in question are nothing more than "laboratory mice" designed to advance understanding of a general class of events. But some empirical phenomena are important for their own sake. The understanding of these phenomena is a principal justification for the scientific enterprise. In the social sciences, issues such as the sources of political or economic stability, the sources of socioeconomic inequality, and the causes of war are all of this type.

Important issues are the subjects of social policy, and social science has a potentially major role to play in these policy debates. In the social sciences, the metatheoretical fallacy often finds its way into policy debates. This happens, for example, when powerful constituencies interpret evidence that market forces affect the development of organizational labor markets as a justification for opposing policy interventions that would increase opportunity for women and minorities. It also occurs when a group interprets evidence that employers do use organizational labor markets as part of a strategy to control workers as a justification for the revolutionary overthrow of existing social arrangements. But when these explanatory fragments are set aside in favor of more realistic, though less parsimonious or elegant understandings of labor markets, the groundwork is laid for more realistic and fruitful social policies.

When a market model is assumed to be correct unless proven wrong, the burden of proof is placed on the shoulders of those who charge that women and minorities are unfairly segregated into lower-paying jobs with less opportunity. Instead, the metatheoretical fallacy can be avoided by recognizing that multiple forces have shaped the structure of present-day labor markets. Among them are forces that cannot reasonably be justified by an appeal to market efficiency. But when oversimplified explanations are abandoned, one must reassess where the burden of proof should lie. I would argue that the burden of proof should not be placed on those who suffer from restricted opportunity. When evidence of widespread inequality exists, employers and ultimately society must either show that the existing arrangements are fair or else take steps to change them.

The results of this study have suggested that nondiscriminatory promotion policies will not by themselves overcome gender and racial inequality in organizational labor markets. If group differences in initial placement exist, neutral promotion policies would tend to maintain these differences. Correcting the recruitment imbalance requires that the gender imbalance in the clerical ranks be ended. A restructuring of this magnitude is beyond the capacity of any single employer, even one so large as the federal government. The gender imbalance in the lower white-collar ranks will not end unless women are able to move into high-paying blue-collar jobs more easily or (what amounts to the same thing) clerical salaries rise enough to attract high-school-educated men. Gender and racial imbalances in educational and vocational preparation and—in the case of gender—the division of labor in the family would also have to disappear. Without such societalwide changes, no policies implemented by an organization, no matter how extensive, are likely to equalize the organizational status of women and men, or of minorities and whites.

Nonetheless, organizational policies can contribute to the goal of equal employment opportunity. Policies that break down barriers between the lower and the upper tiers would be constructive steps. Promotion policies that are truly gender- and race-neutral are also necessary. It is particularly important that talented lower-tier workers be spotted early in their careers. Because the lower grades of upper-tier ladders are themselves training grades, lower-tier workers should not have to work their way to the top of their ladders before they are identified as potential upper-tier material. The longer it takes for management to identify and promote such workers across the tier boundary, the worse will be their prospects for future advancement and the lower their ultimate attainment.

Ultimately, the evidence forces the conclusion that rigid boundaries between the lower and the upper tier cannot be justified on the basis of the character of the work performed. Any qualitative differences in work at the boundary pale before the quantitative differences that differentiate work at all levels of the grade structure. A more accurate organizational chart would arrange positions in functional areas such as personnel, accounting, or engineering in a single line that stretched from the bottom to the top of the organization. This line would be similar to the line that connected the junior messenger and the chief clerical administrator in the classification schedule of the Congressional Joint Commission in 1920.

In an equitable world, of course, not all junior messengers would make it even to the middle of the hierarchy, and promotions to the top would be rarer still. Furthermore, there is no justification for starting all workers at the same level of the hierarchy, even in a world where their boundaries are deemphasized. Workers with unequal levels of education or work experience should be recruited into different levels of the organization, though the advantages that college or graduate degrees currently provide may be excessive. Finally, the influx of college graduates into a hierarchy above the bottom grades would inevitably slow mobility at the levels these graduates usually entered. However, to the extent possible, artificial separations of jobs onto separate ladders should be avoided. Promotion routes from lower-tier to upper-tier positions should be regularized. Early identification of talent should be encouraged. Assessments of promotion potential should be based on job-related criteria rather than stereotypes about gender, race, educational background, or the idea that clerical experience disqualifies an individual for responsible jobs. If these changes could be accomplished, the goal of technical efficiency as well as social justice would be served.

Appendix
The Occupational Content of Clerical and Administrative Work: 1920 to the Present

INTRODUCTION

Chapter 3 argued that the expansion of government was associated with a restriction of clerical ladders to include only the more routine office work. At the same time, the tasks of higher clerical jobs were redefined as administrative in nature and placed on administrative job ladders. This conclusion was reached through an analysis of positions at the boundary between the two occupational groups. More detailed evidence on the bifurcation of administration and clerical work is contained in the changing job descriptions found in the statutes and position classification standards that defined civil service jobs at various points in time. This appendix examines how the changing language of job analysis described clerical and administrative positions.

The major conclusions can be easily summarized. Increasingly over time, job definitions stressed the analytical and professional character of administrative positions, as opposed to the more structured, routine character of lower-level work. These sources confirm expectations in showing a gradient in skill and responsibility from positions at the bottom of the hierarchy to positions at the top. But the evidence suggests that classifiers had difficulty in identifying a qualitative difference in the tasks of positions located near the boundary of the emerging clerical and administrative job ladders. Ultimately, the classifications systems justify the bifurcation through the desirability of greater management control over recruitment and promotion, rather than through attributes of the job tasks themselves.

CHANGES IN THE STATUTORY DESCRIPTION OF CIVIL SERVICE GRADES

In 1853, Congress organized government clerical work into four grades plus the grade of chief clerk (Act of March 3, 1853, 10 Stat. 189, 209). But this act did not create a position classification system in the modern sense of the term (Baruch 1941a). It lacked provisions to ensure that work of comparable difficulty or responsibility would be assigned to equivalent grades. Instead, the act merely provided that the pay for any particular clerical position must come from the menu of choices it designated. The Classification Act of 1923, in contrast, authorized the creation of a duties classification for civil service jobs. This act established five services, three of which were for white-collar employees. The Clerical, Administrative and Fiscal (CAF) Service had 14 grades, the subprofessional service had 8, and the professional service had 6. In 1928, the Welch Act added two grades to the top of the CAF hierarchy and two grades to the professional hierarchy. In 1949, the Classification Act of 1949 merged the three systems into one hierarchy and also added two additional grades to the top of the hierarchy. The general schedule it created is still in use.[1]

Not all administrative positions in the contemporary civil service are managerial in character. Some are specialized staff jobs without formal authority over subordinates. However, substantial supervisory responsibility is one justification for classifying a job as administrative. Although some clerical jobs entail supervisory responsibility, the position classification standards now in use describes the job of clerical workers as fundamentally the processing of transactions, not the supervising of other laborers. By comparison, the language of 1920s statutes suggests that clerical jobs involved more supervisory responsibility than do numerically equivalent grades today.

A comparison of the job descriptions found in the Classification Act of 1923, the Welch Act of 1928, and the Classification Act of 1949 is shown in Table A.1. The description of lower level jobs in the 1923 and 1928 statutes are the same. Differences at higher grades are noted in the left column of the tables. According to the 1923 statutes, clerical work at grades CAF-5 and higher had extensive supervisory responsibility for the work of lower-level clerical employees. Because almost 60% of all classified civil servants in 1928 were in grades CAF-4 or lower (see Figure 2.1), this emphasis is not surprising. The 1949 grade descriptions for

---

[1]The Civil Service Reform Act of 1978, however, created a Senior Executive Service and removed these employees from the 18-grade hierarchy of the general schedule.

Table A.1
A Comparison of Supervisory Language Used to Describe Corresponding
Positions in the Clerical, Administrative, and Fiscal Service
and the General Schedule

CAF-1 Under immediate supervision	GS-1 Under immediate supervision
SP-1 Under immediate supervision	
SP-2 Under immediate supervision	
CAF-2 Under immediate supervision	GS-2 Under immediate supervision
SP-3 Under immediate supervision	
CAF-3 Under immediate or general supervision Supervise a small section performing simple clerical duties	GS-3 Under immediate or general supervision
SP-4 Under immediate supervision	
CAF-4 Under immediate or general supervision Supervise small stenography section	GS-4 Under immediate or general supervision Requires minor supervisory or other experience
SP-5 Under immediate or general supervision Supervise the work of a small number of employees performing work of an inferior grade in the subprofessional service	
CAF-5 Under general supervision Supervise a large stenography section or a large section performing simple clerical work or a small section performing difficult but routine work	GS-5 (NP) Under general supervision Requires supervisory or other experience

(continued)

Table A.1
(*Continued*)

SP-6

Under immediate or general
supervision supervise the work of a
small number of employees holding
positions in Grade 5 of this service

P-1   (P) Under immediate supervision
Under immediate supervision

CAF-6   GS-6
Under general supervision   Under general supervision

Supervise a large or important office   Requires supervisory or other
organization engaged in difficult and   experience
varied work

SP-7

Under general supervision to supervise
the work of a small number of
employees holding positions in Grade 6
of this service

CAF-7   GS-7
Under general supervision as chief clerk   (NP) Under general supervision
to supervise the general business   requiring considerable supervisory
operations of a small independent   training and experience to perform
establishment or a minor bureau or   work of considerable difficulty and
division of an executive department or   responsibility along . . . supervisory
supervise a large or important   lines
organization engaged in difficult and
specialized work

SP-8

Under general supervision, supervise
the work of a small number of
employees holding positions in Grade 7
of this service

P-2   (P) Under immediate or general
Under immediate or general   supervision
supervision . . . with a small number of
assistants

CAF-8   GS-8
Under general supervision   Under general supervision

Supervise a large or important office   To perform very difficult and
organization engaged in work involving   responsible work along . . . supervisory
specialized training on the part of the   lines
employees.
                                             Requires considerable supervisory
                                             training and experience

---

Table A.1

(Continued)

CAF-9
Under general supervision as chief clerk to supervise the general business operations of a large independent establishment or a major bureau or division of an executive department or to supervise a large or important office organization engaged in work involving technical training on the part of employees

GS-9
(NP) under general supervision perform very difficult, responsible work along . . . supervisory or administrative lines

P-3
Under general supervision . . . with a small number of trained assistants

(P) (No supervisory attributes listed for professionals)

CAF-10
Under general supervision supervise a large or important office organization engaged in work involving considerable technical training and experience on the part of the employees

GS-10
Under general supervision perform highly difficult and responsible work along . . . supervisory or administrative lines

CAF-11
Supervise the general business operations of an executive department or supervise a large and important office organization engaged in work involving extended training and considerable experience on the part of employees

GS-11
(NP) To perform, under general administrative supervision . . . work of marked difficulty and responsibility along . . . supervisory or administrative lines.

CAF-11 (WELCH)
(No change in description, though the generic title assigned to positions at this grade was downgraded)

P-4
Under general administrative supervision

(P) (No supervisory attributes listed for professional positions at this grade)

P-4 (WELCH)
Under general supervision

CAF-12
Supervise the design and installation of office systems or be head of a small bureau in case professional or scientific training is not required

GS-12
(NP) under general administrative supervision [to perform] work of a very high order of difficulty along . . . supervisory or administrative lines

(continued)

Table A.1
(Continued)

CAF-12 (WELCH)
  Supervise a large or important office
  organization engaged in work involving
  extended training and experience on
  the part of the employees

P-5
  To act as assistant head of a large
  professional or scientific organization or
  to act as administrative head of a major
  subdivision of such an organization or
  to act as head of a small professional or
  scientific organization

(P) under general administrative
supervision perform . . . work . . .
requiring . . . experience which has
demonstrated leadership . . .

P-5 (WELCH)
  To perform, under general
  administrative supervision, . . . the
  administration of a small scientific or
  technical organization

CAF-13
  Supervise the design of systems of
  accounts for use by private corporations
  subject to regulation by the U.S.
  Government, . . . , or to act as chief of
  a large bureau or a bureau having
  important administrative or
  investigative functions in case
  professional or scientific training is not
  required

GS-13
  (NP) under administrative direction [to
  perform] work of unusual difficulty and
  responsibility along . . . supervisory or
  administrative lines; to serve as
  assistant head of a major organization
  involving work of comparable level
  within a bureau

CAF-13 (WELCH)
  Act as assistant head of a major bureau
  or to act as administrative head of a
  major subdivision of such a bureau or
  to act as the head of a small bureau, in
  case professional or scientific training is
  not required, or to supervise the design
  and installation of office systems,
  methods, and procedures

P-6
  To act as the scientific and
  administrative head of a major
  professional or scientific bureau

(P) to perform, under administrative
direction . . . work . . . requiring . . .
experience that has demonstrated
leadership

P-6 (WELCH)
  To act as assistant head of a major
  professional or scientific organization,
  or to act as head of a small professional
  or scientific organization

Table A.1
(Continued)

CAF-14
Under general administrative direction
[to perform] work of exceptional
difficulty and responsibility
along . . . supervisory and
administrative line

Work more responsible and exacting
than that for CAF-13

CAF-14 (WELCH)
To act as assistant head of a major
bureau, in case professional or scientific
training is not required, or to supervise
a system of accounts for use by private
corporations subject to regulation by
the United States

P-7
[to perform] work more responsible and
exacting than that for P-6

P-7(WELCH)
To act as assistant head of one of the
largest and most important professional
or scientific bureaus or to act as
scientific and administrative head of a
major professional or scientific bureau

CAF-15 (WELCH)
To act as the head of one of the largest
and most important bureaus, in case
professional or scientific training is not
required

P-8 (WELCH)
To act as administrative head of one of
the largest and most important
professional or scientific bureaus

CAF-16, P-9 (WELCH)
Shall include all positions that may be
specifically authorized and appropriated

GS-14
(NP) Serve as head of a major
organization within a bureau

(P) plan, direct, or execute major
administrative or other specialized
programs

GS-15 (NP,P)
Under general administrative direction
work of outstanding difficulty and
responsibility along . . . supervisory
and administrative lines

To serve as head of a major
organization within a bureau, plan,
direct, and execute programs of
unusual difficulty

GS-16 (NP,P)
Under general administrative direction
work of outstanding difficulty and

(continued)

Table A.1
(Continued)

for at an annual compensation in excess of $9,000	responsibility along . . . supervisory and administrative lines; serve as head of a major organization; to plan and direct programs of unusual difficulty and national significance
	GS-17 (NP,P) To serve as the head of a bureau where the position is of a high order among the whole group of positions of heads of bureaus
	GS-18 (NP,P) To serve as the head of a bureau where the position is exceptional and outstanding among the whole group of postions of heads of bureaus.

Note. The text in the table is excerpted from the Classification Act of 1923, the Welch Act of 1928, and the Classification Act of 1949. CAF refers to clerical, administrative, and fiscal; SP to subprofessional; P to professional; and GS to general schedule. NP in parentheses refers to the part of the 1949 grade description that applies more to administrative positions. P in parentheses refers to the part of the 1949 grade description that applies more to professional positions.

this range continued to mention supervisory responsibilities (supervisory experience was listed as a requirement). However, the 1949 descriptions place more emphasis on the clerical and less on the supervisory tasks than did descriptions of comparable grades in the 1923 and 1928 statutes. Contemporary job descriptions, which will be analyzed later in this chapter, make even clearer that supervisory responsibilities are secondary characteristics of clerical jobs in this range. This deemphasis on supervisory tasks for the higher clerical jobs is not surprising, because the lower clerical ranks currently hold fewer than one in six civil servants, as opposed to the 60% figure of the late 1920s.

A comparison of job descriptions for higher grades also shows a downward drift in the managerial and supervisory responsibilities at any given grade. In the language of the 1923 Classification Act, CAF-7 employees supervised the business operations of a minor bureau. CAF-9 employees supervised the general business operations of a major bureau. Civil servants at CAF-11 supervised the general business operations of an executive department or supervised a "large and important" office organization. CAF-12 employees were possibly the head of a small bureau. CAF-13 employees were possibly the chief of a large bureau.

The Welch Act of 1928 added two grades to the top of both the CAF and the Professional hierarchies. It also rewrote the job descriptions of the higher grades, though not the lower ones. The new descriptions suggest a downgrading of responsibility in positions from CAF-11 through CAF-14. The addition of two additional grades (GS-17 and GS-18) to the hierarchy in 1949 corresponded to a further downgrading of the managerial and supervisory responsibilities at grades numerically equivalent to the old ones. A GS-13 employee might serve as assistant head of a major organization within a bureau, which appears to be about equal to the position held by employees at the CAF-11 level in the 1923 system or CAF-12 in the Welch system. GS-14 (serve as head of a major organization within a bureau) appears comparable to CAF-12 (head of a small bureau) or CAF-13 in the Welch system. GS-15 (serve as head of a major organization within a bureau) appears subordinate to CAF-13 (act as chief of a large bureau) in the 1923 system or CAF-14 in the Welch system. GS-16 ("serve as head of a major organization"), or GS-17 ("serve as the head of a bureau where the position is of a high order among the whole group of positions of heads of bureaus"), or GS-18 are all similar to CAF-14 in the 1923 system, or CAF-15 and perhaps CAF-16 in the Welch system. Table A.1 shows that the lengthening of the hierarchy caused a similar downgrading of work done at any given numerical grade in the professional sector. In both the professional and the administrative sector, the work done by middle or higher-graded civil servants in the 1920s system roughly corresponds to work done by employees located two or three grades higher in the general schedule system.

One might argue that the successive restructurings of the grade hierarchy of the civil service are of little substantive importance if they only amounted to a relabeling of the grade numbers of particular positions. However, they have an additional significance as well. The successive restructurings lifted jobs that were at clerical grade levels in the 1920s to grade levels defined as administrative by the end of the 1940s. At the same time, they reduced the scope of work done in the lowest positions unambiguously describable as administrative or professional as the hierarchy above such positions became longer and more densely populated.

COMPARISONS OF POSITION CLASSIFICATION STANDARDS

Comparisons based on grade descriptions are limited to the very general language of the statutes, which provides only a framework for the detailed position classification standards used to classify jobs. Our conclusions can be solidified by examining the actual job descriptions of representative occupations to identify the similarities and changes that have occurred between the 1920s and the present.

At various points during the past two centuries, the federal government has published descriptions of the content of government jobs. The House of Representatives first showed interest in the question in 1818, when it asked the secretaries of state, treasury, war, and navy and the postmaster general to report on the number of clerks working in each department and on their salaries. It also asked them to provide to the Congress

> such information in relation to the respective employment of your clerks, as may best enable them to judge of the amount of compensation proper to be allowed . . . having regard to an equalization, as nearly as practicable, to the compensation among clerks of equal responsibility, in the several departments of government. (U.S. Congress. House 1818: 1)

In response to an 1838 petition to Congress by government clerks seeking a raise in salary and a standardization of their pay, the Congress again queried heads of the Departments of State, Treasury, War, the Navy, and the Interior as well as the postmaster general about the duties of clerks in government (U.S. Congress. Senate 1838c). Congress collected a third set of reports in 1843 (U.S. Congress. House 1943).

But these early reports were not systematic and were made at a time when the number of employees in the government was small. The first exhaustive, systematic classification of government employees was conducted by the Congressional Joint Classification on Reclassification of Salaries and reported to the Congress on March 12, 1920. With the aid of 60 classifiers, 50 researchers, and a support statistical and clerical staff, the committee set out

> to secure the actual facts in the case of every individual position and individual employee as to the present "rate of compensation" and 'character of employment' and wherever possible, working conditions (U.S. Congress. House 1920: 29).

The result was an 800-page report on about 1,700 distinct positions in the government. The report was a systematic one; the goal of the classifiers was to equate positions based on their duties, not titles or pay, because these attributes were not yet systematized. The product of the Congressional Joint Committee can be compared with present position classification standards to study change in the composition of work.

The *Class Specifications for Positions in the Departmental Service* (U.S. PCB 1924) contains a second set of useful descriptions. These specifications applied to the 50,000 positions covered by the Classification Act of

1923. The descriptions in the 1924 class specifications were not re-searched to the same extent as the descriptions produced by the Con-gressional Joint Commission. But they have the advantage of relating job descriptions to the grades of the Classification Act of 1923. There-fore, these descriptions can more precisely be compared with contempo-rary ones. A third source of information can be found in the 1931 field survey of the Personnel Classification Board. This 1327-page report was the largest classification study produced to date (Baruch 1941a). Taken together, these studies contain ample material for comparing the work of clerical and administrative personnel in the prewar era with that performed today.

CONTEMPORARY CLASSIFICATIONS OF PERSONNEL WORK

Contemporary position classification in the federal service is based on a set of principles, which are described in detail in the *Position Classifi-cation Standards*. These standards guide agencies in their classification of positions, a task required by the Classification Act of 1949. The *Standards* state that the determination of a position's job ladder and grade should be based on an analysis of the position's duties. This principle of federal classification is the foundation of a "rank-in-the-job" classification sys-tem, which means that a person's rank in the system depends upon the characteristics of one's job. It is distinguished from the "rank-in-the-man" European systems. In a "rank-in-the-man" system, an employee is recruited into a distinct service and has a personal rank. He or she retains this rank even if he or she temporarily works at a less responsible job (see, e.g., Stahl 1956; Chapman 1959; Halloran 1967).

The *Position Classification Standards* lists a set of nine factors to be used in developing a position classification standard. These factors are described as follows:

1. Knowledge required by the position
2. Supervisory controls
3. Guidelines
4. Complexity
5. Scope and effect
6. Personal contacts
7. Purpose of contacts
8. Physical demands
9. Work environment

Each factor is scored on a set of levels. For example, complexity is measured on six levels:

1. Tasks that are clear-cut and directly related
2. Duties that involve related steps, processes, or methods
3. Various duties involving different and unrelated processes and methods
4. Varied duties requiring many different and unrelated processes and methods such as those related to well-established aspects of an administrative or professional field
5. Varied duties requiring many different and unrelated processes and methods applied to a broad range of activities or substantial depth of analysis, typically for an administrative or professional field
6. Breadth and intensity of effort . . . involv[ing] several phases being pursued concurrently or sequentially with the support of others within or outside of the organization.[2]

The decision whether a job is properly clerical or administrative, and its job ladder and grade, is in theory based on its relationship to the previously listed factors. But the *General Grade Evaluation Guide for Non-supervisory Clerical Positions* (U.S. OPM 1979) gives a general definition of clerical work that captures its essential features. "The work of the clerk is essentially the orderly processing of the papers and performance of the routine work supporting an office or organization" (U.S. OPM 1979: 1). Some person-to-person contact may occur, but "it is not the person-to-person contact but the paperwork which constitutes the essential purpose and characteristics of the clerical position" (U.S. OPM 1979: 4). It further distinguishes two kinds of clerical work, procedural and substantive. Procedural work, which is to be classified in Grades GS-1, 2 or 3

> is work in which the clerk is not directly concerned with the subject matter of the transaction. In other words, the clerk is not responsible for determining the what or why of the transaction but rather assures that the procedures for processing the transaction are followed. (U.S. OPM 1979:3)

Substantive clerical work, to be classified in grades GS-3, 4 and 5

> is work where the clerk is concerned with the subject (or the what and why) of the transaction worked on. Clerks performing such work make certain

[2]These factors are taken from "Instructions for the Factor Evaluation System," a part of the *Position Classification Standards* (U.S. CSC 1977b). Note that many of the position classification standards in effect in the 1980s were written under an earlier, related set of factor guidelines. See *Position Classification Standards for General Schedule Positions* (U.S. CSC 1963a).

289

decisions regarding the adequacy of the content of the transaction rather than limiting their primary concern to whether the proper procedures have been followed. For example, the processing of a voucher may require that the clerk determine the nature of the financial transaction by reference to contracts, general policies, etc; determine if the voucher is properly prepared in terms of legal requirements; and whether or not payment of the voucher should be made. (U.S. OPM 1979: 3)

Abstract principles are often difficult to apply unambiguously in concrete situations. In order to determine how these principles have been applied in practice, this chapter focuses on a pair of job ladders that the *Position Classification Standards* refers to as models for distinguishing upper-level and lower-level nonmanual work. The job ladders in question are GS-203, the Personnel Clerical and Assistance Occupational Series, a clerical job ladder, and GS-201, the Personnel Management Occupational Series, an administrative job ladder. Not only are the principles underlying the classification unusually clear in these two cases, but these positions can also be compared to descriptions of personnel work from the 1920s.

Table A.2 shows how the personnel classification system distinguishes the duties of positions in the Personnel Clerical and Assistance Series (U.S. CSC 1966a, 1966b). The table shows both the general description of tasks at each grade and specific examples of these tasks. The job descriptions in the *Position Classification Standards* do not include the supervisory responsibilities of each position, which therefore are omitted from Table A.2. But the *Standards* reports that the grades of incumbents of the previously mentioned positions can be further increased if they involve significant supervisory responsibilities in addition to the job tasks described in the *Standards*. Positions that are primarily supervisory, that is, those consisting of the supervision of three or more employees but which are not primarily managerial in character are upgraded one or more grades above the grade of the work supervised. The amount of upgrading is a function of the kind and degree of supervision, the scope and variety of operations supervised, and special additional responsibilities.[3]

Table A.2 shows a smooth progression in the level of difficulty and responsibility that characterize the tasks of personnel clerks and assistants from the lower to the higher graded positions. Lower-level cler-

[3]The "Supervisory Grade Evaluation Guide" makes a distinction between supervisory and managerial positions. "The lower end of the continuum tends to be called supervision, and to be related primarily to the direct oversight of people; the higher end of the spectrum tends to be called management, and relates primarily to the direction of programs and multisegment organizations." Managerial positions are rated according to the tasks involved, not the grade level of subordinates (U.S. CSC 1976c: 2).

Table A.2

Duties of Positions in the Personnel Clerical and Assistance Series

Position	Tasks, general description	Supervisory duties	Tasks, specific duties
Personnel clerk, GS-3	Primarily concerned with the *procedural* aspects of personnel transactions.	*	Checking for presence of necessary documents, for completion of all necessary items in each document, and for arrangement of the necessary documents in the proper sequence, contacting appropriate sources to secure missing data or documents, etc.
Personnel clerk, GS-4	Processing of all types of personnel actions except those of an unusually complicated or difficult nature	*	Review supporting documents to check that (a) data are internally consistent, (b) proper regulations have been cited, (c) proposed action is appropriate and conforms to existing laws
Personnel clerk, GS-5	1. Processing the full range of transactions that include a significant proportion of those of a novel or unusually complicated nature 2. Providing some technical assistance for staffing specialists	*	1. (a) (clerical) Processing excepted and temporary appointments, removals and reinstatements (b) (clerical) Explaining regulatory, procedural, and policy requirements applicable to processing personnel actions 2. (assistance) Processing and orienting all new employees
Personnel clerk, GS-6	1. Independently performs substantive processing of a full range of personnel transactions, . . . includ[-ing] . . . transactions of a novel or unusually complicated nature 2. An authoritative local source of information on	*	Processing regulatory and procedural problems concerning reductions in force, excepted appointments, grievances, etc.

Table A.2
(*Continued*)

Position	Tasks, general description	Supervisory duties	Tasks, specific duties
	regulatory and procedural information		
Staffing assis- tant, GS-6	Provides technical assistance for staffing specialists	*	Interviewing and recommending placement of eligibles for several common types of positions, making local reference checks, and conducting postplacement interviews
Personnel assis- tant, GS-7	Assisting personnel specialists by performing technical assistance work. In contrast to GS-6, these assignments are characterized by concern with a variety rather than a relatively few occupations, types of training, or employee relations areas.	*	1. Interviewing and recommending placement of eligibles for a variety of common types of positions (usually of a nonprofessional nature) 2. Setting up courses and conducting training for clerical personnel 3. Advising employees and supervisors on less involved problems of employee conduct . . . and the full range of procedural requirements for filing grievances.
Personnel assis- tant, GS-8+	**	**	**

Note. *Supervisory duties are not specified in the *Position Classification Standards*. The "Supervisory Grade Evaluation Guide" describes guidelines for increasing the grades of positions with supervisory responsibilities. ** These positions "are too few and too highly individualistic to permit presentation of useful descriptions in a standard."

ical workers process routine personnel actions. Higher-level clerical workers process complicated transactions as well as routine ones. Higher-level clerical workers have more contact with other employees than lower-level clerical workers. Employees whose job is primarily that of processing transactions are placed in grades no higher than GS-6.

Technical assistants are located in Grades 6, 7, and 8 or (rarely) higher. These employees help specialists with tasks other than the processing of transactions. They process and orient employees, interview and recommend placement for lower-level positions, train lower-level employees, or advise specialists and employees about simple issues regarding discipline, grievances, leaves, injuries, and so forth. For more complicated problems, personnel specialists rather than technical assistants attend to their solution.

Higher-level personnel positions are placed in the Personnel Management series, GS-201. The personnel clerical and assistance series and the personnel management series are separate job ladders containing jobs in the same functional area, namely personnel administration. The question therefore arises as to how the line is drawn between the two job ladders. What work is to be classified as "clerical" and what work as "administrative"? According to the *Standards,* the distinction is based primarily on the need for and the use of analytical skills and specialized knowledge.

> If the position primarily and clearly requires a high level of analytical ability, an extensive knowledge of and background in a personnel management functional specialty, a good understanding of the interrelationship of the functional specialties, and the capability to deal successfully with many different kinds of personnel management problems, it is classifiable in one of the personnel management series. However, if the position does not require a high level of analytical ability, or does not require an extensive knowledge of and background in personnel management functions and techniques, or does not require the ability to deal with many different kinds of personnel management problems, it is clearly classifiable in the personnel clerical and assistance series. (U.S. CSC 1976d: 4)

The first sentence of the preceding quotation contains the word *clearly* in instructing how job requirements should be used to classify positions onto either the upper-level or lower-level job ladder. However, the distinction in practice may not be clear, especially because personnel management trainees often perform roughly the same tasks as personnel assistants and are located in the same grade range (5, 7 and 9). In such cases, the *Standards* argued that the classification decision should be made according to the purpose of the work assignment and the capabilities of the individual employee.

> The distinction between a personnel assistant and a personnel specialist hinges on work assignments. To understand the distinction clearly, one must consider duties, responsibilities, *and qualification requirements* (italics theirs). This is particularly true in considering a trainee specialist as compared with a personnel assistant, as portions of their overall assignments may very well be identical. In such instances, the background that the individual brings to the

assignment as well as the purpose of the assignment must be considered. The trainee specialist performs work on the basis of his capacity to absorb and interpret instructions and related data, and does so in a temporary stage of development to work of a more judgmental and analytical nature. The personnel assistant may perform some of the same work items, but he does so on the basis of long experience and familiarity with the organization, the positions involved, the applicable procedures and regulations, and pertinent precedent cases. Furthermore, the personnel assistant performs his work on a continuing basis, without additional assignments specifically designed to develop judgmental and analytical skills required for higher-grade personnel specialist work. (U.S. CSC 1966b: 2)

In effect, then, the *Position Classification Standards* acknowledged that near the boundary of the upper- and lower-tier job ladders, it is sometimes not possible to make classification decisions on the basis of the job tasks involved. At that level, there may in fact be little or no difference in work assignments. Rather, the basis for classification must often be the recipient of the assignment and the purpose of the assignment. The trainee is seen as promotable and in need of developmentally useful experience, whereas the assistant is seen as being at a mature level of his or her civil service career, filling a continuing organizational need for the performance of work in his or her speciality. Thus mobility considerations as well as the content of work define the boundary between the two tiers.

The positions of employees in the personnel management series are, as the title of the job ladder suggests, management positions. They typically consist of "placement and staffing, position classification and/or salary and wage administration, employee relations, labor relations and employee development/training, and related clerical and administrative functions."[4] The *Position Classification Standards* contain a set of analytical categories for classifying the work of personnel administrators into grades. Four criteria are used: the level of authority and responsibility, the size of the work force served, the weight and range of problems, and the "operational character" of the program. These terms are defined as follows:

A. The level of authority and responsibility of the program:
   1. Primary policy level, which denotes the policymaking authority normally associated with a department or agency headquarters.
   2. Secondary policy level, a term that normally applies to the

[4]Other specialized personnel positions are described as "staff" positions, but we will not consider them here (U.S. CSC 1966a).

organizational echelon below the department or agency level.[5]

3. Operating level with full delegation of authority. "The term 'operating level' denotes the absence of the types of policy-setting freedom included in the terms 'primary policy level' and 'secondary policy level.' 'Substantially full delegation' presumes that not more than a very few of the most significant personnel decisions are subjected to a prior review at a higher level."

4. Operating level with limited delegation of authority.[6]

B. The size of the work force served:
1. Small: 350–750 employees.
2. Medium: 1000–5000 employees.
3. Moderately large: 7500–15,000 employees.
4. Large: 20,000–50,000 employees.

C. The weight and range of problems served (e.g., variety and complexity of occupations, complexity of organization, unified or separate management controls, intermingling of work forces, dispersion of work force, isolation from labor markets, complexity due to labor relations activities and special missions that place exceptional demands on personnel).

D. The Operational Character of the Personnel Program:
1. Level I—standard technical operation: "At this level, emphasis is on maintenance of a personnel program which fulfills basic requirements by complying with rules, regulations, and procedures. Specialized personnel program functions are conducted in accordance with established concepts, techniques and procedures, with some minor adaptation of guides to local needs."

2. Level 2—positive management-oriented operation: "At this level, the personnel program goes beyond the fulfillment of basic regulatory and procedural requirements. Definite attention is given to serving the personnel needs of management.

---

[5]"in cases where the policies, procedures, and programs formulated by the 'primary policy level' are sufficiently general to permit the next lower organizational level substantial latitude in developing or adapting policies and procedures, and in shaping program operations to meet specific needs" (U.S. CSC 1966a, pp. 9–10).

[6]"On the other hand, many 'operating-level' programs may have considerable limitations placed on their authority. If there are a substantial number or variety of personnel decisions which must have prior approval at a higher level, there is typically a 'materially limited delegation of authority'" (U.S. CSC 1966a, p. 12).

There is awareness that this demands flexibility in operations and a constructive approach to the solution of problems."
3. Level 3—Outstanding management-oriented operation.

The system is then applied in a straightforward way for the grading of personnel officer positions, as can be seen in Table A.3. Managers of relatively simple programs, serving smaller work forces, with less policymaking responsibility, in relatively simple environments, are given lower grades. Increments in any of these four dimensions justify a higher grade. Increments in multiple categories may justify two or more higher grades. The Assistant Personnel Officer assists a personnel officer and participates to some degree in the planning and direction of the personnel program. If he or she is a "full assistant," his or her position is classified one grade below that of the officer he or she assists. The standard does not give much in the way of specific examples and unquestionably the application of these principles to real-world situations can present ambiguities not easily resolved in terms of these categories. But the general implications of the system are clear enough.

Boundary problems arise, of course, at the bottom of the hierarchy, in deciding whether a position is that of a "personnel assistant" or a

Table A.3
Duties of Positions in the Personnel Management Series

Position	Policy level	Operational character	Size	Environment
Personnel officer, GS-11	Operating level	Level 1	Medium	Minimal
			Small	Substantial
		Level 2	Small	Minimal
Personnel officer, GS-12	Operating level	Level 2	Medium	Limited to moderate
			Small	Very substantial
	Secondary policy level	Level 2	Small	Limited to moderate
	Primary policy level	Level 1	Small	Limited to moderate

(*continued*)

Table A.3
(*Continued*)

Position	Policy level	Operational character	Size	Environment
Personnel officer, GS-13	Operating level	Level 2	Medium	Substantial to very substantial
			Moderately large	Limited to moderate
			Medium	Moderate, coordinates lower levels
	Secondary policy level	Level 2	Small	Substantial
			Medium	Limited to moderate
	Primary policy level	Level 1	Medium	Limited to moderate
		Level 2	Small	Limited to moderate
Personnel officer, GS-14	Operating level	Level 2	Medium	Exceptional
			Moderately large	Substantial
			Large	Limited to moderate
	Secondary policy	Level 2	Small to medium	Exceptional
			Medium	Substantial, coordinates lower levels
			Moderately large	Limited to moderate, coordinates lower levels
	Primary policy level	Level 2	Small	Substantial to very substantial
			Medium	Limited to moderate, coordinates lower levels
Personnel officer, GS-15	Operating level	Level 2	Moderately large	Exceptional
			Large	Very substantial to exceptional
	Secondary policy level	Level 2	Medium	Exceptional
	Primary policy level	Level 2	Medium	Very substantial, coordinates lower levels
			Moderately large	Substantial, coordinates lower levels

"personnel officer." In such situations, where the size of the work force is small, the complexity of the task is minimal, and/or the delegation of authority is "abnormally restricted," "consideration should be given to the possible propriety of a GS-9 or 10 classification or to the question of whether the position is, in fact, that of a personnel officer, or is more properly classifiable as a personnel assistant" (U.S. CSC 1966a: 37).

Ironically, the language of the *Position Classification Standards* suggests a continuity of positions from the bottom of the personnel clerical and assistance series to the top of the personnel management series. But the classification system nonetheless divides these jobs into separate job ladders, one for positions that ostensibly have "professional" attributes, one for positions that do not. The separation is justified as much by the career trajectories envisioned for incumbents as by any qualitative distinction of work at the boundary of the tiers.

EARLIER CLASSIFICATIONS OF PERSONNEL WORK

Earlier classification systems also make use of qualitative distinctions when describing positions that collectively carry out the personnel functions of the federal government. But these distinctions between clerks and administrative officers were not as systematically applied as in the contemporary system. Tables A.4 and A.5 illustrate the job descriptions for these positions.

The 1920 Congressional Joint Commission Survey divided "clerk" positions into five titles, in contrast to the four clerical grades and three or so "assistant" positions in the contemporary position classification system. These 1920 clerk positions encompassed the contemporary clerical and the contemporary "assistant" positions and reached to the level of "assistant personnel officer," an administrative position in the contemporary system. In functional terms, both the clerical and administrative hierarchies in the 1920s system were shorter than in the contemporary system. Only the underclerk was restricted to "procedural" clerical tasks. The junior clerk performed procedural and substantive tasks and some technical assistance tasks (e.g., "assisting in the work of training schools"). Senior personnel clerks were engaged in all the tasks of assistants, whereas principal and head clerks were engaged in work that is at the same relative level as the assistant personnel officer in the contemporary system, whose grade would be one lower than that of the officer he or she was assisting. Officer positions were divided into three levels, in contrast to the six or more levels in the contemporary system.

There are of course, ambiguities in this mapping. Although in some ways the job of the Principal Personnel Clerk corresponds with that of

Table A.4

Personnel Positions, 1920 Classification

Position	Tasks, general description	Supervisory status	Tasks, specific examples
Under personnel clerk	Perform, under immediate supervision, simple routine work		
Junior personnel clerk	Perform, under immediate supervision, somewhat specialized yet routine work		Prepare records; compile reports to disbursing officers and the administrative head of the division; prepare correspondence along fully established lines; assist in the work of the training schools
Senior personnel clerk	Perform . . . responsible or important clerical work in connection with the personnel administration of a government organization or branch	1. Supervise the preparation of correspondence regarding official actions 2. Supervise a few employees engaged in clerical work in connection with personnel records, etc.	1. ascertain the availability and suitability of applicants through personal interviews, correspondence, etc. 2. hear and investigate grievances and complaints of employees; assist an administrative head of a bureau or a military officer in personnel matters
Principal personnel clerk	Perform, under general supervision, important work involving supervisory responsibility or the exercise of independent judgment and discretion in connection with the personnel administration of a government organization or branch	1. Conduct the work of his office and fill in for him in his absence 2. Assist a senior or chief personnel officer along specific lines involving supervisory responsibility 3. Supervise the work of a number of stenographers, typists, clerks, etc. engaged in several distinct types of work; supervise a large group engaged in a single line of work	1. Select clerical appointees from certificates issued by the Civil Service Commission 2. Prepare notices concerning the application of decisions and policies in personnel matters

Head personnel clerk	Perform, under direction, work of an executive or of a highly specialized nature, involving large supervisory responsibility or the exercise of mature judgment and discretion in connection with the personnel administration of a government organization or branch	1. Under a senior or chief personnel officer conduct the work of the office and act for him in his absence 2. Supervise personnel clerks, time and pay-roll clerks, file clerks, stenographers, typists, or others engaged on a considerable variety of work 3. Supervise the preparation of recommendations or military orders for appointments, promotions, transfers, reinstatements etc. 4. Direct the preparation or checking of pay rolls	1. Select clerical appointees from certificates submitted by the Civil Service Commision 2. Consider, decide, and dispose of questions concerning absences from official duty, misconduct, discipline, and other questions requiring tact and diplomacy
Personnel officer	Under direction, have responsible and complete charge of the appointment office of a government organization or branch of relatively small size, in which the appointment work requires considerable responsibility, but not the assistance of a large force of clerical assistants, nor the control of a large variety or volume of personnel work		Assist superior officials in personnel matters
Senior personnel officer	Under general administrative direction in a large government organization or branch, have responsible and complete charge of the appointment office, the management of which requires ability and wide experience (1)		Determine and assist other administrative officials in determining broad and difficult questions of personnel policy

(continued)

Table A.4
(Continued)

Position	Tasks, general description	Supervisory status	Tasks, specific examples
		because of the large size of the organization and the number of the subsidiary appointment offices, or (2) because of the wide variety of personnel functions, the volume of work handled, and the number and rank of subordinates directly supervised, or (3) because of the wide range and high degree of independent authority involved, or (4) because of a combination of those or other valid reasons	
Chief personnel officer		Under general administrative direction, have responsibility and complete charge of personnel work involving the broadest responsibility, and requiring long experience, such as managing the central appointment office of the War, Treasury, or Navy Department	1. Determine and assist administrative officials in determining broad questions of personnel policy 2. Act as a point of contact between the Civil Service Commission, the personnel officers of subsidiary administrative units, and other administrative officials of the establishment

Table A.5

Personnel Positions, 1924 and 1931 Descriptions

Position	Supervisory status, examples	Other specific examples
CAF-1 Under clerk (1931)		To fill out personnel cards from the approved applications
CAF-2 Junior clerk (1931)		To keep time records
CAF-3 assistant clerk (1931)		1. To keep personnel records, prepare personnel journals, and to conduct correspondence on personnel matters 2. To interview applicants for employment and to assist them in preparing their applications
CAF-4 Clerk (1931)	Ability to lay out, direct, and supervise the work of others as required	To maintain records or promotions, appointment dates, separations, etc.
CAF-5 Senior clerk (1931)	To serve as chief of the personnel unit in a hospital having a capacity of 450 or more beds, or in a Veteran's Bureau regional office with more than 8,000 active claims classes	1. To maintain all personnel records and to prepare personnel correspondence 2. To interview applicants for employment and to pass on their qualifications, except for medical, nursing, or technical positions 3. To rate or review the ratings of competitors in civil service examinations for positions in the mechanical trades on such elements as physical ability, training, and experience
CAF-6 Principal clerk (1931)		(No mention of personnel functions)

(continued)

Table A.5
(*Continued*)

Position	Supervisory status, examples	Other specific examples
CAF-7 Junior administrative assistant (1924)	Performing the duties of assistant to a personnel officer in a large government organization where the personnel work requires a large force	
CAF-7 Junior administrative assistant (1931)	1. To serve as assistant to the chief of the personnel bureau of the Panama Canal . . . which maintains a force of some 3,000 Americans and 13,000 West Indians employed by the Panama Canal and the Panama Railroad Co. 2. To sign all routine personnel papers for the chief clerk or executive secretary and to act as chief of the personnel bureau for 2 months each year	
CAF-8 Administrative assistant (1931)	1. As chief clerk of a large technical division, Panama Canal, to keep personnel records, arrange leave schedules and relief for employees absent on account of vacation or sickness. 2. To have general supervision over all matters relating to the personnel of a very large office of a U.S. attorney in one of the most important judicial districts, requiring approximately 50 clerical employees	
CAF-9 Senior administrative assistant (1924)	Having general supervision over the personnel office of a large government organization	

CAF-9 Senior admin-
istrative assistant
(1931)

(No mention of personnel functions)

CAF-10 Junior admin-
istrative officer
(1924)

Directing all matters relating to the personnel of one of
the largest departments

CAF-10 Junior admin-
istrative officer '
(1931)

Under the general supervision of a regional supervisor
of accounts, collections, and operations in charge,
with reference to that officer for advice in cases that
present the more complex, unusual, or controversial
questions and involve important matters of policy, but
with considerable individual responsibility for the
soundness of recommendations . . . to outline methods and procedure for accounting, office, and personnel activities. . .

CAF-11 administrative
officer (1931)

1. As district manager, U.S. CSC . . . , individually or
through his immediate organization and hundreds of
civil service boards of examiners, to plan, organize,
direct, supervise, control, and enforce the procedure
and requirements relating to the recruiting of applicants, their examination, rating certification, and appointment in a civil service district

2. To provide, superintend, and enforce an expeditious,
effective, and business-like arrangement for the handling of local appointments in the field service of the
departments

the Assistant Personnel Officer, his or her role in "planning" the program is less clear than his or her role in "directing" it. To take a second example, the 1920 Personnel Officer would arguably be only a borderline administrative position by today's standards. The description of the Personnel Officer suggests that he or she has substantial authority but also suggests that the work force served is small and the program faces "minimal environmental complexity," in contemporary language.

The difficulties in making exact comparisons arise from the changed nature of clerical and administrative work over this period of time. There is much less stress on planning activities in the 1920 classifications. The classification standards distinguished positions according to the level of responsibility and discretion of the incumbents, not—as at present—according to the level of analytical ability and knowledge of personnel concepts, theories, and principles required for the job. Nonetheless, the comparison suggests that employees with the authority of assistant personnel officers in the contemporary civil service were designated as clerks in the 1920s.

Analysis of the personnel hierarchies in the 1924 and 1931 surveys, which are combined in Figure A.5, shows that the position classification language had been modified somewhat since 1920. But the contrast with the present system remains the same. A check of lower clerical jobs shows that even CAF-4 clerks had considerable supervisory responsibilities. The work of the principal clerk (CAF-6) sounds like it falls in the gray area between personnel officer and personnel assistant, where "the size of the work force is small, the complexity of the task is minimal, and/or the delegation of authority is abnormally restricted." The 1924 system defines administrative officer positions as starting in grade CAF-7, the "junior administrative assistant" grade, as compared with GS-11 in the contemporary system. Positions at this grade and higher also included "head clerk" positions, a consequence of the fact that the clerical–administrative boundary was ambiguous at this time. The junior administrative assistant (CAF-7) had duties that read like those of the contemporary Assistant Personnel Officer, whereas the senior administrative assistant (CAF-9)'s responsibilities were similar to those of a contemporary personnel officer. The junior administrative officer's (CAF-10) tasks involved directing personnel operations of an entire executive department.

The 1924 class specifications applied to departmental positions only. The 1931 field survey shows that clerks in the field also had substantial supervisory responsibilities, through the offices in which they worked were generally smaller. For example, senior clerks (CAF-5) in the field might be chiefs of small personnel units. The administrative responsibilities of higher-level personnel workers in the field were greater still, as the excerpts in Table A.5 show.

Personnel management in the federal bureaucracy of the 1920s was comparatively rudimentary (Willoughby 1927; Feldman 1931; Meriam 1935; Macmahon and Millet 1939).[7] But other administrative functions were also rudimentary in their implementation then as compared with now (Willoughby, 1927). Analysis of other job ladders shows that the changes that took place in the area of personnel are very similar to those occurring in other facets of administration. The duties of clerical and administrative personnel in other lines of work in the 1920s had the same attributes as those revealed in Tables A.4 and A.5. Compared with today, the administrative hierarchies were compressed, and higher clerical workers had administrative responsibilities. Other administrative job ladders in the contemporary system read very much like the personnel clerical and assistance series and the personnel management series in the current *Standards*. They show the same stress on the professional character of contemporary administrative jobs and the same systematic approach to the classification of positions shown for personnel work.

The language employed by these classification systems is "ideal typical" in certain respects. The specifications were designed to serve the objective of rational position classification. Although the duties reported in the class specifications were actually performed by civil servants of the time, any particular position did not necessarily have the title given it either in the 1920 report of the Congressional Joint Committee or in the *Preliminary Field Specifications*. The Personnel Classification Board reported in its *Closing Report* that "titles of positions in the field service are in the main unstandardized, particularly across departmental lines, and are inadequate and sometimes misleading (U.S. PCB 1931: 96). This statement is not an exaggeration.

> To those not acquainted with conditions in the service, the report revealed startling discrepancies in titles and salaries of positions. A typical example was the use of 105 different titles for the position of "senior file and record clerk" including "skilled laborer," "Italian verifier" and "boss painter." Salaries for these positions with identical duties ranged from $720 to $2400. (U.S. CSC 1941b: 110)

[7]For instance, the departments at the time were much smaller than today, which would by itself simplify the personnel function. It must be noted, though, that the Veteran's Bureau and the Departments of Commerce and Agriculture each had more than 4000 employees in Washington as of 1928, and the Treasury Department payroll was over 12,000. Thus several of the departments would have a "medium" size work force by today's standards, with the Treasury Department's being "moderately large." Furthermore, it is not universally agreed that postwar personnel management practices are fundamentally dissimilar to the practices of the 1920s (Drucker 1954).

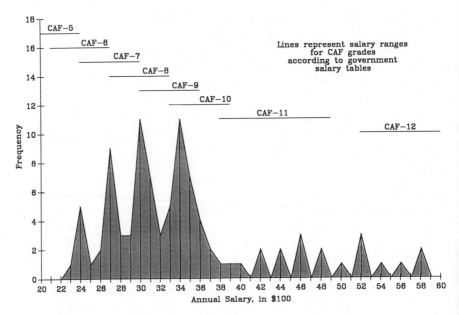

Figure A.1 Salaries and grades of chief clerks, 1927.

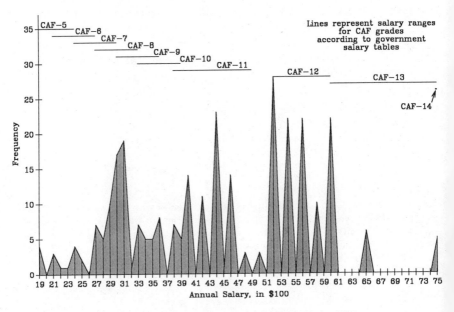

Figure A.2 Salaries and grades of division chiefs, 1927.

The fact that even a "rationalized" system of classification would show ambiguities at the boundary between lower- and higher-level job ladders on the same functional hierarchy suggests that the boundary in the real world was even fuzzier than suggested in the standards.

Some titles, such as chief clerk and division chief were relative in character; the level of responsibility depended upon the scope of the organization of which they were "chief." The 1924 *Class Specifications* of the Personnel Classification Board, released in 1924, suggests that these positions were typically allocated to grades CAF-7, 9, and 11. To determine how titles at the clerical–administrative boundary were actually used at the time, the *Official Register* for 1927 was consulted to examine the grades in which the titles of "chief clerk" and "division chief" could be found (U.S. Bureau of the Census 1927). As noted in Chapter 3, these positions were at the limit of the classified service through the 1920s and were typically filled through promotion from lower-level clerical positions (Low 1900; Mayers 1922; Willoughby 1927). Figures A.1 and A.2, derived from the *Official Register* for 1927 (U.S. Bureau of the Census 1927), show the salaries of chief clerks and a sample of division chiefs.[8] These figures also show the salary range for the CAF grades for 1927.

Figures A.1 and A.2 show the substantial variance in salaries paid both to chief clerks and division chiefs in the late 1920s, a variance that can be partly explained by the size of the organizational unit over which the incumbent presided. Chief clerks were found in Grades CAF-5 through CAF-12, whereas division chiefs were found in grades CAF-5 through CAF-13. The distributions found in Figures A.1 and A.2, which are based on the grade system in place before the Welch Act added two grades to the top of the hierarchy, support the assertion that at least some of the positions accessible to clerks through normal promotion channels within the clerical ranks were quite high in the civil service hierarchy. Figure 2.2 in Chapter 2 showed that, even after the Welch Act was passed in 1928, fewer than 10% of CAF employees were in grades higher than CAF-8. Fewer than 5% were in grades higher than CAF-9, and only 1.1% of all CAF employees were in grades higher than CAF-12.[9]

[8]All employees identified as "chief clerk" in the executive branch of government, excluding the government of the District of Columbia, are included in Figure 4.1. In Figure 4.2, only employees called *chief, head,* or *superintendent* in charge of a *division, unit,* or *section* in the executive departments (not including the independent agencies) is included. It thus undercounts the number of individuals who were in this functional position but is probably a substantially accurate guide to their salary distribution. Note that in 1896, there were already 250 division heads (Commission on Organization of the Executive Branch of Government 1955: 172).

[9]By way of comparison, in 1983, 27% of the full-time white-collar workers were in grades GS-12 and up, 15% were in GS-13 and up, and 7% were in GS-14 and up.

References

Abbott, Andrew, and D. Randall Smith. 1984. "Governmental Constraints and Labor Market Mobility." *Sociology of Work and Occupations* 2:29–53.

Abraham, Katharine G., and James L. Medoff. 1985. "Length of Service and Promotion in Union and Nonunion Work Groups." *Industrial and Labor Relations Review* 38:408–420.

Acton Society Trust. 1956. *Management Succession.* London: Acton Society Trust.

Advisory Committee on Federal Pay. 1979. *Eight Years of Federal White-Collar Pay Comparability* Washington, D.C.: U.S. Government Printing Office.

Albelda, Randy P. 1986. "Occupational Segregation by Race and Gender, 1958–1981." *Industrial and Labor Relations Review* 39:404–411.

Alchian, Armen A., and Harold Demsetz. 1972. "Production, Information Costs and Economic Organization." *American Economic Review* 62:777–95.

Allen, William H. 1912. "Training Men and Women for Public Service." *Annals of the American Academy of Political and Social Science* 61:307–312.

Althauser, Robert P. 1987. "Internal Labor Markets U.S.A.: A Thematic Review." Paper presented at that 1987 Annual Meetings of the American Sociological Association.

Althauser, Robert P., and Arne L. Kalleberg. 1981. "Firms, Occupations and the Structure of Labor Markets: A Conceptual Analysis." Pp. 119–149 in *Sociological Perspectives on Labor Markets,* edited by Ivar Berg. New York: Academic Press.

American Political Science Association. 1913. "Preliminary Report of the Committee on Practical Training for Public Service to the American Political Science Association. *Proceedings of the American Political Science Association,* pp. 301–356.

Aoki, Masahiko. 1984. "Aspects of the Japanese Firm." Pp. 3–43 in *The Economic Analysis of the Japanese Firm,* edited by Masahiko Aoki. Amsterdam: North-Holland.

Appleby, Paul H. 1952. *Morality and Administration in Democratic Government.* Baton Rouge: Louisiana State University Press.

Baritz, Loren. 1960. *The Servants of Power: A History of the Use of Social Science in American Industry.* Middletown: Wesleyan University Press.

Baron, James N., Frank R. Dobbin, and P. Devereaux Jennings. 1986. War and Peace: The Evolution of Modern Personnel Administration in U.S. Industry." *American Journal of Sociology* 91:350–383.

Baron, James N., Alison Davis-Black, and William T. Bielby. 1986. "The Structure of Opportunity: How Promotion Ladders Vary within and among Organizations." *Administrative Science Quarterly* 31:248–273.

Bartholomew, D. J. 1973. *Stochastic Models for Social Processes*. New York: John Wiley & Sons.

Baruch, Ismar. 1944. "Testimony," in *Minutes of Evidence taken before the Commission of Inquiry on Public Service Personnel*. New York: McGraw-Hill.

Baruch, Ismar. 1944. *History of Position-Classification and Salary Standardization in the Federal Service 1789–1941*. U.S. Civil Service Commission, Personnel Classification Division (PCD Manual A-22). Washington, D.C.: U.S. Government Printing Office.

Baruch, Ismar. 1941b. *Position Classification in the Public Service*. Chicago: Civil Service Assembly.

Beard, Charles A. 1916. "Training for Efficient Public Service." *Annals of the American Academy of Political and Social Science* 64:215–226.

Beck, James R. 1960. "High School Recruits—A Neglected Labor Market." *Personnel Administration* 23:40–43.

Becker, Gary S. 1973. "A Theory of Marriage, Part 1." *Journal of Political Economy* 81:813–846.

Becker, Gary S. 1974. "A Theory of Marriage, Part 2." *Journal of Political Economy* 82:S11–S26.

Becker, Howard S. 1970. "The Nature of a Profession." Pp. 87–103 in *Sociological Work*, edited by Howard S. Becker. Chicago: Aldine Publishing Company.

Beckham, A. S. 1930. "Minimum Intelligence Levels for Several Occupations." *Personnel Journal* 9:309–13.

Bell, Daniel. 1973. *The Coming of Post-Industrial Society*. New York: Basic Books.

Bell, H. M. 1940. *Matching Youth and Jobs*. Washington: American Council on Education.

Bellah, Robert N., Richard Madsen, William M. Sullivan, Ann Swidler, and Steven M. Tipton. 1985. *Habits of the Heart: Individualism and Commitment in American Life*. New York: Harper & Row.

Beller, Andrea H. 1980. "The Effect of Economic Conditions on the Success of Equal Employment Opportunity Laws: An Application to the Sex Differential in Earnings." *Review of Economics and Statistics* 62:379–87.

Beller, Andrea H. 1982a. "Occupational Segregation by Sex: Determinants and Changes." *Journal of Human Resources* 17:371–92.

Beller, Andrea H. 1982b. "The Impact of Equal Opportunity Policy on Sex Differentials in Earnings and Occupations." *The American Economic Review, Papers and Proceedings*, pp. 171–75.

Belman, Albert A. 1968. "Trends in Salaries of Classified Federal Workers." *Monthly Labor Review* 91:17–21.

Belsley, G. Lyle. 1947. "Why the Bureaucracy is Belittled." *Personnel Administration* 9:19–23.

Berg, Ivar. 1970. *Education and Jobs: The Great Training Robbery*. New York: Praeger.

Bergmann, Barbara R. 1986. *The Economic Emergence of Women*. New York: Basic Books.

Betters, Paul V. 1931. *The Personnel Classification Board: Its History, Activities and Organization*. Washington: The Brookings Institution.

Bielby, William T., and James N. Baron. 1984. "A Women's Place is with Other Women: Sex Segregation within Organizations." Pp. 27–55 in *Sex Segregation in the Workplace: Trends, Explanations, Remedies*, edited by Barbara F. Reskin. Washington, D.C.: National Academy Press.

Bielby, William T., and James N. Baron. 1986. "Men and Women at Work: Sex Segregation and Statistical Discrimination." *American Journal of Sociology* 91:759–799.

Bills, M. A. 1923. "Relation of Mental Alertness Test Score to Positions and Permanency in Company." *Journal of Applied Psychology* 7:154–56.

Bills, M. A. 1925. "Social Status of the Clerical Worker and His Performance on the Job." *Journal of Applied Psychology* 9:424–427.

Bingham, W. V. 1924. "Intelligence Test Scores and Business Success." *Psychological Bulletin* 21:103–105.

Bingham, W. V. 1939. *Administrative Ability: Its Discovery and Development.* Pamphlet No. 1, Society for Personnel Administration.

Bingham, W. V., and Max Freyd. 1926. *Procedures in Employment Psychology.* New York: McGraw-Hill.

Blachly, F. F. 1925. "Educational Training for Administration in America." *Journal of Public Administration* 3:159–63.

Blau, David M. 1987. "A Time-Series Analysis of Self-Employment in the United States." *Journal of Political Economy* 95:445–467.

Blau, Peter, and O. D. Duncan. 1967. *The American Occupational Structure.* New York: John Wiley & Sons.

Blau, Peter M., and Richard A. Schoenherr. 1971. *The Structure of Organizations.* New York: Basic Books.

Bledstein, Burton J. 1976. *The Culture of Professionalism.* New York: W. W. Norton and Company.

Borjas, George. 1982. "The Politics of Employment Discrimination in the Federal Bureaucracy." *Journal of Law and Economics* 25:271–99.

Bossard, James H. S., and J. Frederic Dewhurst. 1931. *University Education for Business: A Study of Existing Needs and Practices.* Philadelphia: University of Pennsylvania Press.

Brandenberg, George C. 1925. "Personality and Vocational Achievement." *Journal of Applied Psychology* 9:281–292.

Braverman, Harry. 1974. *Labor and Monopoly Capital: The Degradation of Work in the Twentieth Century.* New York: Monthly Review Press.

Brissenden, Paul F. 1929. "Labor Turnover in the Federal Service." Pp. 320–364 in *Report of Wage and Personnel Survey.* Field Survey Division, Personnel Classification Board. Washington, D.C.: U.S. Government Printing Office.

Broadley, H. 1927. "Promotion in the Civil Service." *Public Administration* 5:199–206.

Brooks, Earl. 1938. *In-Service Training of Federal Employees.* Chicago: Civil Service Assembly.

Burritt, Bailey B. 1914. "The Occupation of College Graduates." Pp. 85–88 in *Universities and Public Service,* edited by Edward A. Fitzpatrick. Proceedings of the National Conference on Universities and Public Service. Madison: Cantwell Printing Company.

Burstein, Paul. 1985. *Discrimination, Jobs and Politics: The Struggle for Equal Employment Opportunity in the United States since the New Deal.* Chicago: University of Chicago Press.

Burtt, Harold E. 1929. *Psychology and Industrial Efficiency.* New York: D. Appleton.

Burtt, Harold E. 1926, 1942. *Employment Psychology.* New York and London: Harper & Brothers.

Butler, Richard, and James J. Heckman. 1977. "The Government's Impact on the Labor Market Status of Black Americans." Pp. 235–281 in *Equal Rights and Industrial Relations,* edited by Leonard Hausman. Orley Ashenfelter, Bayard Rustin, Richard Schubert, and Donald Slaiman. Madison, Wisconsin: Industrial Relations Research Association.

Butler, William N. 1954. "Selection and Classification for Clerical Jobs." *Personnel Administration* 17:32–36.

Cain, Glen. 1976. "The Challenge of Segmented Labor Market Theory to Orthodox Theory: A Survey." *Journal of Economic Literature* 14:1215–57.

Campbell, Alan K. 1978. "Civil Service Reform: A New Commitment." *Public Administration Review* 38:99–103.

Campbell, Thomas E. 1932. "Opportunities in the United States Civil Service for College-Trained Men and Women." Pp. 19–24 in *University Training for the National Service*, edited by Morris Lambie. Minneapolis: University of Minnesota.

Carlsson, Gosta. 1958. *Social Mobility and Class Structure*. Lund: CWK Gleerup.

Carpenter, William Seal. 1952. *The Unfinished Business of Civil Service Reform*. Princeton: Princeton University Press.

Cassese, Sabino. 1984. "The Higher Civil Service in Italy." Pp. 35–71 in *Bureaucrats and Policy Making*, edited by Ezra N. Suleiman. New York: Holmes & Meier.

Cathell, D. W. 1890. *The Physician Himself*. Philadelphia: F. A. Davis.

Cathell, D. W. 1905. *The Physician Himself*. Philadelphia: F. A. Davis.

Catherwood, Robert. 1927. "The Next Step in Civil Service." *Public Personnel Studies*. 5:211–217.

Chandler, Alfred. 1977. *The Visible Hand: The Managerial Revolution in American Business*. Cambridge: Harvard University Press.

Chapman, Brian. 1959. *The Profession of Government: The Public Service in Europe*. New York: Macmillan.

Cicourel, Aaron V. 1974. *Theory and Method in a Study of Argentine Fertility*. New York: John Wiley & Sons.

Civil Service Assembly. 1941. *Employee Training in the Public Service*. Chicago: Civil Service Assembly.

Clark, Rodney. 1979. *The Japanese Factory*. New Haven: Yale University Press.

Claxton, P. P. 1914. "Public Service as a Career." Pp. 22–23 in *Universities and Public Service*, edited by Edward A. Fitzpatrick. Proceedings of the National Conference on Universities and Public Service. Madison: Cantwell Printing Company.

Cohen, Michael D., James G. March, and Johan P. Olsen. 1972. "A Garbage Can Model of Organizational Choice." *Administrative Science Quarterly* 17:1–25.

Cohen, Yinon, and Jeffrey Pfeffer. 1986. "Organizational Hiring Standards." *Administrative Science Quarterly* 31:1–24.

Collins, Randall. 1979. *The Credential Society*. New York: Academic Press.

Commission on Organization of the Executive Branch of the Government. 1949. *Task Force Report on Federal Personnel*. Washington, D.C.: U.S. Government Printing Office.

Commission on Organization of the Executive Branch of the Government. 1955. *Task Force Report on Personnel and Civil Service*. Washington, D.C.: U.S. Government Printing Office.

Commission of Inquiry on Public Service Personnel. 1934. *Minutes of Evidence taken before the Commission of Inquiry on Public Service Personnel*. New York: McGraw-Hill.

Commission of Inquiry on Public Service Personnel. 1935. *Better Government Personnel*. New York: McGraw-Hill.

Committee for Economic Development. 1964. *Improving Executive Management in the Federal Government*. New York: Committee for Economic Development.

Committee on Department Methods. 1907. *Report to the President by the Committee on Department Methods. Classification of Positions and Gradation of Salaries for Employees of the Executive Departments and Independent Establishments in Washington*. January 4, 1907. Washington, D.C.: U.S. Government Printing Office.

Congressional Globe. 1834–1873. 46 vols. Washington, D.C.

Conyngton, Mary. 1920. "Separations from Government Service." *Monthly Labor Review* 11:1131–44.

Congressional Record. 1957. Speech by Senator Olin Johnston, March 15, 1957, p. 4748.

Corcoran, Mary, Greg J. Duncan, and Michael Ponza. 1984. "Work Experience, Job Segregation, and Wages." Pp. 171–191 in *Sex Segregation in the Workplace: Trends, Explana-*

tions, Remedies, edited by Barbara Reskin. Washington, D.C.: National Academy Press.

Crick, Bernard. 1962. *The American Science of Politics: Its Origins and Conditions.* Berkeley: University of California.

Curran, Donald C. 1961. "The Civil Service Commission Merit Promotion Program." Unpublished paper in library of the U.S. Office of Personnel Management.

D'Amico, Ronald, and Timothy Brown. 1982. "Patterns of Labor Mobility in a Dual Economy" *Social Science Research* 11:153–75.

Dahlberg, Jane. 1966. *The New York Bureau of Municipal Research.* New York: New York University.

Dahrendorf, Ralf. 1959. *Class and Class Conflict in Industrial Society.* Palo Alto, CA: Stanford University Press.

Danner, Vernice Earle. 1914. "Scientific Criteria for Efficient Democratic Institutions." *Forum* 51:354–64.

David, Paul T. 1952. "The Development and Recruitment of Administrative Leadership in National and International Programs." Pp. 137–167 in *American's Manpower Crisis,* edited by Robert A. Walker. Chicago: Public Administration Service.

David, Paul A., and Peter Solar. 1977. "A Bicentenary Contribution to the History of the Cost of Living in America." *Research in Economic History* 2:1–80.

DePhillips, Frank A. *et al.* 1960. *Management of Training Programs.* New York: Harper.

Deutermann Jr., William V., and Scott Campbell Brown. 1978. "Voluntary Part-Time Workers: A Growing Part of the Labor Force." *Monthly Labor Review* 101:3–10.

Dewey, John. 1914. "The Educational Principles Involved." Pp. 249–254 in *Universities and Public Service,* edited by Edward A. Fitzpatrick. Proceedings of the National Conference on Universities and Public Service. Madison: Cantwell Printing Company.

DiMaggio, Paul J., and Walter W. Powell. 1983. "The Iron Cage Revisited: Institutional Isomorphism and Collective Rationality in Organizational Fields." *American Sociological Review* 48:147–60.

DiPrete, Thomas A., and Whitman T. Soule. 1986. "The Organization of Career Lines: Equal Employment Opportunity and Status Advancement in a Federal Bureaucracy." *American Sociological Review* 51:295–309.

Doeringer, P. B., and M. J. Piore. 1971. *Internal Labor Markets and Manpower Analysis.* Lexington: Heath.

Dore, Ronald. 1973. *British Factory–Japanese Factory: The Origins of National Diversity in International Relations.* Berkeley: University of California Press.

Downing, Paul M. 1981. "A New Goal of Affirmative Action: Percentage Parity between Minority and Women Employees in the Federal Workforce and in the Civilian Workforce." Congressional Research Service: Report No. 81-25.

Drucker, Peter F. 1954. *The Practice of Management.* New York: Harper Brothers.

Duncan, Otis Dudley. 1968. "Social Stratification and Mobility: Problems in the Measurement of Trend." Pp. 675–719 in *Indicators of Social Change,* edited by Eleanor B. Sheldon and Wilbert E. Moore. New York: Russell Sage Foundation.

Dworkin, Ronald M. 1967. "The Model of Rules." *The University of Chicago Law Review.* 35:14–46.

Eaton, Dorman. 1880. *Civil Service in Great Britain: A History of Abuses and Reforms and Their Bearing Upon American Politics.* New York: Harper & Brothers.

Edwards, Richard C. 1979. *Contested Terrain: The Transformation of the Workplace in the Twentieth Century.* New York: Basic.

Eilbirt, Henry. 1959. "The Development of Personnel Management in the U.S." *Business History Review* 33:329–64,.

Ehrenreich, Barbara, and John Ehrenreich. 1977a. "The Professional-Managerial Class, Part I" *Radical America*, 11 (March–April):7–31.

Ehrenreich, Barbara, and John Ehrenreich. 1977b. "The Professional-Managerial Class, Part II" *Radical America*, 11 (May–June):7–22.

Eliot, W. 1910. "The Value During Education of the Life-Career Motive." Address to the National Education Association. Boston. 1910.

Ellul, Jacques. 1964. *The Technological Society*. New York: Knopf.

Emmer, Boris, and John E. Jeuck. 1950. *Catalogues and Counters: A History of Sears, Roebuck and Company*. Chicago: University of Chicago Press.

Emmerich, Herbert, and G. Lyle Belsley. 1954. "The Federal Career Service—What Next?" *Public Administration Review* 14:1–10.

England, Paula. 1982. "The Failure of Human Capital Theory to Explain Occupational Sex Segregation." *Journal of Human Resources* 17:358–70.

England, Paula, and George Farkas. 1986. *Households, Employment, and Gender: A Social, Economic and Demographic View*. New York: Aldine.

Eriksson, Erik. 1927. "The Federal Civil Service under President Jackson." *The Mississippi Valley Historical Review* 13:517–540.

Fabricant, Solomon. 1952. *The Trend of Government Activity in the United States since 1900*. New York: National Bureau of Economic Research.

Fair Employment Practice Committee. 1945. *First Report, July 1943–December 1944*. Washington, D.C.: U.S. Government Printing Office.

Farley, Reynolds. 1984. *Blacks and Whites: Narrowing the Gap?* Cambridge: Harvard University Press.

Faught, Albert Smith. 1920. "Highlights in Twenty Classification Studies." Pp. 48–51 in *Proceedings, 13th Annual Meeting of Assembly of Civil Service Commissions*.

Featherman, David L., and Robert M. Hauser. 1978. *Opportunity and Change*. New York: Academic.

Federal Employee. 1935. "Career System Is Recommended," February, 1956: 9–10,31.

Federal Employee. 1955. "College-Level Exam Program Designed to Step Up Candidates," August, 1955: 20.

Federal Employee. 1956. "Training Bill Urged as Important Step in Federal Service." *Federal Employee*, August, 1956.

Federal Employee. 1958. "Queries and Answers on the New Federal Merit Promotion Plan." *Federal Employee*, May, 1958.

Feldman, Herman. 1928. "A Survey of Research in the Field of Industrial Relations." Unpublished paper.

Feldman, Herman. 1931. *A Personnel Program for the Federal Civil Service*. Washington, D.C.: U.S. Government Printing Office.

Felser, James W. 1947. "Undergraduate Training for the Public Service." *American Political Science Review* 41:507–517.

Finer, S. E. 1952. "Patronage and the Public Service: Jeffersonian Bureaucracy and the British Tradition" *Public Administration* 30:329–360.

Fish, Carl Russell. 1905. *The Civil Service and the Patronage*. New York: Longmans, Green.

Fisher, John. 1945. "Let's Go Back to the Spoils System." *Harper's Magazine* 191:360–368.

Fisher, Bernice M. 1967. *Industrial Education: American Ideals and Institutions*. Madison: University of Wisconsin Press.

Fiske, Edward B. 1987. "M.I.T. Widens Engineer Training." *New York Times*, June 1, 1987. p. 1.

Fitzpatrick, Edward A. 1914. "Introduction." Pp. 9–10 in *Universities and Public Service*, edited by Edward A. Fitzpatrick. Proceedings of the National Conference on Universities and Public Service. Madison: Cantwell Printing Company.

Frederic, Katherine. 1935. *Trained Personnel for Public Service*. Washington, D.C.: The National League of Women Voters.

Fredrickson, George M. 1965. *The Inner Civil War: Northern Intellectuals and the Crisis of the Union*. New York: Harper & Row.

Freeman, Richard, and James Medoff. 1984. *What Do Unions Do?* New York: Basic.

Freidson, Eliot. 1984. "Are Professions Necessary?" Pp. 3–27 in *The Authority of Experts*, edited by Thomas L. Haskell. Bloomington: Indiana University Press.

Freidson, Eliot. 1986. *Professional Powers: A Study of the Institutionalization of Formal Knowledge*. Chicago: University of Chicago Press.

Friedland, Louis L. 1955. "The Career System Revisited." *Personnel Administration* 18:10–24.

Freidrich, Carl Joachim. 1935. *Responsible Government Service under the American Constitution*. Monograph #7. Commission of Inquiry on Public Service Personnel. New York: McGraw-Hill.

Gaus, John M. 1930. "A Study of Research in Public Administration." Draft prepared for the Advisory Committee on Public Administration of the Social Science Research Council.

Gaus, John M. 1949. "A First View: The University-wide Approach." Pp. 189–204 in *The Public Service and University Education*, edited by Joseph E. McLean. Princeton: Princeton University Press.

Gibbon, I. G. 1923. "The Teaching of Public Administration in the U.S.A." *The Journal of Public Administration* 1:41–44.

Gilbertson, H. S. 1914. "The City Managership—A New Career in Public Service." Pp. 88–94 in *Universities and Public Service*. Proceedings of the National Conference on Universities and Public Service. Madison: Cantwell Printing Company.

Gladden, Edgar N. 1967. *Civil Services of the United Kingdom, 1855–1970*. London: Frank Cass & Co.

Glass, D. V., ed. 1954. *Social Mobility in Britain*. London: Routledge & Kegan Paul.

Glazer, Nathan. 1978. *Affirmative Discrimination: Ethnic Inequality and Public Policy*. New York: Basic Books.

Godkin, E. L. 1882. "The Danger of an Office-Holding Aristocracy." *The Century Magazine* 24:287–92.

Goodnow, Frank J. 1900. *Politics and Administration: A Study in Government*. New York: Macmillan.

Gouldner, Alvin W. 1979. *The Future of the Intellectuals and the Rise of the New Class*. London: Macmillan.

Government Positions. 1939. *Government Positions: Adviser's Handbook for Schools, Libraries & Veterans*. Washington, D.C.: Pergande.

Graham, George A. 1935. *Personnel Practices in Business and Governmental Organizations*. Monograph #11. Commission of Inquiry on Public Service Personnel. New York: McGraw-Hill.

Graham, George A. 1941. *Education for Public Administration*. Chicago: Public Administration Service.

Grandjean, Burke. 1981. "History and Career in a Bureaucratic Labor Market." *American Journal of Sociology* 86:1057–1092.

Granick, David. 1972. *Managerial Comparisons of Four Developed Countries: France, Britain, United States and Russia*. Cambridge, Mass: MIT Press.

Granovetter, Mark. 1981. "Toward a Sociological Theory of Income Differences." Pp. 11–

47 in *Sociological Perspectives on Labor Markets*, edited by Ivar Berg. New York: Academic.

Granovetter, Mark. 1984. "Labor Markets and Establishment Size." *American Sociological Review* 49:323–35.

Granville Corporation. 1981. *Upward Mobility Program Assessment: Phase I Report.* Unpublished report submitted to U.S. Office of Personnel Management, Office of Affirmative Employment Programs under Contract No. OPM-65–80, dated October 8, 1981.

Granville Corporation. 1983. *Final Report: Upward Mobility Program Assessment, Phase II.* Unpublished report submitted to the U.S. Office of Personnel Management, Office of Affirmative Employment Programs under Contract No. OPM-65–80, March 9, 1983.

Graves, W. Brooke. 1948. "Efficiency Rating Systems: Their History, Organization and Functioning." U.S. Congress Senate Subcommittee of the Committee on Post Office and Civil Service. Hearings, Efficiency Rating System for Federal Employees, 80th Cong. 2d session, pp. 185–251.

Gray, John H. 1914. "Public Administration and Practical Training for Public Service." Pp. 46–52 in *Universities and Public Service.* Proceedings of the National Conference on Universities and Public Service. Madison: Cantwell Printing Company.

Greenberg, Sally H. 1979. "The Senior Executive Service." Pp. 93–98 in *Recapturing Confidence in Government—Public Personnel Management Reform.* Washington, D.C.: U.S. Government Printing Office.

Griffenhagen and Associates. 1937. *Report on a System of Personnel Administration for the Commonwealth of Virginia.* Richmond: Division of Purchase and Printing.

Griffenhagen, E. O. 1924. "The Origin of the Modern Occupational Classification of Positions in Personnel Administration." *Public Personnel Studies* 2:184–195.

Gulick, Luther, ed. 1937. "Improved Personnel in Government Service." *Annals of the American Academy of Political and Social Science.* Volume 189.

Gulick, Luther, and L. Urwick, eds. 1937. *Papers on the Science of Administration.* New York: Institute of Public Administration.

Haber, Samuel. 1964. *Efficiency and Uplift: Scientific Management in the Progressive Era 1890–1920.* Chicago and London: University of Chicago.

Halaby, Charles N. 1978. "Bureaucratic Promotion Criteria." *Administrative Science Quarterly* 23:466–484.

Halaby, Charles N. 1979. "Job-Specific Sex Differences in Organizational Reward Attainment: Wage Discrimination versus Rank Segregation." *Social Forces* 58:108–27.

Halloren, Daniel. 1967. "Why Position Classification?" *Public Personnel Review* 28:89–92.

Hapgood, H. J. 1906. "College Men in Business." *The Annals of the American Academy of Political and Social Sciences* 28:58–69.

Harston, L. D. 1928. "Intelligence and Scholarship of Occupational Groups. *Personnel Journal* 7:281–285.

Harvey, Donald R. 1970. *The Civil Service Commission.* New York: Praeger.

Haskell, Thomas L. 1977. *The Emergence of Professional Social Science: The American Social Science Association and the Nineteenth-Century Crisis of Authority.* Urbana: University of Illinois.

Haskell, Thomas L. 1984. "Professionalism *versus* Capitalism: R. H. Tawney, Emile Durkheim, and C. S. Pierce on the Disinterestedness of Professional Communities." Pp. 180–225 in *The Authority of Experts*, edited by Thomas L. Haskell. Bloomington, Indiana: Indiana University Press.

Hattery, Lowell H. 1955. "The Prestige of Federal Employment." *Public Administration Review* 15:181–187.

Hawley, Ellis W. 1979. *The Great War and the Search for a Modern Order: A History of the American People and their Institutions, 1917–33.* New York: St. Martin's Press.

Hayes, Lawrence J. W. 1941. *The Negro Federal Government Worker: A Study of His Classification Status in the District of Columbia, 1883–1938.* Washington: Howard University.

Hays, Steven, and Riacher C. Kearney. 1982. "Examinations in the Public Service." Pp. 25–44 in *Centenary Issues of the Pendleton Act of 1883: The Problematic Legacy of Civil Service reform,* edited by David H. Rosenbloom. New York: Dekker.

Heclo, Hugh. 1977. *A Government of Strangers: Executive Politics in Washington.* Washington, D.C.: The Brookings Institution.

Heclo, Hugh. 1984. "In Search of a Role: America's Higher Civil Service." Pp. 8–34 in *Bureaucrats and Policy Making: A Comparative Overview,* edited by Ezra N. Suleiman. New York and London: Holmes & Meier.

Henderson, Richard I. 1979. *Compensation Management: Rewarding Performance.* Reston, VA: Reston Publishing Company.

Hensher, David, and Lester W. Johnson. 1981. *Applied Discrete-Choice Modelling.* New York: John Wiley & Sons.

Hodson, Randy, and Robert L. Kaufman. 1982. "Economic Dualism: A Critical Review." *American Sociological Review* 47:727–39.

Hofstadter, Richard. 1955. *The Age of Reform: From Bryan to F.D.R.* New York: Random.

Hofstadter, Richard. 1964. *Anti-intellectualism in American Life.* New York: Alfred A. Knopf.

Hollander, Herbert. 1968. *Quest for Excellence.* Washington: Current Publications, Inc.

Hoogenboom, Ari. 1961. *Outlawing the Spoils: A History of the Civil Service Reform Movement, 1865–1883.* Urbana: University of Illinois.

Howell, Margaret A., and Anne M. Elledge. 1971. "Evaluating Merit Promotion Plans in the Federal Government." *Public Personnel Review* 32:223–227.

Hutchins, Robert M. 1938. "Shall We Train for Public Administration? 'Impossible'." Reprinted as pp. 227–229 in *Ideas and Issues in Public Administration: A Book of Readings,* edited by Dwight Waldo (1953). New York: McGraw-Hill.

Jacoby, Sanford M. 1983. "Industrial Labor Mobility in Historical Perspective." *Industrial Relations* 22:261–282.

James, H. G. 1915. "Some Reflections on the City Manager Plan of Government." *American Political Science Review* 9:504–506.

Janowitz, Morris, and Dell Wright. 1956. "The Prestige of Public Employment: 1929 and 1954." *Public Administration Review* 16:15–21.

Jenkins, John G. 1935. *Psychology in Business and Industry: An Introduction to Psychotechnology.* New York: Wiley.

Johnson, Eldon L. 1940. General Unions in the Federal Service." *The Journal of Politics* 2:23–56.

Johnson, Terence J. 1972. *Professions and Power.* London and Basingstoke: Macmillan.

Kammerer, Gladys M. 1951. *Impact of War on Federal Personnel Administration, 1939–1945.* Lexington: University of Kentucky Press.

Kanter, Rosabeth M. 1977. *Men and Women of the Corporation.* New York: Basic Books.

Karl, Barry. 1963. *Executive Reorganization and Reform in the New Deal: The Genesis of Administrative Management, 1900–1939.* Cambridge: Harvard University Press.

Karl, Barry. 1974. *Charles E. Merriam and the Study of Politics.* Chicago: University of Chicago Press.

Kaufman, Herbert. 1956. "Emerging Conflicts in the Doctrines of Public Administration." *American Political Science Review* 50:1057–1075.

Kaufman, Herbert. 1965. "The Growth of the Federal Personnel System." Pp. 7–69 in *The Federal Government Service,* edited by Wallace Sayre. Englewood Cliffs, NJ: Prentice-Hall.

Kaufman, Robert L., and Seymour Spilerman. 1982. "The Age Structure of Occupations and Jobs." *American Journal of Sociology* 87:827–851.

Keating, Edward. 1964. *The Gentleman from Colorado: A Memoir.* Denver: Sage Books.

Keene, C. Mansel. 1960. "Careers: On Delivering What We Promise." *Civil Service Journal.* January–March, pp. 5–6, 21–25.

Keller, Morton. 1977. *Affairs of State: Public Life in Late Nineteenth Century America.* Cambridge, Mass. and London: Belknap.

Kenagy, H. G., and C. S. Yoakum. 1925. *The Selection and Training of Salesmen.* New York: Macmillan.

Kestnbaum, Meyer. 1957. "Career Administrators in Government Service." *Good Government* 74:27–29.

Kingsley, J. Donald. 1942. "Recruitment—The Quest for Quality." Pp. 63–70 in *Readings in Public Personnel Administration.* Chicago: Civil Service Assembly.

Kingsley, J. Donald. 1944. *Representative Bureaucracy: An Interpretation of the British Civil Service.* Yellow Springs, Ohio: The Antioch Press.

Kirkland, Edward Chase. 1956. *Dream and Thought in the Business Community, 1860–1900.* Ithaca, N.Y.: Cornell University Press.

Knowlton, Evelyn H. 1948. *Pepperell's Progress: History of a Cotton Textile Company: 1844–1945.* Cambridge: Harvard University Press.

Kocka, Jurgen. 1980. *White Collar Workers in America 1890–1940: A Social-Political History in International Perspective.* London and Beverly Hills: Sage Publications.

Kolensik, Walter B. 1958. *Mental Discipline in Modern Education.* Madison: University of Wisconsin Press.

Krislov, Samuel. 1967. *The Negro in Federal Employment.* Minneapolis: University of Minnesota Press.

Kutscher, Ronald E. 1987. "Overview and Implications of the Projections to 2000." *Monthly Labor Review* 110:3–9.

Lambie, Morris. 1929. "The British Civil Service." Pp. 403–469 in *Report of Wage and Personnel Survey.* Field Survey Division, Personnel Classification Board. Washington, D.C.: U.S. Government Printing Office.

Lambie, Morris. 1932. *University Training for the National Service.* Proceedings of a Conference held at the University of Minnesota, July 14 to 17, 1931. Minneapolis: University of Minnesota Press.

Lambie, Morris. 1935. *Training for the Public Service.* Chicago: Public Administration Service.

Lammers, Cornelius, and David J. Hickson. 1979. "A Cross-National and Cross-Institutional Typology of Organizations." Pp. 420–34 in *Organizations Alike and Unlike,* edited by Cornelius J. Lammers and David J. Hickson. London: Routledge & Kegan Paul.

Larson, Magali Sarfatti. 1977. *The Rise of Professionalism.* Berkeley: University of California Press.

Lazear, Edward. 1979. "The Narrowing of Black–White Wage Differences is Illusory." *American Economic Review* 69:553–64.

Lazear, Edward, and Sherwin Rosen. 1981. "Rank-Order Tournaments as Optimum Labor Contracts." *Journal of Political Economy* 89:841–64.

Leathes, Sir Stanley. 1923. "The Qualifications, Recruitment and Training of Public Servants." *The Journal of Public Administration* 1:343–62.

Leffingwell, W. H. 1925. *Office Management, Principles and Practice.* Chicago and New York: A. W. Shaw Co.

Leonard, Jonathan. 1984. "The Impact of Affirmative Action on Employment." *Journal of Labor Economics* 2:439–463.

Link, Henry C. 1923. "Psychological Tests in Industry." *Annals of the American Academy of Political and Social Science* 110:32–44.

Lipset, Seymour Martin, and Reinhard Bendix. 1959. *Social Mobility in Industrial Society.* Berkeley: University of California Press.

Litchfield, Edward H. 1956. "Notes on a General Theory of Administration." *Administrative Science Quarterly* 1:1–29.

Locke, Edwin. 1976. "The Nature and Causes of Job Satisfaction." Pp. 1297–1349 in *Handbook of Industrial and Organizational Psychology,* edited by Mavin V. Donnette. Chicago: Rand-McNally.

Lockwood, David. 1958. *The Blackcoated Worker: A Study in Class Consciousness.* Fair Lawn, New Jersey: Essential Books.

Lorber, J. 1979. "Trust, Loyalty, and the Place of Women in the Informal Organization of Work." Pp. 371–81 in *Women: A Feminist Perspective,* edited by J. Freeman. Palo Alto, CA: Mayfield.

Low, A. Maurice. 1900. "Does Government Service Pay?" *The Forum* (July) 623–631.

Lowi, Theodore J. 1969. *The End of Liberalism.* New York: W. W. Norton & Co., Inc.

Lupton, Tom, and Angela M. Bowey. 1974. *Wages and Salaries.* Manchester: C. Nicholls & Company.

Macmahon, Arthur W. 1926. "Selection and Tenure of Bureau Chiefs in the National Administration of the United States." Parts I and II. *American Political Science Review* 20:548–582, 770–811.

Macmahon, Arthur W., and John D. Millett. 1939. *Federal Administrators: A Biographical Approach to the Problem of Departmental Management.* New York: Columbia University Press.

MacNeil, Neil, and Harold W. Metz. 1956. *The Hoover Report, 1953–1955: What It Means to You as Citizen and Taxpayer.* New York: Macmillan.

Macy, John W. 1956. "Improving Career Managers in Federal Service Discussed." *Federal Employee.* December, 1956, pp. 8–9, 16–19.

Macy, John W. 1963. "How Should We Obtain an Adequate Public Service?" Pp. 61–74 in *Achieving Excellence in Public Service,* edited by Stephen B. Sweeney and James C. Charlesworth. A Symposium sponsored by the AAPSS and the ASPA.

Macy, John W. 1971. *Public Service: The Human Side of Government.* New York: Harper and Row.

Macy, Robert M. 1954. "A Career in the U.S. Government." *Personnel Administration* 17:17–21.

McClean, John G. 1954. "The Government Climate." Pamphlet No. 8. Society for Personnel Administration.

McClure, Samuel S. 1914. "Public Service as a Career." Pp. 66–77 in *Universities and Public Service,* edited by Edward A. Fitzpatrick. Proceedings of the National Conference on Universities and Public Service. Madison: Cantwell Printing Company.

McFarland, Gerald W. 1975. *Mugwumps, Morals & Politics, 1884–1920.* Amherst: The University of Massachusetts Press.

McMillin, Lucille Foster. 1941. *Women in the Federal Service.* Washington, D.C.: U.S. Civil Service Commission.

Magaziner, Ira C., and Robert B. Reich. 1982. *Minding America's Business: The Decline and Rise of the American Economy* New York: Random House.

Mandell, Milton. 1953. "The JMA Program." *Public Administration Review* 13:106–112.

March, James G., and Johan P. Olsen. 1976. *Ambiguity and Choice in Organizations.* Bergen, Norway: Universitetsforlaget.

Marini, Margaret Mooney. 1980. "Sex Differences in the Process of Occupational Attainment: A Closer Look." *Social Science Research* 9:307–361.

Marshall, Alfred. 1920. *Principles of Economics: An Introductory Volume*. London: Macmillan.

Marx, Fritz Morstein. 1957. *The Administrative State*. Chicago: University of Chicago Press.

Maurice, Marc, Francois Sellier, and Jean-Jacques Silvestre. 1986. *The Social Foundations of Industrial Power: A Comparison of France and Germany*. Cambridge, MA: MIT Press. (Originally published in 1982 under the title *Politiques d'education et organisation industrielle en France et en Allemagne*. Paris: Presses Universitaires de France.)

Mayers, Lewis. 1920. "Some Phases of the Federal Personnel Problem." *American Political Science Review* 14:222–241.

Mayers, Lewis. 1922. *The Federal Service: A Study of the System of Personnel Administration of the United States Government*. New York and London: D. Appleton.

Meriam, Lewis. 1924. "The Uses of a Personnel Classification in the Public Service." *Annals of the American Academy of Political and Social Science*. 103:215–220.

Meriam, Lewis. 1935. "Testimony." Pp. 106–115 in *Minutes of Evidence taken before the Commission of Inquiry on Public Service Personnel*. New York: McGraw-Hill.

Meriam, Lewis. 1936. *Public Service and Special Training*. Chicago: University of Chicago Press.

Meriam, Lewis. 1937a. *Personnel Administration in the Federal Government*. Washington, D.C.: The Brookings Institution.

Meriam, Lewis. 1937b. "The Trend Toward Professionalization." *Annals of the American Academy of Political and Social Science* 189:84–90.

Meriam, Lewis. 1938. *Public Personnel Problems from the Standpoint of the Operating Officer*. Washington, D.C.: The Brookings Institution.

Merkle, Judith A. 1980. *Management and Ideology: The Legacy of the International Scientific Management Movement*. Berkeley: University of California Press.

Meyer, John W., and Bryan Rowan. 1977. "Institutionalized Organizations: Formal Structure as Myth and Ceremony." *American Journal of Sociology* 83:340–63.

Meyer, John, W. Richard Scott, and Terrence E. Deal. 1983. "Institutional and Technical Sources of Organizational Structure: Explaining the Structure of Educational Institutions." Pp. 45–67 in *Organizational Environments: Ritual and Rationality*, by John W. Meyer and W. Richard Scott. Beverly Hills, CA: Sage.

Miller, Ann R., Donald J. Treiman, Pamela S. Cain and Patricia A. Roos, editors. 1980. *Work, Jobs, and Occupations: A Critical Review of the Dictionary of Occupational Titles*. Washington, D.C.: National Academy Press.

Miller, Joanne, and Howard H. Garrison. 1982. "Sex Roles: The Division of Labor at Home and in the Workplace." *Annual Review of Sociology* 8:237–62.

Mitchell, John Purroy. 1914. "The Call for the Conference on Universities and Public Service." Pp. 19–21 in *Universities and Public Service*. Proceedings of the National Conference on Universities and Public Service. Madison: Cantwell Printing Company.

Mitchell, James M. 1952. "Using Federal Manpower Effectively." Pp. 118–127 in *America's Manpower Crisis*, edited by Robert A. Walker. Chicago: Public Administrative Service.

Moe, Ronald C. 1982. *The Hoover Commissions Revisited*. Boulder, CO: Westview Press.

Moses, Robert. 1914. *The Civil Service of Great Britain*. New York: Columbia.

Mosher, Frederick. 1965. Features and Problems of the Federal Civil Service. Pp. 163–211 in *The Federal Government Service*, edited by Wallace S. Sayre. Englewood Cliffs, NJ: Prentice-Hall.

Mosher, Frederick C. 1968. *Democracy and the Public Service*. New York: Oxford University Press.

Mosher, Frederick C. 1971. "The Public Service in the Temporary Society." *Public Administration Review*. 31:47–62.

Mosher, William E. 1937. "The Development of Work Units in Public Administration." Pp. 3–7 in *The Work Unit in Federal Administration*.

Mosher, William E. 1938. "Schools Can Do Much." Reprinted on pp. 229–232 in *Ideas and Issues in Public Administration*, edited by Dwight Waldo (1953). New York: McGraw-Hill.

Mosher, William E., J. Donald Kingsley, and O. Glenn Stahl. 1950. *Public Personnel Administration*. Third Edition. New York: Harper.

Murphy, Lionel V. 1942. "The First Federal Civil Service Commission: 1871–75." *Public Personnel Review* 3:29–39, 3:218–231, 3:299–323.

Nam, Charles B., John LaRocque, Mary G. Powers, and Joan Holmberg. 1975. "Occupational Status Scores: Stability and Change." Pp. 570–575 in *Proceedings of the Social Statistics Section, 1975*. Washington, D.C.: American Statistical Association.

National Academy of Sciences. 1921. "Psychological Examining in the U.S. Army." Chapter 15, "Intelligence Ratings of Occupational Groups." *Memoirs* 15:819–837.

National Industrial Conference Board. 1926. *Clerical Salaries in the United States*. New York: NICB.

National Association of Office Managers. 1954. *Personnel Practices in Factory and Office*. Studies in Personnel Policy No. 145. New York: NICB.

National Association of Office Managers. 1965. *Top Management Organization in Divisionalized Companies*. Studies in Personnel Policy no. 195. New York: NICB.

National Association of Office Managers. 1966. *Personnel Administration: Changing Scope and Organization*. Studies in Personnel Policy No. 203. New York: NICB.

Nenni, Ralph. 1984. "Initial Quality Assessment Survey of Federal Personnel Statistics Program Ten Percent Sample (1962–1980) and Central Personnel Data File (CPDF) Transactions History File (1973–1980)." U.S. Office of Personnel Management Compliance and Investigations Group unpublished manuscript.

Nicholls, Frederick G. *et al.* 1927. *A New Conception of Office Practice, Based on an Investigation of Actual Office Requirements*. Cambridge: Harvard University Press.

Nigro, Felix A., and Lloyd G. Nigro. 1976. *The New Public Personnel Administration*. Itasca, IL: F. E. Peacock Publishers, Inc.

Northrup, Herbert R., and John A. Larson. 1979. *The Impact of the AT&T–EEO Consent Decree*. Philadelphia: University of Pennsylvania Press.

Noyes, Charles E. 1945. "The Profession of Government." *The Antioch Review* 5:16–23.

O'Farrell, Brigid, and Sharon L. Harlan. 1984. "Job Integration Strategies: Today's Programs and Tomorrow's Needs." Pp. 267–291 in *Sex Segregation in the Workplace: Trends, Explanations, Remedies*, edited by Barbara Reskin. Washington, D.C.: National Academy Press.

Olson, Emery E., and Ross Pollock. 1945. "Staffing and Training for Administrative Competence in the Federal Service." *Personnel Administration* 8:8–14.

O'Rourke, L. J. 1930. "A New Emphasis in Federal Personnel Research and Administration." Washington, D.C.: U.S. Government Printing Office.

Ordway, Samuel H. 1938. "Meaning of the Executive Orders of June 24, 1938." *Good Government* 55:61–65.

Ordway, Samuel H. 1942. "Discussion of Federal Recruiting and Examining Problems, with Proposals for Possible Improvement of the Competitive Process." Pp. 44–45 in Volume 3, Part II of *Documents and Reports to Accompany Report on Civil Service Improvement*. The President's Committee on Civil Service Improvement. Letter transmitted February, 1939. Washington, D.C.: U.S. Government Printing Office.

Osterman, Paul. 1984. "White-Collar Internal Labor Markets." Pp. 163–189 in *Internal Labor Markets*, edited by Paul Osterman. Cambridge, MA: MIT Press.

Ouchi, William G. 1980. "Markets, Bureaucracies and Clans." *Administrative Science Quarterly* 25:129–141.

Ouchi, William G., and Mary Ann Maguire. 1975. "Organizational Control: Two Functions." *Administrative Science Quarterly* 20:559–69.

Ouchi, William G., and Alfred M. Jaeger. 1978. "Type Z Organization: Stability in the Midst of Mobility." *Academy of Management Review* 3:305–14.

Owen, Vaux. 1937. "U.S. Should Adopt Progressive Policies Toward Its Employees." *Federal Employee*, November, p. 15.

Owen, Vaux. 1958. "Testimony on Career Executive Program." *Federal Employee.* June, pp. 5–8.

Paget, Richard M. 1957. "Strengthening the Federal Career Executive." *Public Administration Review* 17:91–96.

Parkin, Frank. 1979. *Marxism and Class Theory: A Bourgeois Critique.* New York: Columbia University Press.

Parsons, C. C. 1918. *Office Organization and Management.* Chicago: LaSalle Extension University.

Pear, R. H. 1968. "United States." Pp. 174–187 in *Specialists and Generalists: A Comparative Study of the Professional Civil Servant at Home and Abroad,* edited by Frederick F. Ridley. London: George Allen & Unwin.

Pearson, Norman M. 1945. "Fayolism as the Necessary Complement of Taylorism." *The American Political Science Review* 39:68–81.

Perrow, Charles. 1985. "Review Essay: Overboard with Myth and Symbols." A review of *Organizational Environments: Ritual and Rationality,* by John W. Meyer and W. Richard Scott with the assistance of Brian Rowan and Terrence E. Deal. Beverly Hills, CA: Sage Publications. *American Journal of Sociology* 91:151–155.

Person, H. S. 1924. "Scientific Management: A Brief Statement of Its Nature and History." Pp. 61–74 in *Scientific Management Since Taylor,* edited by E. E. Hunt. New York: McGraw-Hill.

Person, H. S. 1930–35. "Scientific Management." Pp. 603–608 in *Encyclopedia of the Social Sciences.* New York: Macmillan.

Person, H. S. 1940. "Research and Planning as Functions of Administration and Management." *Public Administration Review* 1:65–73.

Pfeffer, Jeffrey, and Yinon Cohen. 1984. "Determinants of Internal Labor Market Arrangements in Organizations." *American Sociological Review* 29:550–72.

Pfiffner, John M. 1946. *Public Administration.* New York: The Ronald Press Co.

Pinfield, Lawrence T. 1986. "A Field Evaluation of Perspectives on Organizational Decision Making." *Administrative Science Quarterly* 31:365–88.

Piore, Michael J. 1975. "Notes for a Theory of Labor Market Stratification." Pp. 125–150 in *Labor Market Segmentation,* edited by Richard C. Edwards, Michael Reich, and David M. Gordon. Lexington, MA: Lexington Books.

Piore, Michael J., and Charles F. Sabel. 1984. *The Second Industrial Divide: Possibilities for Prosperity.* New York: Basic Books.

Polenberg, Richard. 1966. *Reorganizing Roosevelt's Government: The Controversy over Executive Reorganization, 1936–1939.* Cambridge: Harvard University Press.

Pollard, Sidney. 1965. *The Genesis of Modern Management.* Cambridge: Cambridge University Press.

President's Committee on Civil Service Improvement. 1941a. *Report of President's Committee on Civil Service Improvement.* Washington: Government Printing Office.

President's Committee on Civil Service Improvement. 1941b. *Documents and Reports to*

Accompany Report on Civil Service Improvement. Volumes 1, 2, 3a, and 3b. Washington, D.C.: U.S. Government Printing Office.

President's Commission on the Status of Women. 1963. *Report of the President's Commission on the Status of Women.* Washington, D.C.: U.S. Government Printing Office.

The President's Committee on Administrative Management. 1937. *Report with Special Studies.* Washington, D.C.: U.S. Government Printing Office.

President's Reorganization Project. 1977. "Personnel Management Project." 1977. Study Conducted Out of the Office of Management and Budget.

Presidential Task Force on Career Advancement. 1967. "Report of the Presidential Task Force on Career Advancement." Washington, D.C.: U.S. Civil Service Commission.

Procter, Arthur W. 1921. *Principles of Public Personnel Administration.* New York: D. Appleton and Company.

Redlich, F. 1957. "Academic Education for Business." *Business History Review* 31:35–91.

Reeves, Floyd W., and Paul T. David. 1937. *Personnel Administration in the Federal Service.* A part of the report of the President's Committee on Administrative Management. Washington, D.C.: U.S. Government Printing Office.

Reimer, Everett. 1956. "The Case Against the Senior Civil Service." *Personnel Administration* 19:31–42.

Reimer, Everett. 1965. "Modern Personnel Management and the Federal Government Service." Pp. 212–243 in *The Federal Government Service,* edited by Wallace S. Sayre. Englewood Cliffs, NJ: Prentice-Hall.

Reining, Henry. 1956. "The FSEE: The University Point of View." *Public Administration Review* 16:11–14.

Reining, Henry, and Karl E. Stronson. 1942. "An Approach to Public Service Training: Government Internships." *Public Personnel Review* 3:190–199.

Rohatyn, Felix. 1987. "Ethics in America's Money Culture." *New York Times,* June 3, 1987, p. 27.

Roos, Patricia A., and Barbara F. Reskin. 1984. "Institutional Factors Contributing to Sex Segregation in the Workplace." Pp. 235–260 in *Sex Segregation in the Workplace: Trends, Explanations, Remedies,* edited by Barbara F. Reskin. Washington, D.C.: National Academy Press.

Rose, Richard. 1984. "The Political Status of Higher Civil Servants in Britain." Pp. 136–173 in *Bureaucrats and Policy Making,* edited by Ezra N. Suleiman. New York: Holmes & Meier.

Rosen, Sherwin. 1985. "Prizes and Incentives in Elimination Tournaments." *American Economic Review* 76:701–715.

Rosenbaum, James. 1979. "Tournament Mobility: Career Patterns in a Corporation." *Administrative Science Quarterly* 24:220–241.

Rosenbaum, James. 1984. *Career Mobility in a Corporate Hierarchy.* New York: Academic.

Rosenbloom, David H. 1971. *Federal Service and the Constitution: The Development of the Public Employment Relationship.* Ithaca and London: Cornell University Press.

Rosenbloom, David H. 1977. *Federal Equal Employment Opportunity: Politics and Public Personnel Administration.* New York: Praeger.

Rosenfeld, Rachel. 1980. "Race and Sex in Career Dynamics." *American Sociological Review* 45:583–609.

Rosenfeld, Rachel. 1983. "Sex Segregation and Sectors: An Analysis of Gender Differences in Returns from Employer Changes." *American Sociological Review* 48:637–65.

Rosow, Jerome. 1970. "Government Pay Trends." *The Conference Board* (July) 15–22.

Ross, Arthur M. 1958. "Do We Have a New Industrial Feudalism?" *American Economic Review* 48:903–920.

Rumberger, Russell, and Martin Carnoy. 1980. "Segmentation in the U.S. Labor Market." *Cambridge Journal of Economics* 4:117–132.

Sageser, Adelbert Bower. 1935. *The First Two Decades of the Pendleton Act: A Study of Civil Service Reform*. Ph.D. thesis. University of Nebraska.

Saint, Avis Marie. 1931. "Women in Public Service." *Public Personnel Studies* 9:14–19.

Sass, Steven A. 1982. *The Pragmatic Imagination: A History of the Wharton School 1881–1981*. Philadelphia: University of Pennsylvania Press.

Sayre, Wallace S. 1958. "Trends in the Study of Teaching of Public Administration." Pp. 37–43 in *Education for Administrative Careers in Government Service*, edited by Stephen B. Sweeney, Thomas J. Davy and Lloyd M. Short. Philadelphia: University of Pennsylvania Press.

Schlesinger, Arthur M. 1959. *The Age of Roosevelt II: The Coming of the New Deal*. Boston: Houghton-Mifflin.

Scott, W. Richard. 1981. *Organizations: Rational, Natural and Open Systems*. Englewood Cliffs, NJ: Prentice-Hall.

Scott, Walter Dill. 1915. "The Scientific Selection of Salesmen." *Advertising and Selling* 25:5–6, 94–96.

Seidman, Harold. 1980. *Politics, Position and Power: The Dynamics of Organization*. New York: Oxford University Press.

Selznick, Philip. 1957. *Leadership in Administration*. New York: Row, Peterson.

Sewell, William H., and Robert M. Hauser. 1975. *Education, Occupation and Earnings: Achievement in the Early Career*. New York: Academic.

Sewell, William H., Robert M. Hauser, and Wendy Wolf. 1980. "Sex, Schooling and Occupational Status." *American Journal of Sociology* 86:551–583.

Shaeffer, Ruth G. 1972. *Staffing Systems: Managerial and Professional Jobs*. New York: Conference Board.

Shafritz, Jay. 1973. *Position Classification: A Behavioral Synthesis*. New York: Praeger.

Shafritz, Jay M., Albert C. Hyde, and David H. Rosenbloom. 1981. *Personnel Management in Government: Politics and Process*. New York: Marcel Dekker, Inc.

Shepard, Jon M. 1977. "Technology, Alienation, and Job Satisfaction" *Annual Review of Sociology* 3:1–22.

Simon, Herbert. 1945/1957. *Administrative Behavior* (2nd edition). New York: Macmillan.

Simpson, Richard L. 1985. "Social Control of Occupations and Work" *Annual Review of Sociology* 11:415–36.

Slesinger, Jonathan Avery. 1961. *Personnel Adaptations in the Federal Junior Management Assistant Program*. Ann Arbor: Institute of Public Administration, the University of Michigan.

Smiddy, Harold F., and Lionel Naum. 1954. "Evolution of a 'Science of Managing' in America." *Management Science* 1:1–31.

Smith, James P., and Finis Welch. 1984. "Affirmative Action and Labor Markets." *Journal of Labor Economics* 2:269–301.

Smith, James P., and Michael P. Ward. 1984. *Women's Wages and Work in the Twentieth Century*. Santa Monica, CA: Rand Corporation.

Smith, James P., and Finis Welch. 1986. *Closing the Gap: Forty Years of Economic Progress for Blacks*. Santa Monica, CA: Rand Corporation.

Snow, A. J. 1925. *Psychology in Business Relations*. Chicago: A. W. Shaw.

Somers, Herbert. 1954. "The Federal Bureaucracy and the Change of Administration." *American Political Science Review* 48:131–151.

Spero, Sterling D. 1924. *The Labor Movement in a Government Industry*. New York: George H. Doran Co.

Spero, Sterling D. 1948. *Government as Employer*. Carbondale and Edwardsville: Southern Illinois University Press.

Spilerman, Seymour. 1977. "Careers, Labor Market Structure, and Socioeconomic Achievement." *American Journal of Sociology* 83:551–93.

Stahl, O. Glenn. 1956. *Public Personnel Administration*. New York: Harper & Brothers.

Stahl, O. Glenn. 1962. *Public Personnel Administration* (Fifth Edition). New York: Harper & Brothers.

Stahl, O. Glenn. 1963. "Do Present Public Servants Approach the Ideal?" Pp. 25–40 in *Achieving Excellence in Public Service*, edited by Stephen B. Sweeney and James C. Charlesworth. A symposium sponsored by AAPSS and the ASPA.

Stahl, O. Glenn. 1968. "Reformation in Whitehall." *Civil Service Journal* (Oct./Dec.)

Starr, Paul. 1982. *The Social Transformation of American Medicine*. New York: Basic.

Steward, Luther C. 1938. "Our Position on Reorganization Measure Stated by Executive." *Federal Employee* 23(3):1.

Stewart, Frank Mann. 1929. *The National Civil Service Reform League: History, Activities, and Problems*. Austin: University of Texas.

Stewman, Shelby, and Suresh L. Konda. 1983. "Careers and Organizational Labor Markets: Demographic Models of Organizational Behavior." *American Journal of Sociology* 88:637–685.

Stinchcombe, Arthur. 1979. "Social Mobility in Industrial Labor Markets." *Acta Sociologica* 22:217–45.

Stockard, James G. 1956. "The FSEE and the Staffing of Federal Agencies." *Public Administration Review* 16:6–10.

Suleiman, Ezra N. 1974. *Politics, Power and Bureaucracy in France: The Administrative Elite*. Princeton: Princeton University Press.

Suleiman, Ezra N. ed. 1984. *Bureaucrats and Policy Making*. New York: Holmes & Meier.

Suskin, Harold ed. 1977. *Job Evaluation and Pay Administration in the Public Sector*. Chicago: International Personnel Management Association.

Svalastoga, Kaare. 1959. *Prestige, Class and Mobility*. Copenhagen: Glydendal.

Sweeney, Stephen B., Thomas J. Davy, and Lloyd M. Short. 1958. *Education for Administrative Careers in Government Service*. Philadelphia: University of Pennsylvania Press.

Taylor, Frederick. 1903. "Shop Management." Presented at the Spring Meeting, Saratoga, N.Y., June 1903 of The American Society of Mechanical Engineers.

Taylor, Patricia A. 1979. "Income Inequality in the Federal Civilian Government." *American Sociological Review* 44:468–479.

Taylor, Patricia A., and Burke D. Grandjean. 1977. One Percent Extract from the Central Personnel Data File and 10% Extract from the Federal Personnel Statistical Program, Obtained through Funding by the National Institute of Education.

Telford, Fred. 1924. "The Classification and Salary Standardization Movement in the Public Service." *Annals of the American Academy of Political and Social Science* 103:206–215.

Telford, Fred. 1925. "The Content, Form, and Arrangement of the Printed Classification and Compensation Plans." *Public Personnel Studies* 3:42–51.

Thurow, Lester C. 1985. *The Zero-Sum Solution: Building a World-Class American Economy*. New York: Simon and Schuster.

Thurstone, L. L. 1919. "Standardized Tests for Office Clerks." *Journal of Applied Psychology* 3:248–251.

Tolbert, Pamela, and Lynne G. Zucker. 1983. "Institutional Sources of Change in the

Formal Structure of Organizations: The Diffusion of Civil Service Reform, 1880–1935."
Administrative Science Quarterly 28:22–39.

Treiman, Donald J. 1977. *Occupational Prestige in Comparative Perspective.* New York: Academic Press.

Treiman, Donald, and Patricia Roos. 1983. "Sex and Earnings in Industrial Society: A Nine-Nation Comparison." *American Journal of Sociology* 89:612–650.

Tuckerman, L. B. 1932. "Professional Employment in the Bureau of Standards and its Relation to University Training." Pp. 204–231 in *University Training for the National Service,* edited by Morris Lambie. Proceedings of a Conference held at the University of Minnesota, July 14 to 17, 1931, edited by Morris Lambie. Minneapolis: University of Minnesota Press.

Turner, Ralph. 1960. "Modes of Social Ascent through Education: Sponsored and Contest Mobility." *American Sociological Review* 25:855–867.

U.S. Bureau of the Census. 1927. *Official Register of the United States, 1927.* Washington, D.C.: U.S. Government Printing Office.

U.S. Bureau of the Census. 1930. "Enumeration and Classification of Occupations." *Occupations, General Report.* Chapter 1. Washington, D.C.: Government Printing Office.

U.S. Bureau of the Census. 1940. *Occupation Report.* Washington, D.C.: U.S. Government Printing Office.

U.S. Bureau of the Census. 1950. *Occupation Report.* Washington, D.C.: U.S. Government Printing Office.

U.S. Bureau of the Census. 1960. *Occupation Report.* Washington, D.C.: U.S. Government Printing Office.

U.S. Bureau of the Census. 1970. *Occupation Report.* Washington, D.C.: U.S. Government Printing Office.

U.S. Bureau of the Census. 1975. *Historical Statistics of the United States: Colonial Times to 1970.* Washington, D.C.: U.S. Government Printing Office.

U.S. Bureau of the Census. 1980. *Statistical Abstract of the United States.* Washington, D.C.: U.S. Government Printing Office.

U.S. Bureau of the Census. 1986. *Statistical Abstract of the United States.* Washington, D.C.: U.S. Government Printing Office.

U.S. Bureau of Efficiency. 1922. *Efficiency Ratings.* General Circular No. 4. March 25.

U.S. Civil Service Commission. 1884. *First Report of the United States Civil Service Commission.* Washington, D.C.: U.S. Government Printing Office.

U.S. Civil Service Commission. 1885. *Second Report of the United States Civil Service Commission.* Washington, D.C.: U.S. Government Printing Office.

U.S. Civil Service Commission. 1886. *Third Report of the United States Civil Service Commission.* Washington, D.C.: U.S. Government Printing Office.

U.S. Civil Service Commission. 1887. *Fourth Report of the United States Civil Service Commission.* Washington, D.C.: U.S. Government Printing Office.

U.S. Civil Service Commission. 1888. *Fifth Report of the United States Civil Service Commission.* Washington, D.C.: U.S. Government Printing Office.

U.S. Civil Service Commission. 1891. *Eighth Report of the United States Civil Service Commission.* Washington, D.C.: U.S. Government Printing Office.

U.S. Civil Service Commission. 1896. *Thirteenth Report of the United States Civil Service Commission.* Washington, D.C.: U.S. Government Printing Office.

U.S. Civil Service Commission. 1897. *Fourteenth Report of the United States Civil Service Commission.* Washington, D.C.: U.S. Government Printing Office.

U.S. Civil Service Commission. 1898. *Fifteenth Report of the United States Civil Service Commission.* Washington, D.C.: U.S. Government Printing Office.

U.S. Civil Service Commission. 1899. *Sixteenth Report of the United States Civil Service Commission.* Washington, D.C.: U.S. Government Printing Office.

U.S. Civil Service Commission. 1902. *Nineteenth Report of the United States Civil Service Commission.* Washington, D.C.: U.S. Government Printing Office.

U.S. Civil Service Commission. 1909. *Twenty-Sixth Report of the United States Civil Service Commission.* Washington, D.C.: U.S. Government Printing Office.

U.S. Civil Service Commission. 1910. *Twenty-Seventh Report of the United States Civil Service Commission.* Washington, D.C.: U.S. Government Printing Office.

U.S. Civil Service Commission. 1923. *Fortieth Report of the United States Civil Service Commission.* Washington, D.C.: U.S. Government Printing Office.

U.S. Civil Service Commission. 1926. *Forth-Third Report of the United States Civil Service Commission.* Washington, D.C.: U.S. Government Printing Office.

U.S. Civil Service Commission. 1929. *Forty-Sixth Report of the United States Civil Service Commission.* Washington, D.C.: U.S. Government Printing Office.

U.S. Civil Service Commission. 1935. *Fifty-Second Report of the United States Civil Service Commission.* Washington, D.C.: U.S. Government Printing Office.

U.S. Civil Service Commission. 1938. "Research—A National Resource," printed in a report of the National Resources Committee.

U.S. Civil Service Commission. 1939a. *Fifty-Sixth Report of the United States Civil Service Commission.* Washington, D.C.: U.S. Government Printing Office.

U.S. Civil Service Commission. 1939b. *A History of the Federal Civil Service, 1789–1939.* Washington, D.C.: U.S. Government Printing Office.

U.S. Civil Service Commission. 1940. *Fifty-Seventh Report of the United States Civil Service Commission.* Washington, D.C.: U.S. Government Printing Office.

U.S. Civil Service Commission. 1941a. *Schematic Outline and Definitions of Occupational Groups and Series of Classes* Washington, D.C.: U.S. Civil Service Commission.

U.S. Civil Service Commission. 1941b. *History of the Federal Civil Service: 1789 to the Present.* Washington, D.C.: U.S. Government Printing Office.

U.S. Civil Service Commission. 1943. *Sixtieth Report of the United States Civil Service Commission.* Washington, D.C.: U.S. Government Printing Office.

U.S. Civil Service Commission. 1946. *Sixty-Second Annual Report, Fiscal Year Ended June 30, 1949.* Washington, D.C. U.S. Government Printing Office.

U.S. Civil Service Commission. 1948. *Sixth-Fourth Annual Report, Fiscal Year Ended June 30, 1949.* Washington, D.C.: U.S. Government Printing Office.

U.S. Civil Service Commission. 1949a. *Sixty-Fifth Annual Report, Fiscal Year Ended June 30, 1949.* Washington, D.C.: U.S. Government Printing Office.

U.S. Civil Service Commission. 1949b. *Occupations in the Federal Civil Service: A Guide to the Principal Categories of Jobs Filled through the Competitive System.* Pamphlet 3. Washington, D.C.: U.S. Government Printing Office.

U.S. Civil Service Commission. 1950. *Sixty-Sixth Annual Report, Fiscal Year Ended June 30, 1949.* Washington, D.C.: U.S. Government Printing Office.

U.S. Civil Service Commission. 1953. *How Federal Agencies Develop Management Talent: A Management Staff Development Series Prepared from Inventory Data Obtained Directly from the Agencies.* Washington, D.C.: U.S. Government Printing Office.

U.S. Civil Service Commission. 1954. *Seventieth Annual Report, Fiscal Year Ended June 30, 1953.* Washington, D.C.: U.S. Government Printing Office.

U.S. Civil Service Commission. 1955a. *Occupations of Federal White-Collar Workers, 1954.*

Employment Statistics Office. Pamphlet 56. Washington, D.C.: U.S. Government Printing Office.

U.S. Civil Service Commission. 1955b. *Official Register of the United States, 1955.* Washington, D.C.: U.S. Civil Service Commission.

U.S. Civil Service Commission. 1955c. *Seventy-Second Annual Report, Fiscal Year Ended June 30, 1955.* Washington, D.C.: U.S. Government Printing Office.

U.S. Civil Service Commission. 1956a. "A Promotion Survey." Unpublished report.

U.S. Civil Service Commission. 1956b. *Seventy-Second Annual Report, Fiscal Year Ended June 30, 1954.* Washington, D.C.: U.S. Government Printing Office.

U.S. Civil Service Commission. 1956c. *Career Staffing—A Method of Manpower Planning.* Personnel Management Series No. 10. Washington, D.C.: U.S. Government Printing Office.

U.S. Civil Service Commission. 1957a. *Occupations of Federal White Collar Workers* Washington, D.C.: U.S. Government Printing Office.

U.S. Civil Service Commission. 1957b. "Historical Developments in Promotion Programs." Unpublished paper from the Library of the Office of Personnel Management.

U.S. Civil Service Commission. 1957c. *Seventy-Third Annual Report, Fiscal Year Ended June 30, 1954.* Washington, D.C.: U.S. Government Printing Office.

U.S. Civil Service Commission. 1958. *Seventy-Fourth Annual Report.* Washington, D.C.: U.S. Government Printing Office.

U.S. Civil Service Commission. 1959a. *Seventy-Fifth Annual Report.* Washington, D.C.: U.S. Government Printing Office.

U.S. Civil Service Commission. 1959b. "Less Paperwork in Position Classification." Management Series 15. Washington, D.C.: U.S. Government Printing Office.

U.S. Civil Service Commission. 1959c. "The Federal Merit Promotion Program: Its Establishment and Early Operations." A Report to the Subcommittee on Post-Office and Civil Service.

U.S. Civil Service Commission. 1960. *The Government Personnel System: A Summary for Federal Executives and Supervisors.* Washington, D.C.: U.S. Government Printing Office.

U.S. Civil Service Commission. 1961. *Occupations of Federal White-Collar Workers, October 31, 1959.* Washington, D.C.: U.S. Government Printing Office.

U.S. Civil Service Commission. 1963a. *Position Classification Standards for General Schedule Positions.* Washington, D.C.: U.S. Government Printing Office.

U.S. Civil Service Commission. 1963b. "Classification Principles and Policies." Personnel Management Series Number 16. Washington, D.C.: U.S. Government Printing Office.

U.S. Civil Service Commission. 1964a. *Federal Workforce Outlook: Fiscal Years 1964–68.*

U.S. Civil Service Commission. 1964b. "An Analysis of Promotion Plans, Programs and Guidelines." Unpublished paper, Bureau of Programs and Standards. U.S. OPM Library.

U.S. Civil Service Commission. 1966a. "Personnel Management Series, GS-201." *Position Classification Standards.* TS 62. Washington, D.C.: U.S. Government Printing Office.

U.S. Civil Service Commission. 1966b. "Personnel Clerical and Assistance Series, GS-203." *Position Classification Standards.* TS 62. Washington, D.C.: U.S. Government Printing Office.

U.S. Civil Service Commission. 1967. *Federal Careers for Women.* Washington, D.C.: U.S. Government Printing Office.

U.S. Civil Service Commission. 1968a. *Grade Trend of Federal Civilian Employment Under the General Schedule: 1964–1968.* Pamphlet SM 32-68. Washington, D.C.: U.S. Government Printing Office.

U.S. Civil Service Commission. 1968b. *85th Annual Report*. Washington, D.C.: U.S. Government Printing Office.

U.S. Civil Service Commission. 1968c. "Some Features of the Revised Federal Merit Promotion Policy." Unpublished paper by the Bureau of Recruiting and Examining, OPM Library.

U.S. Civil Service Commission. 1968d. *Study of Employment of Women in the Federal Government*. Washington, D.C.: U.S. Government Printing Office.

U.S. Civil Service Commission. 1970a. *Upward Mobility for Lower-Level Employees*. Washington, D.C.: U.S. Civil Service Commission.

U.S. Civil Service Commission. 1970b. "Identifying Underutilized Skills in the Work Force." Bulletin No. 713–15, dated July 23, 1970.

U.S. Civil Service Commission. 1970c. *Occupations of Federal White-Collar Workers, October 31, 1969 and October 31, 1970*. Washington, D.C.: U.S. Government Printing Office.

U.S. Civil Service Commission. 1971. *A Pacesetting Year: U.S. Civil Service Commission Annual Report, 1971*. Washington, D.C.: U.S. Government Printing Office.

U.S. Civil Service Commission. 1972. "A Final Report Submitted by the Job Evaluation and Pay Review Task Force of the U.S. Civil Service Commission."

U.S. Civil Service Commission. 1973a. "Equal Employment Opportunity Plans." Federal Personnel Manual System Letter No. 713–22, dated October 4, 1973.

U.S. Civil Service Commission. 1973b. *Current Federal Workforce Data, Fiscal Years 1970, 1971 and 1972*. Washington, D.C.: U.S. Civil Service Commission.

U.S. Civil Service Commission. 1973c. *Biography of an Ideal: A History of the Federal Civil Service*. Washington, D.C.: U.S. Government Printing Office.

U.S. Civil Service Commission. 1973d. "Promotion and Internal Placement." Chapter 335 of *Federal Personnel Manuel*.

U.S. Civil Service Commission. 1974a. "Upward Mobility for Lower-Level Employees." Federal Personnel Manual System Letter No. 713–27, dated June 28, 1974.

U.S. Civil Service Commission. 1974b. *Employee Training in the Federal Service Fiscal Year 1973*. Washington, D.C.: U.S. Government Printing Office.

U.S. Civil Service Commission. 1976a. *Occupations of Federal White-Collar Workers*. Washington, D.C.: U.S. Government Printing Office.

U.S. Civil Service Commission. 1976b. *Upward Mobility through Job Restructuring*. Personnel Management Series No. 26. Washington, D.C.: U.S. Civil Service Commission.

U.S. Civil Service Commission. 1976c. "Supervisory Grade-Evaluation Guide." *Position-Classification Standards*. TS-23. Washington, D.C.: U.S. Civil Service Commission.

U.S. Civil Service Commission. 1976d. "Part II—Nonsupervisory Personnel Positions, GS-2-1." *Position Classification Standards*. TS-25. Washington, D.C.: U.S. Government Printing Office.

U.S. Civil Service Commission. 1977a. *Occupations of Federal White-Collar Workers*. Washington, D.C.: U.S. Government Printing Office.

U.S. Civil Service Commission. 1977b. "Instructions for the Factor Evaluation System." *Position Classification Standards*. TS-27, May 1977. Washington, D.C.: U.S. Government Printing Office.

U.S. Civil Service Commission. 1978. *Occupations of Federal White-Collar Workers*. Washington, D.C.: U.S. Government Printing Office.

U.S. Commission on Civil Rights. 1970. *Federal Civil Rights Enforcement*. A Report of the United States Commission on Civil Rights to the U.S. Congress.

U.S. Comptroller General. 1975a. "Upward Mobility Programs in the Federal Government Should be Made More Effective." Report to the Congress, April 29, 1975.

U.S. Comptroller General. 1975b. "Classification of Federal White-Collar Jobs Should be Better Controlled." Report to the Congress, December 4, 1975.

U.S. Comptroller General. 1977. "Problems in the Federal Employee Equal Employment Opportunity Program Need to Be Resolved." Report to the Congress, September 9, 1977.

U.S. Congress. Senate. 1836a. Senate Documents, 355, 24th Congress, 1st session. May 3, 1836.

U.S. Congress. 1836b. Senate Documents 362. 24th Congress, 1st session. May 9, 1836.

U.S. Congress. 1838a. Senate Documents, 71. 25th Congress 2d sess. Jan. 3, 1838.

U.S. Congress. 1838b. Senate Documents, 239. 25th Congress, 2d sess. Feb. 26, 1838.

U.S. Congress. 1838c. Senate Documents, 436. 25th Congress, 2d session, May 15, 1838.

U.S. Congress. 1852a. Senate Executive Documents 69. 32nd Congress, 1st session. April 27, 1852.

U.S. Congress. 1852b. Senate Executive Documents, 95, 32d Congress, 1st session. July 6, 1852.

U.S. Congress. 1874. Senate Executive Documents. 53, Appendix F, p. 188. 43rd Congress, 1st session. April 15, 1874.

U.S. Congress. 1948. Senate. Hearings before the Subcommittee of the Committee on Post Office and Civil Service. Eightieth Congress, Second session on S. 1848, S. 1849, S. 1930, S. 1931, and S. 1949. Washington, D.C.: U.S. Government Printing Office.

U.S. Congress. 1957. Senate. Hearings before a Subcommittee of the Committee on Post Office and Civil Service. Eighty-Fifth Congress, First Session, on S.27, S.734 and S.1326. May 20, 21, 22, 23, and 27, 1957. Washington, D.C.: U.S. Government Printing Office.

U.S. Congress. House. 1818. 15th Congress, 1st sess., House Document 194.

U.S. Congress. House. 1836a. 24th Congress, 1st sess., House Document 247. May 4, 1836.

U.S. Congress. House. 1836b. 24th Congress., 1st sess., House Report 641. May 10, 1836.

U.S. Congress. House. 1842. House Reports 741, 27th Congress, 2d session, May 23, 1842.

U.S. Congress. House. 1843. House Reports, Vol IV 294, 27th Congress, 3rd session, March 2, 1843.

U.S. Congress. House. 1920. Report of the Congressional Joint Commission on Re-classification of Salaries. March 12, 1920. Washington, D.C.: U.S. Government Printing Office.

U.S. Congress. 1923. "The Classification Act of 1923." Public Law No. 516. 67th Congress.

U.S. Congress. 1924. Report by Lewis Meriam on the role of the Bureau of Efficiency in undermining the 1923 Classification Act, published in the Congressional Record, 68th Cong. 1st sess, 2/12/24, pp. 2290–2310.

U.S. Congress. 1972. Legislative History of the Equal Employment Opportunity Act of 1972. H.R. 1746, P.L. 92–261.

U.S. Congress. 1976. History of Civil Service Merit Systems of the United States and Selected Foreign Countries together with Executive Reorganization Studies and Personnel Recommendations. Compiled by the Library of Congress Congressional Research Service for the Subcommittee on Manpower and Civil Service of the Committee on Post Office and Civil Service. U.S. Congress, House. 94th Congress, 2nd session. 12/31/76.

U.S. Department of Labor. 1939. Dictionary of Occupational Titles, First Edition. Washington, D.C.: U.S. Government Printing Office.

U.S. Office of Personnel Management. 1973. "Promotion and Internal Placement." Federal Personnel Manual, Chapter 335. Washington, D.C.: U.S. Government Printing Office.

U.S. Office of Personnel Management. 1979. "General Grade Evaluation for Nonsupervisory Clerical Positions." *Position-Classification Standards*. TS-34. Originally issued 1961. Washington, D.C.: U.S. Government Printing Office.

U.S. Office of Personnel Management. 1981. *Handbook of Occupational Groups and Series of Classes*. Washington, D.C.: U.S. Government Printing Office.

U.S. Office of Personnel Management. 1983. *Occupations of Federal White-Collar and Blue-Collar Workers*. Washington, D.C.: U.S. Government Printing Office.

U.S. Personnel Classification Board. 1924. *Class Specifications for Positions in the Departmental Service*. Washington, D.C.: U.S. Government Printing Office.

U.S. Personnel Classification Board. 1929. *Report of Wage and Personnel Survey* Field Survey Division. House Document No. 602, 70th Congress, 2d Session. Washington, D.C.: U.S. Government Printing Office.

U.S. Personnel Classification Board. 1930. *Preliminary Class Specifications of Positions in the Field Service* Field Survey Division. Washington, D.C.: U.S. Government Printing Office.

U.S. Personnel Classification Board. 1931. *Closing Report of Wage and Personnel Survey* Washington, D.C.: U.S. Government Printing Office United States.

Valenzuela, Arturo. 1984. "Parties, Politics, and the State in Chile." Pp. 242–279 in *Bureaucrats and Policy Making*, edited by Ezra N. Suleiman. New York: Holmes & Meier.

Van Riper, Paul P. 1958. *History of the United States Civil Service*. Evanston, IL: Row, Peterson and Company.

Veysey, Laurence. 1965. *The Emergence of the American University*. Chicago: University of Chicago Press.

Viteles, Morris S. 1921. "Tests in Industry." *Journal of Applied Psychology* 5: 57–63.

Viteles, Morris S. 1967. "Morris S. Viteles." Pp. 417–449 in *A History of Psychology in Autobiography*, Volume 5, edited by Edwin G. Boring and Gardner Lindzey. New York: Appleton-Century-Crofts.

Wagner, David G., and Joseph Berger. 1985. "Do Sociological Theories Grow?" *American Journal of Sociology* 90:697–728.

Waldo, Dwight. 1948. *The Administrative State: A Study of the Political Theory of American Public Administration*. New York: The Ronald Press Co.

Waldo, Dwight. 1955. *The Study of Public Administration*. New York: Random House.

Walker, Harvey. 1935. *Training Public Employees in Great Britain*. New York: McGraw-Hill.

Walker, Harvey. 1945. "The Universities and the Public Service." *American Political Science Review* 9:926–933.

Wallace, Phyllis A. 1976. *Equal Employment Opportunity and the AT&T Case*. Cambridge, MA: MIT Press.

Warner, W. Lloyd, Paul P. Van Riper, Norman H. Martin, and Orvis F. Collins. 1963. *The American Federal Executive: A Study of the Social and Personal Characteristics of the Civilian and Military Leaders of the United States Federal Government*. New Haven: Yale University Press.

Watson, John B. 1927. "Can Psychology Help in the Selection of Personnel?" *Printer's Ink* 139:69–78.

Weber, C. O. 1922. "The Psychology of Employment" *Administration* 3:6–14.

Weber, Gustavus A. 1919. *Organized Efforts for the Improvement of Methods of Administration in the United States*. New York: D. Appleton and Company.

Weick, Karl E. 1976. "Educational Organizations as Loosely Coupled Systems." *Administrative Science Quarterly* 21:1–19.

Welch, Finis. 1981. "Affirmative Action and Its Enforcement." *American Economic Review* 71:127–33.

Whipple, Guy Montrose. 1910. *Manual of Mental and Physical Tests: A Book of Directions Compiled with Special Reference to the Experimental Study of School Children in the Laboratory or Classroom.* Baltimore: Warwick and York, Inc.

Whipple, Guy Montrose. 1916. "The Use of Mental Tests in Vocational Guidance." *Annals of the American Academy of Political and Social Science.* 65:193–204.

White, Leonard. 1926. *Introduction to the Study of Public Administration.* New York: Macmillan.

White, Leonard. 1932. "General Discussion." Pp. 291–292 in *University Training for the National Service,* edited by Morris Lambie. Minneapolis: University of Minnesota Press.

White, Leonard. 1933. *Trends in Public Administration.* New York: McGraw-Hill.

White, Leonard. 1934. "Address before the American Political Science Association." December 28, 1934.

White, Leonard. 1935a. *Government Career Service.* Chicago: University of Chicago.

White, Leonard. 1935b. "The British Civil Service." Pp. 1–54 in *Civil Service Abroad: Great Britain, Canada, France, Germany,* authored by Leonard White, Charles Bland, Walter Sharp, and Fritz Marx. New York: McGraw-Hill.

White, Leonard. 1937a. *Government Careers for College Graduates.* Chicago: Civil Service Assembly.

White, Leonard. 1939. *Introduction to the Study of Public Administration.* Revised edition. New York: Macmillan.

White, Leonard. 1948. *The Federalists: A Study in Administrative History.* New York: Macmillan.

White, Leonard. 1951. *The Jeffersonians: A Study in Administrative History.* New York: Macmillan.

White, Leonard. 1953. "Centennial Anniversary." *Public Personnel Review* 14:3–7.

White, Leonard. 1954. *The Jacksonians: A Study in Administrative History, 1829–1861.* New York: Macmillan.

White, Leonard. 1956. "The Case for the Senior Civil Service." *Personnel Administration* 20:4–9.

White, Leonard. 1958. *The Republican Era: 1869–1901: A Study in Administrative History.* New York: Macmillan.

Wiebe, Robert H. 1967. *The Search for Order: 1877–1920.* New York: Hill & Wang.

Williamson, Oliver. 1975. *Markets and Hierarchies: Analysis and Antitrust Implications.* New York: Free Press.

Williamson, Oliver. 1985. *The Economic Institutions of Capitalism.* New York: Basic.

Willoughby, W. F. 1927. *Principles of Public Administration with Special Reference to the National and State Governments of the United States.* Washington, D.C.: The Brookings Institution.

Wilmerding, Lucius. 1935. *Government by Merit.* Commission of Inquiry on Public Service Personnel Monograph 12. New York: McGraw-Hill.

Wilson, Woodrow. 1887. "The Study of Administration." *Political Science Quarterly.* 2:197–222.

Wilson, Woodrow. 1901. "Democracy and Efficiency." *Atlantic Monthly* 87:289–99.

Wolf, Wendy, and Neil D. Fligstein. 1979. "Sex and Authority in the Workplace." *American Sociological Review* 44:235–52.

Woodruff, Clinton Rogers. 1914. "Civil Service Reform as a Factor in Making Public Service a Career." Pp. 78–84 in *Universities and Public Service.* Proceedings of the

National Conference on Universities and Public Service. Madison: Cantwell Printing Company.

Wright, Albert Jr. 1918. "Scientific Criteria for Efficient Democratic Institutions." *Scientific Monthly* 6:237–41.

Wright, Erik Olin. 1985. *Classes.* London: Verson.

Wynia, Bob L. 1972. "Executive Development in the Federal Government." *Public Administration Review* 32:312–313.

Yerkes, Robert. 1922. "What Is Personnel Research?" *Monthly Labor Review,* 14:11–18.

Youmans, E. Grant. 1956. "Federal Management Intern Career Patterns." *Public Personnel Review* 17:71–78.

Young, Philip. 1955. "Address of Philip Young, Chairman, U.S. Civil Service Commission, to the Kansas City Federal Personnel Conference at Kansas City, MO., on September 29, 1955."

Young, Philip. 1956. "The Federal Service Entrance Examination." *Public Administration Review* 16:1–5.

Zucker, Lynne, and Carolyn Rosenstein. 1981. "Taxonomies of Institutional Structure: Dual Economy Reconsidered." *American Sociological Review* 46:869–884.

Index

Tournament model (*Cont.*)
  internal labor markets and, 4
  promotion and, 167
Training
  equal employment opportunity and, 219
  federal civil service and, 106–107
  postwar policies and, 146–149
  See also Education
Train-then-place strategy, 201, 219
Transfers, 123
Turnover rates, 121. *See also* Job tenure;
  Seniority

Unemployment, 211
Unions
  classification and, 109
  federal civil service and, 108
  personnel reforms and, 74
  promotion and, 147
  status and, 25
  tiered personnel systems and, 132
  See also National Federation of Federal
    Employees (NFFE)
Universities
  federal civil service and, 125–126
  public administration and, 143
  research bureaus and, 112–113
University education. *See* College education; Education

Vacancies, 120–125. *See also* Promotion;
  Recruitment
Vertical mobility. *See* Mobility

Veterans, 132, 136–137, 140
Vietnam War, 206, 210–211

Wages and salaries
  classification systems and, 163
  clerical–administrative boundary and,
    53–56, 58
  early civil service and, 49
  equal employment opportunity and, 209
  federal civil service, 100–101
  labor force composition and, 35–36
  personnel reform and, 74
  sex variation in, 231
  team production and, 4
  transfers and, 123
Welch Act of 1923, 35, 278
White-collar hierarchy, 31–45
  composition of labor force, 31–39
  promotions and, 39–44
White-collar work
  federal civil service, 22–28
  professionalism and, 15
Women
  clerical–administrative boundary and,
    57–58
  clerical work and, 62
  equal employment opportunity and,
    197, 203–204
  promotion and, 124
  status attainment model and, 2
  wages and, 231
  See also Equal employment opportunity;
    Sex differences